Strictly Right

Also by John R. Coyne Jr.

The Kumquat Statement: Anarchy in the Groves of Academe

The Impudent Snobs: Agnew vs. the Intellectual Establishment

*Fall In and Cheer: A Thoughtful, Often Irreverent
View of Contemporary American Politics*

The Big Breakup: Energy in Crisis (with Patricia S. Coyne)

Also by Linda Bridges

The Art of Persuasion: A National Review Rhetoric for Writers
(with William F. Rickenbacker)

Strictly Right

William F. Buckley Jr. and the American Conservative Movement

Linda Bridges
and
John R. Coyne Jr.

BICENTENNIAL
1807
WILEY
2007
BICENTENNIAL

John Wiley & Sons, Inc.

Published by John Wiley & Sons, Inc., Hoboken, New Jersey
Published simultaneously in Canada

Photo Credits
Thomas A. Bolan: page 261; courtesy of Christopher Buckley: page 304; courtesy of Priscilla L. Buckley; pages 11, 31; courtesy of William F. Buckley Jr.: pages 17, 21, 34, 59, 77, 140, 209, 235, 282; courtesy of ISI: page 57; Jan Lukas: pages 136, 175, 178, 203, 248; Alice V. Manning: page 100

Wiley Bicentennial Logo: Richard J. Pacifico

For general information about our other products and services, please contact our Customer Care Department within the United States at (800) 762-2974, outside the United States at (317) 572-3993 or fax (317) 572-4002.

Wiley also publishes its books in a variety of electronic formats. Some content that appears in print may not be available in electronic books. For more information about Wiley products, visit our web site at www.wiley.com.

Library of Congress Cataloging-in-Publication Data:

Bridges, Linda.
    William F. Buckley Jr. and the American conservative movement/Linda Bridges and John R. Coyne, Jr.
        p. cm.
    Includes bibliographical references and index.
    ISBN 978-0-471-75817-4 (cloth)
    1. Buckley, William F. (William Frank), 1925– 2. Journalists—United States—Biography.
    I. Coyne, John R. II. Title.
    PN4874.B796B75 2007
    070.92—dc22
    [B]
                                                                                    2006029441

Printed in the United States of America

10 9 8 7 6 5 4 3 2 1

To Priscilla Buckley and Bill Rusher,
and in memory of Jim Burnham—
teachers, colleagues, friends

Contents

Acknowledgments

Our thanks, first, to our editor, Hana Lane, for coming up with the idea for this book, and for her encouragement and guidance. Then to Priscilla Buckley, Bill Rusher, Frances Bronson, Dorothy McCartney, and Lee Edwards for their encouragement and for supplying needed bits of information. No one helped us with the typing—but a word of thanks to Jaime Restrepo, Bill Buckley's resourceful computer guru, for rescuing one of the authors from time-consuming glitches. Finally, at risk of presumption, thanks to Bill Buckley himself, for his personal kindnesses to the authors, for his professional example, and for the central role he has played in shaping the social, political, and intellectual life of our nation.

Prelude

An old friend of Bill Buckley's once observed, "You realize, he is a rather *dramatic* man." So his method of divesting himself of his stock in National Review, Inc. was entirely in character. The divestiture, planned for June 2004, had been months in the works and had involved several colleagues and lawyers. A new entity, Constitutional Enterprises Corporation, had been set up, and its board of directors carefully chosen. Investment banker Dusty Rhodes, who had become *NR*'s president after early retirement from Goldman Sachs, would be chairman of the new board. The other members would be Van Galbraith, another investment banker, a friend of Buckley's since their sophomore year at Yale, and a long-serving chairman of the *National Review* board; Daniel Oliver, former Federal Trade Commissioner, a friend since Buckley's campaign for mayor of New York in 1965, and Galbraith's successor as chairman of the *NR* board; Christopher Buckley, novelist and founding editor of *Forbes FYI*, WFB's only son, and a member of the *NR* board for four years; and Austin Bramwell, the youngest member of *NR*'s board, Yale 2000, and a newly minted lawyer.

Although many people knew the divestiture was coming, the actual ceremony was planned with a secrecy worthy of Blackford Oakes. Buckley divulged all the details only to the two people responsible for carrying them out: *NR* publisher Ed Capano and WFB's longtime personal secretary, Frances Bronson. The party would take place at Paone's, an Italian restaurant near *NR*'s Manhattan office; Paone's was founded just two years after the magazine and has been a favorite gathering place ever since. The new directors and a few out-of-towners were asked to save the date, but weren't told why. Three dozen other colleagues and former colleagues were invited by telephone . . . *the day of the party.* These are busy people—journalists, presidential speechwriters, lawyers—but the only ones who didn't come were those who were unavoidably in places like Switzerland or Seattle.

And so, on June 29, 2004, after a lovely meal of serenata (a pasta specialty of Paone's) and veal spiedini, in the presence of people ranging from the newest editorial associate to a woman WFB had known since earliest consciousness—his older sister and longtime managing editor, Priscilla Buckley—he handed over to Dusty Rhodes the stock certificate for the magazine he had founded forty-nine years earlier and actively run for most of its life, and most of his adult life. There were toasts and reminiscences, and Priscilla gave a long and hilarious account of the early days of *National Review.* A pianist chosen by Buckley, the personable Bob Dawson, played between toasts; when Buckley stood up to speak, Dawson swung into "Can't Help Loving That Man." There was a wistfulness to the evening, as Buckley took one more step into retirement, but also enormous good cheer, as those assembled were reminded how important *National Review* and its founder have been in their lives.

In the two years since that evening, Buckley has persisted in using the word "retirement" to describe his situation, though he is scarcely retired in any normal sense of the word. At the time of the party he had just completed the publicity appearances for his little book *The Fall of the Berlin Wall*, for Wiley's Turning Points series. He was about to launch the publicity campaign for *Miles Gone By: A Literary Autobiography*, put out by Regnery, which had published his first book fifty-three years earlier. That morning he had written his syndicated column, as he does every Tuesday and Friday. He was in the midst of revising the manuscript of his new novel, *Last Call for Blackford Oakes*, which would be published by Harcourt early in 2005. And he was actively involved in planning the celebrations that would mark *National Review*'s fiftieth anniversary in 2005.

Still, active though he remains, the divestiture and the anniversary provide a punctuation mark, an occasion for taking stock of a career that has spanned the entire second half of the twentieth century and the beginning of the twenty-first, and that changed the face of American politics. At *NR*'s twenty-fifth anniversary party, one month after Ronald Reagan was elected president, George Will said: "Before there was Ronald Reagan there was Barry Goldwater, and before there was Barry Goldwater there was *National Review*, and before there was *National Review* there was Bill Buckley with a spark in his mind, and the spark in 1980 has become a conflagration." Five years later, at the thirtieth anniversary party, Reagan himself said: "You and I remember a time of the forest primeval, a time when nightmare and danger reigned and only the knights of darkness prevailed; when conservatives seemed without a champion. And then, suddenly riding up through the lists, came our clipboard-bearing Galahad: ready to take on any challengers in the critical battle of point and counterpoint. And, with grace and humor and passion, to raise a standard to which patriots and lovers of freedom could repair."

A pretty good description, that. And besides, what conservative wants to quarrel with Ronald Reagan?

1

Life before *National Review*

In 1954, the twenty-eight-year-old Bill Buckley started lining up funding for a magazine that would "stand athwart history, yelling Stop," as he would write in the Publisher's Statement in the first issue of *National Review*. By "history" he meant the growth of centralism, collectivism, and secularism here in the United States and, abroad, the marching on of Communism through the world.

But the name of Ronald Reagan's "clipboard-bearing Galahad" was not yet a household word. Oh, he was known here and there—as the author of two highly controversial books, one criticizing his alma mater, Yale, and the other defending Joe McCarthy. He was remembered in the Ivy League as one of the most brilliant debaters it had ever produced. But in the rest of the country a lot of people, being invited to support this new venture, were asking, *Just who is this William Buckley?*

Although Buckley comes across as solidly New England, his family's immediate roots were in the South. His Buckley great-grandparents—the husband a Protestant, the wife a Catholic—had immigrated to Canada from Ireland (County Cork) in the 1840s, settling in southern Ontario. Their son John, a big, gentle, tough-minded man, married a devout Catholic girl, Mary Ann Langford, whose parents had emigrated from Ireland (County Limerick) at about the same time as the senior Buckleys. They started their married life near Hamilton, Ontario, where they had grown up. But John was troubled by allergies in that lush farming country, and so he and Mary Ann made their way to the austere semidesert of southern Texas, where he became a sheep rancher and the sheriff of Duval County.

John and Mary Ann had two daughters and four sons, of whom William Frank, born in July 1881, was the second. John died young, age fifty-four, not as sheriff gunned down by a desperado but of a stroke, leaving his strong, determined, and loving wife to bring up the younger children. Will was in college by that time, at the University of Texas at Austin; with financial help from his older sister, Priscilla, who worked in the land office, he was able to complete his studies, including a law degree. (Their older brother, John, had been stabbed to death as a teenager.)

There were more Mexicans than Anglos in the Buckleys' hometown of San Diego, Texas, and the children had grown up fully bilingual. After practicing law for two years in Austin, Will decided, at age twenty-seven, to try his luck in Mexico. He first worked for a prominent lawyer in Mexico City ("a crook," he later called the man), then moved to Tampico, on the Gulf Coast, where he set up a law practice with his younger brother Claude, newly graduated from the University of Texas; they were soon joined by their youngest brother, Edmund.

There are two stories from that period, told by a Mexican friend of Will Buckley's named Cecilio Velasco, that say a lot about his personality and character. The first incident occurred a few weeks after Velasco started working for Buckley & Buckley. When Will Buckley hired Velasco, he gave him two pieces of advice: in a law office, there is no such word as "can't"; and no matter what he was asked to do, he should never say "no." So one day when Buckley asked Velasco if he could take down a contract in shorthand, filling in for a secretary who was out sick, Velasco said, "Of course." Buckley dictated; Velasco scribbled, and then went away to start typing. When he brought in the finished product, it was evident to Buckley that Velasco in fact could not take shorthand. It was equally evident that he had absorbed the gist of what Buckley wanted to say, and that he had expressed it well. "Not so bad," Buckley said. "Next time you can dictate it to yourself." Their friendship lasted the rest of Buckley's life.

The second had to do with a safe. A Mexican friend told Buckley that he urgently needed five thousand pesos and asked if he could make him a loan. Buckley checked with his cashier and found that he had a total of $250 in the office safe—in those days, equal to about five hundred pesos. So he went to his bank and signed a note for five thousand pesos, payable in fifteen days, and turned the money over to his friend. Then and throughout his life, the word was out: if a friend, or the widow of a friend or former employee, needed money, Will Buckley would somehow find it.

The Buckley brothers did reasonably well representing oil companies that had interests in Mexico, and before long Will, who found the practice of law "the most trying thing in the world," was letting Claude and Edmund handle most of the law business while he himself started working in oil and in real estate. Then, in the summer of 1917, Will went to New Orleans on business and met the twenty-two-year-old Aloïse Steiner.

Aloïse's father, Aloïs Steiner, was secretary-treasurer of a company that made sugar-refining equipment. His parents had come to New Orleans from northern Switzerland not long before the Civil War. Aloïse's mother, May Wassem Steiner, was of Swiss and German descent. May's paternal grandfather, John Henry Wassem, had served in the Hessian army for six years before emigrating in the 1830s; a piquant detail: his discharge papers listed him as being six feet eight. All branches of both families were devout Catholics.

New Orleans in those days was full of Southern belles, but even in that company Aloïse and her sisters, Vivian and Inez, were notable. Aloïse was also a talented storyteller, weaving endless yarns to amuse her little brother, Jimmy ("Alla's serials," he called them). The Steiner sisters managed to retain all their lives an innocence that greatly amused the next generation. One story has Aloïse and Vivian, both in their seventies, both widowed, sitting on the porch and chatting while Vivian filled out some sort of medical form. Industriously going down the list of ailments, Vivian raised her head and said, "Darling, as girls did we have gonorrhea?"

After a courtship lasting only a few days, Will and Aloïse were engaged; as Aloïse later told the story to one of her granddaughters, "I said to him, I said, 'Mr. Buckley, I will just have to think about it—Yes!'" They married at Christmastime and settled down in Tampico, fully intending to make their home there. But the political situation in Mexico was becoming dangerous. In 1911 the long-ruling Porfirio Díaz had been overthrown by Francisco Madero, who in turn was overthrown by Victoriano Huerta. In 1914, President Wilson—against the advice of the former ambassador to Mexico, Henry Lane

Wilson—decided that he knew better than the Mexicans who should be their president. Saying, "We have gone down to Mexico to serve mankind if we can find out the way," President Wilson abetted the left-wing, anti-Catholic Venustiano Carranza in his attempt to oust Huerta. Years later, an American who had been in Mexico at the time told two of Will Buckley's children, Aloïse and John, a story about their father. It was in 1916, the American said, and the U.S. Marines had landed at Vera Cruz, the next major port south of Tampico. But there was no U.S. military presence in Tampico itself, and the revolutionaries were threatening the American residents. There was a German gunboat in the river—but how to attract its attention? As Mexican riflemen waited on rooftops, "your father," the American told young Allie and John, "went out into the middle of the silent square and started hurling obscenities in Spanish such as we never thought to hear from him . . . and he deliberately provoked their fire." The German naval captain heard it and led an expedition to rescue the Americans.

By the time Buckley was asked to testify before the Senate Foreign Relations Committee in 1919, Wilson's protégé, Carranza, had come to power. The following year he was ousted by his former ally Alvaro Obregón, who substituted left-wing anti-Catholic tyranny for the oligopoly of the Church and the large landowners that had existed under Díaz. The mass of the people were no longer technically "peons," but they were no better off materially than they had been before, and they were not allowed to practice their religion. Obregón promptly expropriated whatever Huerta and Carranza hadn't, and he started expelling "pernicious foreigners"—including the Buckleys. This was under Article 33 of the revolutionary constitution; when, years later, Will told his children about those days, he would say it was better to be 33-ed than .30-.30-ed.

By November 1921, when the Buckleys were exiled from Mexico, Will and Aloïse had three children—Aloïse, John, and five-week-old Priscilla. Will had had over $100,000 in assets (the equivalent of somewhere near $3 million in 2006 dollars), most of it now gone. But he had an idea: Venezuelan oil. And he had enough money left to open an office in New York City and, in 1923, to buy a beautiful old house with many acres of land in Sharon, a village in the hills of northwestern Connecticut. A country boy himself and an outdoorsman, he had no desire to raise his growing family—Allie, John, and Pitts, as Priscilla was nicknamed, were soon joined by Jimmy and

Jane—in a Manhattan townhouse with a postage-stamp backyard. The house in Sharon was called Great Elm and still is, although the magnificent tree that gave it its name succumbed to Dutch elm disease in the 1940s, and the house itself has been divided into condominiums, two of which remain in the family.

When the Buckleys' sixth child was born—on November 24, 1925, in New York City—Will finally gave in to Aloïse's wish that he name a son after himself. Their plan was temporarily foiled by an officious priest who maintained that "Frank" was not a proper Christian name (since it wasn't a saint's name), and who therefore christened the baby "William Francis Buckley." At age five, Billy insisted on taking his father's full name.

Will Buckley's Venezuelan venture, Pantepec, was prospering, necessitating frequent travels on his part; Aloïse sometimes went with him, sometimes stayed home with the children and the large household staff: "Mademoiselle" (Mlle Jeanne Bouchex, the children's governess and Aloïse's deputy); the groom, Ed Turpin; several gardeners and farmhands; and a dozen indoor servants (including, by the time Billy was born, two Mexican nurses). Then in 1929 Will decided it would help in raising money for his oil exploration to spend some time in Europe, so he packed up his family and took them to France. (The family now included two-year-old Patricia; another little girl, Mary Ann, had been born apparently healthy, but died in her mother's arms when she was two days old.) They lived part of the time in Paris, near the Bois de Boulogne, and part in Saint-Firmin, near Chantilly, where nine-year-old John delighted in testing his American fishing skills on *perche* and *brochet*. It was on a later visit to Paris that Aloïse was approaching yet another *accouchement* (the term she tended to use even when not in France). Trish's birthday, April 23, was also approaching, and she was hoping the new baby would be born on that day. Aloïse walked around carrying heavy suitcases to hasten the event, but the baby, Maureen, asserted her individuality at the outset by waiting till April 24 to emerge.

Three-year-old Billy, who until then had been virtually monolingual (not in English but in Spanish), had his first formal schooling in French. Could the roots of his idiosyncratic way with language—including his frequently remarked love of unusual words—be found here? One thinks of his friend Vladimir Nabokov, with an equally brilliant and idiosyncratic style, who could read English before he could read his native Russian.

After a couple of years Will Buckley moved the family to England. The older children (*les grands* or *los grandes,* depending on whether you were being hailed by Mademoiselle or by Nana or Filipa, the Mexican nurses) were sent to Catholic boarding schools: Allie and Priscilla to St. Mary's Convent, Ascot; John and Jim to the Oratory Preparatory School in Reading. The younger ones (*les petits* or *los pequeños*), Jane, Billy, and Trish, went to Catholic day schools in London. While at Reading, Jim was actually caned, not once but twice, leading to huge indignation on the part of his siblings and providing, forty years later, a crucial element in Blackford Oakes's formation (although Jim's were ordinary canings, not the work of an anti-American sadist like Blackford's headmaster, and Jim dismissed the incidents philosophically instead of raging at them).

In 1933, Will brought his family back to Sharon and went full-bore on implementing his pedagogical ideas. He was the sort of man who wants what he wants when he wants it (how appropriate that it's his third son, and not the easygoing John or Jim, who is his namesake). And what he wanted now was to produce offspring who shared his love for beauty and learning. So he engaged tutors to follow his curriculum, including music teachers, one of whom would become a lifelong member of the Buckley circle. When the children first saw the petite and pretty twenty-four-year-old Marjorie Otis, they promptly dubbed her "Old Lady." She was one of the three music teachers who developed in the young Buckleys a lasting love of music, and she remained a friend of theirs—a very close friend of Bill, Trish, and Priscilla—until her death as a very old lady indeed, aged ninety-four.

But even during the "school year," it was by no means all work, no play. There were stables, with enough horses for all (the year Bill took part in the Good Hands competition at the National Horse Show in Madison Square Garden, the other young riders included Edward Albee and Jacqueline Bouvier); the swimming pool beckoned until autumn edged toward winter; and the hunters in the family—John, and later Bill, and later still Reid (Priscilla didn't take up hunting till she was an adult)—could go out with a dog early in the morning for pheasants, and get back in time for their studies.

In the mid-1930s Will started taking his family to Camden, South Carolina, for part of the winter. He rented houses for several years before he found the one he wanted to buy. The house was oddly named

Nine little Buckleys and their parents at Great Elm (and Carol will make ten, but not for another five years). Left to right, front row: Bill, ASB, Maureen, Priscilla, Jane, Reid, John; back row: Jim, Allie, Trish, WFB Sr.

Kamschatka, after the remote peninsula in Siberia, because when it was built, before the Civil War, it was so far out of town as to seem quite inaccessible. It was in Camden that the young Buckleys became acquainted with the Southern part of their heritage. When youngest brother Reid returned to the States after years of living in Spain, that's where he settled, and youngest sister Carol now lives nearby.

While the family was still growing, the number of children actually present in the household started diminishing. One by one, as they entered their teens, they were sent off to boarding school. The boys went to Millbrook in Millbrook, New York—not as prestigious as the St. Grottlesex schools, but (a) it was just a few miles from Sharon, (b) it permitted its pupils to go home for weekends, and (c) the founding headmaster, the formidable Mr. Pulling, met with Mr. Buckley's approval. (The way Bill tells the story, decades later Mr. Pulling asked Bill and his wife, Pat, to address him as "Edward." Bill hemmed and hawed; Pat, with her characteristic directness, said, "Are you crazy, Mr. Pulling?") The girls went to various schools—some to Nightingale-Bamford in Manhattan; some to Ethel Walker in Simsbury,

Connecticut, due east of Sharon; and Carol to the Convent of the Sacred Heart in Noroton, Connecticut, on Long Island Sound.

A person who grew up in a small family has to work at understanding the dynamics of a large family. In the Buckleys' case, eldest daughter goes from being an only child to being big sister, first of one brother, to whom she is very close, then of an assortment of younger brothers and sisters. Kid brother, alternately protected and teased by older siblings, soon becomes big brother to one, eventually four, younger siblings, to the youngest of whom he is godfather. Youngest daughter, born five years after her nearest sibling, grows up not in a house full of cacophony and movement, but in one from which most of her elders have gone off to school—or even college, or war—and when they *are* home, she's convinced that she'll never catch up to the brilliance of their dinner-table conversation.

In a large family the children form alliances and subgroups. Priscilla tells how, when teased by John or Allie or by neighbor children, she or Jim would defiantly announce that he or she had a "powerful friend" who would intercede; to this day, correspondence between Jim and Priscilla is addressed to "PF," and signed "PF." One might have expected Jane, the eldest of *les petits*, to pair off with Billy, but in fact it was Tish (as he calls her—to most people she's Trish) with whom he was "paired from infancy."

And the heads of this household? Father loving but strict, rather shy though a great teller of tales from his youth, and formal in manners even for a member of his more formal generation. Mother a fount of unconditional love. When each of the parents died, the family organized a memorial volume, with contributions by family and friends. In the case of Mrs. Buckley, who spent her last years in deepening senility, Priscilla wanted to make sure the grandchildren knew that this was only a tiny part of her story. And so Priscilla and Old Lady write of Aloïse Buckley as she was in the early 1930s, a woman irresistibly charming and seemingly scatterbrained, but who very efficiently manages the household of servants and farmhands and tutors while her husband is off managing his businesses. Then on Friday evenings, Priscilla writes, she is seen "rushing excitedly to the front door . . . as the car drives up with Father as if this is the best thing that has ever happened to her. Which it was. And she knows it. And he does."

Both parents are devout Catholics in their very different ways, he quiet and undemonstrative, she telling of her prayer life as unselfconsciously as if she were relating a conversation with a neighbor. Both are

deeply patriotic, although completely comfortable in other climes—
rooted cosmopolitans, you might call them. And both are conservative, he more philosophically and with a libertarian bent (the crusty
libertarian Albert Jay Nock was a great friend of his and a frequent
visitor at Great Elm), she more intuitive and traditional. Their children all grew up as conservative, Catholic, rooted cosmopolitans, saving their rebellions for the world outside Great Elm and Kamschatka.

When Bill graduated from Millbrook in 1943, he was only seventeen,
not yet eligible for the draft. But there was no point starting at Yale
and then having to leave in mid-semester, and so he spent a few
months at the University of Mexico improving his Spanish before he
was inducted into the army.

Will Buckley had vigorously opposed America's entry into the
war and supported Charles Lindbergh and America First; his children
had enthusiastically shared his views. But once the United States was
in the war, the Buckleys were Americans first, and by the time Bill was
drafted, John was on active duty in the army in North Africa; their
first brother-in-law, Ben Heath (Allie's husband), was in the army air
corps attached to the Pentagon; and Jim was in the navy in the
Pacific. Bill describes his own service as "brief and bloodless." He
started out at Fort Benning, Georgia, where, like his fictional characters Sebastian Reinhard and Ed Coady in *Nuremberg: The Reckoning*,
he was among the young soldiers chosen for the honor guard escorting President Roosevelt's body onto the train in Warm Springs. When
the war ended, Bill was sent to Fort Sam Houston, Texas, to take
charge of a group of men awaiting demobilization.

"Here love had died between me and the army," says Captain
Charles Ryder at the beginning of Evelyn Waugh's *Brideshead Revis-
ited*. For Bill, there was no love to die. His recollections of army life
emphasize the bullying, the petty deprivations, the forced camaraderie with men with whom he had not much in common. But he
toughed it out, and, by his own account, it gave him something crucial—something that observers from our present vantage point can
see as fundamental to his adult personality. As a boy he didn't have
many friendships outside his own family. As a teenager at Millbrook,
he did have a few close friends, especially an English boy sent as a
"bundle from Britain" to escape the Blitz, the future historian Alistair
Horne, who remains one of his closest friends. But in general, as Bill

wrote in a long letter to his father, "I was not very popular with the boys." He ascribed this to his youthful dogmatism: "I could not understand another point of view; it seemed to me that anyone who was not an isolationist or a Catholic was simply stupid. Instead of keeping these sentiments to myself, I blurted them out and supported them upon the slightest provocation."

What he learned in the army was "the importance of tolerance, and the importance of a sense of proportion about all matters—even in regard to religion, morality, and so on. Some friends I made whom I really prized were atheistic, and even immoral. But I learned, nevertheless, that regardless of the individual's dogmas, the most important thing as far as I was concerned was the personality: would his friendship broaden your horizon or provide you with intellectual entertainment?" In those few sentences are contained the essence of what would separate *Firing Line* from all the shouty, more-heat-than-light talk shows that came along in the 1970s and 1980s. Those sentences also answer the question asked by so many puzzled fans: How can you be friends with _____ [fill in the blank]? John Kenneth Galbraith, Mike Wallace, Henry Kissinger, and dozens of other public figures who at the least are not movement conservatives, and some of whom are out-and-out leftists. Indeed, you can count on the knuckles of one finger the people (aside from Stalin, Hitler, Mao, et al.) whom Buckley truly despises: Lowell Weicker, Gore Vidal—oh yes, and Ralph Schoenman, assistant to Bertrand Russell in his notorious "war crimes" campaign against the United States, whom Buckley called a "cretin" on *Firing Line*.

This same trait has proved to be one of his great strengths as a novelist: the ability to portray with understanding and even affection the bad guys, most notably Blackford Oakes's longtime antagonist, Boris Bolgin.

In 1946 Bill was demobilized and entered Yale. John and Jim had graduated from Yale before going off to war. After being demobbed, John (like Ben Heath) had gone straight into the family oil business, but when Bill arrived as a freshman, Jim was back in New Haven, at the law school; Reid would arrive as a freshman two years later.

Yale's contribution to the war effort, as Bill has written, was to commit itself to matriculating after the war any young man it accepted who was called up to active service right after high school. Hence

Bill's class was the largest in history (this remained true even after Yale started admitting women in the late 1960s), and he and three roommates shared a suite meant for two in Davenport College. One of Bill's roommates, Richie O'Neill, would later lend Blackford Oakes his engineering expertise, along with a marvelous anecdote, given to Blacky in *Saving the Queen*. As Bill tells the nonfiction story: "[Richie] came early to the decision that he needed to do something to tame the fastidious dean of the Engineering School. . . . When Richie slept in one Monday, he found on Tuesday a summons to the office of Dean Loomis Havemeyer. . . .

"'Why did you miss your class yesterday, Mr. O'Neill?'

"'Diarrhea, sir.' Richie smiled.

"He was thereafter immune to summonses from that office."

Yale bristles with extracurricular activities, many of them probably as important to one's future life as what goes on in the classroom. There are singing groups and senior societies, the Political Union and the *Daily News*, organized sports and the debate team. Bill "heeled" (tried out) as a freshman for the *Daily News* (an experience he gives to Harry Bontecou in *The Redhunter*, transposing it from Yale to Columbia, and to Reuben Castle and Justin Durban in the Midwest in *The Rake*). He also was active on the debate team and in the Political Union, and he eventually joined the Elizabethan Club, the Fence Club, and the society to which both candidates in the 2004 presidential election belonged, Skull & Bones. But Bill emphatically did not follow the father of one of those candidates, George H. W. Bush (class of '48), onto the baseball team. Patriotic to the core, Bill is nonetheless un-American in his utter lack of interest in organized sports. Indeed, the only team sport that has ever appealed to him is ocean racing. He did not see a major league baseball game until 1994, and he went then only because ACLU chief Ira Glasser wouldn't drop the subject. A few years later someone else invited him to a game, and he replied, "No thanks. I've already been." Nor did he think himself qualified to join one of the singing groups, but he loved listening to them, and the Whiffenpoofs have entertained at many a *National Review* party.

And he made friends, lifelong friends—most of them fellow students, but also faculty members: economics professor Glenn Saxon, *Daily News* business manager Francis Donahue, Dante scholar Thomas Bergin. As Buckley put it in his toast at his class's forty-year reunion, "Most of my friends I met forty-odd years ago, met them

within a radius of two hundred yards of where I am now standing."
One of these men, L. Brent Bozell Jr., a tall, raw-boned, redheaded
Nebraskan, became his partner on the debate team. According to
debate coach Rollin Osterweis, they formed a devastating one–two
combination, with Bozell offering eloquent prepared statements and
Buckley engaging in the cut-and-thrust that *Firing Line* viewers
would come to know so well. In the fall of 1949, Oxford sent over a
crack debating team, Robin Day and Anthony Wedgwood-Benn, to
take on the Ivy League. (Day would become a leading print and television journalist; Wedgwood-Benn gradually metamorphosed into
far-left Labour politician Tony Benn, dropping parts of his name and
his official biography as he went.) The two young Englishmen were
wiping the floor with their American opponents—until they came to
Yale. According to Osterweis, Bozell and Buckley had an English
style of debate—that is, they relied more on eloquence and wit than
on the sheaves of facts and figures typical of American debaters. Taking the negative side on the topic "Resolved: the Americans should
nationalize all their non-agricultural industries," Buckley and Bozell
trounced the Oxford team 3–0.

Early in their friendship, Bill had introduced Brent to the sister he
was closest to, Trish. The two redheads quickly fell in love, and they
married in December of Brent's senior year (Trish, not having lost
time to the war, had already graduated). Bill's work on the *Daily
News* yielded another romance between one of his friends and one of
his sisters, with less fortunate results. Bill and Tom Guinzburg heeled
together for the OCD (Oldest College Daily) and, luckily for their
friendship, had different agendas. Guinzburg wanted to become
managing editor, because he was interested in collecting news and
putting out the paper. Buckley wanted to become chairman (editor-
in-chief), because he wanted to write the editorials. That is how it
eventually worked out, and Guinzburg and Buckley were happy with
the arrangement, even if many liberal readers of the OCD were less
than happy with Buckley's editorials. Then Tom Guinzburg and Jane
Buckley fell in love. Guinzburg was Jewish, and Will Buckley ordered
Jane to break off the relationship. Bill agreed with his father, and his
friendship with Guinzburg naturally suffered (although it was later
mended, and continues to this day). Buckley's first biographer, John
Judis, who is Jewish, describes Will Buckley as a "virulent" anti-
Semite—although he absolves Bill of any such charge, and he records
that when the Fence Club rejected Tom because he was Jewish, Bill

A banquet organized by outgoing *Daily News* editor Buckley, to which he had invited the presidents of half a dozen major East Coast universities. The head table, left to right: Dwight David Eisenhower of Columbia, Tom Guinzburg, James B. Conant of Harvard, WFB, Charles Seymour of Yale (speaking), John D. Macomber, Harold Dodds of Princeton, Gary Ellis, Harold Stassen of the University of Pennsylvania.

refused to join the club until it relented and accepted his friend. Bill himself would later write that his father did indeed partake of the country-club anti-Semitism prevalent in his day. But Will Buckley also had a rational objection to a marriage between a Catholic and a Jew, and it was this objection that Bill shared: How could they worship together? What would be their children's religious upbringing? Guinzburg later reflected that had there not been opposition, his and Jane's romance would probably have faded in a season. But as it was, the temperature was pretty chilly in the OCD office during the rest of his and Bill's tenure.

Time-consuming as the newspaper, the debate team, and the Political Union were, Buckley did manage to attend his classes, majoring (like his future friend Ronald Reagan) in economics. The classes were often wonderful experiences; he recalls especially philosophy professor Robert Calhoun, who "spoke the kind of sentences John Stuart Mill wrote," and history professor Lewis Curtis, whose "description of the Battle of Jutland could have had a long run off Broadway." But classes were often maddening, with religion frequently belittled and collectivism exalted; many of Yale's economics professors would have regarded the free market as the devil's work, except that that would have been too close to a religious expression.

Matters came to a head on Alumni Day of Buckley's senior year—February 22, 1950. He had been chosen by the faculty to be the student speaker that day. Instead of writing, as he later put it, the usual "good old Yale" kind of speech, he decided to address head-on the "policy of educational *laissez-faire,*" which held that it was an attack on "academic freedom" to insist that freedom is better than tyranny, the free market better than socialism and central planning, Christianity better than secular humanism. The problem, he said, was not that all Yale professors, by any means, were hard-left atheists; it was that official Yale refused to say that one set of opinions was better than another.

Buckley brought a copy of his speech, as required, to the University News Bureau forty-eight hours before the Alumni Day celebration. Within two hours, he had been tracked down by a leading alumnus and urged to alter his "indictment of the administration." He was told that "the alumni simply wouldn't *understand* it . . . they'll leave the place thinking Yale is communistic." Buckley refused to alter more than a few sentences, but he did offer to withdraw as speaker. This offer was met, he says, with "hurt feelings" and urgings to rewrite his speech; finally it was President Charles Seymour himself who, when Buckley refused to write a milder speech, accepted his withdrawal.

The next act of this drama was on Class Day, part of the graduation festivities. Buckley had been elected by the Yale Class Council to be the speaker, and the administration, though apprehensive, did not try to persuade the students to change their vote. This time Buckley did not engage in open aggression against the administration, though he did call for Yale to return to espousing Western civilization and celebrating America as "an oasis of freedom and prosperity."

While Buckley was, as he put it, "getting some learning" and stirring up Yale, big things were happening in the wider world. At home, the war had decisively ended the Depression, but it had not ended the New Deal, which had been launched to counter the Depression. The war had also caused major changes in the status of women. Many of those who had done "men's work" during the war slipped gratefully back out of the labor market, but certain professions, having been opened, would never be closed again. Priscilla Buckley was one of the first women to hold a responsible position at United Press, thus launching her sparkling journalistic career. And the unequaled prosperity and rapid suburbanization following the war were causing great shifts in the social landscape.

The end of the war also brought ferocious debate over how to handle our wartime ally, Josef Stalin, and his sympathizers in the States. In the half-decade after the war, the Soviet Union methodically enslaved, one after another, East Germany, Albania, Bulgaria, Romania, Poland, Hungary, Czechoslovakia, and, briefly, Yugoslavia (which broke free of the Soviet Empire in 1948 but did not throw off Communism). In 1949 Mao Tse-tung drove Chiang Kai-shek and his Nationalists out of Mainland China. Two weeks after the class of 1950 graduated, North Korean tanks swept across the 38th parallel toward Seoul, embroiling the United States in yet another war. This one, however, was not officially a war but a "police action" under the auspices of the new United Nations, in whose founding a State Department functionary named Alger Hiss had played a substantial role. In 1948 Whittaker Chambers, an editor at *Time*, accused that same Alger Hiss of being a Communist spy, and two years later Senator Joseph McCarthy, seeking an explanation of how so many countries had fallen under Communist domination, accused dozens of State Department officials of being Communists or Communist sympathizers. By no means all of those who defended Hiss and excoriated Chambers and McCarthy were Communists, or even Communist sympathizers, strictly speaking; a new breed, the anti-anti-Communist, was born, and thus was launched one of the fiercest ideological battles in American history. Meanwhile, thanks partly to several Communists who were *not* State Department officials—the Rosenbergs, David Greenglass, Klaus Fuchs—the Soviets quickly ended our monopoly on atomic weapons. The Cold War—what James Burnham would call the Third World War—was under way.

In this war, Buckley was an enthusiastic recruit. Before his graduation, he had been approached by the CIA via his Yale mentor, the legendary political science professor Willmoore Kendall. Kendall introduced him to Burnham, who was an outside contractor with the CIA. Burnham in turn introduced him to a man whose name would later become all too well known, the dashing OSS veteran and popular novelist E. Howard Hunt. Buckley gladly signed up with the new agency. However, before he started his training, he had some unfinished business at Yale.

He also had some unfinished personal business. He and Brent Bozell had spent the summer of 1949 in Saskatchewan, working for one of the Buckley oil companies. Trish Buckley, meanwhile—by now engaged to Bozell—had gone to Vancouver to visit a Vassar class-mate, Patricia Taylor. (Happy coincidence—or perhaps the Invisible Hand—had been at work in bringing the two Patricias together, since Trish was the first Buckley girl not to go to Smith.)

Pat was, and is, glamorous, beautiful, and imperious. During sophomore year at Vassar, Trish had told her family about her Cana-dian friend: "Pat looks like a queen, she acts like a queen, and is just the match for Billy." During her visit to Vancouver two summers later, Trish contacted Bill and Brent and extended the Taylors' invita-tion to spend a few days with them. As the story is told, they arrived in Vancouver on a Sunday and were due to leave the following Thurs-day, but Bill postponed his departure by a day. On Thursday evening, Pat—already an intense card player—was involved in a canasta game when Bill asked her sister to get Pat to join him in the library. As John Judis reconstructs the scene, Pat did come. "'Bill, what do you want?' she asked. And he said, 'Patricia, would you consider marriage with me?' She said, 'Bill, I've been asked this question many times. To the others I've said no. To you I say yes. Now may I please get back and finish my hand?'" Whether it happened just that way or not, the story is pure Pat.

Pat's father, Austin Taylor, had made a not inconsiderable fortune in gold, oil, and timber, and he had large stakes in Vancouver real estate. He and his wife, Kathleen (known as Babe), were noted phi-lanthropists, her special focus being on the Red Cross. Austin Taylor ran what was regarded as the finest stud farm in British Columbia; he regularly took his family down to Pasadena, California, for the Santa Anita meets, at which his horses did very well. Decades later, Pat sur-prised a houseful of guests on Kentucky Derby day by betting on Sunday Silence against the favorite, Easy Goer, because, she explained, Sunday Silence's trainer, Charlie Whittingham, had trained for her father. Sunday Silence won by two and a half lengths.

There was one snag in the proposed marriage: the religious ques-tion again. Only this time it was Pat's parents, of Northern Irish descent, objecting to their Anglican daughter marrying a Roman Catholic. Negotiations were protracted, but finally it was worked out that the sacrament of marriage would be celebrated on July 6, 1950, at the RC cathedral in Vancouver, with the archbishop presiding; then

The reception on the Taylors' lawn; in background, to Bill's left: Babe Taylor, the mother of the bride.

at the reception, on the Taylors' vast lawn in the center of Vancouver, the Anglican bishop would bless the new couple. Austin and Babe Taylor became very fond of their son-in-law, and he devoted to them.

After what Bill has described as a "hedonistic" honeymoon in Hawaii, the young couple set up housekeeping in Hamden, Connecticut, a suburb of New Haven. Pat worked on developing the culinary skills for which she was later renowned, and also a dramatic theme that has run throughout their marriage. As Bill later put it, his own culinary function "was to turn off the pressure cooker when the sound rang out, while Pat would hide under the staircase, assuming a fetal position, resignedly awaiting the explosion, and, as resignedly, her impending widowhood." Bill, meanwhile, taught Spanish part-time at Yale and grappled with his first book, exploring the same issues he had raised in his aborted Alumni Day speech: the promulgation in Yale classrooms of centralism, secularism, and socialism.

He was encouraged in his work by Frank Chodorov, a friend and disciple of Will Buckley's friend Albert Jay Nock, and by his own mentor at Yale, Willmoore Kendall. Kendall was a brilliant political theorist; he was also a born contrarian. Buckley has mused that if the Yale political culture had been solidly conservative, Kendall would probably have remained the quasi-Trotskyist he had been as a young

man. Now, as Buckley worked on his book, Kendall read the manuscript and made suggestions, many of which Buckley incorporated.
One of these proved to be among the most controversial lines in the
book. "I believe that the duel between Christianity and atheism is the
most important in the world," Buckley had written. "I further believe
that the struggle between individualism and collectivism is"—and
then Kendall suggested, and Buckley accepted, the phrasing: "the
same struggle reproduced on another level." This would lead to
heated accusations that Buckley had no regard for the poor and was
not Catholic but "Calvinist" in his economics.

The manuscript was finished by April 1951, and Buckley started
searching for a publisher. A Chicago conservative named Henry Regnery, who had started a publishing house just a few years earlier,
enthusiastically accepted the manuscript, eventually titled *God and
Man at Yale*. The eminent journalist John Chamberlain (Yale '25),
who had met Buckley while visiting his alma mater, agreed to write
the introduction.

Publication of *God and Man* was scheduled for the fall, but meanwhile there was the commitment to the CIA. Following the protocols
under which he enlisted, Buckley has written almost nothing of his
own experiences in the agency, but we can safely assume that his
training was much like that given to Oakes in *Saving the Queen*. Also,
one imagines that Buckley's motivations were much like those he
gives to Oakes: a desire to fight for freedom and against despotism.
And Pat thought a CIA career in exotic places sounded "fascinating"—certainly more glamorous than cooking in Hamden, Connecticut, while her husband sweated over his Royal typewriter.

Bill and Pat spent the summer of 1951 in Washington, D.C.,
where Bill learned about safe houses and observation techniques and
how to hand over a document unobserved. Then they were sent to
Mexico City, where Bill reported to his recruiter, Howard Hunt.

The Buckleys and the Hunts became close friends, and the Buckleys enjoyed life in Mexico City. They hooked up with many old
friends of Will Buckley's, and Pat found a house whose yard had space
for a wonderful garden. But fascinating it wasn't. Bill was a deep-
cover agent, like Blackford. But whereas Blacky's first assignment
propelled him into a stay at Windsor Castle, an affair with the Queen
of England, and finally a nerve-throbbing aerial battle of wills, Bill's

assignment involved pretending to work in an export–import business while infiltrating the student political movement in Mexico City. The work was achingly slow, the payoffs small, and Bill started to feel there were better ways to put his talents to use in the cause of freedom.

Then, in October 1951, *God and Man* hit the bookstores, and nothing would ever be the same.

Henry Regnery had ordered an initial print run of five thousand, a modest but respectable number. He had to order a second printing within days. *God and Man* became a best seller—but it cost its publisher dearly. Blaming Regnery for accepting so radical a book, the University of Chicago took away from him the lucrative contract he had just won to publish the Great Books series. But Regnery was steadfast. As Buckley puts it, "I still have the letter from him, advising me that he had devoted the night before—after seeing the first rash of reviews—to rereading the book. He concluded that he had been correct to publish it and, so far as I know, never gave another thought to his decision to launch the book."

Buckley himself came under withering attack—not only from official Yale, but also in publications ranging from the *New York Post* and the *St. Louis Post–Dispatch* to the *Atlantic Monthly* and *Saturday Review*, the *Yale Law Journal* and the *Northwestern Law Review.* One of the high points was the conclusion of the piece by Frank Ashburn—headmaster of Brooks School and a Yale trustee—for *Saturday Review*: "The book is one which has the glow and appeal of a fiery cross on a hillside at night. There will undoubtedly be robed figures who gather to it, but the hoods will not be academic. They will cover the face."

What Klan-like recommendations had Buckley made? They boiled down to, first, recognizing that Yale had been founded to produce patriotic, Christian leaders of America, an end that was being subverted by an extreme understanding of "academic freedom," and, second, fostering a return to that original purpose by giving alumni a say in running the institution that had formed them and that they so generously supported. In the course of the controversy over the book, the Reverend Henry Sloane Coffin said to Buckley, "Why do you want to turn Yale education over to a bunch of boobs?" Buckley comments, "Since Mr. Coffin had been chairman of the Educational Policy Committee of the [Yale] Corporation, it struck me that if indeed the alumni were boobs he bore a considerable procreative responsibility."

On the strength of *God and Man*, and of Buckley's handling of the attacks on it, two of the three existing right-wing periodicals, *The American Mercury* and *The Freeman*, offered him editorial positions. He also had speaking offers galore. And so, in March 1952, he and Pat returned to the States from Mexico, this time to New York City, and he accepted the offer from the *Mercury*.

Pat, three months pregnant, started scouting for a house. As much as Bill loved his hometown of Sharon, it was too far from New York City for a daily commute; equally important, it wasn't on the seacoast, and Bill had dreamed since age thirteen of one day owning an oceangoing sailboat. After several weeks of prowling the New York and Connecticut coastline, Pat rang Bill triumphantly one day: she had found it. It was in Stamford, Connecticut, with a broad lawn sloping down about a furlong to Long Island Sound. Bill has referred to the house as "ugly but comfortable." Some may beg to differ with the first part of that description. The house at Wallacks Point doesn't have the classical elegance of Great Elm or Kamschatka; it is an asymmetrical Mediterranean-style structure with walls of pink stucco. But to anyone who loves the Italian lakes, with their villas perched on the hillsides, it is quite beautiful. Bill and Pat were safely ensconced in their new home by the time Christopher Taylor Buckley was born, in September 1952.

That year, 1952, was of course a presidential election year, after a generation of Democratic dominance. From a right-wing point of view, the outgoing Democratic administration could have been far worse—but it could have been far better. There was prosperity, to be sure, but President Truman had done nothing—nor was it likely that the man who had been FDR's last vice president would have done anything—to roll back the previous decade's centralization and growth of government. To Buckley and his colleagues, the New Deal, and even Truman's milder Fair Deal, were the antithesis of the spirit of local control and voluntarism that, in Tocqueville's analysis, had made America great. Abroad, the administration's goal was containment (George Kennan's term), not rollback. Truman had complaisantly followed, at Potsdam, the outline drawn up at Yalta, and in subsequent years, as Stalin gobbled up one Central European country after another, the United States scarcely protested. But Truman did call a halt when Soviet-backed guerrillas started making headway in

Greece, which Roosevelt and Churchill had not conceded as being within the Soviet sphere of influence; he enunciated the Truman Doctrine, and the Republican Congress backed him up. The Marshall Plan, begun and carried out on Truman's watch, had brought Western Europe to its feet and very probably saved it from going Communist. And when the Soviets attempted to force West Berlin into Communist East Germany by starving it out, Truman did take the advice of the military governor of Germany, the bold and resourceful General Lucius D. Clay. Clay proposed a massive airlift to save the embattled city from the Soviet blockade, and Truman authorized him to go ahead. But in Korea, when General Douglas MacArthur simply raised the question of taking the war to North Korea's backers, the Red Chinese, Truman summarily called him home and dismissed him as commander of the United Nations forces.

Truman could have run again in 1952, being grandfathered under the 22nd Amendment. But the controversies over Communists in his administration, the battle with the Dixiecrats on the one hand and Henry Wallace on the other in 1948, and the stalemate in the Korean War had taken their toll. He lost the New Hampshire primary to Tennessee senator Estes Kefauver and soon afterward announced that he was not a candidate for reelection. At the end of the day, Illinois governor Adlai Stevenson—Truman's favored candidate—won the nomination at the Democratic convention in Chicago.

On the Republican side, the standard-bearer for many on the right was Senator Robert Taft of Ohio, who represented a small-town heartland conservatism. However, some (including Buckley) who had shared Taft's isolationism in the late 1930s worried that his isolationism now would blind him to the seriousness of the worldwide Communist threat. The more liberal wing of the party, meanwhile, was determined to stop Taft. Although two men who had come up through the political ranks were already in the race—California governor Earl Warren and former Minnesota governor Harold Stassen—the GOP liberals made the bold move of recruiting a man who had never held elective office, but who was widely and deeply popular. In January 1952 Senator Henry Cabot Lodge announced that he was placing on the New Hampshire ballot the name of Dwight David Eisenhower, the victorious Supreme Commander of the Allied Expeditionary Force in Europe.

Ike did well in the primaries. At the Republican convention, which like the Democrats' was held in Chicago, he won on the first ballot, after Stassen released his delegates. Eisenhower then handily defeated the far more liberal Stevenson in November, 55 percent to 45 percent, and 39 states to 9.

The right was not sanguine about the prospects of Ike's rolling back the New Deal/Fair Deal, but he did seem set on prosecuting the Cold War, especially when he named John Foster Dulles, hardline brother of CIA director Allen Dulles, to be his secretary of state.

Against this backdrop, what was the state of the conservative movement? Put bluntly, there wasn't one. There was—as, in their different accents, Robert Taft and Willmoore Kendall maintained—a widespread intuitive conservative sensibility in the country, despite the general acquiescence in FDR's enormous concentration of power in Washington, D.C. But in discussions of political theory, the term "conservative" was only starting to be used. Indeed, as of 1950, the few intellectuals who were describing themselves as "New Conservatives" applauded the welfare state as necessary to save capitalism. The leading light of this kinder, gentler New Conservatism, Peter Viereck, said of *God and Man* that Buckley was not conservative but reactionary. Buckley replied that if being conservative meant accepting the New Deal, then he was content to be reactionary. Not until Regnery published Russell Kirk's *The Conservative Mind* in 1953 would the future movement start to coalesce around that term.

Meanwhile, schools of thought that would soon be part of that movement existed here and there, but they seldom worked in concert with one another. Most prominent, as of the early 1950s, were the libertarians, aka classical liberals. They believed that the best polity was one of ordered liberty—individual liberty and responsibility, with one man's safety and property protected from his neighbor's expansiveness by the rule of law. This tradition—the tradition of John Locke and Adam Smith, which played so large a role in the American founding—had taken a beating from the socialists and progressives in Britain and America from the 1890s on, and particularly during the Depression. But it had never died out, and it got a tremendous boost at the end of World War II from books published by two refugees from Hitler-controlled Austria. F. A. Hayek's *The Road to Serfdom* (1944) and Ludwig von Mises's *Bureaucracy* (1944) and *Human Action* (1949) were hailed by such progenitors of the American conservative movement as John Chamberlain, Henry Hazlitt, William Henry Chamberlin, and John Davenport.

This school of thought—what we might also call conservative libertarianism, or classical libertarianism—was partly intertwined with, partly at odds with, a more radical libertarianism. Whereas Hayek and Mises saw the need for enough state power to protect A's private property— the basis, in their view, of personal liberty—from B's incursions, Nock called the state "our enemy," and Chodorov—described by Buckley as of 1950 as "a gentle, elderly anarchist"— wrote that "taxation is robbery."

It was from the libertarian side of the right wing that the first organizations of premovement conservatism sprang. In 1953 the radical libertarian Chodorov founded the Intercollegiate Society of Individualists (*individualism* here being contrasted to collectivism, not to community), with the conservative libertarian Buckley as its first president. Earlier, in 1946, the classical liberal Leonard Read had started the Foundation for Economic Education. Read was not content with criticizing statism—he felt the need to forward a positive "free-market, private-ownership, limited-government philosophy." He quickly won the support of Hayek, and he put Mises on FEE's payroll. The following year, Hayek himself founded a more exclusive group, the Mont Pelerin Society, which soon was exercising influence way out of proportion to its size. As the young Milton Friedman put it, "The importance of that [founding] meeting was that it showed us we were not alone." This was a step away from Nock's gloomy libertarianism, which depicted those who rejected statism and progressivism as "the Remnant." That image has emotional appeal, but it's the romantic appeal of the lost cause. It isn't going to change a country's direction. What Friedman saw in Mont Pelerin was libertarians prepared to cease being a lonely remnant.

The next major strand of right-wing thought was traditionalism. The traditionalists who would play the biggest roles in the early days of the conservative movement were Russell Kirk and the more esoteric Eric Voegelin. Kirk delineated the conservative philosophy of Edmund Burke and his intellectual descendants, a philosophy that celebrated a hierarchical, nonrationalistic social order and "affection for the proliferating variety and mystery of traditional life." Voegelin wrote in opposition to the modern "gnostics," who, in his most famous phrase, had "immanentized the Christian eschaton"—that is, promised heaven on earth if only the Communists (or the Jacobins, or the American Progressives) had their way. Working alongside Kirk and Voegelin were such thinkers as the great Episcopal priest Bernard Iddings Bell (though he was seen more as a churchman than as a political philosopher) and Berkeley professor Robert Nisbet (though he was seen more as an academic sociologist). And coming at the Great Tradition—Athens and Jerusalem—from his own angle was the University of Chicago's Leo Strauss, the founder of one of the most influential schools of right-wing thought.

A somewhat different breed of traditionalist was the Southern Agrarian. The Agrarians' manifesto, *I'll Take My Stand*, had been published in 1930. One of their younger adherents, Richard Weaver, was a respected professor of English at the University of Chicago in the early 1950s; he had published his seminal *Ideas Have Consequences* in 1948. Two others, Cleanth Brooks and Robert Penn Warren, were leading exponents of New Criticism in the English Department at Yale, where Reid Buckley was studying. The Agrarians believed that despite the fearful stain of slavery, the antebellum South had sustained the values of what C. S. Lewis called Old Western Man. As Weaver put it, the South had been "the last non-materialist civilization in the Western world."

The third strand of right-wing thought was anti-Communism. This category may seem redundant, since by definition libertarians are anti the ultimate embodiment of statism, and traditionalists are anti the enemy of Western civilization. But an important component of the inchoate conservative movement was people who were anti-Communists first, before they found any specific niche on the right. These were, mostly, men and women who had been Communists or Trotskyists and had turned against totalitarianism; they knew from the inside how truly evil it was. In this category were figures as disparate as Whittaker Chambers, James Burnham, Freda Utley, and Max Eastman.

Besides the handful of right-wing organizations existing in the early 1950s, there was an equally small number of explicitly right-wing publications. *The American Mercury*, where Buckley was working, had been founded by the radical libertarian H. W. Mencken in the 1920s. It was now edited by William Bradford Huie, a courageous Alabamian who opposed Jim Crow. In 1950, a group of classical libertarians—Henry Hazlitt, John Chamberlain, and Suzanne La Follette—had revived *The Freeman*, founded, also in the 1920s, by radical libertarian Albert Jay Nock. And in 1944 classical libertarians William Henry Chamberlin, Frank Hanighen, and Felix Morley had started *Human Events*, the Washington weekly, still going strong today, focusing on national politics and policymaking.

By 1953, when Buckley left *The American Mercury* to collaborate with Brent Bozell on a book about Joe McCarthy, this small galaxy of conservative publications was in turmoil. *The Freeman*, plagued by internal dissent, was starting to wobble out of control. Forrest Davis, who had earlier persuaded McCarthy that General Marshall was a Communist, got control of *The Freeman* and alienated all his fellow editors and most of the stockholders. After a mass resignation of *Freeman* editors, Leonard Read's FEE put up the money to save the magazine—but purely as a journal of free-market economics, not as a commentator on the whole political, economic, and cultural scene.

That was a disappointment to those who loved *The Freeman* as it had been, but it was nothing like what happened to *The American Mercury*. It, too, was having financial trouble, and the owners turned to a Connecticut millionaire named Russell Maguire. Maguire had a good track record of backing right-wing causes and politicians. Unfortunately, it soon transpired that his primary interest was anti-Semitism. Huie resigned as editor, and the *Mercury* headed for the fever swamps.

Even before the decline of *The Freeman* and *The American Mercury*, an Austrian expatriate named William S. Schlamm had decided that a new right-wing magazine was needed. Schlamm was one of several former leftists turned fervent anti-leftists who had been harbored by Henry Luce in his Time–Life empire (others included Whittaker Chambers and John Chamberlain). Indeed, Schlamm had for a while been Luce's personal foreign policy advisor.

Schlamm had tried to get Henry Regnery's backing, but Regnery remained unconvinced of Schlamm's ability to launch a new magazine and hold it together. In 1953 Schlamm decided to try another tack. He had noticed Buckley—as who could not, among those who followed public controversy?—and proposed that the young man spearhead the new venture. Schlamm's genuinely brilliant insight was that someone just starting out in public life would have a better chance than an established figure of getting other established figures to come into his tent. As Buckley later put it, "It was much easier for a 29-year-old to be editor in chief of a magazine with these giants than for a 39-year-old or a 49-year-old, because people are willing to do favors and be condescending toward someone who is 25 years younger than they." But sometimes the condescension grated. Decades later, long after Schlamm had returned to Austria, mutual friend Erik von Kuehnelt-Leddihn said to Buckley one evening, "You know that Willi loved you like a son."

"Yes," said Buckley. "The problem is he treated me like a three-year-old son."

In any case, Buckley could do nothing with Schlamm's idea until he and Bozell had completed *McCarthy and His Enemies*. Aloïse Heath's account of that collaboration was meant to be humorous, and succeeded—but there was truth beneath the humor. "Bill," Allie wrote in the family newsletter, "spent half the summer of 1953 in Stamford, moodily writing his share of *McCarthy and His Enemies*, and the other half in Sharon, quarrelsomely rewriting Brent Bozell's. Brent, *McC. and H. E.*'s coauthor, vice-versa'd both geographically and emotionally." Among other things, the book had to be exhaustively researched if it was not to succumb to the same charges launched at the senator himself. As Buckley later put it, "Eighteen months of research and writing is a long enough time to spend seeking out an eighth allegory in Dante's *Inferno*; it is a very very long time to spend on the question whether Esther Brunauer was ever a member of the Joint Anti-Fascist Refugee League."

Also, although Buckley said nothing about it in public at the time, he and Pat suffered a devastating personal loss early in the course of this project. The pregnancy that had produced Christopher was actually Pat's second; the first had been ectopic. She now suffered a second ectopic pregnancy, putting an end to her and Bill's hopes of a larger family. This is not a topic Bill has often spoken or written about—though fifty years later, in *Last Call for Blackford Oakes*, he gave the circumstance of one successful pregnancy and two ectopics to the engaging Nina and Lindbergh Titov. Once Pat's social career took off, many people assumed that she had deliberately not had more children lest the pregnancies spoil her figure and interfere with the scheduling of charity balls. But that was not at all her agenda. Whether Bill and Pat would have emulated Will and Aloïse Buckley with ten children (as Ben and Allie Heath and Brent and Trish Bozell were doing), or stayed closer to the three of Austin and Babe Taylor, who knows? But life would have been very different for Bill and Pat, and for Christopher.

In any case, in the fall of 1953 the young authors completed their manuscript, all 250,000 words of it, considerably more than Henry

Eight of the Buckleys, grown up, with spouses; they are in the patio, a Mexican touch that WFB Sr. had added to Great Elm. Left to right, front row: John, Bill, Jim; second row: Brent, Trish, John's Ann, Pat, Priscilla, Jim's Ann, Allie; back row: Jane and Bill Smith, Betsey and Reid, Ben Heath.

Regnery thought marketable. They hired Schlamm to cut 75,000 words and write a prologue, and the book was published in March 1954, one month before the Army-McCarthy hearings began. It was not a book that said much about McCarthy personally. As Buckley's comment about Esther Brunauer suggests, it was a painstaking sifting of the evidence concerning people McCarthy had, in one way or another, targeted. And it by no means concluded that the senator was always right. McCarthy himself apparently understood the authors' need to distance themselves from some of his forays, but his wife, Jeanie, thought any such formulations disloyal, and she tried, unsuccessfully, to undercut the project with Regnery. Even so, after Edward R. Murrow's first major attack on McCarthy, the senator asked Buckley if he would go on Murrow's show to refute the charges. Buckley said yes, but Murrow's people refused. So McCarthy, by now drinking heavily, attempted his own refutation and was pummeled by Murrow. He never recovered.

It was not until 1998, in his novel *The Redhunter*, that Buckley wrote extensively about Joe McCarthy as a human being. The portrayal there is of a man passionately patriotic, intuitive rather than logical, temperamentally a gambler, and the more tenacious the more he was challenged. McCarthy was also, according to Buckley and many other friends, a splendid companion, but one whose salt never lost its savor. Once at a party he was being pursued by a large woman who had some information to pass on to him. Unfortunately, she had a habit of standing very close to her interlocutor, all the while spilling cigarette ashes on her ample bosom. McCarthy sidled up to Frank and Elsie Meyer and growled, "Keep her away from me—she *breasts* me."

Like *God and Man*, *McCarthy* got good notices in the few existing right-wing publications, and fire and brimstone from the left. Even those liberals (like Dwight Macdonald) who had had good things to say about *God and Man* panned *McCarthy*. The orthodoxy within the liberal intelligentsia had hardened: of Joe McCarthy, *nothing* good could be said.

On the other hand, there were plenty of people in the country who were not liberal intellectuals and who were interested in hearing what McCarthy's young defenders had to say. Buckley had not been officially invited back to Yale since *God and Man*, but now he and Bozell were asked to debate two law school professors, Vern Countryman (who had attacked *God and Man*) and Fowler Harper. In a jam-packed Woolsey Hall, the pro-McCarthy team, according to the next day's Yale *Daily News*, won resoundingly. A few weeks later, when Buckley spoke at the National Republican Club in Manhattan, a thousand people gathered inside the hall and more than a thousand outside in Bryant Park, listening over loudspeakers. The reaction was tumultuous. As in his days on the Yale debate team and the *Daily News*, so would it be throughout Buckley's adult career: the spoken word and the personal presence would be as important in furthering his mission as the written word.

After *McCarthy and His Enemies* was published, Bozell, who had obtained his law degree from Yale, went to work on McCarthy's defense team in the Senate censure hearings, and Buckley continued to do some speechwriting for the senator. But for Bill, it was time for the next thing. He and Pat went to visit Willi and Steffi Schlamm in Vermont, and Bill and Willi started to outline their plan.

They agreed on the type of magazine they wanted to put out— something modeled on *The Freeman*, which would include running commentary on the events of the day as well as less ephemeral political and economic analysis and cultural and social observation. They agreed that Buckley would be the editor-in-chief and—crucial point—would own all the voting stock, so that warring parties could not scuttle the new journal, as they were in the lengthy process of doing to *The Freeman*. Of course, Schlamm never assumed his own role would be truly subordinate. As he wrote with breathtaking candor to his old friend and colleague Whittaker Chambers, whom he was trying to recruit for the editorial board, the senior editors would "establish satrapies in the magazine, domains in which each of us editors is acknowledged as the supreme authority (although all of us, in technical ultimate decision, will listen to the editor-publisher who hires and fires us)." And, third point, the appealing young American Buckley rather than the sardonic, heavy-featured, Austrian-accented Schlamm would be the principal money-raiser. This was a role Buckley did not relish (and has continued not relishing for the succeeding fifty years that he has performed it). As he wrote to his father's friend and colleague Dean Reasoner, "I think I also told you that I am a rotten salesman, and that I have always conceived of Hell as the place where people of my temperament are required to spend eternity going from person to person selling something."

But sell he did. Few of his papers from that period have survived—he did not yet have, after all, a permanent office and a personal secretary—and so we don't have the sort of detailed record of his movements that we have for later years. But he was on the road a lot. At *NR*'s forty-fifth anniversary party, Christopher Buckley recalled his child's-eye view of the magazine's founding. "'Founding Mother,' I would say, 'where is Founding Father *tonight*?'" Buckley sought out people with money and conservative inclinations in the Midwest, the Deep South, and Texas, as well as in the New York area. An important—and slightly surprising, even then—source of support was Hollywood. Buckley had met screenwriter Morris Ryskind—like Burnham, Schlamm, et al., a former leftist turned anti-Communist—while giving a talk in Los Angeles on the McCarthy controversy. Ryskind liked him, agreed with him, and did everything he could to help launch the new magazine. Half a world away, in Paris, where she was working for United Press, Priscilla Buckley was introduced to Adolphe Menjou. "Are you any relation of Bill Buckley?" the dapper actor asked.

"Why, yes. He's my brother."

"What a charming, talented young man," Menjou replied, and proceeded to tell Priscilla's lunch guest, Gloria Swanson, about Bill's

Where's Founding
Father tonight? Home!

meetings with a group of men that included Ward Bond, Bing Crosby, and John Wayne. (Buckley did not meet Ronald Reagan until several years later, but Reagan was an early subscriber to the magazine.)

The money came in, but more slowly than Buckley and Schlamm had hoped. They reckoned they would need $550,000 to cover expenses until they had built up a subscriber base. As of September 1955 they had $290,000 from outside sources, plus $100,000 put up by the magazine's first and most enthusiastic backer, WFB Sr.

Meanwhile, there was the need to recruit some colleagues, and here, too, there were snags. Buckley and Schlamm hoped to pick up some of the former *Freeman*ites left without a home after their mass resignation. John Chamberlain was, as Buckley and Schlamm had hoped, entirely sympathetic with their plans. However, by the time they started recruiting editors, he had accepted a position with *Barron's*. With two young daughters to support, his wife, Peggy, strongly opposed his leaving *Barron's* to join the fledgling venture. Ralph de Toledano similarly declined to leave *Newsweek*. And Whittaker Chambers, besides having suffered a serious heart attack, doubted that the magazine, if it ever got off the ground, could do much to affect the great struggle then going on. "It is idle," he wrote to Buckley, "to talk about preventing the wreck of Western civilization. It is already a wreck from within."

But Suzanne La Follette was willing to come aboard. A cousin (once removed) of Fighting Bob La Follette, the old Progressive senator, she had worked for the original *Freeman* under Nock in the 1920s. She had veered left in the 1930s, but had been jolted by the Stalin purges—especially the trial of Leon Trotsky—and had come back to right-wing libertarianism. She had been the founding managing editor of the new *Freeman* in 1950. Now she was hired to be the founding managing editor (though listed on the masthead simply as one of five editors) of the *National Weekly*, as Buckley and Schlamm were planning to call their magazine. (As it turned out, that name was already copyrighted and they had to choose another—providentially, since *National Review* survived as a weekly for fewer than three years before finances obliged it to go fortnightly.)

James Burnham was also willing. Tall, courtly in manner, the son of a prosperous Chicago railroad man, he had degrees from Princeton and Oxford and had been a professor of philosophy at New York University. During his association with the American Workers Party, cofounded by his friend and NYU colleague Sidney Hook, he spent some vacation time as a union organizer (to the distaste of his elegant wife, Marcia, who did not like muddy boots in her front hall). While teaching aesthetics and Thomist philosophy at NYU (one of his courses was called "Aquinas and Dante"), he had become Leon Trotsky's leading spokesman in the United States. In later years he liked to say that his beliefs had not changed, just his perception of how best to put them into practice. Swallowing that may take a few grains of salt, but Burnham could provide surprising illustrations. For example, he once started a column with the dictum "Who says A must say B" and concluded with "Who wills the ends wills the means." He took pleasure in pointing out that the former was the Trotskyist, the latter the Thomist formulation of the same statement. (Burnham trained young colleagues at *NR* to say "Trotskyist," not "Trotskyite." In his memory, his former pupils still do.)

Buckley had first met Burnham in June 1950, when Kendall introduced them in the course of recruiting Buckley into the CIA. One month later, Buckley took Burnham's *The Coming Defeat of Communism* with him to Hawaii for beach reading during his and Pat's honeymoon.

By the time Buckley and Schlamm were recruiting colleagues for the new magazine, Burnham had cut himself off from most of his old associations. He had broken with Trotsky early in the war, over the "Old Man's" defense of Stalin's invasion of Poland and Finland.

Most of his post-Trotskyist colleagues were liberal anti- (and often ex-) Communists of one stripe or another—Dwight Macdonald, Mary McCarthy, Sidney Hook. He rattled this coterie with an essay published in *Partisan Review* titled "Lenin's Heir"—that is, Stalin. Burnham's argument was that Stalin, not Trotsky, was Lenin's true heir—his point being not that Stalin was better than Trotsky, but that Lenin was as bad as Stalin. However, his ironic ode to Stalin's Jove-like "insolence and indifference and brutality" was bizarrely misread, first by Dwight Macdonald and then by George Orwell, as signifying, in Orwell's phrase, "a sort of fascinated admiration." Fascinated, yes; admiration, never.

Still, there was no permanent split with Macdonald at that time, and Burnham remained on the advisory board of *Partisan Review*. In 1949 he was recruited by a Princeton classmate, Joseph Bryan III, to do contract work for the CIA's covert operations division, for which he took a leave of absence from NYU and moved his family to Washington, D.C. During this period, he helped found the Congress for Cultural Freedom, mobilizing anti-Stalinist leftists against the Soviets' phony "peace" initiatives. He eventually resigned from NYU to work for the Congress full-time.

Then along came Joe McCarthy. Burnham had no great love for McCarthy himself and disapproved of his methods, both on intellectual grounds and as likely to harm the anti-Communist cause. But he agreed with McCarthy that the Soviets were being abetted by Americans in high places and that these should be ferreted out. And he held in contempt those who treated McCarthy as if he were Torquemada, Savonarola, and Hitler rolled into one. In opposition to the anti-anti-Communists, Burnham became what he called an "anti-anti-McCarthyite." But this made him, to use his own word, an "anomaly" at *Partisan Review*, the Congress for Cultural Freedom, and even the CIA. Howard Hunt later revealed that he had been ordered by Frank Wisner, the legendary but increasingly unstable head of covert operations, to have nothing more to do with Burnham. One by one Burnham was fired by, or preemptively resigned from, these entities; he ceased to have contact with many old friends on the left except in the public prints. When Buckley came to call on him at his farmhouse up on the hill above Kent, Connecticut, a village a few miles south of Sharon, Burnham was more than ready to join up.

There was one last snag: Marcia Burnham, surprisingly, went to Buckley and urged him not to hire her husband. He had wrecked every organization he had ever belonged to, this formidable woman told the twenty-nine-year-old aspiring editor, and he would wreck this one. Providence was at work again. Buckley did not take her advice, and Burnham would prove to be the most loyal deputy a man could have.

Incorporation papers had been drawn up (by, as it happens, William Casey, Esq.—the same William Casey who would later be Ronald Reagan's director of central intelligence). April 1955 had been set for the launch date, even though *National Review* was still short on funds. And then WFB Sr., who had previously suffered a couple of minor strokes, had a major one, leaving him in a coma for several days and partially paralyzed thereafter. Bill rushed down to Charlotte, North Carolina, to join his mother and siblings in the hospital vigil, and the launch was postponed until November.

2

Forging the Conservative Movement

A printer had been found: Wilson & Co. in Orange, Connecticut. Wilson served also as compositor—in those pre-computer days, typesetting was emphatically not a do-it-yourself proposition, as the intricate, gargantuan Linotype machines required highly skilled operators. Office space had been found, in a rundown building at 211 East 37th Street in Manhattan. The building was unsalubriously located right on one of the exits from the traffic-choked Queens-Midtown Tunnel. However, it was also conveniently located just two blocks away from the elegant townhouse occupied by Catawba, the company tying together the various Buckley oil enterprises. Catawba extended its hospitality whenever *National Review* needed a place for a formal meeting or an editorial lunch with outside guests. (If Buckley was lunching alone with someone, it might be at an Upper East Side French restaurant called Voisin or at the venerable German Lüchow's, both of which advertised in *NR* for many years, or at the New York Yacht Club or the Yale Club.) A small production staff had been assembled, headed by *Freeman* alumna Mabel Wood and including Maureen Buckley, just a year out of Smith College, and her school chum Reggie (née Rosamond) Horton. And Buckley had acquired his first personal secretary—the omnicompetent Gertrude

Vogt, who had spent many years in the book review section at the *New York Herald Tribune* and who sought to impart some of her own formidable self-discipline to the new enterprise.

The first issue of *National Review: A Weekly Journal of Opinion* was put to bed on November 11, thirteen days before its editor/publisher's thirtieth birthday. (Volume I, Number 1 was formally dated November 19, 1955, such being the conventions in magazine publishing.) "A blue-bordered oasis in a sea of desolation," one early reader called it, and for several years that narrow blue border was the only decoration on the cover. Those first, thirty-two-page issues (dropping to twenty-four pages within the first six months) were printed on butcher paper, and *NR*'s layout was only slightly less austere than *The Freeman*'s. The columns of type were relieved only by the occasional line drawing (usually by the courtly Hungarian expatriate Alois Derso) or cartoon (in the beginning, the gorgeous steel-engraving style of C. D. Batchelor, soon joined by the chaotic jagged lines of John Kreuttner). As in *The Freeman*, each issue began with a few pages of unsigned editorials before going into signed material. The magazine was heavily column-driven; in a typical issue there would be three main articles, framed by eight or ten columns (by Buckley, Burnham, Schlamm, Kendall, Bozell, and Kirk, plus Sam M. Jones from Washington, Freda Utley on "the figure the United States is cutting abroad," Frank Meyer on academic journals, Jonathan Mitchell on labor and business, and Karl Hess on the liberal press). There would be one long book review per issue, and half a dozen short ones. John Chamberlain had agreed to write the lead book review every other issue; on the alternate weeks, the lead might be written by Burnham or Richard Weaver or John Dos Passos or one of several others—most of the editors and contributors listed on the masthead wrote reviews from time to time. Among distinguished reviewers not on the masthead were Philip Burnham, longtime editor of *Commonweal* (and younger brother of Jim); Cleanth Brooks; Roy Campbell, the South African author and adventurer (he didn't just write about bullfighting, he actually fought bulls in the south of France); and William Henry Chamberlin, foreign correspondent for the *Christian Science Monitor*. Chutzpah time: an early issue featured Senator Joseph R. McCarthy on Dean Acheson's memoirs (the review was actually written by Brent Bozell).

From the start, humor and style were as much a part of the magazine as exposition of political principles and analysis of current events.

Two of the first issue's cover articles are humorous in manner, though serious in substance. In "How to Raise Money in the Ivy League," Aloïse Heath explains that the way to do it is to write a letter to fellow alumni/ae warning that "the Best College in the World harbors pink professors." When Mrs. Heath tried it, money poured into Smith College's coffers and hate mail onto her desk. In "They'll Never Get Me on That Couch," Morrie Ryskind tells of the difficulties of social life in Hollywood if one is (a) conservative and (b) unpsychoanalyzed. The Publisher's Statement in that first issue is where the line, endlessly quoted, about standing athwart history first appeared. But the statement also contains less often cited gems: "There never was an age of conformity quite like this one, or a camaraderie quite like the Liberals'. Drop a little itching powder in Jimmy Wechsler's bath and before he has scratched himself for the third time, Arthur Schlesinger will have denounced you in a dozen books and speeches, Archibald MacLeish will have written ten heroic cantos about our age of terror, *Harper's* will have published them, and everyone in sight will have been nominated for a Freedom Award." This, in the formal statement launching a new magazine!

And from the start, the magazine was deliberately eclectic in its choice of editors and contributors. There would be room for adherents of every major strand of right-wing thought: libertarians and Burkeans, free-marketeers and Southern Agrarians, Madisonians and European monarchists. The only categories excluded were racists, anti-Semites, and "kooks."

Very early, a species called "the *National Review* conservative" came to be taxonomized. How could that be, with such a wide range of colorations? Basically, a *National Review* conservative was (and is) one who (a) is not automatically excluded for one or more of the reasons listed above, and (b) is willing, even if it requires the gritting of teeth, to work with the other members of the group. Thus, when Russell Maguire took *The American Mercury* anti-Semitic, Buckley issued an order: No one who appeared on *The American Mercury*'s masthead could appear on *National Review*'s. Such a person could write for *NR* as long as his own writing was not anti-Semitic; but masthead, no. Max Eastman, on the other hand, the redoubtable biographer of Trotsky, was welcomed at *NR* despite his atheism, and he appeared on the initial masthead. But, as Buckley later wrote, Eastman was not merely an atheist but a "God-hater." He soon decided that the Christianity of too many of his colleagues was too evident, and so he decamped. Ayn Rand, another God-hater, never wrote for the magazine—and after Whittaker Chambers's lacerating review of *Atlas Shrugged* in December 1957, she made it known that she would walk out of any room Buckley walked into. On the opposite end of the right-wing spectrum was Peter Viereck, self-styled "New Conservative." Viereck had come by his opinions honestly, in reaction to his father's pro-Nazism, but he wound up closer to Adlai Stevenson than to Robert Taft, and he was extolled by Arthur Schlesinger Jr. as part of the "Vital Center." Frank Meyer took the trouble to read him out of the conservative movement, but he was always a movement of one.

With all that, the "*National Review* conservatives" on the first masthead ranged widely enough—from near-anarchists Chodorov and Hess to classical libertarians Chamberlain and Meyer, to traditionalists Kirk and Bozell and Southern Agrarian Weaver, to self-described "majority-rule democrat" Kendall, to anti-Communists Burnham, Utley, and Eugene Lyons.

As *NR*'s second publisher, William A. Rusher, would later put it, Buckley's "getting all these lions, tigers, and bears to lie down with each other, in the name of battling liberalism, was an immense accomplishment." Rusher was referring partly to the different subspecies under the "*NR* conservative" rubric. But he was referring also to the temperaments of some of the founding editors. Schlamm feuded with Kendall and was suspicious of Burnham's influence on Buckley. La Follette frequently clashed with Kendall over his insouciantly idiomatic grammar and word usage; his locally famous retort was: "Suzanne, when people get around to making dictionaries, they come to people like me to find out what to put in them." Russell Kirk was chagrined to find himself on the same masthead as Frank Meyer, who had begun his review of *The Conservative Mind* for *The Freeman* with the words, "Russell Kirk's books, in declining order of importance, are . . ." and then proceeded to list them chronologically. Kirk stayed on the masthead for just four issues, then withdrew. But he continued to write his "From the Academy" column for the next twenty-five years. (Two years after *National Review* was founded, Henry Regnery backed Kirk in the founding of *Modern Age*, a conservative quarterly that published many of the same people as *National Review* but with a more scholarly tone.)

Some of these disputes (Kendall versus anyone, Schlamm versus almost anyone) were largely a matter of personal style. Others, like

Meyer versus Kirk, were founded on deeply cherished principles. To Kirk, "individualism" was "social atomism," and liberty had to bow before "tradition and sound prejudice." To Meyer, "Liberty is the political end of man's existence because liberty is the condition of his being." But despite all the disputes, the magazine continued publishing, attracting subscribers and advertisers as it went.

It also, just a few months into its existence, attracted the notice of the intellectual left. In February 1956 John Fischer, the editor of *Harper's,* weighed in with a lengthy analysis of the new magazine and its personnel—"or rather psycho-analysis," as Buckley described it in his reply; in the April *Commentary* Dwight Macdonald offered a striking mixture of suavely urbane dismissal and vitriolic, adjective-laden attack, titled "Scrambled Eggheads on the Right"; and in the July *Progressive* Murray Kempton tut-tutted over the magazine's utter boringness.

Macdonald's essay is the most often quoted of the three; a couple of samples will give the flavor. "Here are the ideas," Macdonald wrote, "here is the style of the *lumpen*-bourgeoisie, the half-educated, half-successful provincials . . . who responded to Huey Long, Father Coughlin, and Senator McCarthy. Anxious, embittered, resentful, they feel that the main stream of American politics since 1932 has passed them by, as indeed it has, and they have the slightly paranoiac suspiciousness of an isolated minority group. For these are men from underground, the intellectually underprivileged who feel themselves excluded from a world they believe is ruled by liberals (or eggheads— the terms are, significantly, interchangeable in *NR*) just as the economic underdog feels alienated from society." Golly! Or this about James Burnham, Thomist philosopher and aesthetician: "a spectacular backslider from Trotskyism . . . whose intellectual horizon has steadily narrowed to a kind of anti-Communism as sterile and doctrinaire as the ideology he fights."

Buckley devoted more than five thousand words to his reply, which analyzed the three essays in some detail and then summed up: "The kind of criticism levelled at *National Review* by Messrs. Fischer, Macdonald and Kempton leaves little doubt, it seems to me, as to the nature of our offense. *National Review* is neither supine nor irrelevant. It does not consult Arthur Schlesinger, Jr., to determine the limits of tolerable conservative behavior, nor does it subsist on mimeographed clichés describing The Plot to Destroy America. It has gathered together men of competence and sanity who have, quietly and with precision, gone to work on the problems of the day and turned over many stones, to expose much cant and ugliness and intellectual corruption. It is to be expected that They should set the hounds on us."

For *National Review*'s first couple of years, Buckley was spending virtually all his working time at the magazine. But even for someone who works as hard as he does, "working time" isn't coextensive with "time." In 1954 he and his brother-in-law Austin "Firpo" Taylor (so nicknamed because he was born the day Firpo fought Dempsey) had bought a forty-two-foot cutter. They and their friends sailed *The Panic* up and down the New England coast, both cruising and racing. Then in 1956 they did their first Newport-Bermuda race—not threatening any of the leaders, but placing respectably for their class.

Not long afterward Bill led a dozen friends and siblings (including Priscilla, Maureen, Brent, and Trish) up to Pico Peak in Vermont to try skiing. As the story goes, they rented equipment and, after zero lessons, took the chairlift up to the top. Pico is not the highest mountain in the Northeast, and the trails from the top, while rated black (most difficult), are nothing compared to, say, Superstar at neighboring Killington. Still, it's a wonder that they all made it down alive—and more of a wonder that half the party signed up for lessons that same day and became avid skiers.

Buckley also made sure there was a lively social life involving *National Review* and its circle. The editorial meeting every Tuesday morning was followed by editorial lunch. This was usually at Catawba's offices, until an Italian American pop singer named Nicola Paone started a little restaurant nearby, and it quickly became an *NR* favorite. There might be one or more guests—writers with whom the magazine wanted to make contact (future contributors Arnold Beichman and Ernest van den Haag turn up on early lists), European visitors (Otto von Habsburg, Erik von Kuehnelt-Leddihn), or local supporters of the magazine (the military historian Hoffman Nickerson, whose second wife, Bonnie, had been Hilaire Belloc's research assistant). On Tuesday evening, after a full day's work, the core of the editorial-writing team would repair to one or another restaurant—it might be French, or Italian, or Chinese—for dinner. On Wednesday evening, after the editorial section in manuscript form had been given to the printer's messenger, the whole editorial/production department plus members of the business staff, notably Bill Rusher and Jim McFadden, would gather for editorial drinks, trading stories for an hour or so before dispersing to their several dinners.

And there were parties, over which Pat presided with the brilliance that was becoming legendary. The most ambitious was the Christmastime Messiah Party, which involved staff and friends trundling out to Wallacks Point to listen to a recording of *Messiah* and then partake of a lavish buffet.

All of this could not keep fissures from developing, but in the absence of rending differences it did—and still does, as we write, even though Bill has substantially retired from the magazine—promote a sense that we are indeed a band of brothers, friends as well as colleagues.

From the perspective of the Sixties—whether the radical Sixties or the swinging Sixties—the Eisenhower years were bland, traditionalist, oppressive, emblematic of the traces that had to be kicked over. So what was there for a new conservative magazine to stand athwart?

Plenty, alas. The men and women who started *National Review* hadn't expected much of Eisenhower, and not much is what they got. True, as of November 1955, all the real disasters overseas had happened on Truman's watch—the Soviet Union's salami-slicing of Central Europe; the Communist takeovers in China and North Korea; the preemption by executive fiat of any attempt by MacArthur to reverse the takeover in North Korea; the Soviets' development, partly via spy activity in the West, of atomic weapons. However, the few effective counterattacks were also under Truman—the establishment of NATO; the Truman Doctrine; the Berlin airlift. John Foster Dulles, as Ike's secretary of state, bowwowed more fiercely than Dean Acheson had done as Truman's, but what did the new administration actually accomplish in the way of rollback? Nothing. It did give aid and comfort to the Nationalist Chinese who had fled to Taiwan; it called a halt to the Korean War with the border no farther south than when the Communists invaded; it engaged in (or permitted Allen Dulles's CIA to engage in) various activities to help forestall indigenous

Communist takeovers in Western Europe. But this was all (to borrow from the title of Burnham's 1953 book) containment, not liberation.

This was high among the reasons *NR* seriously considered backing a challenge to Eisenhower's renomination in 1956. It was no coincidence that the third main article in Volume I, Number 1, was a devastating analysis of the temptations to appeasement (what fans of summitry had dubbed the "Spirit of Geneva") by California senator William Knowland, the conservatives' likeliest candidate had they gone ahead with the challenge.

On the domestic front, many of the things the magazine opposed most forcefully were the fault not of the Eisenhower administration, but rather of the courts or the cultural elites: social engineering, "progressivism" in grade school education, secularism and collectivism in the universities, excessive power given to labor unions. But the administration had done nothing to roll back the government apparatus installed by the New Deal/Fair Deal. And *NR*'s editors would not forget that in the great domestic battle between the anti-Communists and the anti-anti-Communists, when Eisenhower had finally had enough, he turned his ruthlessness not against the Communist sympathizers still squatting in his government, but against Joe McCarthy.

From *National Review*'s perspective, Ike had two big things going for him. The first was that he was not Adlai Stevenson (or even Nelson Rockefeller or Henry Cabot Lodge). That is, though not a principled conservative, he was not a dyed-in-the-wool liberal, either. He didn't roll back the Roosevelt/Truman government expansions, but—except for his interstate highway system—he mostly didn't treat the taxpayer's money as if it presumptively belonged to Washington.

The second was his vice president. Conservatives didn't confuse Richard M. Nixon with Russell Kirk or Friedrich von Hayek. But, as Buckley would later write, "at the earliest conspicuous moment in his career, he had been spotted as the man who believed Whittaker Chambers, and disbelieved Alger Hiss." Chambers never lost his regard for Nixon, and his opinion counted for a great deal with Buckley. So when, in late 1955 and early 1956, a Dump Nixon movement started in the left wing of the Republican Party, and when Eisenhower did not move decisively to quash it, conservatives got busy. In the weeks leading up to the New Hampshire primary, *NR* repeatedly reminded its readers (sometimes in the editorial section, sometimes in Sam Jones's Washington column) of the importance of keeping Nixon on the ticket, and other conservative voices around the country did the same. When, in March, twenty-two thousand New Hampshire Republicans wrote in Nixon's name on their ballots as their choice for VP, the Dump Nixon movement collapsed.

Even so, *NR* could only hold its nose when considering a second Eisenhower term. "General Eisenhower," Buckley himself wrote in a signed article in March, "is a good man. He is not a doctrinaire, or an adventurer who would commit the nation's destiny in pursuit of one beguiling horizon, or a redeemer cocksure of his afflatus. That is not a part of the Eisenhower program, for it is not a program administered either by traitors, or adventurers, or charisma-conscious political evangelists or, even, cynics. Therein its strengths—its only strengths." In October, the magazine published a two-man symposium on the question: "Should Conservatives Vote for Eisenhower–Nixon?" Yes, said Burnham: because on almost every point the Eisenhower administration is at least marginally better than the Democratic alternative, and because for conservatives to abstain or vote for a third party would "serve only to isolate conservatives still further from the life of the nation." No, said Schlamm: because "Mr. Eisenhower is not the first Republican President elected since 1928. He is the first Democratic President elected on the Republican ticket." Therefore, "For conservatives, the strategic job in this year's election is to break" Eisenhower's control over the party; "that control . . . can be broken only by defeating Mr. Eisenhower."

Burnham's resolve to vote for the ticket was sorely tested, and Schlamm's position strengthened, by two events that took place halfway around the world in the fortnight before the election. On October 23, Hungarians rose up against their Soviet oppressors. The rebels believed that they had been encouraged by Radio Free Europe (though the head of RFE claimed that the station was merely extolling the virtues of freedom, not advocating an attempt to achieve it) and that American troops, or at least matériel, would soon be arriving. On October 29, Israel sent troops across the Sinai Desert, attempting, in concert with Britain and France, to regain control of the Suez Canal, which Nasser had nationalized in July. In the case of Suez, Eisenhower categorically condemned the "resort to force" by our allies. In the case of Hungary, he murmured vague appreciation of the desire for freedom; when, on November 4, the Red Army, after a tactical retreat, turned around and began massacring the lightly armed Hungarians, Eisenhower did: nothing. He did not even—as editorials by Buckley forcefully reminded *NR*'s readers—instruct our delegates to the UN to press for a condemnation of the Soviet Union. Indeed, the U.S. delegation helped block any meaningful UN action in Hungary, while on Suez we actively collaborated with the Soviets against the nations we called our allies.

Hungary brought out, even more sharply than the concurrent U.S. election, the differences of temperament and approach among *NR*'s editors and leading contributors. They all agreed, of course, in deploring the Soviet attack and the weak Western response. But they differed enormously in tone. Schlamm and his close friend Erik von Kuehnelt-Leddihn—an aristocratic Austrian monarchist and *NR*'s principal European correspondent—launched passionate denunciations. Schlamm: "Europe, now that the Hungarian witnesses to man's indomitable hunger for freedom are buried, remembers its last forty years of blundering illusion and stupid surrender." Kuehnelt-Leddihn: "Perhaps everything will be saved—except honor. This is the reaction of every impartial observer of the Hungarian tragedy, which, excepting the drama of the Warsaw rising in 1944, is the most monstrous single happening in modern history." Buckley deployed searing irony: "We wish a national moratorium could be declared on verbal and written criticism of Communism and Communists. We wish that every politician, every orator, every editorial writer, every preacher would, one morning, stop deploring any act of the Soviet Union, or aspect of Communism. In the sudden stillness, we would realize how empty has been our 'opposition' to Communism, for in that stillness we would hear, in dreadful clarity, only the bustling wheels of normalcy, and know the absence of any meaningful act of resistance; and, without the solace of our rhetoric, we might be ashamed." Bozell imagined a conversation between Eisenhower and John Foster Dulles: "'It's just that I wish those people hadn't counted on us. Even though you're right, it kind of haunts you—you know.' 'I know, Mr. President. I admit it haunts me, too—even though I know you're right. There is one consolation: certainly no one will ever misunderstand us in the future.' 'That is certainly true.'" And Burnham couched his own denunciation in terms of a mordant prudence: "Withdrawal from *all* the satellites, not merely from Hungary, should be made the first demand in all contexts. It could properly be made a condition to every negotiation with Moscow on any subject. With the present situation in East Europe inhibiting effective Soviet counteraction toward the West, the demand for withdrawal can be put forward, with a minimum risk, in the sharpest terms: even, if Western leadership could face its responsibilities, as an ultimatum."

More important than the differences in tone were the differences in concrete recommendations, and these brought a long-simmering dispute to the boil.

Schlamm from the start of *National Review* had found Burnham to be too much of a Realpolitiker. Burnham had found Schlamm to be an unrealistic purist. And though Buckley's own inclinations were often closer to Schlamm's, he had come to trust Burnham more. At *National Review*'s offices there are several sets of "marked copies" of the magazine—bound volumes in which the author of each unsigned editorial is noted. Buckley and Burnham from the start were the workhorses of the editorial section, assisted by regular contributions from Suzanne La Follette, economist Jonathan Mitchell, Maureen Buckley, and, starting in February 1956, Priscilla Buckley. Far less regular were the contributions by Schlamm and Kendall. But in Schlamm's case the problem wasn't laziness: he was submitting plenty of editorials, but Buckley judged many of them unusable.

Now, in December 1956, just after the magazine's first birthday, Burnham dropped a depth charge into the office water cooler: a characteristically calm, analytical column in which he explained why, in the present circumstances, the best chance of achieving the liberation of Central Europe lay in "neutralizing" it—that is, demanding the removal of Soviet troops from the Captive Nations, and making that possible for the Kremlin by removing American troops from West Germany and creating a reunified, demilitarized Germany.

Most of Burnham's colleagues were appalled. Schlamm, whether more appalled than most or whether seeing a strategic opportunity, went ballistic. He (along with La Follette) demanded that Buckley kill that column and threatened to resign if he did not. Heated arguments were followed up by memos. Eventually, Buckley wrote an editorial, titled "Wait and See," in which he distanced the magazine from Burnham's proposals but at the same time invited Burnham to elaborate on them and invited the other editors to reply. "Does *National Review* buy the proposal?" Buckley wrote. "Certainly not on the strength of what we have heard to date. But we shall not close our minds on the subject. We shall encourage serious discussion of the proposal in future issues. . . . Such a discussion will surely be fruit-ful, for it will be a discussion of means between men who share the relevant fundamental assumptions: that coexistence is immoral, unde-sirable, and, in the long run, impossible; that we are dealing with an implacable enemy whose revolutionary fervor burns as hot as ever, and whose designs on the men of the West, and their institutions, remain the same."

After Burnham's own follow-up, Schlamm was allowed first crack at him. His essay concluded: "The supercharged Spirit of Geneva which [Burnham] now wishes on Dr. Adenauer—not in spite but, mind you, because of the Hungarian slaughter!—is the specter of our own perdition. Hard anti-Communists, even when afflicted by a spell of *ennui*, will not sacrifice the certainty which has formed their char-acter, and has established their decisiveness, to the intellectual kick of a 'new' and 'interesting' idea."

Meyer and Bozell followed, also in pretty tough terms (although neither of them laid down ultimatums to Buckley). The only partici-pant who thought Burnham's idea had merit was the political philosopher Gerhart Niemeyer (who, perhaps not coincidentally, was German-born). Niemeyer closed his piece with a cheerful exhortation and a statement not entirely accurate: "On with the discussion, gen-tlemen. Minds are still open."

This extended symposium patched things up for the moment, which was Buckley's immediate goal. For anyone familiar with his career as debater and polemicist, this will sound very odd indeed, but he hates confrontation over personal matters. Over ideas, absolutely—bring on all comers. But the unspoken rule of Great Elm and Kam-schatka—avoid personal unpleasantness; avoid forcing anyone to say something painful—was deeply internalized.

Buckley could not easily forget that the magazine had been Schlamm's idea in the first place. Also, Schlamm's columns—"For-eign Trends" and "Arts & Manners"—were very popular with *NR*'s readers. But Schlamm had proved undisciplined as an editorial writer, whereas Burnham was reliable and often brilliant. And Schlamm's shouting and ultimatums were profoundly distasteful to Buckley and other staffers, particularly his sisters Priscilla and Maureen.

Buckley's first effort at finding a modus vivendi was to tell Schlamm to keep writing his columns but stop participating in the editorial meetings or writing for "The Week" (as the editorial section was called and still is, even though the magazine soon became a fortnightly). Schlamm sullenly acceded, coming down from his Vermont home each week only long enough to see a play or two and produce his copy. Then one day in the summer of 1957, he found he no longer had an office: Buckley, acutely aware of his own shortcomings on the business side, had hired Bill Rusher as publisher. The quarters at 211 East 37th had only four real (though tiny) offices with closable doors. It was clear that the publisher had to have one of them, and equally clear (to Buckley, but not to Schlamm) that a man who spent only one or two days per week in New York did not.

Schlamm issued one more ultimatum, pointing out—heartbreakingly, except that he had brought this breach on himself— that the magazine was as much his lifeblood as it was Buckley's. Buckley agreed to hold a meeting to settle matters, and he asked John Chamberlain (who by now was listed as an editor on *NR*'s masthead, although he had not joined the staff full-time) to take part. Chamberlain was one of Schlamm's oldest American friends, from Time–Life days, and he was the most irenic presence imaginable. But even Chamberlain could not prevail against the combination of Schlamm's principled disagreement with Burnham and his personal resentment of Burnham's having supplanted him in Buckley's confidence. And so the very man who had wisely urged Buckley to keep all the voting stock in his own hands ran right up against his own protective barrier. In the fall of 1957 Willi and Steffi Schlamm departed for Europe, where Willi resumed his German-language career. A few years later, visiting the States, he made an overture, which Buckley accepted, lunching with him and Chamberlain. After that, Schlamm contributed occasional pieces to *NR* from Europe.

Schlamm's writing is not much remembered in America today. His early work, for Henry Luce, was mostly published anonymously, and his theater reviews for *NR* (like John Simon's film reviews twenty years later) could be heavy-handed in their scorn. But Schlamm was a coiner of brilliant aphorisms, a couple of which Buckley still loves to quote: "The trouble with socialism is socialism. The trouble with capitalism is capitalists"; and (with regard to some concerned group or another) "Scientists are the people who first build the Brooklyn Bridge and then buy it." But within *NR* circles, Schlamm's earthly immortality was conferred by his rival, Burnham, who over the years compiled a set of "Laws" that he perceived as governing life. Number 6 is: "In every enterprise there is a Schlamm."

Even before the arrival of Rusher and the departure of Schlamm, there had been a fair amount of shuffling and changing on the staff as the new publication found its feet. The initial business team had been a disaster. Subscription renewal notices didn't get sent out, the book-keeper couldn't keep books, the advertising salesman didn't sell. Then one day a jaunty young man just out of the army arrived at 211 East 37th, saying that he had newspaper experience, he had read the magazine from the very first issue, and he wanted to join up as a sol-dier in the conservative movement. Buckley hired James P. McFadden on the spot, and he became indispensable, doing all sorts of necessary jobs on the publishing and promotion sides that no one had known were necessary. About a year later, a tough-minded and highly effi-cient Italian girl from Queens, Rose Caniano Flynn, took over the bookkeeping from the sweet but incompetent Miss Fairclough.

On the editorial side, Priscilla Buckley was still in Paris when the first issue of *National Review* arrived in her mailbox in November 1955. But she had already decided that it was time to leave the news-room at United Press and return Stateside. She adored—still adores—Paris, but the hours at UPI were killing and the pay low. More important, her father had never fully recovered from his stroke in April, and France was a long way from home in those days before commercial jet travel. Priscilla had not entirely decided what she would do after UPI, but Bill wasn't slow in letting her know, through typically circuitous Buckley "family channels," that he had a maga-zineful of intellectuals, and what he needed was a professional jour-nalist. By February 1956 she was sending in editorial items; in July she came to New York and joined the staff full time.

Besides doing her share of the editorial writing, Priscilla became the on-staff investigative reporter. One of her first signed articles brought in not a few CMSs (cancel-my-subscription letters). It was titled "Siberia, U.S.A.," and in it she examined and found wanting the theory making the right-wing rounds that the federal government had a plot "to get rid of political dissenters and critics on the right, particularly those who favored the Bricker Amendment [to limit the United States' activity abroad], by deporting them to Alaska." One of the CMSs conjectured that "Miss Buckley had remained in France too long, and acquired socialistic notions." Other topics she covered included fluoridation, a public school boondoggle in Westchester County, New York, and the efforts by the Soviet Union to lure back a group of émigrés living in New Jersey.

Willmoore Kendall, the initial editor of the Books section, proved lazy and unimaginative in his assignments; before long he had not too grudgingly given up a task he found onerous to Frank Meyer, who wanted it. And Whittaker Chambers, after so many years of courtship, and to Buckley's great joy, signed on almost immediately after Schlamm departed—whether *propter hoc* or just through a coincidental upswing in his health. Chambers started coming up to New York every week from his farm in Westminster, Maryland, bringing not the gloom that the Weltschmerz of his writing would suggest but large-hearted good cheer. He didn't actually contribute that many words to the magazine, but he was a healing presence after the angry, sardonic Schlamm.

Two of Buckley's younger hires in that period proved more mixed. Garry Wills, a seminary dropout, was a brilliant young historian and cultural critic. Buckley hired him to take over the theater reviewing that Schlamm had done, and also to do general editorial work. Wills didn't claim to be a conservative—he called himself a "distributivist," a follower of the socioeconomic theory developed by G. K. Chesterton, whose work would be the subject of Wills's first book. Frank Meyer tried to explain to him, as to others under Chesterton's spell, that as an essayist, as a poet, Chesterton was wonderful; as a socioeconomic theorist, he was a wonderful poet. Wills did much fine writing for *NR*, but despite all Meyer's efforts he never really became a movement conservative, and in the turmoil of the late 1960s he would veer sharply left.

The other young man, John Leonard (the future editor of *The New York Times Book Review*), innocently provoked a confrontation that had a very happy result—in fact, that may have been instrumental in *National Review*'s long-term survival. Buckley, to borrow a phrase from W. H. Auden, "worships language and forgives everyone by whom it lives," and he had been bowled over by something the young Leonard had written in a Harvard student publication. Buckley asked Leonard to lunch, offered him a junior editorial job, and only then asked, "You aren't by any chance a conservative?" The answer was no, but Buckley gave him the job anyway—and Suzanne La Follette hit the ceiling. She had already been on Schlamm's side in the Burnham dispute; she didn't enjoy her run-ins with Kendall anywhere near so much as Kendall did; and she had another young candidate for the editorial assistant slot (Allan Ryskind, son of Morrie; Allan instead went on to a fine career at *Human Events*). In April 1959 La Follette, who was nearing retirement age anyway, resigned—but far less stormily than Schlamm. The magazine gave her a farewell dinner, and she stayed in touch.

Meanwhile, Bill had asked Priscilla to take over Suzanne's job. If the opportunity had not presented itself for another couple of years, Priscilla might have been gone—not out of any sort of disloyalty, but simply as an appropriate career move for someone who was seeing her old UPI buddies go to high-paying jobs at prestigious glossies. Since in retrospect it seems clear that Priscilla had as much as Bill himself to do with keeping *National Review* going over the years, this was a very fortunate move indeed by the young editor-in-chief.

And *National Review* needed all the good fortune it could get. It had survived the Schlamm-Burnham crisis, but a financial crisis had raised its head. Circulation had hit eighteen thousand by the magazine's first anniversary, but then had crept up by only another thousand over the next year and a half. McFadden and Rusher had tightened up operations considerably, but money was running out. And so they took a drastic step on the expense front. In July 1958 *NR* went to a "summer schedule" of fortnightly publication. When the summer ended, the summer schedule didn't, and in October it was announced that the magazine (formerly twenty-four pages, now up to thirty-two) would continue to be produced every two weeks, with an eight-page *NR Bulletin* appearing in the alternate weeks—for an additional subscription fee. As McFadden put it for internal consumption, "Remember—you may be paying more, but you're getting less."

On the income front, Rusher and McFadden persuaded Buckley to launch a fund appeal. Before *NR* began publishing, Schlamm had argued that if it could reach twenty-five thousand subscribers, those subscribers would not let it die. For whatever reason, circulation—stalled at nineteen thousand since November 1956—took off in that same summer of 1958. By February 1959 it had reached twenty-nine thousand, and Schlamm was proved right. The fund appeal became a permanent feature of *National Review.* The staff has had to field caustic comments over the years from some recipients of the fund-appeal letter, to the effect that a publication that champions capitalism oughtn't to stay in business if it can't pay its own way. Buckley early on found the intellectual justification he needed, and it has proved satisfying to those readers who regard *NR* as being in a different category from most commercial magazines, whether *The New Yorker* or *Sports Illustrated*, *Esquire* or *Good Housekeeping*. As Buckley recently recalled that first fund appeal, "When spirits were very low, I was rescued by an epiphany. Don't laugh! It was—it is—that *National Review* is, supremely, an educational enterprise. I wrote then [in 1958] to you to say that there are enterprises in life that simply aren't devised to generate profits. We accept them as institutions that need to be patronized, because they do vital work. It is vital to educate our children, vital to care for our health, vital to maintain our churches (and our mosques, as President Bush would no doubt instruct his speechwriters to phrase it). *National Review* is such an enterprise."

During this crowded season of change and adjustment, Bill and his siblings had to face a deeper transition: the death of their adored father. Will and Aloïse had had a good summer in Bad Gastein, an old-style resort in Austria, near Salzburg. Will found relief there from his hay fever, and he benefited from the hot springs. As a result of his stroke three years earlier, he could read only with difficulty, but every two weeks, when the new issue of *National Review* arrived, Aloïse would start reading it aloud to him, and she would report back to Bill on his spirited reactions to the good news and bad, and to the prose in which it was couched. Son Reid and daughter-in-law Betsey brought their young family over for part of the summer; they were living in Spain, where the American dollar went much further than at home for a novelist wrestling with an abundant imagination and not much income. Will, who had always loved the company of small children, greatly enjoyed playing with little Hunt, Jobie, and Lizzie.

In late September, Will and Aloïse made their way to Le Havre and boarded the SS *United States* to sail back home. Early on the morning of Sunday, September 28, two days before the ship was to dock in New York, Will suffered a serious stroke. Whatever might or might not be possible today, in 1958 there was no way to get a passenger in mid-Atlantic speedily to shore. Will was mostly unconscious, unaware of what was happening, but Aloïse had to watch the agonizing hours slip by, waiting for full hospital treatment. On

Tuesday morning, thanks to some string-pulling by old friend and comrade-in-arms Ralph de Toledano, Bill was able to ride on the Coast Guard cutter out into New York Harbor to meet the ship and escort his parents to Lenox Hill Hospital.

It may well be that nothing could have been done even if the stroke had taken place five minutes away from the hospital. In any case, Will Buckley died the following Sunday, October 5. As Bill wrote in the book of recollections published by the family, "After Monday, the last day aboard the *S.S. United States*, he did not have a moment of consciousness; or a moment's apprehension. There had been plenty, in the last [three] years, against which to exercise his enormous reserves of courage: a paralyzed left side, the treatment—and the inevitable condescension—that is meted out to all cripples; yet he was never heard by any living soul, including the woman in whom he confided everything, and reposed all his trust, to utter a single word of complaint—against the pain, the boredom, the humiliations, the immobility. But at the end, he was not called upon to suffer more."

Meanwhile, at *National Review*, the changes were working well. Frank Meyer quickly turned his editorship of the book section into a sort of salon—all the more impressive because he lived not in a major city but in Woodstock, New York, about ninety miles north of Manhattan and not reachable by train. And yet young conservatives, and not so young conservatives, would happily make the trek for the joy of Frank and Elsie's company. Those who visited the Meyers at their snug, book-filled house on Ohayo Mountain Road recall the endless talk, starting in the kitchen while Elsie cooked, moving to the dinner table, and continuing from there. It might be political philosophy (Frank always took a hard line; characteristically, his column for the magazine was called "Principles & Heresies"), it might be practical politics (Which, if any, of the current candidates comes close to embodying our principles?), or it might involve competitive recitation of memorized poetry.

In any case, the talk would stretch far into the night. Frank was one of our genuine eccentrics. He would go to bed about dawn, and arise at what for other people was the end of the workday. He told Priscilla that this habit had developed out of a conviction that he must be on guard, lest some of his former comrades come after his

Frank and Elsie Meyer, at home in Woodstock.

family one night. Elsie downplayed this, but Frank had been pretty high in the counsels of the Party, and the CPUSA was not as independent of Stalin as it liked to make out.

Whatever the reason, Frank was a nocturnal animal. He was also a telecommuter before telecommuting should have been feasible. There were no fax machines in those days, no e-mail, no FedEx or Express Mail. There wasn't even direct-dial long-distance telephone service in many localities, including Woodstock. But there were telephone operators. The phone company understandably put its less experienced people on the night shift; night operators in Woodstock got a quick, intensive training course at Frank's hands. And there was a local man who was willing to drive down to the city every (or, soon, every other) Wednesday with the edited copy for the book section.

By such means, Frank stayed in touch with probably a wider network of people than anyone else at *NR*, Bills Buckley and Rusher included. Besides the visitors he encouraged, he deployed the telephone to an extent practically unheard of in the late 1950s and early 1960s. His first call of the day was always to Priscilla, checking in. She would say that she knew Frank had insomnia if this occurred before 5:00 P.M. Then he would start calling his stable of reviewers. Guy Davenport, his principal fiction reviewer for many years, recalled that inevitably Frank would call him just before dinnertime, just as something on the stove was reaching a critical point; but such was his regard for Frank that Guy did not simply tell him not to call at that hour. And Frank would call Brent Bozell. The philosophical dispute between Meyer and Bozell was roughly the same as the one between Meyer and Kirk; the difference is that Meyer and Bozell were close friends. Willmoore Kendall—the master of the one-sentence description—defined an emergency phone call between Frank Meyer and Brent Bozell as one that interrupted the regular phone call between Frank Meyer and Brent Bozell.

Meyer brought an amazing variety of people into the magazine through his book section: apolitical belletrists like Joan Didion (she eventually became political—the wrong way, from *NR*'s point of view), deep political thinkers like Eliseo Vivas and Ellis Sandoz, libertarians like David Brudnoy. He even got W. H. Auden to write for the magazine—a wonderful review of *The Image of the City and Other Essays* by Charles Williams. Unfortunately, an editorial item in the same issue stirred Auden's wrath (it was a derogatory remark about J. Robert Oppenheimer), and so that review was his one and only appearance in *NR*.

One of the few phrases in Dwight Macdonald's "Scrambled Egg-heads" that many *NR* types would agree with was his description of Willmoore Kendall: "a wild Yale don who can get a discussion into the shouting stage faster than anybody I have ever known." There was a lot more to Kendall than that, but it was true as far as it went.

Kendall leavened his intellectual pursuits with earthier ones—he was a heavy drinker and a serious womanizer. In 1956 he was received into the Catholic Church, with Buckley serving as his godfather. At the reception afterward, Father Stanley Parry—an occasional contributor to *National Review* and a leading conservative philosopher—said to Bill, "You know, probably the best thing that could happen to Willmoore would be if he ran his car into a tree on his way home tonight. Because he'll never again be so close to a state of grace."

Jeffrey Hart has written of Kendall's prodigious drinking; he has also quoted Kendall as saying—rather condescendingly, one gathers—that Burnham would consume only a single weak martini before dinner (not quite true, by the way) out of regard for his formidable brain. One wonders what Kendall might have produced had he had a tiny bit of regard for his own formidable brain.

One of *NR*'s first frolics: a booby prize for Arthur Schlesinger Jr., who had incautiously taken part in an *NR* contest under his own name. Left to right: Priscilla Buckley, Suzanne La Follette, Jim Burnham, ADA (named for Schlesinger's beloved Americans for Democratic Action), Willmoore Kendall, Bill Buckley.

As for women, he cut a swath. Even in still photographs, you can see that devil-may-care glint in his eyes, the rakish smile. Part of *NR*'s internal history is the Willmoore Kendall Memorial Couch. One morning Gertrude Vogt arrived very early, went down to Suzanne La Follette's office to retrieve some document—and found Willmoore and a young editorial assistant in flagrante on the long brown leather couch. Gertrude told Suzanne about it as soon as she came in; Suzanne went to Bill as soon as *he* came in and intoned in her deep voice: "I will have no fornication on my couch." She demanded Willmoore's firing; Bill took Willmoore down to the corner pub, the Fireside, to hash it out. He wound up obtaining Willmoore's pledge not that he but that the girl would never set foot in *National Review*'s offices again. The girl remained Willmoore's *maîtresse-en-titre* and housesitter until, a year or so later, he returned from a trip abroad with a brand-new wife. Priscilla, meanwhile, wrote up the incident in a memo to Maureen, who had married and retired from the magazine. Priscilla's memo concluded: "Aren't men silly?"

*   *   *

While the business team at NR tackled the deficit internally, Bill Buckley had started looking for other sources of revenue. One of the most promising financially was the lecture circuit, which had the additional advantage of spreading the conservative message more widely. Buckley had done a fair amount of public speaking since leaving Yale, but most of it wasn't very remunerative—it was either publicity for one of his books, or favors for local Catholic organizations that had befriended him, and he them, during the McCarthy battles. But the real lecture circuit—hiring out, through an agent, to speak at colleges and to business and civic groups—is another matter entirely. As Buckley would later explain, even the highest-paying magazines don't come close to offering the compensation per hour that one routinely gets by writing a speech to be given, with suitable modifications, at two dozen venues over the next month. And so he signed up with an agent named Catherine Babcock and started hitting the lecture trail twice a year, spring and fall, logging a schedule that gives one jet lag just reading it. Here's a page from his calendar for 1962:

January 8: 8:05 A.M.: fly to Indianapolis
6 P.M.: Dinner with the Indiana Conservative Club's leaders and contributors; address on HUAC

January 9: To Bloomington, Indiana
12 noon: address, "Aimlessness in American Education"
6 P.M.: Dinner, second address

January 10: 10 A.M.: Indianapolis Athletic Club
8 P.M.: lecture, "A Dynamic Conservative Program vs. Current Liberalism"

January 11: 9 A.M.: fly to Houston
8 P.M.: lecture, "The Liberal Ideology and U.S. Foreign Policy"

January 12: 10:45 A.M.: fly to Lafayette, La., for the Newman Forum of the University of Southwestern Louisiana

January 13: 8:26 A.M.: fly to Austin via San Antonio
8 P.M.: Address for the Texas Union Speaker Program

January 14: 6:21 P.M.: fly to San Francisco via Dallas

January 15: 9:35 A.M.: fly to Spokane via Portland
8 P.M.: Public lecture sponsored by the Anti-Communist Freedom Fighters

January 16:   10 A.M.: Talk for the student body of Gonzaga University
               5:30 P.M.: fly to Seattle

January 17:   12 noon and 8 P.M.: "The Liberal Mind," for Young
               Americans for Freedom at the University of Washington

January 18:   8 A.M.: fly to Los Angeles
               6:30 P.M.: Black-tie dinner sponsored by the Executives'
               Dinner Club of Beverly Hills and Bel-Air

January 19:   Cocktails and dinner for Californians for Goldwater

January 20:   Steve Allen show

January 21:   1:30 P.M.: fly back to New York

Buckley also, in January 1959, started a tradition that would continue for more than forty years: going to Switzerland for six or eight weeks every winter to write a book. Having started his book-writing career with a bang right after Yale, he had put it aside entirely while first raising the money for and then actually starting *National Review.* For the first two years of the magazine's existence, he did no writing except for its pages. Now, taking along some research materials and a couple of previously written essays ("The Liberal Mind" and "The Age of Modulation"), he set out with Pat and Christopher for the Saanen valley. That first year, the Buckleys shared a chalet with Alistair and Renira Horne and their daughters in Saanenmöser, a village on the eastern end of the T-shaped Saanen valley, of which the more famous Gstaad forms the north-south stroke. (Horne was familiar with the area from his schooldays: before being sent to Millbrook, where he and Bill became friends, he had studied at Le Rosey, the international boarding school in Gstaad.) Bill's modus operandi, as it evolved, was to work in the morning, have lunch with someone and ski in the afternoon, then work until dinnertime. Not exactly a "vacation," but the break he needed from everyday duties if he was going to return to writing books.

That 1959 book was *Up from Liberalism*, a study of how American liberaldom thought and behaved. Buckley offered the manuscript to Henry Regnery, who thought it needed more fleshing out; Buckley disagreed and tried it out on a small New York conservative publisher, McDowell, Obolensky, which accepted it. It was widely, and often heatedly, reviewed, and it brought Buckley back into the limelight.

In the book, Buckley draws his case studies from battles over issues ranging from internal security investigations to forced integration of schools to federal spending. He has a great deal of fun at the expense of Eleanor Roosevelt, Arthur Schlesinger Jr., the influential TV critic John Crosby, and numerous others ("Following Mrs. Roosevelt in search of irrationality is like following a burning fuse in search of an explosive; one never has to wait very long"). But probably the most damning criticism he exercises is simply quoting from his subjects' own utterances. This, for example, from Mrs. Roosevelt herself, in her question-and-answer column in the *Woman's Home Companion*: A correspondent writes, "In a recent column you defended your right to shake hands with Mr. Vishinsky [Soviet ambassador to the United Nations, and sometime prosecutor in Stalin's purge trials] and Senator McCarthy. Would you also have felt it was right to shake hands with Adolf Hitler?" To which ER replies: "In Adolf Hitler's early days I might have considered it, but after he had begun his mass killings I don't think I could have borne it." Or this from John Crosby: "Blacklisting is the shame of a mighty industry," and those who go in for it are "unjust, un-American, and . . . pretty close to being criminal." Or this from Richard Rovere: "This story is sworn to by men of good repute. Governor Faubus [the segregationist governor who resisted the integration of the Little Rock schools] . . . addressed a crowd in an Arkansas town and ranted against the President, the Supreme Court, the N.A.A.C.P., and just about everything else. When he had done, a great shaft of light pierced the roof of the meeting hall, and lo, Jesus Christ appeared. He said that He was the resurrection and the life, that those who set man against man shall not enter the Kingdom of Heaven, that the meek and the peacemakers are blessed. The mob was quiet while He spoke; when He finished, there was a great shout through the hall— 'Nigger-lover!'"

Of course, Bill Buckley was able to devote three or four months a year to lecturing and book-writing only because Priscilla Buckley, Jim Burnham, and Bill Rusher were willing and able to hold the fort— which by now had moved from the cramped, uncomfortable quarters at 211 East 37th to a turn-of-the-century nine-story apartment building a knight's move away, two blocks down and one block over, at 150 East 35th.

The new building was not much less shabby than 211, having been abused through decades of penny-pinching, but it had good bones—a façade handsome enough to lead to rumors that it was by McKim, Mead, and White; inside, solid plaster walls and solid oak doors, giving a privacy never to be had at 211—and it was located on a pleasant tree-lined block no farther from Catawba than the old building. Each floor had four suites of differing sizes (as apartments, they had been a studio, two one-bedrooms, and a two-bedroom), and *NR* initially took part of the first floor, most of the second, and all of the third. One of the oddities of having offices in a former residential building was that, as someone—probably the aphoristic Willmoore Kendall—put it, we had as many bathrooms as we had full-time staffers. By the time the present authors arrived at *NR*, in the late 1960s, the old claw-footed bathtubs were being pulled out and replaced with filing cabinets, but McFadden kept one with plumbing intact for chilling wine and beer for parties.

NR's staffers over the years would differ as to the pleasantness or un- of our abode. Some (especially those who worked on the eighth floor and had to deal with the unreliable elevator) were hopeful every time the lease came up that we would finally move to a "normal" office building. Others agreed with Jeanne Wacker, a former philosophy professor who became our copyeditor in the mid-1970s, that "This is exactly how a journal of opinion should look." Or with the British visitor who said, "At all costs, you must keep these offices. *The Spectator* just isn't the same since it moved." Well, we pro-150ers enjoyed our little rabbit warren for nearly forty years before the old landlord died and his son sold the building.

In the world outside *NR*'s walls, after Hungary the balance of power between the United States and the Soviet Union had settled down to an uncomfortable, nuclear-shadowed stalemate. County fairs throughout America featured exhibits of bomb shelters, and American schoolchildren were drilled in hiding under their desks when the air raid siren sounded (*so* helpful against nuclear attack) and wondered, some of them, if they would live to grow up.

Soviet troops advanced no further in Europe, even when Khrushchev started making threatening noises about West Berlin. But Macmillan's "winds of change" were blowing through Africa, and the Soviets were eager to move in on the countries that the Western colonialists were leaving, such as Algeria, the Congo, and Ethiopia. Nasser had been a Soviet client ever since the Suez crisis in 1956.

Then, on January 1, 1959, a guerrilla army that had been fighting in the Cuban mountains for three years succeeded in ousting the dictator Fulgencia Batista. American conservatives held no brief for

Batista but observed that the leader of the guerrillas, one Fidel Castro, was a leftist and that several of his close associates were Communists. American liberals rushed to embrace Castro and to proclaim that he was an indigenous reformer. Time soon told: indigenous he was, but a Communist he also was, or became. He quickly put Cuba under a totalitarian pall that the corrupt Batista would never have dreamed of, and he offered his country to Moscow as an outpost in the Western Hemisphere. As Burnham put it: "That Fidel Castro was once an idealist still seems likely, though it was three years ago that this journal first challenged his fitness to rule. But few can now deny that that idealism dried up inside of him somewhere along the way, perhaps on the triumphant march from Oriente Province to Havana; that it was consumed by a lust for power and transmuted into a petulant tyranny."

On the other side of the world, Red China announced that it intended to annex the little free islands of Quemoy and Matsu. In this case, Eisenhower and John Foster Dulles hung tough, and Mao Tse-tung backed down. But the threat was still there. North Korea, meanwhile, was still in the Communist camp, and Ho Chi Minh was continuing his efforts to bring South Vietnam into that same camp.

These were some of the salient points on the foreign landscape as America headed into the 1960 election campaign. On the domestic side, as in 1956, the liberal agenda was being advanced more by the intellectuals and, increasingly, the Supreme Court under Earl Warren than by the executive or legislative branches of the federal government. But the Eisenhower administration had made no counter-moves, and Vice President Nixon hadn't raised a voice in dissent. He had, however, given a sturdy performance against Khrushchev in Moscow in July 1959—the "kitchen debate"—which conservatives chalked up in his favor. And with Bill Knowland having given up his Senate seat to run for governor of California, and then having lost to Edmund G. "Pat" Brown, there was no obvious conservative candidate—although a few people, including Brent Bozell and Bill Rusher, were becoming interested in a second-term senator from Arizona, Barry M. Goldwater. Meanwhile, on the left side of the Republican Party, Nelson Rockefeller was busily jockeying for position.

The debate between Burnham and Schlamm during the 1956 campaign had put in black and white a crucial issue for those who would apply political philosophy to the real world. After the political process has done its initial sifting, do you go for what Buckley would come to call the "rightwardmost viable candidate," even if "rightwardmost" in the case at hand is barely right of center? That's what Burnham argued in 1956, in behalf of Eisenhower. Or do you, with Schlamm, say that if the only "viable" candidate—the one who because of incumbency or some other advantage seems to have a lock on the Republican nomination—is not rightward enough, you abstain or go for a third-party alternative? Is giving your support to a candidate who is in no real sense a conservative diluting your principles? Or since, as Chambers put it, "to live is to maneuver," are we better off supporting the Republican candidate, however unappealing? These are questions that *NR* and its editors, writers, and readers would face again and again over the next decades—indeed, as much today as ever.

3

Goldwater for President

As *NR* geared up for the election campaign, other matters demanded attention. In August 1959, having earlier rejected the
idea, President Eisenhower invited Chairman Khrushchev to visit the
United States, and Khrushchev accepted.

As Buckley has explained in numerous fund-appeal letters, *National
Review* has never seen its purpose as merely publishing so many pages
per issue and collecting so many dollars in subscription and advertising revenue. It has always sought to spread the word in whatever way
possible. So, in the early days, it hosted occasional *NR* Forums.
These might be debates (for example, Buckley versus the *New York
Post*'s James Wechsler on the proposition "Resolved: That liberalism
should be repudiated"); they might give a platform to a visitor seldom heard in America (for example, Jacques Soustelle, once a great
ally of de Gaulle's, who turned against *le grand Charles* when he turned
on Algeria). Many conservatives who came of age in New York City in
the late 1950s have said how much these affairs meant to them.

However, the *NR* Forums were comparatively low-key. Khrushchev's visit demanded something more, and Buckley got the idea of
hiring Carnegie Hall for a rally. This operation was the origin of Bill
Rusher's observation, "Buckley thinks you can accomplish anything
with a couple of phone calls." Rusher, who was assigned to make the
calls, attests that it wasn't quite that simple. But it came off. On the evening of September 17, 1959, the twenty-eight-hundred-seat Carnegie

Hall was filled nearly to capacity. Eleven speakers would discourse on why Eisenhower should not have invited Khrushchev and why the American people should not welcome him. Buckley was last on the program. Just read on the printed page, this is one of his great speeches. In the supercharged atmosphere in that hall, it had the audience ready to march on the White House.

Buckley begins with a wonderfully ornamented account of Khrushchev's arrival:

> I deplore the fact that Khrushchev is traveling about this country, having been met at the frontier by our own prince, who arrived with his first string of dancing girls, and a majestic caravan of jewels and honey and spices; I mind that he will wend his lordly way from city to city, where the Lilliputians will fuss over his needs, weave garlands through the ring in his nose, shiver when he belches out his threats, and labor in panic to sate his imperial appetites. I mind that Khrushchev is here, but I mind more that Eisenhower invited him. I mind that Eisenhower invited him, but I mind much more the defense of that invitation by the thought leaders of the nation.

Buckley then takes apart, one by one, the reasons offered by the administration and the press why Khrushchev should come to the United States, and gives his own reasons why he should not:

> That he should achieve orthodox diplomatic recognition not three years after shocking history itself by the brutalities of Budapest; months after endorsing the shooting down of an unarmed American plane [a C-130 transport plane that wandered into Soviet airspace—more than a year before Francis Gary Powers's U-2]; only weeks since he last shrieked his intention of demolishing the West; only days since publishing in an American magazine his undiluted resolve to enslave the citizens of free Berlin—that such an introduction should end up constituting his credentials for a visit to America will teach him something about the West that some of us wish he might never have known.

And then the swelling chords of the peroration:

> Ladies and gentlemen, we deem it the central revelation of Western experience that man cannot ineradicably stain himself, for the wells of regeneration are infinitely deep. No temple has ever been so profaned that it cannot be purified; no man is ever truly lost; no nation is irrevocably dishonored. Khrushchev cannot take permanent advantage of our temporary disadvantage, for it is the West he is fighting. And in the West there lie, however encysted, the ultimate

resources, which are moral in nature. Khrushchev is *not* aware that the gates of hell shall not prevail against us. Even out of the depths of despair, we take heart in the knowledge that it cannot matter how deep we fall, for there is always hope. In the end, we will bury him.

When Nixon won the 1960 nomination, lines were drawn at *National Review*. Chambers having resigned from the editorial board the previous fall, Burnham was alone in supporting Nixon for election. Burnham was opposed by Kendall, Meyer, Bozell, Rusher, and—though uncomfortably—Buckley. When the time came for the official editorial, giving or withholding the magazine's endorsement, Buckley wrote it himself. And he wound up neither endorsing nor rejecting Nixon; instead, the editorial is a plea, directed as much to Buckley's colleagues as to *NR*'s readers, for the purists and the maneuverers each to admit that the other position is one a conservative can reasonably take.

On November 8, Nixon lost to Kennedy by a whisker—the margin, many believe, being contributed by the graveyards of Chicago, under the control of Mayor Richard J. Daley—and conservatives started looking ahead. In the issue following the election, Meyer and Bozell both wrote columns saying, in effect, *Look where Realpolitik got us. Goldwater in '64!*

The Kennedy administration was marked from the beginning by foreign crises: the Bay of Pigs, the Berlin Wall, the Cuban Missile Crisis, the escalating war in Vietnam. This was the height of the Cold War—a dismal time for human freedom but offering great material for a future novelist. The Berlin Wall and the Missile Crisis are central to two of the best Blackford Oakes novels, *The Story of Henri Tod* and *See You Later Alligator*; Buckley would revisit Berlin in the nonfiction *Fall of the Berlin Wall*. And one of the protagonists in his first non-Oakes novel, *Brothers No More*, is on the scene in Vietnam when the Ngo brothers are assassinated. (Around 1959 the American press started to refer to the South Vietnamese government as the "Diem regime." But the family name of Ngo Dinh Diem and his brother Ngo Dinh Nhu was Ngo.) These crises make it tempting to speculate how things would have turned out if Nixon had won. To be sure, when Nixon finally did become president, he greatly disappointed conservatives by toasting Mao Tse-tung and Chou En-lai, committing détente with Leonid Brezhnev, and abandoning South Vietnam. But what might he have done had he and the nation not just lived through the upheavals of the 1960s?

Kennedy had campaigned on youth and vigor, the call of the New Frontier. In his inaugural address, he spoke of the need to "pay any price, bear any burden, meet any hardship, support any friend, oppose any foe, to assure the survival and the success of liberty." But in the first chance he got to do just that—an invasion of Cuba by a group of anti-Castro exiles, planned under Eisenhower—his administration failed miserably.

Kennedy himself had told his advisers he wanted to maintain "plausible deniability": that is, he wanted to be able to deny, to Khrushchev, or the UN, or the *Washington Post*, that the United States had anything to do with the invasion. In fairness to Kennedy, the "Cuba Project," as it was called internally, was already flawed by the CIA's own desire for deniability. But then, in meeting after meeting, Secretary of State Dean Rusk pressed for further changes in the plans. The original idea was for Brigade 2506 to land near the city of Trinidad on the south coast of Cuba, where there were already active anti-Castro forces at work. At Rusk's urging, the landing area was changed to the totally unsuitable Bay of Pigs several miles further west. Then the promised U.S. air cover was reduced from forty bombing sorties (to which President Kennedy had initially agreed) to thirty-two. At the very last minute the number was reduced to eight.

Decades later, after the relevant papers were declassified, a colonel involved in the Cuba Project, Jack Hawkins, wrote an article for *NR* detailing the successive disastrous decisions, and finally telling of his own increasingly frantic efforts to reach Dean Rusk, McGeorge Bundy, anyone in authority, to get them to abort the invasion if they weren't going to do it properly. But his superiors wouldn't listen, and so he could only stand by as the reports came in of hundreds of brave men being shot down or captured as they ran out of ammunition.

Would Nixon and his advisors have done better? We'll never know. Nixon did say to Kennedy, in a visit to the White House just after the Bay of Pigs, that he would recommend a full-scale U.S. invasion of Cuba: "I would find proper legal cover and I would go in." Now, it's easy for a man out of office to say something like that, but he did *think* to say it. And under Nixon, Rusk and Robert McNamara, the impresario of incremental escalation, would not have been secretaries of State and Defense. And—double-edged irony—Henry Cabot Lodge, dubbed Henry Sabotage by Clare Boothe Luce, would not have been ambassador to Saigon, busily undercutting the Ngo regime, because he would have been vice president of the United States.

*   *   *

For several years after the founding of ISI, there were no new national organizations on the right. Then in 1958 a retired candy manufacturer from Belmont, Massachusetts, Robert Welch, founded the John Birch Society, an organization devoted exclusively to fighting Communism. It was named after an American missionary (and intelligence officer) killed by Communist guerrillas in China at the very end of World War II—described by the Birch Society as the first American victim of the Cold War. The new group attracted many bona fide conservatives—including Adolphe Menjou and Roger Milliken, early supporters of *National Review*; Medford S. Evans, who had been on *NR*'s masthead from the beginning; and, as Barry Goldwater wryly put it, nearly his entire Arizona constituency.

At first *NR* had no serious problem with the Birch Society. Then Welch sent Buckley his new book, *The Politician*, in manuscript. This work was based on the assumption that President Eisenhower was a "dedicated, conscious agent" of the international Communist conspiracy. Welch was essentially making the same assumption Forrest Davis had made about George Marshall: he has to have been working for the Communists for them to have gained so much ground on his watch. Buckley and his colleagues rejected the assumption now as they had then, and they started thinking about whether *NR* had a duty to repudiate the Birch Society publicly. Meanwhile, the classic rejection of Welch's position came from Russell Kirk: "Eisenhower's not a Communist—he's a golfer."

In the early 1960s, *NR* conservatives started feeling the need for organizations of their own. Young Americans for Freedom grew directly out of the 1960 Republican convention. There was already in that election cycle, although it is not widely remembered, a small Goldwater-for-president movement. Goldwater's *Conscience of a Conservative* (actually written by Brent Bozell) appeared not in 1964, as most of us think we recall, but in the summer of 1960. There was an active Youth for Goldwater organization at the Republican convention in Chicago that year. Marvin Liebman, an ex-Communist PR man who by that time was close to *NR* and WFB, was at the convention working for Congressman Walter Judd of Minnesota, whom many conservatives were pushing for vice president. (Liebman also worked with Judd on the Committee of One Million, in defense of Taiwan;

the later joke had it that Liebman *was* the Committee of One Million.) Liebman ran into the young Goldwaterites and was impressed by them, especially by David Franke and Douglas Caddy. He raised with Buckley the subject of a conservative youth organization. Buckley was enthusiastic, and the two young men were hired, Franke as an editorial assistant at *NR* and Caddy by Liebman's PR firm. They were charged with laying the groundwork for the new organization.

Plans were made, invitations were sent out, and the founding conference of Young Americans for Freedom was scheduled for the weekend after Labor Day 1960 at Great Elm. The invitees were mostly students—undergraduate, grad, and law—but with leading roles for a couple of slightly older men: M. Stanton Evans (son of Medford S.; Yale '55; already the acclaimed young editor of the *Indianapolis News*) and Lee Edwards (Duke '54; he had started out with the *Washington Times Herald*, and served now as press secretary to Senator John Marshall Butler of Maryland). Evans drafted YAF's founding document, the Sharon Statement, and Edwards would be the founding editor of its monthly magazine, *The New Guard*. Robert Schuchman (Yale Law '61) was YAF's first national chairman, taking the chair at the Sharon conference. Evans and Edwards went on to become, and are still, important members of the conservative movement. Schuchman's friends all expected him to be one of the conservative leaders of his generation, but shockingly he died of a stroke just six years later, at age twenty-seven.

In any case, the conference—with Aloïse Buckley the titular hostess, and Bill and Priscilla present but tactfully letting the younger people run the show—was a stunning success. The young Americans went back to their campuses to beat the drums for freedom—and most of them, not incidentally, for Barry Goldwater. This was a phenomenon largely overlooked by commentators so fixated on the growth of the New Left as to miss the parallel growth of a New Right.

At the same time, two young Irish New Yorkers named J. Daniel Mahoney and Kieran O'Doherty started testing the waters for a New York Conservative Party. *NR* the previous year had published an editorial explaining why a national third party would be a bad idea but suggesting that third parties in individual states—ones where the local Democratic and Republican Parties were virtually indistinguishable—might be quite effective. The idea was not to supplant the Republican Party but to draw it to the right. New York was propitious for such a venture, since the state election laws permit a candidate to run on more than one party's ballot line. In fact, New York already had a vigorous Liberal Party; and tellingly—this is one of the things that animated Mahoney and O'Doherty—with Republicans like Nelson Rockefeller and Jacob Javits in the field, the Liberals often endorsed not the Democratic but the Republican candidate.

Buckley was receptive to the Conservative Party idea, McFadden helped out with advertising and Liebman with publicity, and Meyer wrote the founding statement of principles. Mahoney and O'Doherty decided not to make their launch till after the New York City mayoral election of 1961, in which, with only-in-New-York chutzpah, Democrat Robert Wagner, the incumbent, ran and won on a reform platform. So the new Conservative Party was launched in 1962. Its first two campaigns didn't go far, but starting in 1965 the Conservative Party would change the face of New York politics—and the lives of several of the Buckleys.

In 1960 an old friend of Bill Buckley's—Tom Wallace, Yale '55, an editor at Putnam's—suggested that Buckley was ready to move from small conservative publishers to a mainstream house, namely Putnam's. Wallace signed him to edit a book called *The Committee and Its Critics*. The book, subtitled "A Calm Review of the House Committee on Un-American Activities," covers everything from the Hiss case to *Operation Abolition*, a film about a 1960 riot against HUAC in San Francisco. The contributors are mostly *NR* editors (Buckley, Burnham, Kendall, and newcomer William F. Rickenbacker) or associates (Karl Hess, Ralph de Toledano, Stan Evans, lawyers C. Dickerman Williams and George N. Crocker, and the young Ross Mackenzie, later to be the editor of the *Richmond News Leader*), but there is also Irving Ferman, former chief counsel to the ACLU, contributing "A Comment by a Civil Libertarian." The work is a skillfully arranged mixture of scholarship, analysis, and polemic, and it did well enough for Putnam's to sign Buckley the next year to put together a collection of his own previously published journalism.

Rumbles Left and Right would prove to be the first of eight or nine such collections (depending on whether you count the autobiographical *Miles Gone By* in this category). Among the contents: Buckley's Carnegie Hall speech against Khrushchev; a searing account of how *New York Times* reporter Herbert Matthews covered up for Fidel Castro (the article is titled: "Herbert Matthews and Fidel Castro: I Got My Job through the *New York Times*"); "An Evening with Jack Paar," recounting Buckley's first run-in with Gore Vidal; the elegiac

"The Last Years of Whittaker Chambers"; and the essay Buckley has described as "my *Hamlet*, my Gettysburg Address, my Ninth Symphony," the one that has been reprinted far and away more times than any other, "Why Don't We Complain?" For the dust jacket, Buckley came up with one of those effronteries—to use a favorite Buckley word—that delight or infuriate, according to the eye of the beholder: he quoted, as if it had been spoken seriously, a remark dripping with irony that Arthur Schlesinger Jr. had made during a debate: "[Buckley] has a facility for rhetoric which I envy, as well as a wit which I seek clumsily and vainly to emulate." Schlesinger went apoplectic when told of the blurb, but Buckley refused to remove it. It took the shared experience of a mind-numbing State of the Union address by Lyndon Johnson six years later (recounted in *Let Us Talk of Many Things*) to put the two men back on speaking terms.

Meanwhile, in January 1962, just before Buckley left for Switzerland to produce *Rumbles*, he was contacted by Harry Elmlark of the Washington Star Syndicate, who wanted to talk with him about writing a newspaper column. Elmlark was a liberal and didn't think much of Buckley's politics, but his assistant had included Buckley's name on a list of possible columnists sent out to newspaper editors around the country and had received an enthusiastic response. With some foreboding—and over the objections of Jim Burnham, who worried that it would take too much time away from the magazine—Buckley agreed to a trial contract.

On April 1, 1962, he started writing the once-a-week column, called "A Conservative Voice." The first few columns covered subjects ranging from the fellow-traveling C. P. Snow to the American media's invidious use of the term "right-wing"; from JFK's price controls on steel to upheavals in the Congo and Algeria. After four months the syndicate renamed the column "On the Right," as it has been known ever since. Getting the column was a milestone in Buckley's career. For the first time he was reaching not just the self-selected people who would come to a debate or buy a book or subscribe to *National Review*, but a whole range of newspaper readers nationwide.

That same winter, the editors—that is to say, Bill and Priscilla Buckley and Jim Burnham, over the objections of Bozell, Meyer, Rusher, and Rickenbacker—decided it was time to separate *National Review* conservatism from the John Birch Society. (Rudolph Bing once said of his own tenure at the Metropolitan Opera, "It is a democracy run by one man.") The objectors said, in essence, that with so many enemies on the left, we shouldn't be picking fights on the right. Buckley's argument was that we precisely needed to pick a fight with someone we believed was damaging the conservative cause. As he put it in the excommunicating editorial (which, after much discussion, was aimed not at the John Birch Society per se, but at Robert Welch),

> The fact of the matter is that Mr. Welch, by what Russell Kirk has called "an excess of zeal, intemperance, and imprudence," promotes a split in the conservative movement—by asking for the tacit support of men who cannot in good conscience give it, who, moreover, feel that to give it is to damage our chances of success. "Cry wolf often enough," Mr. Kirk wrote to Mr. Welch, "and everyone takes you for an imbecile or a knave, when after all there *are* wolves in this world." If we are to win the war against Communism, we have no less a task before us than to change national policy. Nothing is clearer than that Mr. Welch is not succeeding in doing anything of the sort, precisely because, by the extravagance of his remarks, he repels rather than attracts a great following.

One thing Buckley did before going ahead with the editorial was attempt to obtain Barry Goldwater's approval. Goldwater was reluctant, pointing out that he personally knew many JBS members who were entirely sound. But the way in which the published version was couched permitted him, in a letter to the editor printed in the following issue, to congratulate the magazine on the editorial while pursuing the distinction between Welch and the rank and file: "Mr. Welch is only one man, and I do not believe his views, far removed from reality and common sense as they are, represent the feeling of most members of the John Birch Society. . . . Because of this, I believe the best thing Mr. Welch could do to serve the cause of anti-Communism in the United States would be to resign.

"I am sure you realize this is a difficult suggestion for me to make, for I am well acquainted with Mr. Welch's dedication. However, we cannot allow the emblem of irresponsibility to be attached to the conservative banner."

In the next issue, a short, well-crafted letter to the editor appeared: "You have once again given a voice to the conscience of conservatism. As always the voice is clear and repudiates the easy downhill path of expediency (that path is so crowded with Liberals these days). Now we shall eagerly await a Liberal definition of Left and far Left." The letter was signed, "Ronald Reagan, Pacific Palisades, Cal."

*   *   *

Barry Goldwater actually had no political ambitions for himself, apart from continuing to serve his home state in the Senate and encouraging like-minded young politicians, such as John Tower, newly elected senator from Texas. However, he was judged by most observers to have performed nobly at the 1960 convention. His job, once Nixon had been nominated, was to give a speech reaching out to Northeastern liberals on behalf of Southwestern conservatives, and he succeeded. (Though Brent Bozell grumbled in *NR* that Goldwater had gone too far in the direction of patting his supporters on the head and telling them to grow up and get behind Nixon-Lodge.) Goldwater became known as Mr. Conservative, and in the eyes of many on the right he was now the hope for the future. From *National Review*'s side, the leader of the Goldwater-for-president movement was publisher Bill Rusher.

Like Buckley and Bozell, Rusher had, as an undergraduate (Princeton '42), been a leading debater; unlike them, he had also engaged in political organizing, in the conservative wing of the Young Republicans. After several years in a big New York law firm, he had gone to Washington as counsel to the Senate Internal Security Subcommittee, run in masterly fashion by James Eastland of Mississippi. In 1957 Rusher was thinking of coming back to New York, and Buckley collared him for *National Review*, of which Rusher was a charter subscriber. Besides heading up the business side of the magazine, Rusher had senior editor rank, in terms of taking part in editorial discussions.

Successive generations of young staffers found Rusher's precise ways and his insistence on certain points of political rectitude to be somewhat comic. (Both Bill and Priscilla Buckley have recounted the legendary practical joke at his expense—a total rearrangement of his office, switching every movable object from its carefully appointed place. This was masterminded by Bill Rickenbacker, who was more senior than a "young staffer," but whose intellect was equaled only by his mischievousness.) However, none of us ever doubted Rusher's knowledge or his connections, and these he now deployed on behalf of the Goldwater-for-president movement. He was one of twenty-two men who met in a Chicago motel room in 1961 to form, as Rusher later put it, "the nameless committee that, incredibly, would capture the Republican party in 1964 and hand its presidential nomination to Barry Goldwater." The senator didn't say he would run but

Toast time at Priscilla's forty-second birthday party: Jim McFadden receives his marching orders from WFB, watched by Pat, as Maureen O'Reilly listens to Marvin Liebman.

he didn't order the committee to stop, and in March 1962 Marvin Liebman worked with YAF to organize a huge rally for Goldwater (eighteen thousand in attendance) at Madison Square Garden.

Elsie Meyer later recalled her embarrassment that evening, as her husband let out all the stops in a rabble-rousing speech of a sort she hadn't heard him give since they left the Communist Party. She also recalled Brent Bozell's speech. He had already started making "gnosticism" the centerpiece of his indictment of the current American culture. Of course he was right. But he forgot that public speakers have to be not only right, but understood. People who didn't catch the reference to Eric Voegelin but knew some medieval history wondered if he was saying the Albigensians were making a comeback. People who weren't aware of either Voegelin or the Albigensians tended to mistake the word for a more familiar one. Elsie overhead one woman at the Garden congratulating Brent on his condemnation of "agnosticism."

But the rally was an immense success, an event that could not be overlooked. "For the first time," Rusher later wrote, "the media were forced to acknowledge that sine qua non of democratic politics: significant numbers."

*   *   *

Not long after the Goldwater rally, Bozell decided it was time to buckle down to the book he had been working on in odd moments, an analysis of the Warren Court. He had already suspended his *NR* column; now he took the pregnant Trish and their eight children to Spain (where Reid and Betsey were still living, as Reid worked on his sprawling, brilliant first novel, *The Eye of the Hurricane*). Brent did complete *The Warren Revolution* while in Spain. He also fell in love with a type of Catholicism he had not known before.

Bozell had been devout ever since his conversion as a teenager, and indeed he had occasionally found his cradle-Catholic brother-in-law and editor-in-chief insufficiently obedient (as when Buckley wrote a scathing editorial, "A Venture in Triviality," about Pope John XXIII's encyclical *Pacem in Terris*). But now Bozell got to know some Carlists, Spanish monarchists who believed the Church should play a large role in the country's political life. In June 1963 Bozell resigned from *National Review*'s editorial board, and when he returned to the States later in the year, he brought the Carlist idea home with him along with his manuscript. In years to come it would profoundly affect his relationship with Buckley, with the American conservative movement, and indeed with America.

Meanwhile, Yale had finally, in 1961, worked itself up to taking a very unusual step: it bought up the contract of a tenured professor who had been a thorn in its side, Willmoore Kendall. Kendall had remarked a decade earlier that whenever he asked for a leave of absence Yale was "insultingly cooperative." Now he and Yale were free of each other at last. Kendall went first to Stanford as a visiting professor, and then on to the relatively new, and explicitly Catholic, University of Dallas. He remained a senior editor of *National Review*, but he stopped contributing unsigned editorials, and his signed pieces (mostly book reviews) slowed to a trickle. In the fall of 1963, the other senior editors held a routine Agony (known locally as "the quarterly meeting held three times a year"). They went down the masthead, as they routinely did at Agonies, seeing if anyone should be moved up, down, or off. Kendall's nonperformance was remarked, and Buckley the next day wrote him a routine letter suggesting that he should move from Editor to Contributor.

Kendall's reply was anything but routine. He wrote with bitter irony that the title of "Contributor" would be too great an honor, and he resigned from the magazine altogether. He communicated with Buckley only once more: to ask, "Godson to Godfather," that

Buckley pray for him upon the Vatican's granting him two simultaneous annulments, permitting him to make sacramental his marriage to
his true love, Nellie. Three years later, Kendall died at age fifty-seven,
of a heart condition exacerbated by his prodigious drinking.

Buckley had intended, in 1963, finally to tackle the book he had been
planning to write but had put off throughout the formative years of
National Review. It was to be a "big book," not reacting to a particular phenomenon, like *God and Man* or *McCarthy*, but exploring his
understanding of the conservative philosophy. The book was tenta-
tively called *The Revolt against the Masses*, and it was to build on the
seminal work by the Spanish traditionalist José Ortega y Gasset, *The
Revolt of the Masses.* But Buckley's time in Switzerland in 1963 was
taken up by the exigencies of writing his column and getting it to
New York in those days before e-mail or even fax. (For the first
decade or so of "On the Right," whenever Buckley was away from
150 East 35th Street, whether in Switzerland or on the lecture circuit, the only way of filing the column was by telephone dictation.)

By 1964, even though the column was now three times a week,
Buckley and his staff had mastered the routine, and he set off for
Switzerland with his friend Hugh Kenner in tow. Buckley's intention
was to bounce ideas off the polymathic literary critic, and also to
teach him to ski.

The snow was poor, and the skiing project was not a wild success.
Neither was the book. By the end of the trip, Buckley had produced
only ten thousand words—about one-tenth the length of *Up from
Liberalism*. Buckley later diagnosed his problem as a sense that time
seemed to have passed his thesis by: he had expected America "to
realize that it has to go back to serious thought, and away from these
distracting frivolities with which we had been preoccupied. Exactly
the opposite happened. Instead of going against the masses, we went
right into a situation where the masses tyrannized—the Berkeley campus blowup."

However, it appears that Buckley was also, whether he fully realized it or not, finding out something about his métier. A decade earlier, working on *McCarthy*, he had learned that he doesn't have the
scholarly temperament—not for him the excitement, as Nabokov put
it, "at the rocket of an asterisk, the flare of a 'sic!'" Now he learned
that he is not fundamentally a political philosopher. That is, he is not
a system-builder, an abstract thinker. His job is to apply the scholars'

findings to the current questions, and to bring the results to as wide an audience as possible, using the force of his personality as well as the written word.

Still, it took a while for him to assimilate this. Over the next few years he still spoke occasionally of *Revolt* as a work in progress. But it has never seen the light of day—one of the very few pieces of writing that he abandoned without bringing to fruition.

What Buckley called "the Berkeley campus blowup" began innocently enough, in the fall semester of 1964, when the Free Speech Movement grew out of student protests against the banning of political groups on campus.

Today, it's commonly assumed that the FSM was solely a creation of the left. But in fact, students of all political and ideological stripes— including Youth for Goldwater and Young Americans for Freedom— and students with no stripes whatsoever took part in demonstrations demanding that the university lift that ban. The movement would soon be captured by Students for a Democratic Society and other leftist groups, and given fuel by the war in Vietnam and muscle by peripheral groups like the Black Panthers. But at its birth, the FSM represented a broad variety of student concerns. Most of these had nothing to do with national politics. Instead, they centered on the way the university itself was run. One point of contention was the quality of teaching, primarily being conducted by teaching assistants standing in for high-priced faculty. Another was the increasingly remote and authoritarian administration of the University of California, the chancellor of which, Clark Kerr, had recently praised what he called "the multiversity" (and what Russell Kirk called "Behemoth U") as a great laboratory, and compared its students to lab rats. It wasn't only leftists who cheered when FSM leader Mario Savio said, "We're the raw material! But we're a bunch of raw material that don't mean to have any process upon us, don't mean to be made into any product, don't mean to end up being bought by some clients of the University, be they the government, be they industry, be they organized labor, be they anyone! We're human beings!"

In a panel discussion during *NR*'s fiftieth anniversary celebration in October 2005, liberal pundit Jeff Greenfield asked Buckley whether he regretted his own and his magazine's hard resistance to the civil rights movement. Yes, Buckley said, he realized in retrospect that he and his colleagues were relying too much on normal political processes as outlined in the Constitution to fully incorporate blacks into American public life, when in fact the political processes in many Southern states simply did not permit blacks to participate. He had illustrated this point, in an article written two decades before his exchange with Greenfield, by telling the story ("a national joke," he says, "of my youth and, I suspect, of my parents' youth") of the elderly black man who comes to the polling place in, say, Alabama and is given the literacy test. It is a page of Sophocles, in the original. The official asks the old man if he knows what it says. "It says here," says the man, folding his bifocals and putting them back in his pocket, "it says here that no nigger's going to vote here today."

Buckley's second thoughts as expressed to Greenfield are generous, but in fairness to the younger Buckley and his colleagues, one should remember the context of the times. The constitutional issues were real. The concept of states' rights could be and often was used by racists for their purposes, but it is also a fundamental principle of the American Republic, which at its founding was a union of states and not a unitary entity. From a modern conservative point of view, states' rights are a bulwark against the concentration of power in Washington. As veteran journalist James Jackson Kilpatrick put it in NR's "A Program for a Goldwater Administration," "Certain functions of government, for good or ill, were intended to be the States' own business; the States were to experiment, to try new approaches, or to leave it to their people whether particular problems were to be tackled at all. This was the genius of the federal idea; it was part of the vitality of the whole design. But within the federal harem, the States today are merely eunuchs; they are pitiful satellites around a federal sun. . . . The daily Federal Register bristles with executive orders that subvert the States; and a dissenting Justice Harlan offers eloquent authority for the Supreme Court's steady march toward that 'monolithic society which our federalism rejects.'"

In the early 1960s, the white politicians who were promoting ambitious civil rights measures were the same ones who were promoting ambitious intervention by Washington, D.C., in every aspect of life. And many of the black activists, notably Martin Luther King Jr., were allied with the hard left. Bill Rusher was aware, from his Senate subcommittee work, that two of King's closest associates, Stanley

Levison and Hunter Pitts "Jack" O'Dell, were high-ranking members of the Communist Party. Also, King did not endear himself to conservatives with comments like, "We see dangerous signs of Hitlerism in the Goldwater campaign."

By the end of 1962, President Kennedy was looking vulnerable, and F. Clifton White—the man behind that "nameless committee"— asked Senator Goldwater's permission to put his name forward for the Republican nomination. Goldwater flatly refused. In February 1963, half of the original twenty-two met again in Chicago.

"It was one of the strangest political caucuses I have ever attended," Rusher later recalled. "The people in the room were sincere, idealistic conservatives; but they were also realists, and they were well aware that without Goldwater's consent, or at least his willingness to refrain from a specific repudiation, our efforts on his behalf were bound to be futile. And yet . . . the political desperadoes assembled in that room felt sure they were on to something. They sensed in their bones that the Republican party was ready for Goldwater and for conservatism, if only Goldwater could be made ready for the GOP."

Then it happened. "Disconsolately we picked at the problem. The argument was dismally circular. At last, somewhere over my left shoulder, a voice with a midwestern or southwestern twang cut through the gloom: 'Let's draft the son of a bitch.'

"A muffled voice of reason posed the inevitable question: 'What if he won't let us draft him?'"

To which the first speaker shot back: "Then let's draft him *anyway!*"

Thus was born the National Draft Goldwater Committee, headed by Clif White. When the formation of the committee was formally announced in February 1963, Goldwater's response, according to Rusher, "was, though grumpy, at least bearable."

Rusher thought Burnham and Buckley, plus some of their junior colleagues, didn't take Goldwater seriously enough, and certainly didn't take the draft effort seriously enough. At editorial meetings, when he reported on the progress of the nameless committee, there would be knowing looks around the table—until one day the *New York Times* reported on the committee's efforts. This gave rise to another Rusher dictum: "No editor of *National Review* believes anything until he reads it in the *New York Times.*"

*   *   *

Back then, in the early 1960s, there was plenty of bustling behind the scenes between presidential election years, but as far as the general public was concerned political campaigns weren't the ridiculously protracted affairs they are now. (When Muskie "peaked too soon" in the 1972 cycle, "too soon" was January 1972, not sometime back in 1969.) So for most of 1963, even if he had been an active candidate, Goldwater would not have been expected to do much more than what he did: attend to his Senate business and his Arizona constituency. Then came November 22. Americans of all sorts and conditions—ones who had loved JFK and thrilled to every photograph of the First Family, and ones who were looking forward to voting against him a year thence—truly mourned their young President. As *NR* put it (in an unsigned editorial written by Buckley), "The grief was spontaneous and, in most cases, wholly sincere. Not because Mr. Kennedy's policies were so universally beloved, but because he was a man so intensely charming, whose personal vigor and robust enjoyment of life so invigorated almost all who beheld him."

Liberals may have felt the immediate loss more keenly, but in the political short and middle term it was conservatives who suffered more. Kennedy had been slipping in the polls, and he had not done well at getting his New Frontier programs through Congress. Now, all of a sudden, Lyndon Johnson, who as majority leader had been the Senate's consummate operator, was in the Oval Office. LBJ skillfully invoked the memory of the slain President to ram through spending bill after spending bill, plus the Civil Rights Act of 1964 (it had been introduced in 1963 but had stalled under Kennedy). Johnson announced the goals of his Great Society in May 1964, and he was going to be virtually unbeatable in November. Whoever the Republicans nominated was doomed to a kamikaze run against a ghost.

Goldwater knew it; at some level most of us who worked for him knew it. And yet to be young and a conservative in 1964 was very heaven. We had a candidate who actually stood for something other than business as usual. We wore our AuH_2O pins proudly, and we bought our copies of *The Conscience of a Conservative* and extras to give away (it eventually sold three and a half million copies). We cheered when Goldwater stood up at the Republican Convention at the Cow Palace in San Francisco and said, "I would remind you that extremism in the defense of liberty is no vice. And let me remind you also that moderation in the pursuit of justice is no virtue."

Those are the words, written by political science professor Harry Jaffa (borrowing from Cicero) and highlighted in Barry Goldwater's acceptance speech, that would soon be carved by Democrats and their allies in the national media into the tombstone of the Goldwater campaign. Those words, which in a better day would have been heard as strong and unexceptionable statements of patriotic truth by a great American patriot, were just not acceptable in the postassassination political world.

From then on, with the media in full cry, the campaign careened from one perceived disaster to another, from Social Security to the TVA. Whether Goldwater would have campaigned differently if he had had a realistic chance, we will never know. Maybe ("There are words of mine floating around in the air that I would like to reach up and eat," he once said), maybe not. As Buckley put it decades later, in a speech to the Goldwater Institute in Phoenix,

> I remember the fascination we all felt during his famous campaign of 1964. Our standard bearer was disdainful of any inducements to bloc voting. Sometimes he even gave the impression that his design was to alienate bloc voters. He had no such thing in mind. He was simply engaged in acts of full disclosure of the architectural splendor of his views, at once simple in basic design, and artful in ornamentation. Campaigning in St. Petersburg, Florida, a center for senior citizens, he deplored the excesses of the Social Security program. Then he chose Knoxville, Tennessee, to wonder out loud whether the TVA—Tennessee's greatest shrine—was really a very good idea. Then on to Appalachia, where he deplored the Depressed Areas program.

Matters weren't helped by the fact that early in 1964, Goldwater had turned his back on the Draft Goldwater Committee, which had done all the work to get him to that point, and placed a group of not-ready-for-prime-time Arizona pols in control of his campaign.

Despite their clear edge, the Democrats fought one of the dirtiest campaigns in living memory. Goldwater was regularly accused of racism for his votes against the civil rights bills. The accusations were probably disingenuous. They were certainly belied by the fact that Goldwater had personally directed, back in the 1930s, that his family's department store be integrated, as to both staff and customers. At the local level, Goldwater rallies, using the slogan "In your heart you know he's right," were overflown by small planes trailing banners,

"In your guts you know he's nuts." More famous—though it aired only once—was the TV commercial showing the little girl pulling petals off a daisy; when she gets toward the last one, her voice is replaced with a voiceover countdown, and then the explosion and the mushroom cloud, with Lyndon Johnson's voice in the background: "These are the stakes. To make a world in which all God's children can live, or to go into the dark. We must either love each other, or we must die." Lyndon Johnson, well-known lover of mankind! And finally an anonymous male announcer: "Vote for President Johnson on November 3. The stakes are too high for you to stay home."

On September 11, 1964, Buckley addressed the national convention of Young Americans for Freedom. In that talk, he took his audience to the depths and then raised them to a new plateau. It had been expected that he would urge the young conservative activists to redouble their efforts to win for Goldwater. But Buckley had something very different in mind. It is worth dwelling for a moment on that speech, both a sober appeal to reason and a work of pure rhetorical drama.

"I wish," he said,

> to speak to you on two subjects. The first has to do with the role of the conservative movement at this juncture in American history, when . . . we labor under the visitation of a freedom-minded candidate for the presidency of the United States. I say labor, because the nomination of Barry Goldwater, when we permit ourselves to peek up over the euphoria, reminds us chillingly of the great work that has remained undone. A great rainfall has deluged a thirsty earth, but before we had time properly to prepare the ground.

Then came the line that stilled the large audience: "I speak of course about the impending defeat of Barry Goldwater."

Those in attendance say there were gasps, then total silence, as Buckley continued:

> The beginning of wisdom is the fear of the Lord. The next and most urgent counsel is to take stock of reality. Reality, during a political campaign, sometimes suggests the advisability of dismissing strategic considerations in favor of tactical imperatives, which call for cultivating, in the Goldwater camp, the morale of an army on the march. Our morale is high, and we are marching. But the morale of an army on the march is that of an army that has been promised victory. It is wrong to assume that we shall overcome; and therefore it is right to reason to the necessity of guarding against the utter disarray that sometimes follows a stunning defeat. It is right to take

thought, even on the eve of the engagement, about the potential need for regrouping, for gathering together our scattered forces.

Then the high rhetoric, with stunning metaphors, precisely chosen and exactly right:

The election of Barry Goldwater would presuppose a sea change in American public opinion; presuppose that the fiery little body of dissenters of which you are a shining meteor suddenly spun off nothing less than a majority of the American people, who suddenly overcame a generation's entrenched lassitude and, prisoners all those years, succeeded in passing blithely through the walls of Alcatraz and tripping lightly over the shark-infested waters and treacherous currents, to safety on the shore.

Finally the conclusion, focusing on the debt of gratitude owed to Barry Goldwater:

The glorious development of this year was the nomination of a man whose views have given the waiting community a choice. The opportunity is golden to take the advantage we have got. It is an advantage that has been given us primarily as the result of the gallant efforts of Senator Goldwater. His disposition to sacrifice his career [by giving up his Senate seat] in order to give us these few months to take our point to the people from a national platform is an act of political nobility. . . . Now is precisely the moment to labor incessantly to educate our fellow citizens. The point is to win recruits whose attention we might never have attracted but for Barry Goldwater: to win them not only for November 3 but for future Novembers: to infuse the conservative spirit in enough people to entitle us to look about, on November 4, not at the ashes of defeat but at the well planted seeds of hope, which will flower on a great November day in the future, if there is a future. . . .

We dishonor the Goldwater movement if we permit ourselves to speak to those recruits we gather as though the walls of Agincourt were hollow eggshells which will come crumbling down under the pressure of our heroic rhetoric. . . . The enemy is made of sterner stuff. So are we, and we must prove it by showing not a moment's dismay on November 4 in the likely event that the walls have stood firm against our assault. On that day we must emerge smiling, confident in the knowledge that we weakened those walls, that they will never again stand so firmly against us.

The Goldwater campaign did indeed end in electoral disaster, with Barry Goldwater carrying only six states and losing to Lyndon

Johnson in the popular vote by 61 to 39 percent. "But to say that," as Rusher puts it, "and stop there, is to overlook almost entirely the real political significance of 1964. . . . It laid the foundations for everything that followed. Before 1964, conservatism was . . . a political theory in the process of becoming a political movement; after 1964, and directly as a result of it, conservatism increasingly became the acknowledged political alternative to regnant liberalism—almost fated, in fact, to replace it sooner or later."

And that, in the end, is exactly what it did. But before that happened there would be a great pause in the orderly march to conservative hegemony, a political hiatus—or, as Rusher later put it, "a long detour" at the hands of Richard M. Nixon.

At the high point of the Goldwater campaign—the very day the candidate was to be nominated—personal disaster struck the Buckley family and a wide circle of friends.

Maureen Buckley, who had done so much to keep the editorial department sane in *National Review*'s first three years, had met and fallen in love with a young businessman named Gerald O'Reilly. They married in 1958 and immediately began producing the next generation; one of Priscilla's classic stories involves her, unmarried and with no experience of midwifery, being called on to assist in the unexpectedly speedy birth of Maureen's second child, who was named, appropriately, Priscilla.

On July 16, 1964, Maureen's part-time maid, Georgia Cobb, who also worked for Aloïse Buckley and Priscilla at their apartment in Manhattan, came as scheduled to the O'Reilly home in Scarsdale. Georgia found Maureen unconscious on the dining room floor, with her five children milling around uncomprehendingly. Georgia called 911 and Gerry; the doctors did their best, but eventually the word reached the editorial department: Maureen, young, vibrant Maureen, had had a cerebral hemorrhage and was not expected to live through the night.

Bill Rickenbacker was detailed to get hold of Bill Buckley at the Republican Convention. He reached Bill Rusher, who had delighted in Maureen's company at the magazine and had even dated her a few times before she met Gerry. Rusher's personal sorrow added to the grimness of his task: finding Buckley on the convention floor and telling him what had happened. As Rusher recalls it, "When he heard my news, his face seemed to freeze into an expressionless mask. 'Get me to a telephone,' he said quietly." Bill reached Priscilla, who confirmed the report; he told her he would be on the next plane to New York. "So Bill Buckley," Rusher concludes, "who had done so much to lay the intellectual foundations of the movement that was triumphing that evening at the Cow Palace, was winging eastward out of San Francisco, his thoughts altogether elsewhere, when the convention nominated Barry Goldwater as its candidate for President of the United States."

To Maureen's siblings, her death was not only a profound personal loss but also a shocking intimation of mortality. Except for Mary Ann, whom none of them had even seen, they had all grown up healthy, and the boys had come safely through the war. Among them they had produced four dozen healthy children. The loss of their father had been painful, but the pain was mitigated by knowing that after his years of suffering, he was ready to go home to God. This was different. "Until this time," Priscilla later wrote, "we had seemed, as a family, golden, untarnished by time or tragedy." Now a shadow had fallen.

Two years later, John Buckley's wife, Ann, died at age thirty-eight of a stroke, leaving three children; and in January 1967 Aloïse Heath died, age forty-eight, also of a stroke, leaving ten children. Bill, in his obituary, quoted one of Aloïse's children: "Nothing will ever be fun again." Well, it would, but not right away.

For Maureen, as for their father, Bill and Priscilla edited a volume of recollections by family and friends. For Aloïse they published a collection of her own writings, *Will Mrs. Major Go to Hell?* They also started a tradition, which continues to this day, of publishing one of Aloïse's Christmas pieces in the magazine each December. *NR* still gets letters every year from delighted readers making Aloïse's acquaintance for the first time.

4

The Raging Sixties

I n *Up from Liberalism*, commenting on the apathy of "the Silent Generation," Buckley wrote, "It seems to me that there will not again be a robust political life in the undergraduate world until the student becomes convinced that *it matters* what he thinks about public problems." When he wrote those words, in 1959, that must have seemed a pipe dream. As the 1960s wore on, it became a nightmare.

In retrospect, Americans tend to remember the student radicalism of the Sixties as having been triggered by mounting deaths of American soldiers in Vietnam, and the black radicalism of the Sixties as having been triggered by continuing segregation and oppression. In fact, the student upheavals began *before* the heavy American involvement in Vietnam. The Berkeley protests were triggered by policies of the University of California's administration. When Students for a Democratic Society began in 1962, the main issues listed in its founding document, the Port Huron Statement (written by a future Mr. Jane Fonda, Tom Hayden), were the oppression of Negroes in the South, the Cold War, and the mechanization of modern life ("men still tolerate meaningless work and idleness"). There was no mention of Vietnam. As for black radicalism, while some of the civil rights–era protests had turned violent, the full-scale riots in our cities began only *after* passage of the Civil Rights Act. (Revolution of rising expectations?) The mid-Sixties saw the transition from

"We Shall Overcome" to "Get Whitey"; from "Peace and Love" to "Kill the Pigs."

It was in this overheated atmosphere, in the spring of 1965, that Buckley gave a speech at a communion breakfast of the Holy Name Society of the New York City Police Department. Buckley had spoken to the society before, with the outside world taking no notice. But this time it was one month after the attempted march from Selma to Montgomery. Ten days after the aborted march, a white Northern woman, Viola Liuzzo, was driving her car along a lonely stretch of Alabama road, far from the areas protected by the National Guard. She had with her in the passenger seat a young black militant. Mrs. Liuzzo was shot and killed by an unknown gunman. In his speech, Buckley commented on the huge press coverage given Mrs. Liuzzo's death and examined what this said about the press's assumptions about the South. "Why, one wonders," he asked, "was this a story that occupied the front pages from one end [of the country] to another, if newspapers are concerned with the unusual, the unexpected? Didn't the killing merely confirm precisely what everyone has been saying about the South? . . . Who could have been surprised by this ghastly episode?"

Just as Bill's sister Aloïse, ten years before, had inadvertently learned how to raise money for the Ivy League, so Bill now learned how he could reliably get his name onto the front pages. BUCKLEY PRAISES POLICE OF SELMA/HAILED BY 5,600 POLICE HERE AS HE CITES "RESTRAINT" was the *New York Times* headline. The *New York Post* reported: "Laughter and more applause greeted Buckley's query, 'Didn't the killing confirm what some elements in the South said would happen?' . . . The cheers were even louder when Buckley criticized Mrs. Viola Gregg Liuzzo, the slain Detroit mother of five, for going to the march on Montgomery." (The *Post* has since been turned into a right-wing paper by Rupert Murdoch, but back then it was owned by a staunch liberal, Dorothy Schiff.) The charges—both against Buckley and against his NYPD audience—were easily refuted: a tape had been made of the proceedings, and independent reporters listened to it and confirmed Buckley's account of what he said and how the police reacted. (This was an early big story for John Leo, just starting his journalistic career. He disagreed with much of what Buckley said, but nonetheless was offended by the media's misreporting.) But Buckley had been stung, on his own behalf and that of the police, who were major targets in that season, called "pigs" and frequently accused of brutality.

It so happened that 1965 was a mayoral election year in New York City, and it was looking as if the Republican candidate would be John Vliet Lindsay. Lindsay was a clean-cut, good-looking Yale classmate of Jim Buckley's; Lindsay's twin brother, David, had also been in their class and remained a close friend of Jim's. But John Lindsay had gone into the Rockefeller wing of the New York Republican Party. He was a four-term congressman representing the so-called Silk Stocking District on Manhattan's East Side, and he was hoping to use the mayoralty as a springboard to nothing less than the White House. He was thus already precisely what the Conservative Party had been formed to oppose. Add to that the fact that he had pointedly disavowed his party's presidential ticket in 1964, and he was ripe for opposition from the right. As Buckley would put it in a press conference that spring, "The two-party system presupposes an adversary relationship between the two parties. That there is no such relationship in New York, Mr. Lindsay makes especially clear when he proposes as running mates members of the Liberal and Democratic Parties. . . . Mr. Lindsay, described by *The New York Times* as being 'as liberal as a man can be,' qualifies for the support of the Liberal Party and the Republican Party only if one supposes that there are no substantial differences between the Republican Party and the Liberal Party. That there should be is my contention."

Among *NR*'s senior staff at the time, only Bill Rusher was legally a resident of New York City. But all the others, except Frank Meyer, spent several days a week there, and they paid NYC income taxes on their *NR* paychecks. They could see that the city was a poster child for failed liberal policies. In May, Buckley wrote a column giving a ten-point program on which an enterprising person could run for mayor; it included items (some of which he later modified or abandoned as he learned more about the subject) like reimbursing neighborhoods for the cost of private watchmen to supplement the hard-pressed police force; giving special incentives to black and Puerto Rican entrepreneurs; cracking down on double parking during business hours (this may sound trivial, but not to anyone who has tried to make his way through New York traffic); taking away the monopoly power of trade unions; preserving the neighborhood schools; and putting welfare recipients to work. When the editors decided to run that column in the magazine, Priscilla suggested using BUCKLEY FOR MAYOR for the streamer—the little eye-catching phrase that diagonals across the upper left-hand corner of *NR*'s cover.

When Dan Mahoney received his copy of the magazine, he called Buckley and asked, Do you mean it? Buckley's first reaction was, No, of course not. His second was, Well, why not?—provided, that is, that a mayoral race wouldn't cost too much money, and wouldn't take too much time away from either the magazine or his other commitments. And provided also that he would be allowed to run a "paradigmatic" campaign—one that would not play to bloc politics, but would allow him to state his understanding of how conservative principles applied to the many problems facing the city.

Mahoney agreed, and the campaign was launched. (Interestingly, mayoral candidates in New York City do not need to be legal residents of the city for tax or voting purposes.) From the beginning, there was no pretense that winning was possible. Asked how many votes, "conservatively speaking," he expected to get, Buckley replied, "Conservatively speaking, one." At another time, asked what he would do if he won, he famously replied, "Demand a recount."

The mayoral year was also the year of the great newspaper strike. For anyone who cares about print journalism, this was a disaster, reducing the number of outlets in what had once been a great newspaper town from six to three. (In the 1920s there had been twelve.) But it was a boon to the Buckley campaign. For a crucial part of the summer, television was the principal medium of the mayoral contest, giving the candidates direct, unmediated exposure to the voters. This sharpened the contrast between Buckley's performance and those of Lindsay and the hapless Democratic candidate, Comptroller Abe Beame. (Beame finally became mayor eight years later, just in time to preside over the collapse of the city's finances—not primarily his fault, but the fault of generations of bad management and corruption. This was the crisis that yielded the famous *New York Daily News* headline FORD TO CITY: DROP DEAD.)

Buckley sternly refused to play to bloc voters, to the point of refusing to march in the Pulaski Day parade, even though Poland and the other Captive Nations were of far more pressing concern to him than to either of his opponents. But he knew where his natural constituency lay: white ethnics, who felt that their paychecks were being gobbled up by taxes for which they were not getting, in return, good educations for their children or safety in their neighborhoods and in the subways. These were the people who a decade earlier had been portrayed lovingly by Jackie Gleason & Co. in *The Honeymooners*, and who a decade later would be lampooned by Norman Lear in *All in the Family*.

The stereotype of someone of Buckley's background is that he would regard the outer boroughs—as Manhattanites call 80 percent of their city, namely the Bronx, Queens, Brooklyn, and Staten Island—as "drive-through" territory. That is, you go through them only to get to the airport, or to your country place. But in fact Buckley had paid many visits to these boroughs in the course of his speaking career. His correspondence includes more than one letter expressing gratitude that a wealthy young Ivy Leaguer had taken the trouble to travel to some remote spot for a communion breakfast or a parish book club meeting. Now it turned out that one of Buckley's running mates, the candidate for president of the City Council, Rosemary Gunning, was from Queens, and the other, the candidate for comptroller, Hugh Markey, was from Staten Island. The fact that both were Catholics of Irish descent, and that Buckley was a Catholic of Irish descent (half, actually, but no one seemed to notice the Swiss/German half), was cause for much scorn from the press, which assumed that the Conservatives had deliberately chosen the candidates because of their demographics. This was the same press that saw nothing remarkable in the other candidates' frantic efforts to "balance their tickets"—that is, choose running mates because of their demographics: in the case of the WASP Lindsay, an Irish Catholic and a Jew; in the case of the Jewish Beame, an Irish Catholic and an Italian Catholic.

But the attendant accusations of racism and general evil were quite startling. "For weeks," intoned the *New York Times* editorial page near the end of the campaign, "William F. Buckley Jr. has been pandering to some of the more brutish instincts in the community, though his appeals to racism and bigotry have been artfully masked." "He is no racist himself," the *Times* conceded a week later, in response to a letter to the editor from Buckley, "yet, he delights the prejudices of certain listeners by slurs on Negroes." How did he do this? There were four principal charges in the indictment: (1) He frequently quoted from Nathan Glazer and Daniel Patrick Moynihan's scholarly and widely respected *Beyond the Melting Pot* on matters such as the illegitimacy rate among urban blacks. (2) He was on record as having a high regard for the police force and as opposing the establishment of a (presumptively hostile) Civilian Review Board to weigh accusations of police brutality. (3) He was on record as having a high regard for his running mate Mrs. Gunning, who had been a leader in the movement to preserve neighborhood schools (that is, preserve them from racial busing). (4) He called on politicians, black and white alike, to disavow Adam Clayton Powell Jr., Abyssinian Baptist minister and ten-term U.S. congressman representing Harlem. Powell regularly went on junkets (at taxpayer expense) with a pretty secretary or two (at taxpayer expense); he elevated one of these secretaries to the status of wife and sextupled her salary (at taxpayer expense, and also violating a congressional rule by basing her not in his district or in Washington, D.C., but at his vacation home in Puerto Rico). Most important, he urged his fellow Northern blacks to take to the streets in violent protest of conditions in the South.

To the ladies and gentlemen of the press, the case was clear: even if Buckley wasn't a racist, these were appeals to "the prejudices of certain listeners"—that is, his (mostly Catholic) ethnic supporters.

Being thrown into outer darkness by the press is no fun, even for a professional polemicist. And there was a good deal of tedium in the televised debates with two far-from-scintillating opponents. But there was also the joy of combat, as related in one of the most memorable sentences of Buckley's book about the campaign, *The Unmaking of a Mayor*: "A good debater is not necessarily an effective vote-getter: you can find a hole in your opponent's argument through which you could drive a coach and four ringing jingle bells all the way, and thrill at the crystallization of a truth wrung out from a bloody dialogue— which, however, may warm only you and your muse, while the smiling paralogist has in the meantime made votes by the tens of thousands."

Other aspects of the campaign also had their delights. Buckley wrote about the camaraderie on the young campaign team—his brother Jim as campaign manager; Neal Freeman, whom he had hired away from Doubleday the year before, as general personal assistant (he was known around *NR* as "the keeper of the body"); Dan Mahoney and Kieran O'Doherty, the seasoned political operatives on the team; and various young volunteers, some of whom would go on to play large roles, though often behind the scenes, in the conservative movement. Daniel Oliver had started reading *National Review* while in the army learning Russian at the Monterey Defense Language Institute; he was now studying law at Fordham. Agatha Schmidt, a recent graduate of Marymount College, was the daughter of Godfrey Schmidt, who had served as counsel to Cardinal Spellman; he had also hosted, in the 1950s, "Cocktails for Conservatives," a series of gatherings that brought right-wing New Yorkers together. David Stuhr, a young professor of finance (Yale '60), had been one of the organizers of a Buckley appearance at the Yale Political Union and had stayed in touch.

On election day, Buckley received 13.4 percent of the vote—a total of 341,225 votes more than, "conservatively speaking," he had predicted. Staten Island—which he would describe as, "so to speak, my *querencia*; a relatively neurosis-free, ethnically reposed enclave in Greater New York, unsundered by ideology, tension, urban jitters"— gave him 25.2 percent of its vote; Manhattan gave him 7.2 percent; the other three boroughs, in the teens.

Whether or not this campaign is what scuttled Lindsay's presidential ambitions, the effect on Buckley's own career was incalculable. As Neal Freeman put it, "It made him a star. . . . In 1964 you would travel anywhere in the country with Bill Buckley and both of you were anonymous. By 1965, you couldn't walk twenty-five feet in an airport without the autograph hunters."

The first concrete result was a contract (from Viking, now run by his old Yale friend Tom Guinzburg) for a book about the campaign. In January 1966 the Buckleys left for Saanenmöser accompanied by Aggie Schmidt, who had been the campaign secretary, and Dave Stuhr, who had helped with some of the position papers. They brought with them stacks of written matter—position papers, newspaper commentary, internal campaign memos. With the help of his young researchers Buckley produced his offbeat classic, *The Unmaking of a Mayor*. He could afford to be candid in a way that no one who wanted to achieve elective office could, and so this is a deliciously revealing account of the humbuggeries of modern politics, mixed with serious reflection on the problems of urban society A.D. 1965.

The second result of the campaign was *Firing Line*. Buckley and Freeman had been talking for a year about the possibility of launching a television show, Buckley versus a string of liberal opponents. They had come up against a concentrated lack of interest from television executives. The Buckley-Beame-Lindsay debates changed all that. Suddenly WOR-TV in New York came to *him*, and *Firing Line* was born.

Its producer was a big, loud, savvy New York Jewish liberal named Warren Steibel; somewhat to the surprise of both of them, he and Buckley quickly became friends. Steibel took a suite on the fourth floor of 150 East 35th Street and started lining up guests. *Firing Line* hit the airwaves in April 1966.

The first dozen guests were all certified members of the American left, but they had been imaginatively chosen and their interactions with Buckley were wonderfully diverse. Some of the exchanges were heated, such as the one over Vietnam with the aged lion of the left, Norman Thomas—six-time presidential candidate on the Socialist ticket—and the one, also over Vietnam, with Yale professor and antiwar activist Staughton Lynd, who had recently visited Hanoi on behalf of the antiwar movement. (Graffito seen on the Yale campus at about this time: "Staughton Lynd reads *National Review*.") Buckley was sometimes accused of incivility—in not being more deferential to the old and nearly blind Thomas; in the deliberate provocativeness of his brief introductions of his guests ("[David] Susskind is a staunch liberal. If there were a contest for the title of Mr. Eleanor Roosevelt, he would unquestionably win it"). But there was always serious substance in the conversation—on Vietnam and the Communist threat generally with Thomas and Lynd; on affirmative action with James Farmer, founder of the Congress of Racial Equality; on HUAC with John Henry Faulk, who claimed to have been victimized by the committee. There were also some surprisingly genial hours spent on contentious subjects—with Bishop James A. Pike, that season's wild card in the Episcopal Church, on school prayer; with television personality Steve Allen on capital punishment; with Leo Cherne, chairman of Freedom House, on Joe McCarthy. And for a show that was, as one TV executive put it to Buckley and Steibel, low on "production values," some of those tapes provide a startling reminder of the culture of the late Sixties—Timothy Leary, the high priest of LSD, appearing not in a suit and tie but in flower-child garb; Allen Ginsberg, hair crinkling all over the place, dark eyes sparkling, playing his little harmonium and doing his Hare Krishna chant.

Even when heated, the shows never descended to the shouty name-calling of too many later political talk shows. (Buckley engaged in that once, to his continuing chagrin—not on *Firing Line*, but on network convention coverage, with Gore Vidal in 1968.) And though

Buckley was usually sharing the screen with liberals (not always—guest number 13 was Clare Boothe Luce, guest number 15 Barry Goldwater), a conservative voice was now being beamed into the living rooms of millions of people who hadn't thought to pick up a small blue-bordered journal of opinion, and Buckley himself had become a national celebrity.

Bill and Pat Buckley's *home*, ever since they moved there in 1952, has been the house at Wallacks Point. An interviewer once asked Bill: If you could live anywhere in the world that you wanted, where would you live? And he answered: "Where I live." But Bill worked in Manhattan, and he quickly found that there are nights when you just don't want to get on that train, and so a pied-à-terre was needed. The first was a small but lofty-ceilinged apartment in the East 30s; the second, once Bill and Pat decided to put Christopher in a Catholic day school in the city, was a much larger apartment in the East 70s. Then, with Bill's increased visibility brought about by the mayoral race, and with Pat getting more deeply involved in charity work and social events, it was time for an apartment suitable for serious entertaining. Pat started hunting, and soon she had found The One: a maisonette at 73rd and Park that had belonged to Dag Hammarskjöld. (Rush Limbaugh made great sport of the "maisonette" business at *NR*'s 45th anniversary dinner; it's New York real estate talk for an apartment that is on the ground floor and has its own separate entrance from the street.)

As you enter, you're in a smallish foyer, facing a large hall with a spiral staircase. Bill's Challis harpsichord has sometimes lived in the foyer, sometimes under the staircase. During the period, in the 1960s and early 1970s, when he regularly rode a Honda motorscooter between 73rd Street and 35th Street, it would be parked, to Pat's annoyance, in the foyer. (At the office, to Bill Rusher's annoyance, it would be parked in the third-floor hallway. WAR tried to convince WFB that this was an illegal fire hazard. He never succeeded, but the Honda finally went when the state enacted a helmet law that Bill considered draconian.) To the right of the hall are a study/drawing room, painted Pat's signature red, where dinner guests gather for cocktails, and a large salon. The salon is where the Bösendorfer piano lives; it belonged to Pat's mother, and she likes to say, "That piano is the reason Bill married me." To the left of the hall, there are a dining room with two round tables, each seating twelve; a small cloakroom; and the kitchen and maid's rooms. Upstairs, master bedroom and bathroom, smaller bedroom, and smaller-still study (this, as opposed to the "red room" downstairs, is the working study, the one that in the 1960s housed Bill's typewriter, and now houses his computers and all their paraphernalia).

The walls are covered with paintings, which at first glance seem to be lit from inside, so artfully done are the tightly focused little spotlights installed in the ceiling. Many of the paintings are by Raymond de Botton, whom Bill discovered in a gallery in Saanen in 1965 while Pat was in hospital there recovering from a bad skiing injury. ("Mrs. Buckley?" a nurse asked one day. "The *late* Mrs. Buckley," Pat managed to say.) When, a few years ago, Pat completely redecorated, the shimmery abstract paintings of another of Bill's favorites, Robert Goodnough, replaced the assortment of representational paintings in the dining room. And on every surface are photographs in silver frames—Bill and various siblings aged less than ten, Pat as a radiant young mother, Captain Bill on his sloop *Cyrano*, a sidelong closeup of David Niven, and (one of Bill's favorite photos—he used it in both *Let Us Talk of Many Things* and *Miles Gone By*) a backview of Christopher and his wife, Lucy, escorting Bill out of the ballroom after *NR*'s thirty-fifth anniversary party, at which he announced his retirement as editor-in-chief.

As Bill put it recently when the NYC taxing authorities tried to claim 73rd Street was his principal residence, "How could my principal residence be a place where there isn't room for my son and his family to stay overnight?" But at the time Pat found the apartment, Christopher was heading off to Portsmouth Abbey, a boys' school (at that time—it's now co-ed) run by the Benedictines in Rhode Island. The apartment's vocation, which it has fulfilled splendidly, was not as a home but as a venue for entertaining.

Through the decades the *NR* circle and the New York social circle have frequently mingled there. It might be to watch election returns, though by no means all the Buckleys' social friends are conservatives (as one of them put it while accepting the 2004 invitation, "If Bill and Pat are happy, I won't be, and vice versa"). Or it might be to listen to one of Bill's favorite pianists or harpsichordists, ranging from a supertalented amateur like Larry Perelman to the internationally renowned Rosalyn Tureck and Fernando Valenti. (Tureck shocked Bill—but such was his regard for her that he acceded—by refusing to use his beloved Bösendorfer, with its lush Romantic sound, for a Bach recital, demanding instead that a Steinway, with its harder, more brilliant edge, be brought in.)

The Christmas party gradually changed in the new venue. For the first few years the tradition of listening to a recording of *Messiah* continued. Then, starting in the early 1970s, although it was still called the Messiah Party, the music might be Fernando Valenti playing Scarlatti on the harpsichord, or a church choral society whose director Bill knew singing Christmas music, or, in more recent years, a jazz pianist. But always there was a sumptuous buffet supper, topped off by an array of Pat's signature desserts.

As you drive up the mountain road from Château d'Oex to Gstaad, just before the village of Rougemont, you pass a sixteenth-century château. A friend who stayed with the Buckleys in Saanenmöser recalls Bill saying, "Wouldn't it be wonderful to live there?" Not long afterward, it came to pass.

It's not easy for a foreigner to buy property in the canton of Vaud, but the American diplomat and philanthropist Edward Tuck (best known for organizing the restoration of the Trophée des Alpes on the French Riviera) had acquired the château between the world wars. His nephew, also Edward Tuck, had inherited it and discreetly rented it out for a few months of the year. Now Bill got his chance to take the château for two of those months.

There must be a formal front door somewhere, but guests normally entered via the kitchen, presided over by the brilliant but self-effacing Julian Booth. A hallway leads to the public rooms—an enormous living room, paneled in the light-colored wood traditional in that part of Switzerland, where Bill, with Tuck's permission, installed a piano; a large drawing room; and a dining room with a heavily carved refectory-style table. Beneath the living room is the huge room Bill made his study and atelier—a few years before, at the urging of Clare Luce, he had taken up painting. Visitors have described this room as a "cellar," because you have to go downstairs from the main floor to get to it. However, because the land falls away toward the river valley, it is fully windowed, looking out toward Bill's favorite ski run, the Videmanette.

When Bill first rented the château he had recently made friends with John Kenneth Galbraith, who became one of his favorite debating

The château, seen from
the Videmanette side.

partners. Ken and Kitty Galbraith had discovered Gstaad some years earlier, when Ken was representing the United States at some long-drawn-out conference in Geneva. They came every winter, and now they introduced the Buckleys to David Niven, who would become a close friend of them both. One other introduction had less happy results, though it led to one of Pat's great lines. The Galbraiths brought Ted Kennedy for a visit one afternoon, but then they had to go farther down the valley while he returned to Gstaad. The area is well served by railway, but Kennedy asked whether he might borrow a car. "You certainly may not," said Pat. "There are three bridges between here and Gstaad."

Through the Galbraith/Niven connections the Buckleys entered the circle of the "Gstaad royals"—some reigning monarchs, like Prince Rainier of Monaco and, later, King Juan Carlos of Spain; some deposed, like King Constantine of Greece, or scions of a deposed family, like Prince Nicholas Romanoff of Russia. Parties with the royals led to some inter-Buckley friction. Bill and his sisters Priscilla and Jane, who had started coming to Gstaad for two weeks each winter, took the attitude Bill gives to Blackford in *Saving the Queen*.

"Do I have to curtsy?" Sally asks Blackford before a state dinner at the White House, her old roommate having become the Empress of Sinrah.

"Americans don't curtsy."

"Not even to the Queen of England?"

"Not even to the Queen of England. . . . Sally, we are a *republican* country."

Pat, however, was for many of those years a loyal subject of the Crown, and even since she became an American citizen she has retained her ideas of how to behave toward royalty. Pat curtsies.

But their friends were by no means all titled expatriates or celebrity birds of passage. Early in the Buckley/Horne sojourns in Saanenmöser, Bill and Alistair made friends with the baker's daughter, who delivered the bread each day. Anita Jutzeler was an expert skier (asked once how old she was when she learned to ski, she said, "I can't remember a time when I didn't ski"), and the men pointed out to her that if she got her certification, they could hire her as a guide. She did, and they did. Her future husband, Peter Matti, of a prominent Saanen family, also skied with the Buckleys and Hornes; he would lead the stronger skiers, eventually including Christopher and his childhood friend Danny Merritt, into hors-piste territory—off the groomed trails. And these friendships led to others among the local population, notably with Nina Schneller, a ski-school colleague of Anita's.

There was just one qualification: potential friends had to be able to speak English, French, or Spanish. For all the time Bill has spent in the German-speaking part of the Saanen Valley—and although he has written two novels and one nonfiction book set predominantly in Germany—he takes a *J'y suis, j'y reste* attitude toward language. His German is confined to words like *Zeitgeist* and *Weltanschauung;* in ordering a meal in Gstaad, he resolutely speaks French even when it becomes clear that the German-speaking waiter's second language is English.

In early 1964, as the Goldwater campaign was just getting started, a young Hoosier named Don Lipsett floated the idea of a new conservative organization. Lipsett, who had been part of *NR*'s early, unsuccessful business team, had found his niche as Midwest Director of the Intercollegiate Society of Individualists (as ISI was still called—it would soon be renamed the Intercollegiate Studies Institute), working with conservative students and faculty to battle the liberals on their campuses. What the movement needed, Lipsett judged, was an organization where conservatives of all stripes and all ages could meet and talk—that's all. The Philadelphia Society's founding documents even state that "The Society should sponsor no resolutions, political statements, or corporate programs of action."

Receiving the blessing of his employer, ISI president Vic Milione, Lipsett organized some preliminary regional meetings in 1964. Then, after Goldwater's defeat, the young entrepreneur proposed a meeting between Buckley and economist Milton Friedman—the first meeting, as it happens, between the future friends. Also present were Frank Meyer and Edwin J. Feulner Jr., the future head of the Heritage Foundation, at that time still a graduate business student at Wharton. In 1991 Buckley would tell the society, "It was almost thirty years ago that Ed Feulner and I each put up fifty dollars to incorporate the Philadelphia Society. I swear, I never got a bigger bang for a buck." Feulner agrees with the second part of that statement but asks to correct the first part: the hundred dollars, he says, all came from Buckley; Feulner's contribution was to take it to the bank and open the account.

In any case, the first national meeting was set for February 1965 in Chicago—pretty near the center of the country and close to Lipsett's Indiana base. Twenty-five years later, a rather-full-of-himself young NR staffer, editing an article on that year's Philly Soc meeting, inserted a sentence to the effect that the society had started out as a club for Midwestern car dealers but was now a serious organization (meaning that it now had lots of Washington policy wonks). The offending sentence was quickly excised by an older colleague—but let's look at it for a moment. Part of the society's point has always been that there are no admission requirements beyond a keen interest in conservative ideas. No advanced degrees required, no publication history. Probably it has had car dealers—perhaps it has now, and why not? But look at the lineup of speakers for the first national meeting: Milton Friedman, Frank Meyer, Stanley Parry, Brent Bozell, Stefan Possony, Robert Strausz-Hupé, Richard Cornuelle, LeBaron R. Foster, G. Warren Nutter, Russell Kirk, George Stigler, Eliseo Vivas. A couple of those people have since dropped off most of our radar screens; one of them has since won a Nobel Prize. But the list is basically a who's who of American conservatism, A.D. 1965. Some car dealers!

The society has gone on to bring sustenance to thousands of conservatives, young and old. Not having a publishing arm, it is less well known than its older cousin, ISI, or its younger cousin, the Heritage Foundation. It is simply, as long-serving treasurer Dave Stuhr puts it, a place where we can "recharge our batteries." Or as Buckley put it in his address to the society's fortieth anniversary meeting, "We are devoted here to the proposition that what we do and say and write *does* matter, does have effect. . . . It could even be held, with utmost seriousness, that the work of the Philadelphia Society—and this is testimony primarily to our meetings here with one another—is itself proof of our substantiality."

One of the bright spots in the Goldwater campaign had been the work of Ronald Reagan. He was a well-known figure, having for eight years hosted the popular *General Electric Theater* on television. And during those years, he had become more and more active in public affairs. When asked in 1964 if he would serve as co-chairman of the California Goldwater-for-president organization, he instantly said yes. He gave speeches for Goldwater around the state; one of the present authors heard him at Dodger Stadium on a warm summer evening and was bowled over. Late that summer, a group of conservative California businessmen, led by Holmes Tuttle (who, as coincidence would have it, was a high-end car dealer), offered to film the speech—formally titled "A Time for Choosing," but informally known as The Speech—for nationwide showing. Goldwater's Arizona Mafia wanted to nix it—they thought Reagan would ruffle too many feathers. But after a phone call from Reagan, Goldwater reviewed the film himself. Having seen it, he gave his okay. It brought in thousands of pledges of support that first evening and was shown again and again on television and at rallies in the last few days of the campaign. It brought $8 million into the Goldwater campaign.

Three weeks after the election, *NR* published a little symposium, with comments by George Bush (the elder), Ambassador John Davis Lodge, Ronald Reagan, Russell Kirk, and Gerhart Niemeyer. Of Reagan, the editors wrote, "There are those who believe he should campaign two years hence for the governorship of California. Including us."

Reagan himself would have preferred to campaign on someone else's behalf, but when group after group that he spoke to in 1965 said he was the one, he finally agreed to run. Now, in the same season that *Firing Line* began, Reagan was doing just that, against two-term incumbent Pat Brown. Brown had earlier defeated some pretty impressive politicians—Bill Knowland and Richard Nixon—and he thought he had an easy run against a mere actor. But the actor, stung by accusations that he could only mouth other people's words (in fact, he had started writing most of his own material a decade earlier, when speaking on behalf of General Electric), decided to stop routinely giving prepared speeches and rely instead on Q&A. He proved enormously effective at this, and his issues—the growing unrest on California's university campuses; the state's out-of-control taxation, crime rate, and welfare rolls; increasing air and water pollution— resonated with the people. As Reagan says in his autobiography, "I knew [Brown] knew he was in trouble" when he made a truly outrageous television commercial. It didn't have the "production values" of the LBJ daisy commercial, but it was right up there in sliminess. It showed Governor Brown telling a group of schoolchildren, "I'm running against an actor, and you know who killed Abe Lincoln, don't you?"

Reagan carried the flag for the cause—for our institutions and for our country—with dash and total conviction, combining conservative substance and celebrity style, with just a touch of that go-to-hell panache that characterized Bill Buckley's 1965 mayoral campaign. On November 8 the former actor defeated the old-line pol by almost a million votes—58 percent to 42 percent—and conservatives stopped brooding about 1964 and started thinking of the future.

The future was looking brighter than the present. The summer of 1965 had seen the Watts riot in Los Angeles—six days of looting, arson, and violence, featuring rock throwing, rifle fire, and Molotov cocktails; thirty-five wound up dead and hundreds injured. There were smaller riots that summer in Chicago and Springfield, Massachusetts. In 1966 we had been promised a "long hot summer," and so it was; there were 103 officially recorded riots that summer, starting in Newark (twenty-three dead), then Detroit (forty-three dead), and eventually spreading to cities as small as Fresno, California, and Nyack, New York. On the campuses, the sit-ins and protests of the early Sixties had given way to harder-edged demonstrations. In that passage in *Up from Liberalism* in which Buckley had written of his hopes for "a robust political life in the undergraduate world," he was envisioning something like his own undergraduate days, when it seemed "that every individual exertion, every point scored, every pamphlet distributed, every polemic delivered, contributed to the crystallization of an historical impulse." But that is not what the mid-Sixties activists had in mind.

Vietnam, as we have noted, was not the initiating cause of the student rebellions, but as the decade wore on it became the focus. In April 1965, SDS organized the "March on Washington to End the War in Vietnam," and students at campuses across the nation staged their own protests.

Some of the kids' elders egged them on, notably professor Noam Chomsky at MIT, professor Herbert Marcuse at UC San Diego—and New York senator Robert F. Kennedy. Observers speculate as to whether Kennedy was motivated by cynical political calculation or survivor's guilt at his brother's death. Whatever the reason, the former hard-boiled counsel to Joe McCarthy's Senate committee and hard-boiled attorney general in his brother's administration started weeping on the Jack Paar show and transmuted himself into a leader of the peace-and-love generation. As Murray Kempton put it on *Firing Line*, "It seems to me that his radicalism is a total hangup on the young." Two years before the 1968 election Bobby started distancing his late brother from the Vietnam War. He famously said that donating blood to the Vietcong would be a very American thing to do. Kennedy, incidentally, was one of the few prominent liberals who refused to appear on *Firing Line*. When Buckley was asked why he thought that was, he replied, "Why does the baloney reject the grinder?"

One of Governor Reagan's first major confrontations had to do with the University of California. As governor, Reagan became ex officio a member of the UC Board of Regents. As Buckley told the story in a major essay in *National Review* ("A Relaxing View of Ronald Reagan"), Reagan had no sooner been inaugurated than one of his fellow regents told him that they were planning to demand the resignation of Chancellor Clark Kerr, the man who had likened his students to "lab rats." The regent told the new governor that he and his colleagues were prepared to hold off for a few months if firing Kerr immediately would embarrass Reagan. As Buckley reports it, Reagan basically said, "Go ahead, and God bless you." When the duly appointed regents duly acted, the press exploded with accusations that the know-nothing actor/governor was daring to interfere with academic freedom. But Kerr was out, and Reagan and the other regents weathered the storm.

The winds of change were not confined to secular society. The Second Vatican Council had come to a close in 1965, and the results of its decisions gradually percolated throughout the Catholic world. It would not be until 1970 that the New Order of the Mass was formally issued, but already by 1966 the American hierarchy had mostly replaced Latin with the vernacular and had instituted many liturgical changes—to Bill Buckley's intense mortification.

It was partly that he missed the language and ritual he had come to love during daily Mass at the school he briefly attended in England, St. John's, Beaumont. And it was partly the quality of the translations and liturgy that replaced the old Mass. One of Buckley's most remarkable sentences was drawn out of him by the new liturgy:

> Really, the new liturgists should have offered training in yoga, or whatever else Mother Church in her resourcefulness might baptize as a distinctively Catholic means by which we might tune off the fascistic static of the contemporary Mass, during which one is either attempting to sing, totally neglecting the prayers at the foot of the altar, which suddenly we are told are irrelevant; or attempting to read the missal at one's own syncopated pace, which we must now do athwart the obtrusive rhythm of the priest or the commentator; or attempting to meditate on this or the other prayer or sentiment or analysis in the Ordinary or in the Proper of the Mass, only to find that such meditation is sheer outlawry which stands in the way of the liturgical calisthenics devised by the Central Coach, who apparently judges it an act of neglect if the churchgoer is permitted more than two minutes and 46 seconds without being made to stand if he was kneeling, or kneel if he was standing, or sit—or sing—or chant—or anything if perchance he was praying, from which anarchism he must at all costs be rescued: "LET US NOW RECITE THE INTROIT PRAYER," says the commentator: to which exhortation I find myself aching to reply in that "loud and clear and reverential voice" the manual for lectors prescribes: "LET US NOT!"

The New Order did not shake Buckley's faith, and it never tempted him to join any group of traditionalist schismatics, like the Lefebvrists. But it did seriously dampen his pleasure in the practice of his faith—until he found a modus vivendi with a small group of friends, one of them a priest who is willing to say the Mass in Latin.

Unless you were a Black Panther or a Weatherman, 1968 was one of the worst years in American history.

We were clearly at sea in Vietnam. Incremental escalation was a disaster, militarily and on the home front. The United States had shackled itself by agreeing to do nothing serious to interdict the North Vietnamese troops and matériel pouring in down the Ho Chi Minh Trail through Laos and Cambodia, and we had no strategy for victory. As Burnham put it, "You can't win a war unless you are willing to kill enemy soldiers. President Johnson seems prepared to lose, very slowly and with great dignity."

At home, the idea that the university campus was a place for scholarship and learning had gone by the boards. It was now a place where you chanted, "Hey hey, LBJ, how many kids will you kill today?" and "Ho Ho Ho Chi Minh, the NLF is gonna win." (This slogan was for many years listed in *NR*'s in-house style book, to make sure that if we quoted it, we quoted it correctly. One of Bill Buckley's foibles is a tin ear for popular culture. He once tried to rewrite a quotation from Yogi Berra, and he routinely quoted this line as "Ho Ho Ho, Ho Chi Minh, the NLF is bound to win.")

The cities were still reeling from the riots of 1965 and 1966. Then on April 4, 1968, Martin Luther King was assassinated. He was a great man; he was a man with whom conservatives had serious differences. It happened that two weeks after King's death Buckley was scheduled to speak to the American Society of Newspaper Editors. He told them: "Me, I say this: that more significant by far than the ghastly murders of John Kennedy and Martin Luther King, acts committed by isolatable and isolated men—more significant by far is the spontaneous, universal grief of a community which in fact considers itself aggrieved. That is the salient datum in America: not that we bred the aberrant assassins of John Kennedy and Martin Luther King, but that we bred the most widely shared and the most intensely felt sense of grief: such grief over the loss of Mr. Kennedy and Mr. King as is felt over the loss of one's own sons."

Bobby Kennedy had leapt into the presidential primary race just a few days before King was shot, emboldened by the surprisingly strong showing in New Hampshire of the antiwar Senator Eugene McCarthy. Two weeks after Kennedy entered the race Lyndon Johnson announced that he would not run for reelection, and his Vice President, Hubert H. Humphrey, took his place. As the climactic California primary approached, *NR* commissioned James Jackson Kilpatrick to write a profile of RFK, and it was devastating—all the falsifications of his own record and his late brother's, the distancing of himself from the Democratic regulars to whom he owed so much, the identification with the radicals. It was going to be the cover story in the issue that would go to press two days after the California primary. The cover art was a cobra's body with Bobby's head.

On the night of Tuesday, June 4, most New Yorkers turned off the TV and went to bed once it was clear that Kennedy had won. At 5:30 the next morning Priscilla Buckley's phone rang. It was Jim McFadden: *Have you heard the news? . . . I'll get a cab and pick you up in an hour.*

At 7:00 Priscilla's private line at the office rang—it was Kilpo. *Can I help?* Yes, said Priscilla, please come. He grabbed the next Shuttle from Washington, D.C., to New York; it was he who wrote the editorial on the shooting, as he memorably put it, "out of the alembic of a deadline hour."

When Burnham arrived at the office, he called a mini-conference and, in his analytical way, went over the possibilities: RFK dies before the issue comes out . . . RFK lives, but is brain-damaged . . . RFK is not as badly wounded as is feared, but he is still the victim of a foul attempt. . . . Whatever happened, Burnham and his colleagues concluded, *NR* could not afford to let that cover story see the light of day. Missing an issue would be bad, but going ahead with the Kennedy material would be suicidal.

Today, four decades later, if worse came to worst, you could simply scan in an excerpt from the *Federalist Papers* to fill the space. Not so in 1968. Providentially, two articles had been set in type several weeks earlier and then held to make room for something more timely. The copyeditor, Pat Carr, was assigned to read every page of the magazine that had already been locked up. So ubiquitous was Kennedy that year that Pat found invidious references to the junior senator from New York on virtually every page of the magazine—even in Russell Kirk's column. Corrections had to be phoned to the printing plant for all of these. (If the fax machine had been invented by this time, *NR* didn't have one.) It was a Stakhanovite effort (to use a word that Bill cheekily picked up from the Communists), but the editorial staff managed it.

Oh, and why have we not mentioned Bill Buckley until that last parenthesis? Because he was off sailing in the Aegean. He finally heard the news at around 3:00 P.M. New York time on Wednesday and breathlessly called Priscilla to find out what the magazine was doing. For once she was not indulgent with her little brother. "We're too busy to talk," she told him, and hung up.

During that season of unrest and upheaval both of the present authors were students in California: she as an undergraduate at the relatively peaceful University of Southern California, he doing graduate work at the heart of the madness, at Berkeley. Berkeley had never really gone back to normal after the Free Speech demonstrations in 1964. And by 1968, campus radicals had developed a symbiotic relationship with the Black Panthers (formally, the Black Panther Party for Self-Defense), founded by Huey Newton, Bobby Seale, and Eldridge Cleaver in Oakland in 1966, after the killing of Malcolm X.

The images from that decade, already difficult to evoke, are images that once assailed the emotions—a girl pushing a flower into a guardsman's rifle barrel; glass from smashed windows glittering along Telegraph Avenue; the screams and gunshots and bloodshed of People's Park; the almost sexual frenzy of the five thousand students and street people packed into Sproul Plaza as Eldridge Cleaver whipped them up, something like contempt gleaming in his hard, slitted eyes.

It was a decade of rage, of screams, of tears. There were tears for John Kennedy. There were tears for Martin Luther King. There were tears for Robert Kennedy. There were tears for the students at Kent State. Throughout the country, the emotions were raw and everywhere apparent, and as the decade progressed they turned increasingly hard. The Sixties began with the love of the flower children and ended with a hatred that many still called love. Charles Manson and his girls, who swam easily in the radical sea of the Sixties, butchered their victims in the name of love, and Bernardine Dohrn applauded. At a rally in Flint, Michigan, in 1969, Dohrn, dubbed by J. Edgar Hoover "La Pasionaria of the lunatic left," put it elegantly: "Dig it. First they killed those pigs, then they ate dinner in the same room with them. They even shoved a fork into a victim's stomach. Wild!" (Today, married to erstwhile Weather Underground bomber turned college professor Bill Ayers, Dohrn is an icon of the Chicago educationist establishment—guaranteed to radicalize your kids correctly, and who said Marxists can't sip tea?)

It had become a cliché on the liberal left to say that the right had created "an atmosphere of hate and fear" in which violence was inevitable. For over two decades, professors such as Richard Hofstadter and Daniel Bell—the latter coming to be considered a conservative by his peers—routinely warned us against rightist paranoid politics and "violence cults on the Right." But then came the violence of the Sixties, and, as Senator S. I. Hayakawa later pointed out, our intellectual establishment, like the British at Singapore, discovered that their guns had been trained in the wrong direction. (Hayakawa had been president of San Francisco State College during the worst of those years, 1968–1973.)

"The American riots of the 1960's baffled political historians for lack of a clearly defined purpose," wrote Theodore White in 1968. ". . . For generations, violence had threatened America from the native American right—the menace always perceived on the lunatic fringe of reaction where Ku Klux Klan, American Nazis and Minutemen muttered, rumbled and mobilized as phantom marauders. But when the real marauders, in the 1960's, took to the streets, they came not from the 'right' but from the 'left' in the most liberal administration in history, while the thinkers looked the other way."

Professor Marcuse called it a natural reaction to something he named "repressive tolerance." Other academics explained that campus and street violence was equivalent to what the university did to students and blacks and what the government was doing in Vietnam. Some of the more radical among them took Frantz Fanon as their text: "Violence alone, violence committed by the people, violence organized and educated by its leaders, makes it possible for the masses to understand social truths and gives the keys to them."

For the most part, among the comfortably tenured faculty members of various institutions of higher learning, this was a little extreme. Instead, in the spirit of what Marcuse called "the new sensibility," they asserted that violence could only be committed by institutions, not by individuals protesting institutionalized violence.

Perhaps. But at places like Berkeley in 1968, students lived on a daily basis with what looked very much like violence. Classes were disrupted as a matter of course, and it was not uncommon for those protesting such disruptions to be badly roughed up. Buildings were occupied, bombs exploded, and bricks sailed through library and classroom windows. At one point, even the faculty club was attacked, leading to some startlingly counterrevolutionary comments from a few professors.

Throughout the Bay Area, 1968 was a year of spiraling violence. There was a devastating series of riots in Berkeley and Oakland, spilling over into San Francisco, as the New Left moved off the campus and into the streets. The antiwar movement at Berkeley had become unapologetically pro-Hanoi, actively rooting for North Vietnamese victories and refusing to discuss the consequences of such victories for the young Americans without college deferments who were fighting in Vietnam.

The civil rights movement had splintered into violent black racist groups that increasingly took pleasure in savaging whites on Bay Area campuses. The peace marches had become wild trashing raids, with the clenched fist replacing the peace sign. The Weatherman faction of SDS and other New Left groups, among them the Black Panthers, had begun to arm; and those sweet songs of protest sung by Joan Baez and her imitators had given way to the Rolling Stones' "Street Fighting Man."

And all of this was a dress rehearsal, preparing for the great confrontation that was to occur in Chicago in August, where the most extreme and violent of the New Left groups turned the Democratic National Convention into a war zone. There, what has frequently been described as a "police riot" broke out, the "pigs," as they were called by sensitive young rioters, reacting under extreme provocation. One policeman later described how, trapped in his overturned truck and afraid the rioters were going to torch it, he burst out swinging his nightstick in all directions. Not everything the police did in Chicago can be excused, to be sure. (In Berkeley, where the police force was heavily manned by young college types, the cops seldom bruised a student.) But as Michael Lerner, a former FSM leader, pointed out, while those demonstrators in the streets of Chicago were our children, so too were those "pigs."

Even Bill Buckley did something totally uncharacteristic in that crazed season—he lost his cool and threatened violence, on nationwide television no less.

The previous fall, an ABC executive had approached him about the network's coverage of the upcoming conventions. The executive said he and his colleagues had in mind a twenty-minute segment each evening with two commentators, a liberal and a conservative. They wanted Buckley as the conservative and asked if he had any suggestions for the liberal. He named several names, and then said he "wouldn't refuse to appear alongside any non-Communist . . . as a matter of principle," but that he didn't want to appear with Gore Vidal, "because I had had unpleasant experiences with him in the past and did not trust him." Whether or not that remark had anything to do with persuading ABC that Buckley-Vidal would be great theater, choosing Vidal is of course exactly what it did.

The exchanges—four in Miami for the Republican convention and four in Chicago for the Democratic—were acrimonious from the start. There was personal sniping from both sides. In the first exchange, Buckley reacted to Vidal's description of the GOP as "a political party based almost entirely upon human greed" by saying: "Now the author of *Myra Breckinridge* is well acquainted with the imperatives of human greed." Vidal replied: "If I may say so, Bill, before you go any further, that if there were a contest for Mr. Myra Breckinridge, you would unquestionably win it. I based the entire style polemically upon you—passionate and irrelevant."

There was also, from Vidal, a constant stream of highly questionable assertions—about Nixon's record, about Reagan's record, about the behavior of the radicals in Chicago. These dubious descriptions and quotations were the more infuriating because whenever Buckley tried to correct one of them, Vidal patronizingly called *him* a liar. Some were not easily refutable under the circumstances—Buckley's research folder, in August 1968, did not include notations as to how Senator Nixon had voted on a farm bill in 1951. Others were more obvious, in that thousands of people had heard Vidal's "absolutely well-behaved" protestors shouting "F—— LBJ! F—— Mayor Daley!" ABC had even, a few minutes earlier, shown footage of some of them tearing down an American flag and raising a Vietcong flag in its place.

That was the background for the final confrontation, which Vidal began by saying, "As far as I am concerned, the only crypto-Nazi I can think of is yourself." To which Buckley famously replied: "Now listen, you queer. Stop calling me a crypto-Nazi or I'll sock you in your goddamn face and you'll stay plastered."

The incident shook Buckley, so much so that he wrote a fifteen-thousand word article analyzing it, which *Esquire* published the following August. Vidal wrote his own article, also published by *Esquire*, in which he made assertions that provoked Buckley to sue for libel. Legal delays being what they are, it was not until 1972 that *Esquire* settled out of court, publicly apologizing to Buckley and reimbursing him for his $95,000 in legal expenses.

While the kids were rampaging and the Democrats were splitting apart and George Wallace was bringing his own brand of anger into the 1968 race, the Republicans were conducting a primary campaign. Michigan governor George Romney and Illinois senator Charles Percy had been early favorites on the liberal side of the party; as the convention approached they had faded and Rockefeller was moving up. On the conservative side, Rusher and some of his colleagues from the Draft Goldwater campaign were beating the drums for Reagan. Reagan himself, having served fewer than two years of his term as governor, was saying that he was willing to be California's "favorite son" but would not actively campaign for the nomination. And there, in the middle, was Richard Milhous Nixon.

Early in the electoral cycle Nixon had received Barry Goldwater's endorsement. In 1967, Nixon arranged a meeting with Buckley. Then and a few weeks later, when Nixon appeared on *Firing Line*, Buckley was impressed by his grasp of the issues. Buckley also was not put off by what Nixon told him in the car on the way to the taping. Nixon said he had learned two things from his own 1962 gubernatorial race in California and from Goldwater's presidential race in 1964. As Buckley later quoted him: "'Barry Goldwater found out you can't win an important election with only the right wing,' Mr. Nixon said to me in 1967. . . . 'But I found out in 1962 that you can't win an election without the right wing.'"

Willmoore Kendall and Brent Bozell, who had so bitterly opposed Richard Nixon in 1960, were long since gone from *National Review*. Frank Meyer, who had also opposed him, was cautiously hopeful, on the grounds that Nixon "has an honorable anti-Communist record" and "if Nixon is nominated, he will owe it to conservative support." And Bill Rusher was more or less resigned to the unlikelihood of Reagan's changing his mind so long as Nixon was in the race, since challenging Nixon at that point would have split the party. Rusher did permit himself later to speculate what would have happened if Nixon had stuck with the lucrative law practice that he had taken up after his 1962 loss. "American history would have been spared a great many tragic missteps," Rusher wrote, "if Richard Nixon had adhered to his resolve to turn his back on politics and live the good life in New York. It seems likely that Ronald Reagan would have won the 1968 nomination . . . and the presidency that fall. With the conservative movement in full and early blossom, there would have been a far different, and far better, outcome in Vietnam. There would have been no Watergate, and no presidential resignation under threat of impeachment."

But that is not the course that history did take, and Buckley and Burnham in their columns, and in occasional editorials, were favorable toward Nixon. In the issue after the convention, *National Review* published an editorial (by Burnham) that began: "If Richard Nixon conducts his Presidential campaign as brilliantly as he did his campaign for his party's nomination, he should be the winner in November; and if he thus confirms his mastery of the political process, we shall have reason for confidence in his ability to direct the affairs of the nation."

One thing *NR*'s editors never considered was supporting George Wallace's third-party candidacy. Wallace was soliciting conservative votes, and *National Review* found that he often said sensible things— on matters, for example, like encouraging entrepreneurs to build factories in poor areas rather than encouraging poor people (blacks especially) to flock to overcrowded cities. But on the basis of his whole history, the editors judged that Wallace was not a conservative but a New Deal statist with a populist touch; and on the basis again of his history, and of supporters whom he did not repudiate, they judged him a racist. Two of the more acrimonious *Firing Line*s were taped in that year, one with Wallace himself, one with Judge Leander Perez of Louisiana, a Wallace supporter. Accusations of racism are thrown around so loosely that it's startling to come upon the real thing, undiluted:

PEREZ: "In the first place, I am not a racist . . ."

BUCKLEY: "Well . . . have you been widely misquoted? For instance, you're quoted as having said, 'Yes, the Negro is inherently immoral—yes, I think it's the brain capacity.' Is that a misquotation?"

PEREZ: "It's not a misquotation. It's the truth."

BUCKLEY: "Uh-*huh*."

PEREZ: "Because I know Negroes. We have a number of Negroes in our community, and I know that basically and mentally they are immoral."

No one claimed that Wallace himself agreed with everything Perez said, but neither did Wallace repudiate his support. Add such things to his record as governor, and *NR* decided to explicitly reject Wallace's candidacy. The editors even commissioned Goldwater to write an article to that effect. The type on *NR*'s cover read:

Memo to: American Conservatives
From: Barry Goldwater

PLEASE DON'T THROW AWAY YOUR VOTE BY VOTING FOR
GEORGE WALLACE.

Three weeks later, Richard Nixon won the presidency—and, rather more gratifyingly for *NR* types, Barry Goldwater, after a four-year hiatus, was heading back to the Senate.

In the great cacophony of the Sixties, through all the chattering and shouting and arguing among various gradations of leftist theory, came one clear, consistent, and extraordinarily distinctive voice, articulating the instinctively understood concepts of the Western tradition. The voice was Bill Buckley's, and alone among the journals of the day, *National Review* was speaking to and for students on campuses across the country who had no other voice or spokesman. The day-to-day violence with which those at Berkeley lived naturally affected their daily lives, and for many it became a central fact of existence, triggering strong and sometimes emotional reactions. For some, it meant throwing in with the revolutionaries or dropping out altogether. For others, it meant protesting the protests. For one of the authors of this book, it meant attempting to describe to the world outside what was really happening at Berkeley. This writer sent a series of articles over the transom to *National Review*.

The articles were accepted, and as Buckley put it in his introduction to the resulting book, *The Kumquat Statement* (a play on the title of *The Strawberry Statement*, by radical Columbia student James Simon Kunen), this writer "quickly attracted a considerable audience . . . distinguished less by those who look merely for an additional reason to inveigh against the Young Revolutionists than by those who were truly grateful to someone who, by objective transcripts of what was going on, gave us insight not only into the quite incredible lengths of what some of the students were doing, but into the far more unimaginable lengths to which so many members of a faculty formally committed to reason and meditation were disposed to go."

It goes without saying that the writer was enormously flattered— and humbled—by those words. But beyond ego gratification, it should be noted that in them Buckley states a theme that character- izes his comments on the period. He seldom blames "the kids" for their excesses. Rather, he lays the blame on those charged with their education.

In a column, "An Evening with the Kids," in May 1969, he writes of giving a speech on a campus torn by unrest. It's an outdoor set- ting, SDSers on one side, black militants on the other, both groups attempting to prevent the majority of students from hearing the speaker. But he presses on and finishes his speech, "to much applause from the thousands, which is their way less of complimenting the speaker, than of rebuking the demonstrators."

During one of the delays, Buckley had whispered to the student next to him: "Why do you people put up with it?" Because, the stu- dent answered, "the last time we ejected one of these people, the chancellor gave us hell. We just can't do anything, period. Especially if they're black."

After the speech and an abbreviated question-and-answer period, Buckley writes, "The speaker reaches the sanctuary of the automobile, and the evening ends, the speaker confirmed in his suspicion that there is nothing at all wrong with the overwhelming majority of the students, whose intimidation is less the result of the raucous minority, than the result of the intellectual and moral abdication of their faculty and deans, who are made, like their cousins in Ithaca, out of Cornell jelly."

In November 1968, at the height of the unrest—and one week after Richard Nixon won the presidency—Bill Buckley came to San Fran- cisco. It was during that trip that he invited one of the writers of this book, *NR*'s Berkeley correspondent, to Trader Vic's, where after sev- eral hours of Navy Grogs and wonderful conversation, he asked the writer to come to work for *National Review*. And it was also during

that trip that he taped a *Firing Line* show with Eldridge Cleaver, convicted rapist, author of *Soul on Ice* (in which he explained, to the sat-
isfaction of most of the Berkeley professoriate, that his rapes of white
women were for ideological purposes), and presidential candidate of
the Peace and Freedom Party.

Cleaver was huge that year. His hard-eyed talks advocating the
killing of pigs played to overflow crowds at Sproul Plaza and other
Bay Area venues. It seemed no one had the standing, or the guts, to
take him on. As Senator Hayakawa put it, "White liberals, in their
hunger for humiliation, will take as revealed truth anything an angry
black man says."

And then Bill Buckley came riding into town, all alone and totally
unafraid, into the heart of the New Left revolution.

"Concerning Mr. Cleaver's activities and those of his party,"
Buckley wrote after his conversation with Cleaver,

> one can suggest only the flavor of his approach. Ronald Reagan, for
> instance, is, in Mr. Cleaver's language, "a punk, a sissy, and a coward,
> and I challenge him to a duel to the death or until he says Uncle
> Eldridge." Those who take a little clandestine pleasure at that kind
> of thing said about Ronald Reagan might however find a little bit
> off-putting the *Black Panther Journal* published after the assassina-
> tion of Bobby Kennedy, which ran a drawing of Mr. Kennedy as a
> dead pig. . . .
>
> I asked Mr. Cleaver whether he finds it consistent with his ide-
> ology to encourage the assassination of Mr. Richard Nixon, who,
> after all, is the chief pig-elect. Mr. Cleaver replied that he would not
> publicly encourage the assassination of Mr. Nixon because the pigs
> would come after him if he did, but that privately he would do so,
> satisfied as he is that Nixon deserves to die, as did the pig Kennedy.
>
> Had enough? Ah, but your stomachs are not as strong as those
> of the more educated members of the community, like the faculty
> members of the University of California who have invited Mr.
> Cleaver to give a course for credit at the Berkeley campus. Actually
> they really wouldn't want him for President; they are just getting
> their kicks without confronting the consequences: a venture in ide-
> ological onanism.

It's difficult today to describe just how heartening this performance, and others like it, were for those of us who felt besieged by a
mindless radicalism, unable to find anyone in any position of authority or responsibility willing to stand with us. As Buckley was later to

say, looking back on the Sixties, "I thought it was an exhilarating time, even though, more clearly than at any other time I can think of, the country was really coming apart."

One good thing came out of the infatuation of trendy liberals with the Black Panthers: the elevation of Tom Wolfe into a cultural icon of the right. Wolfe had come out of the New Journalism, which included writers as disparate as Gay Talese and Hunter Thompson. Wolfe's "Kandy-Kolored Tangerine-Flake Streamline Baby," written for *Esquire,* had brought him attention as a rising young writer, but it was "Mau-Mauing the Flak-Catchers" and, especially, "Radical Chic," for *New York* magazine, that made him a star. As Christopher Buckley recently put it, "I didn't know it was *legal* to write that way."

Here is Wolfe on the famous party at Leonard Bernstein's apartment for some New York–based Black Panthers: "*Mmmmmmmmmm-mmmm.* These are nice. Little Roquefort cheese morsels rolled in crushed nuts. Very tasty. Very subtle. It's the way the dry sackiness of the nuts tiptoes up against the dour savor of the cheese that is so nice, so subtle. Wonder what the Black Panthers eat here on the hors d'oeuvre trail? Do the Panthers like little Roquefort cheese morsels rolled in crushed nuts this way, and asparagus tips in mayonnaise dabs, and *meatballs petites au Coq Hardi,* all of which are at this very moment being offered to them on gadrooned silver platters by maids in black uniforms with hand-ironed white aprons?"

Not long afterward Wolfe made his first appearance on *Firing Line,* already wearing the white suit that would become his trademark. Comrades in arms, he and Bill Buckley soon became friends.

On the other hand, 1968 opened a rift between Buckley and another of his favorite writers, Garry Wills. Wills had already moved away from *National Review* professionally. He had dropped off the masthead in early 1967, though he continued to contribute book reviews and the occasional article. In January 1968 *Esquire* published a long piece by Wills titled "Buckley, Buckley, Bow Wow Wow," which many Buckley fans at the time found puzzlingly unpleasant, given that the author was supposed to be a friend of the subject. The peg was a debate at Yale between Buckley and William Sloane Coffin. Wills spent some time in New Haven in the weeks before the debate and interviewed a number of Yale fixtures, including Coffin himself. The day of the debate, he starts out at 150 East 35th Street and accompanies Buckley through his chores for the magazine and then on the road to New Haven, winding up with the debate itself. Wills does quote Francis Donahue, business manager of the Yale *Daily News*, as saying, "If I had my choice of all men—including the Pope—and could pick just one to be my brother, I'd take Bill. I never worked with a more considerate or a fairer man." But right up at the front of the article, Wills quotes Mrs. Coffin as saying, "He has the charm of someone who is always saying, 'Look how charming I am.' But under it all he's such a *cold fish*." And Wills quotes Coffin himself as quoting the late Mrs. Paul Weiss: "One day, when he was an undergraduate, Victoria narrowed her eyes at him and voiced the real insight on Buckley: 'Bill,' she said, 'why are you so scared?' Buckley's running scared." Bill himself didn't object to the article, but many of his admirers were indignant.

Meanwhile, as 1968 bubbled and boiled, Wills found himself in increasing sympathy with the radicals. *NR* went ahead and sent him to Chicago as planned, to report on the Democratic convention; his report was published, but many readers thought it should not have been, or at least not without some excisions. Buckley explained his editorial decision in his "Notes & Asides" column in the magazine: "And then there was some vehement criticism, though not so much as one would suppose, of the use of the four-letter word for sexual intercourse. The question whether to print it was not taken lightly, because we are on the side of those who are on the side of decorum provided there isn't too much antimacassar dripping about. But it simply isn't possible any longer to *portray* what is going on in so many situations around the country without portraying also the verbal licentiousness of the participants."

But on too many issues—the black riots, the Vietnam war, left-wing Catholic radicals like the Berrigans (brothers Daniel and Philip, both priests, both on the FBI's Ten Most Wanted list for their antiwar activities)—Wills had moved away from *National Review*. He continued to write for Frank Meyer's book section for several years, but only on books (two new translations of the *Odyssey*; a biography of Hilaire Belloc) that did not touch on the points of separation.

As Wills turned further left—and acquired a newspaper column in which to make his views more widely known—he and Buckley stayed in touch. But after every Wills column that was, from the *National*

Review perspective, egregiously radical, Buckley would impose on himself a period of *x* days of abstinence from contact with Wills—just as, whenever he caught himself inhaling one of his beloved after-dinner cigars, he would impose a similar period of abstinence. Eventually all contact ceased—although, just in the past few years, Buckley and Wills have renewed relations.

With the black and student rebellions going on at home, and with Vietnam filling our outward-looking radar screen, Americans were paying only peripheral attention to the events in Czechoslovakia. In January 1968, Alexander Dubcek was elected first secretary of the Communist Party. He immediately started a program of "regeneration," aimed, he said, at strengthening Communism in Czechoslovakia. However, his program included loosening press censorship; giving the courts, the trade unions, and various economic enterprises increased autonomy; and permitting some political freedom for four non-Communist parties. He called his program the Prague Spring.

As early as March, the Kremlin gave Dubcek a warning. The warning was repeated in July and again in early August. On August 20 (six days before the Democratic Convention in Chicago) the tanks rolled in—Soviet forces augmented by troops from all the fraternal Warsaw Pact powers. The Soviets were not as brutal as they had been in Hungary in 1956. Unlike Imre Nagy, Dubcek wasn't killed, but only sent to the countryside and put under house arrest; his fellow citizens were punished selectively, not slaughtered wholesale. But the message was clear. It was articulated as the Brezhnev Doctrine: No nation, once corralled into the Soviet empire, would ever be permitted to leave it. The embattled Johnson administration scarcely noticed.

In the fall of 1968, Buckley wrote an article for *Esquire* called "The Politics of Assassination," exploring the ramifications of the killing of Kennedy, King, and Kennedy. That article had a leisurely opening sentence, to which Hugh Kenner mightily objected. Buckley had written: "Robert F. Kennedy had a way of saying things loosely, and it may be that that is among the reasons why so many people invested so much idealism in him, it being in the idealistic (as distinguished from the analytical) mode to make large and good-sounding generalities, like the generality he spoke on April 5 after the assassination of

Martin Luther King, two months exactly before his own assassination." Kenner swung into action in a letter to Buckley: "Garry [Wills] under pressure tends to deliquescent metaphor (vide his Miami piece, *NR*) as does WFB to filigree syntax (vide current *Esquire*, first sentence, which while it parses [to say which is to say that a chicken coop does not collapse] resembles less a tensioned intricacy in the mode of M. Eiffel than it does a toddler's first efforts with Tinkertoy)." The two men had a lengthy exchange, which Buckley published in *NR*, ending with: "WFB urbi et orbe, Jan. 1, 1969: Who's right?"

One of the present authors, by this time a junior at USC, was up to her ears in semester-end work. Only after final exams did she produce her syntactical analysis and send it off to *National Review*. It arrived too late to be printed with the rest of the letters on that exchange, but to her surprise she received a letter from WFB himself—*Where are you going to school and what are you going to do when you get out?* She replied promptly this time, and was even more surprised to get a phone call from Frances Bronson, who had just succeeded Gertrude Vogt as executive secretary. Mr. Buckley was going to be in Los Angeles on a speaking engagement; could Miss Bridges meet him on April 16? And so, on the appointed afternoon, she drove to the home of Pat's sister, Bill (as she was confusingly nicknamed in childhood) Finucane, in the Flintridge hills, just a few miles from where the Taylors used to stay for the Santa Anita meets.

Greeted by Bill F. and a friendly Labrador retriever, she was ushered into the study, where Bill B. was on the phone to his mother. Presently he rang off and turned to his guest. Would she come to *NR* as a summer assistant and then, if everything worked out, return after graduation for a permanent job? Well, yes, she would. And then conversation turned to the topics of the day—What is the temper on the USC campus? Did the Watts riots affect you? How is Reagan viewed on campus?

In 1969, when she and the coauthor of this book arrived at 150 East 35th Street from their separate corners of California, there had just been a changing of the guard. Rickenbacker—partly chafing at the regard Buckley accorded to Burnham, partly restless and wanting to devote more time to his investment newsletter—had just resigned as a senior editor, but he stayed in touch. He continued to write for the magazine, and he would return as a senior editor for a couple of years in the late 1970s. (He also, in 1991, coauthored a little book about writing, *The Art of Persuasion*, with one of the present authors.) Arlene Croce had also resigned. Croce had come to *NR* as production editor, succeeding Mabel Wood, and had quickly worked her way up to senior editor. She had sound political sense and had done much good editorial work, but her real love was dance. When *The New Yorker* offered her a slot as a critic, she never looked back.

Meanwhile, Jeffrey Hart had just come on board as a senior editor. Hart was a professor of English at Dartmouth, specializing in the eighteenth century—the literary people like Dr. Johnson, but also the political philosophers, above all, Burke—and in what he calls the "high modernism" of the twentieth century—Eliot, Pound, Joyce, but also more popular writers like Fitzgerald and Hemingway. Hart had first written for Meyer's book section in 1963, and in 1965 he produced a book, *The American Dissent: A Decade of Modern Conservatism*. It focused on the developing conservative understanding on several major issues, mostly as seen in *National Review*'s pages, and it was excerpted in *NR*'s tenth anniversary issue. Publishing in *National Review* made Hart a marked man with his left-wing colleagues. It also made him a hero to conservative Dartmouth students, and he would serve as their mentor even after his retirement decades later.

In 1966, Brent and Trish Bozell launched a new Catholic conservative magazine, *Triumph*. It was heartily welcomed by *National Review*, in an editorial written by Buckley, as filling an important niche. After all, while *NR* was edited by a Catholic, it was in no sense a Catholic publication. Our first religion editor, Will Herberg, was a Jew, and the senior editors, as of 1966, included two Catholics, one lapsed Catholic, one nonobservant Jew, and one lapsed Episcopalian.

But as America wobbled through the late Sixties, buffeted by the radical protests and the bad news from Vietnam, Bozell turned in the direction of the Carlism he had fallen in love with in Spain. Back in 1960, he had engaged in a memorable exchange with his friend and adversary Frank Meyer on the question, Freedom or virtue? Meyer held that the primary political good was freedom, which men could then use to pursue virtue. Bozell held that virtue was the primary good, and that freedom was at best a means, at worst a hindrance.

Now Bozell started seeing America itself as the problem and conservatism as no solution—conservatism is, he wrote, "an inadequate substitute for Christian politics." He repudiated his own book *The Warren Revolution* because, as Buckley put it in his answering editorial, "His thesis now is that the republic of the Founding Fathers was doomed because of their failure adequately to enthrall the city of man to the city of God." With one exception (a reminiscence following Frank Meyer's death), Bozell would not write for *NR* again until, two decades later, he had come through his own personal hell (a lengthy battle with manic depression) and emerged as a very holy man, and one reconciled to his native land.

Young Americans for Freedom, founded in such high spirits in Sharon, had almost immediately run into difficulties. Within a year, one of its young founders was trying to take it into the Rockefeller camp; another was trying to take it over to the John Birch Society. Buckley, Rusher, and Liebman put out those fires, but YAF was still prey to internal contentions. These burst to the surface in 1969, when Buckley was scheduled to deliver the keynote address to YAF's annual convention.

By this time the "fusion" of traditionalism and libertarianism that Meyer had eloquently described back in 1960 (it was Bozell, in an answering article, who put scornful suffixes on Meyer's noun and created "fusionism" and "fusionists") had become the norm among those who considered themselves *National Review* conservatives. Each of us might lean more in one direction, but we saw ourselves as making common cause with those who leaned the other way.

Now, a radical libertarian faction of YAF had declared war against the organization's more traditionalist leadership. The libertarians' hero was Karl Hess, who, as Buckley put it, "had served as a speechwriter for Barry Goldwater and was now a vociferous advocate of total repudiation of government." Hess's critique of America, from the extreme libertarian side, mirrors Bozell's from the Catholic traditionalist side: "To really love this land," Hess writes, "one must first learn to loathe this nation and the system for which it stands." He describes his former *NR* associates as "false and authoritarian friends" who have led YAF astray, and warns that "order"—as in Hayek's "ordered liberty"—means "State dictation and State-controlled property." One of Hess's admirers, Jerome Tuccille, later reported that "the high point" of YAF's 1969 convention in St. Louis was a meeting of people from various libertarian organizations with counterparts on the radical left, including "two SDS anarchist chapters." Summing up, Tuccille wrote, "The most important thing to emerge from this convention is that, for the first time, the most influential forces on the Libertarian Right will be working to establish an open . . . coalition with the New Left in their common struggle to resist the abuses of the United States government."

Buckley, speaking to the convention, proceeded to appeal to logic, reason, and the need to make distinctions. "I rue the unnecessary distance this country has traveled away from freedom for its citizens," he told his audience. "YAF was founded among other things to brood over that excess, and to keep it constantly before the minds of the public. But to assume that young Americans, or old Americans, could have any freedom at all in the absence of a measure of sacrifice toward that common affection which lifts our society into being is to assume that each one of us is omnipotent, and to prove that each one of us is omnipotent only in the capacity to fool oneself, and to make oneself a fool."

In the end, the message went largely unheard. This was neither the time nor the place for logic, reason, or distinctions. This was the high point of a decade of high emotions, a time when on the campuses and in government the men chosen to lead us were fooling themselves, and making themselves fools, and the young people assembled in St. Louis were no wiser than their elders.

5

The Long Detour

R ichard Nixon had at last reached, in the words of his hero Disraeli, "the top of the greasy pole"—but what was he to do there?

Perhaps the most important charge given to Nixon—the primary
reason he was elected—was to calm the nation, to end the war in
Vietnam and put down the insurrection at home. By this time it was
not just SDS and its Weatherman offshoot that wanted an immediate
pullout from Vietnam. Many ordinary young men—and their parents—wanted that as well. As *NR* put it in an editorial (written by
Jeff Hart): "The Vietnamese war has been botched, both tactically
and strategically. It involved failures of mind before it produced a
lesion of will. . . . And so it is difficult to get very angry with a college
senior who is reluctant to risk his life for free elections in a remote
Asian country."

National Review's position on the war, outlined in a major editorial, "What Next in Vietnam?" and fleshed out in many other
writings, principally by Jim Burnham, was that (a) stopping the
Communists' advance was important, not just to the South Vietnamese but to the entire free world; (b) the strategy and tactics the
United States had been employing—using large-scale fighting units
against will-o'-the-wisp guerrillas; failing to interdict the Ho Chi
Minh Trail—were guaranteed to fail; and (c) it was not too late to
win—winning being defined as leaving South Vietnam strong
enough to defend her own borders—provided we changed to a

proven counterinsurgency strategy such as the one the British had successfully used in Malaysia.

Whether the fault lay more with Nixon or more with the generals on the ground, and whether anyone could have gotten the American people behind a reoriented strategy in the poisonous atmosphere Nixon inherited from Johnson, the fact is that it didn't happen. The fall of 1969 saw the first pullouts of American troops and, at home, the first of the "Moratoriums" against the war in Vietnam, which were to disrupt American campuses for the next year and a half. By the time these demonstrations (held on the fifteenth of every month) finished, even sleepy USC was suffering frequent bomb threats (though, unlike Berkeley, never a real bomb). On the campuses Nixon and his national security advisor, Henry Kissinger, quickly took the place of Johnson and McNamara as public enemies number 1 and number 2.

On the domestic front, Buckley and his colleagues watched the new administration closely for signs and portents. *NR* applauded the appointment of Warren Burger to succeed Earl Warren as Chief Justice, and the nomination of Clement Haynsworth to succeed Abe Fortas. (We did not applaud when Haynsworth went down in flames and was replaced by Harry Blackmun, although no one at the time foresaw *Roe v. Wade.*) Nixon took his first major domestic policy initiative in August 1969 with the announcement of welfare reform, revenue-sharing with the states, and the streamlining of a congeries of job training programs. *NR* was cautiously hopeful, although aware that a program like revenue-sharing could wind up meaning more, not less, federal involvement in local affairs.

And always, always, there was the awareness that Nixon was not One of Us. "On the whole, then," said one editorial, "at the six-month mark, a conservative tendency: which, a few unreconstructed skeptics have been heard to murmur, could be a Machiavellian effort to defuse conservative outrage at acceptance of defeat in Vietnam." "The favorite Nixon political strategy," said a second editorial, "—a simultaneous envelopment from both the right and the left flanks— makes it difficult at times to figure out just what's what on the Potomac front." And a third: "With his undoubted genius at playing Left against Right, he has once again disarmed opponents on both flanks."

In the same issues of *NR* in which these early evaluations of the Nixon presidency were appearing, Arlington House, a new, energetic conservative publisher, was running ads for a book called *The Emerg-*

ing Republican Majority by Kevin Phillips. Phillips, who had served on the staff of New York congressman Paul Fino and who would soon join the Nixon staff, had studied the 1965 mayoral race and now pointed to Buckley's strong showing as evidence of a rich new source of Republican votes. The Buckley candidacy had demonstrated that working-class and middle-class ethnic Americans who had traditionally given their votes to the Democratic Party were desperately looking for somewhere else to go as the Democrats moved left. Buckley, to be sure, didn't treat this constituency as in any normal sense a "voting bloc." He said the same things to them that he said to Wall Street audiences or college audiences. But these voters liked the conservative principles and policies he articulated.

William Gavin, one of Richard Nixon's first speechwriters, puts it this way: "Bill Buckley's campaign was like one of those daring commando raids into enemy territory in which it is discovered that many in the captive population are on our side, but not yet strong enough to revolt. By the time Nixon made the invasion itself in 1968, a lot of other things had happened that dictated when and where and how he would exploit what Bill had found. But Bill brought back the intelligence."

Unfortunately, Nixon put the task of building his new political majority in the hands of H. R. Haldeman and John Ehrlichman. During the first term other advisors who had once been close to Nixon were gradually frozen out by these two, who increasingly controlled access. Others, like Pat Buchanan—the one true conservative among the top staff—were too close to Nixon personally to be denied access. However, their influence on policy was minimized.

Haldeman and Ehrlichman, Bill Rusher maintains, "shared Nixon's disdain for the burgeoning conservative movement" and set out to construct "a coalition that would be anti-liberal, but more ambiguous and . . . more attractive than out-and-out conservatism." That coalition would take many forms, but in the first two years of the Nixon administration it was built on the "silent majority"—libertarian Otto Scott's term for those hard-working, productive Middle Americans who had unexpectedly turned out for Bill Buckley in 1965, and who were now turning out in increasing numbers to applaud Vice President Spiro Agnew.

For the 1970 congressional elections, Nixon staffers were instructed to play the social themes, the four A's—acid, abortion, anarchy, and amnesty. It was during this campaign that Agnew gave some of his most memorable speeches. These were written in great part by Bill Safire and Pat Buchanan, although Agnew enjoyed chipping in. In that regard, he claimed to the end that "effete corps of impudent snobs," the famous phrase from an earlier speech, was his alone.

Interestingly, it was this sort of phrase that prompted Bill Buckley, who was offended by even the faintest whiff of Wallaceite populism, to suggest that Agnew be more careful with his rhetoric, in terms both of content and of rhythms. This suggestion sent Agnew's volatile press secretary, Vic Gold—himself a fine writer and an occasional contributor to *National Review*—into a frenzy. "Goddamn it, Bill," he shouted at one hapless staffer, who was apparently expected to serve as a stand-in for Buckley, "how about this? How about 'a goddamn effete corps of impudent goddamn snobs'? How's that for rhythms?"

But the "Buckley Democrats" loved Agnew's rhetoric. An unsigned *Wall Street Journal* editorial, written in January 1970 by Bob Bartley and titled "Assaulting the Aristocracy," put it this way: "The heart of the Agnew phenomenon is precisely that a class has sprung up in this nation that considers itself uniquely qualified ('the thinking people') and is quite willing to dismiss ordinary Americans with utter contempt ('the rednecks')." Agnew had touched a chord with Bartley's "ordinary Americans," and it was a chord that energized Nixon, who urged his staff to learn from the vice president's appeal.

Despite that appeal, however, the 1970 election results were less than spectacular for the Republicans—a gain of two seats in the Senate, a loss of nine in the House, and a loss of eleven governorships.

For *National Review* conservatives there was a personal interest in one of these races. In New York, the Senate seat that had briefly been Bobby Kennedy's was being contested. When a senator dies, it's up to the state's governor to appoint a successor, and Nelson Rockefeller had as a matter of course appointed a fellow Republican, Charles Goodell. As a congressman Goodell had been comparatively conservative, but when he entered the Senate he tacked left. The Conservative Party thought he was worth challenging, and they picked Jim Buckley, who had served as campaign manager in Bill's mayoral race, to be the candidate, in a three-way race with Democrat Richard Ottinger.

Buckley campaigned hard on the issues, and money poured in from conservatives around the country. Agnew helped out—it was he who dubbed Goodell "the Christine Jorgenson of the Republican Party," causing an outraged Governor Rockefeller to ask the White

House to keep the vice president out of New York. But the White House arranged for Jim Buckley to be photographed with Agnew at a New York luncheon, and the word got out that the president preferred the Conservative Buckley to the Republican Goodell.

Jim Buckley is a quiet man, with none of the panache of his younger brothers, Bill and Reid. But he is thoughtful, a man of deep character, and he resonated with the voters.

That of course is not the way the liberal media saw it. They hauled out the same racism charge they had used against Bill five years before. Among other things, they were set off by Jim's campaign slogan, "Isn't it about time *we* had a Senator?" By "we," the people who thought up the slogan meant "tax-paying, law-abiding citizens." The media took it to mean "whites angry with civil-rights gains." To the *New York Times*, Jim Buckley and his supporters were "ruthless night-riders of the political Right." To the *New York Post*, Buckley was a "symbol of all the primitive forces that would turn back the political clock, encourage repression and deepen the alienation now felt by the young and dispossessed"; he made a "naked appeal to the spirit of repressive right-wing reaction now shadowing the nation."

Producing the cover for the issue of *NR* that went to press just before the election was an exhilarating experience for one of the present authors. It was a quiet afternoon in late October. The senior editors were not yet in town for the editorial meeting. Bill swooped into the editorial department after lunch, calling out, "Pitts! Linda! I need you in the conference room." He picked up our old Royal typewriters, one in each hand, by hooking two fingers through the frame surrounding the keys. (A 1940s-model Royal weighs thirty-five pounds.) At least he didn't bound up the stairs with them—we waited for the elevator.

When we and our typewriters were settled in the conference room (he went and fetched his own once he had put ours down), he told us what was up. We were going to write headlines for a mock *New York Times* front page. They would be the headlines the *Times* would least want to print the day after the election—the "Nightmare Edition," he called it. We started tapping away, our work interrupted by laughter as finished headlines were read out. The top story began: BUCKLEY SWEEPS SENATE RACE—and lo! two weeks later Jim Buckley actually did win. The second lead was less prescient: 3 MAJOR UPSETS: / KENNEDY, MUSKIE, / GORE ALL LOSERS. A few days after the issue was published, Bill's buddy Abe Rosenthal, managing editor of the *Times*, weighed in with a deadpan critique of the wording and layout.

At the end of the day, Jim took 39 percent of the vote in the three-way race and became, as Bill and Priscilla call him to this day, "the sainted junior senator from New York." The liberal press couldn't stand it. Robert Mayer began his *Newsday* column: "It crept in during the night. It was hanging over the city when we awoke yesterday, gray and imponderable, like the fog. Morning became afternoon and still it would not go away, the shame, the burden, the thorny crown of collective guilt." This is the moment the New York Conservative Party was born for.

Bill, meanwhile, was becoming increasingly visible at a variety of levels. He was ever more in demand as a commencement speaker; he won Best Columnist of the Year Award in 1967, and *Firing Line* won an Emmy in 1969; he was invited to join the Bohemian Grove, a club for movers and shakers in business, politics, and the arts, whose members convene at their "camp" north of San Francisco every summer; and Nixon appointed him to the commission overseeing the United States Information Agency. In the popular culture, his props and mannerisms, so well known from *Firing Line*—the clipboard and red pen, the mobile eyebrows and flickering tongue, the drawly intonation—were imitated by popular comedians like David Frye and Robin Williams. Bill wrote occasionally for *Playboy*, to the great disgust of some of his admirers: *Why would you let your writing be published in a magazine that opposes everything you stand for?* His answer: *Because I decided it was the only way to communicate my views to my son.*

In September 1970 he reached a TV pinnacle: he was the celebrity guest on *Laugh-In*. It was a classic performance on both sides:

HENRY
GIBSON: Mr. Buckley, I have noticed that whenever you appear on television, you're always seated. Is that because you can't think on your feet?

WFB: It's very hard to stand up carrying the weight of what I know.

WFB: The producer of *Laugh-In* wrote me an irresistable letter. To begin with, he promised to fly me out on an airplane with two right wings.

That same season Putnam's suggested that he write a book simply chronicling a week in his life. That book, *Cruising Speed*, may have provided the first occasion for a reviewer to observe that Buckley didn't explore his *feelings* on this or that. Asked about this, Bill would reply that he is not much given to introspection, and this has become a routine part of descriptions of him, by others and by himself. But the comment cannot be true in the way it's usually taken. He may not *enjoy* introspection; he certainly, with a very few exceptions, does not make the fruits of it a matter of public record. But he is a practicing Catholic of pre–Vatican II vintage, and it is simply inconceivable that he does not regularly make his confession, which requires prior introspection. The difference is that sacramental confession is between the penitent and the priest and God; it is not vouchsafed to the readers of *Playboy*, the *New York Times*, or even *National Review*.

In any case, *Cruising Speed* records the shape of Bill's everyday life as it was when the present authors arrived at *National Review*. The weekly rhythms were supplied by the magazine's schedule and by Bill's own Monday-Wednesday-Friday column. Seasonally, he would hit the speaking trail for about a month each spring and fall (back in January 1964, when "On the Right" increased to three times a week, *National Review* announced that WFB was retiring from the lecture circuit; that particular retirement lasted one season); at Christmastime he would go with Pat (and with Christopher, until he graduated from Portsmouth Abbey and set off for six months on a merchant freighter) and usually a couple of friends to sail in the Caribbean; in late January, it was off to Switzerland; and in August, a week or two's sail along the New England or Canadian coast. *Firing Line* tapings were shoehorned into this framework, as were occasional longer articles. And this all had to be fitted together with Pat's schedule. She was by now a stellar organizer of charity events—as she puts it, "raising money for things I believe in," principally the Fashion Institute at the Metropolitan Museum and the Memorial Sloan-Kettering Hospital. She was appearing on best-dressed lists, and photos were frequently published of her wearing outfits by, and going to parties with, designers like Bill Blass and Oscar de la Renta.

Meanwhile, back at the office, we knew we would see our Fearless Leader at least two days every magazine week when he was in town. Depending on what else was on his plate that day, he might scoot in on his little Honda, or he might arrive by limousine, driven by Tom Cooney or Jerry Garvey. Tom and Jerry were firemen who didn't work the same shift, and therefore could switch off as Bill's driver. (Jerry soon retired from the department and started driving for Bill full-time; thirty-five years and three or four limousines later, he's still behind the wheel.)

The Tuesday morning editorial conference was a high point of the fortnight. Bill raised everyone's energy level, and we all hoped to come up with something that would amuse him. We also enjoyed the theater of the occasional clashes between Jim Burnham and Bill Rusher over such matters as the Greek colonels (whom Burnham supported) and the white regimes in Rhodesia and South Africa (which Rusher supported). After a few minutes of general chitchat, Bill would call on us for our lists of editorial topics. Rusher would go first, then Burnham, Priscilla, and Jeff Hart, and then the junior editors. When the present authors arrived at *NR* in 1969, these meetings took place at a table in Bill's office, with junior staffers filling every corner of the room. In 1970 Jim McFadden moved his promotion department from the adjoining suite up to the eighth floor, and Aggie Schmidt, who had joined *NR* as full-time research director right after *Unmaking of a Mayor* was finished, organized the creation of a conference room. It had much more space than Bill's office, but the new table and chairs were huge, and so it was not much less crowded.

When we had finished reading out our lists, Bill would exchange his red pen for Priscilla's blue or black one and parcel out writing assignments. Then Bill and the senior editors (including, ex officio, WAR and Priscilla) would head for Paone's for lunch, sometimes inviting one or another of the juniors, while the rest of us grabbed sandwiches and settled down at our Royals. Bill often scheduled *Firing Line* tapings for Tuesday afternoons, but he would come back to the office to look at any copy that had been turned in, and then he and the senior editors would go uptown for dinner.

Editorial dinners had changed drastically when the Buckleys acquired the 73rd Street apartment. In the early days of the magazine, Bill would go out for a shop-talking meal in a restaurant with Priscilla, Jim Burnham, maybe Bill Rusher, and, for the brief time he spent at the magazine, Whittaker Chambers. Now the dinners were dinner parties presided over by Pat, with all the senior editors (except of course Frank Meyer), one or more outside guests, and, if there was room, some of the junior editors (Pat maintains a strict limit of twelve at table for regular editorial dinners). While meant for enjoyment, and deeply enjoyed, these dinners were also meant to be informative. Often the next day's "On the Right" would be based on the dinner-table conversation.

Wednesday morning Bill would start by writing his column. One of the present authors, her first summer with the magazine, went to Bill one such morning to ask him to autograph a book for a friend back home. Sure, he said. But then, handing her his just-typed column, he said, "Cut a hundred words out of that—but don't kill any of the jokes." Trembling, she sat down to do so. Her cuts passed the test.

When Bill signaled he was ready to resume editing, Priscilla would send accumulated material up in the dumbwaiter that connected their offices, his on the third floor, hers on the second. The excitement of the deadline would build through the day, its audible symbol being the *clunk* of the dumbwaiter and the ringing of bells to signal that something was coming. Priscilla would let us see our edited work before giving it to the typists to produce a clean copy for the Linotypists. We were all anxious to see what Bill had done to our writing—and both abashed and admiring when we saw how he had improved it with a few flicks of his red pen. At some point Bill would wander down to Priscilla and Jim's office and pull a chair up to a corner of her desk to go over "Notes & Asides" material; their conversation was punctuated by frequent laughter.

If Bill didn't have another engagement, he would join us for ordered-in sandwiches in the conference room. The most memorable of these lunches was the time Bill's wine merchant had sent him a bottle that another customer had returned, saying it was corked; Mr. Sokolin couldn't now sell it, so he might as well make a present to a loyal client. None of us, including our discriminating editor-in-chief, thought the wine was spoilt at all. In fact, we thought it was quite wonderful. We hadn't known ahead of time, and so hadn't planned our menus accordingly, but one of the present authors can attest that 1949 Lafite-Rothschild goes superbly with peanut butter and bacon on a toasted English muffin (an unlikely sounding but delicious sandwich that Bill had introduced us to).

Back to work, and at some point Priscilla would disappear for the cover conference with Bill and art director Jimmy O'Bryan. More writing and editing, and then at 4:30, finished or not, we convened to put the editorial section together. Bill's way of doing this was subtractive. He would start by getting the count on the total material written: someone would read off the number of lines for each editorial, and he would enter them in his little Swiss calculator, which looks like a pepper mill with numbers on the outside. Then he would go through the editorials, deciding which had to run now and which could hold. Meanwhile, Priscilla was spreading out sheets of typing paper, each containing one editorial paragraph, in a set order (serious domestic, then serious foreign, then economics, then cultural, then offbeat). Once the conference room was in place, she would do this decorously on the shelf that ran around three sides of the room on top of the file cabinets. But until 1970, the only place to do it was Bill's office floor—fortunately carpeted, since Priscilla and Bill had to get down on their hands and knees to look over the paragraphs thus arranged.

When Bill had chosen the editorials and put them in order, he would start prowling along the paragraphs: "That can hold. . . . That can hold"—decisively turning over the unfortunate rejects. A few minutes of wrestling with the count, and then Bill would triumphantly read out the offbeat opening and closing paragraphs (often by Tim Wheeler, who filed his copy from his farm in Indiana). Bill would number the whole lot, and one of us would take it downstairs for the printer's messenger.

By the time we returned upstairs someone would have deployed bottles and glasses, and the conference room was ready for editorial drinks. Often Bill would invite a guest. It might be Erik von Kuehnelt-Leddihn, who was a charming raconteur, although we had to stifle giggles at his command, of which he was very proud, of American idiom ("So's your Aunt Matilda!" was a favorite phrase of his; also, "That's not *regular*!"); or Taki Theodoracopulos, a young Greek, the scion of a shipowning family, whom Bill had met in Gstaad, and who was tired of just being rich and wanted to become a journalist; or the producers of *Laugh-In*. Often Jim McFadden would come down and delight us with stories of the old days at *NR*. And usually Bill Rusher would make an appearance, intoning, hand still on doorknob, "*Drinking* again?"

We would need to work hard the next morning, correcting the final proofs. But for this moment we felt that helping to put out Bill Buckley's magazine was the best game in town.

Back in 1965, according to Bill Rusher, Nixon had "told a group of reporters . . . that 'the Buckleyites' were 'a threat to the Republican Party even more menacing than the Birchers.'" Needless to say, this caused an uproar among the "Buckleyites." It was the job of Pat Buchanan—who had been hired as Nixon's ambassador to the right wing, of which he himself is a charter member—to get Nixon down from that tree. The "clarification" eventually hammered out by Buchanan was that "Mr. Buckley, by his repudiation of the Birch Society in his magazine and syndicated column, had thereby made himself a much stronger candidate and a greater threat to the Republican candidate, Representative Lindsay."

In its way, this was true enough, although as with so many Nixonisms, fact and fiction awkwardly crowd one another. At any rate, as Rusher says, "The episode seems to have taught Nixon the danger of antagonizing the conservative movement." But it had not, as of the 1968 campaign, seemed "to have occurred to him to make common cause with it." That changed, up to a point, with the 1970 elections. The results were deeply disappointing to Nixon and his staff, and it was apparent that more than Agnevian rhetoric was going to be required to build the new majority Kevin Phillips had foretold. As Robert Mason puts it in *Richard Nixon and the Quest for a New Majority*, "Many members of [the] conservative movement were not unequivocally pledged to the cause of the new majority. Their approach to politics often emphasized an anti-Communist foreign policy and a laissez-faire domestic policy. Nixon shared neither guiding principle, so his relationship with movement conservatives was at best uneasy."

To quiet that uneasiness, and impressed with the performance of Jim Buckley and the New York Conservative Party, Nixon moved to solidify his relations with Bill Buckley. He invited Bill and Pat, along with Conservative Party leaders Dan Mahoney and Kieran O'Doherty and their wives, for a visit to his retreat in the Bahamas. He promised Bill he would speak at *National Review*'s fifteenth anniversary party, and he would have done so, had he not been obliged to attend the funeral of Charles de Gaulle. When Bill visited Nixon in the White House shortly thereafter, Nixon discussed individual articles that had appeared in *National Review*'s anniversary issue (thanks in no small part to Pat Buchanan's advance briefing).

After that or another Oval Office meeting, Bill recounted a classic Nixon moment. The subject of Ronald Reagan came up, and Bill said, "Well, you know, Mr. President, I think a large part of Reagan's strength comes from the fact that he simply doesn't care what the *New York Times* says about him." Nixon turned to Haldeman and said, "*I* don't care what the *Times* says about *me*, do I, Bob?"

Nixon also arranged for Buckley to meet Vice President Agnew, who actually read *National Review* himself, without briefing, and had

Before the Fall: Spiro Agnew with WFB at the 1972
Conservative Party dinner.

developed a great admiration for it—an admiration that extended to
Buckley, whom Agnew considered to be one of the most important
and influential thinkers of the time. Later, Agnew would come to
admire a number of other thinkers and policy shapers—*Commentary*
writers and Harvard professors, among them Irving Kristol and Daniel Boorstin. For a brief moment, just before the fall—when James
Reston of the *New York Times* referred to Agnew as the personifica-
tion of "the old American verities"—that admiration was warmly
reciprocated. But right to the end, which came so quickly and unexpectedly, it was Buckley whose good opinion Agnew most valued.

In December 1970 Agnew appeared on *Firing Line*, and later
that month Buckley asked him to speak at a luncheon for top corporate executives at 73rd Street. Among the guests were James Roche,
chairman of General Motors; Edgar Speer, president of U.S. Steel;
Fred Borch, chairman of General Electric; and one of the authors of
this book. Agnew had asked that the writer be invited to the luncheon and then insisted that he be seated next to him, which required
that one of the corporate chairmen be moved to the other table. And
when the vice president ended his talk by exhorting the corporate
leaders assembled to buy the writer's just-published book, *The
Kumquat Statement*, the pleasure was especially intense. (The whole

story of the last-minute invitation is told in Priscilla Buckley's wonderful memoir, *Living It Up with National Review.*)

For the writer, that luncheon led eventually to a position as the vice president's chief speechwriter, a position he held until Agnew's resignation. But for the purposes of this book, it indicated that despite Buckley's early reservations about Agnew's rhetoric and his strong populist appeal, a bond had been forged between Spiro Agnew and Bill Buckley and *National Review.*

Unfortunately, Vice President Agnew was not setting administration policy. For the first two years of his presidency Nixon had done reasonably well on the economic front. True, he had not rolled back the Great Society—"the dozen, hundreds of programs, agencies, Job Corps, Vistas, Offices of Equal Opportunities, Headstarts, Human Resources Administrations, etc., many of which never worked, many more of which work only haltingly," as *NR* put it editorially back in 1969. But he had done a certain amount to streamline it, and he had a rock-solid group of advisors, led by George Shultz of the Chicago School of Business. On the foreign front, he had proved "steadfast . . . in resisting the great pressures upon him to desert Southeast Asia," as *NR* put it in 1971, although there were serious worries that we were falling behind the Soviet Union militarily.

Then, in the summer of 1971, the blows fell, one after another. There was the revelation of Henry Kissinger's secret trips to Peking. That was followed closely by the announcement that President Nixon himself would pay summit visits to Peking *and* Moscow. And then, in response to continued inflation, unemployment, and a weak dollar, Nixon went on television August 15 to announce his New Economic Policy ("a rather ominous name," Burnham pointed out editorially: the original NEP was launched in 1921 by V. I. Lenin). The central features of NEP II were wage and price controls, the severing of the dollar from any approximation to the gold standard, and a new "flexible" tariff policy. Frank Meyer took on the whole package in his "Principles & Heresies": "The parallel between the course we are following and that which England has followed since World War II is sad to contemplate. Welfare and comfort, the decay of armaments, devaluation, withdrawal from a leading status in the world—all in one degree or another are here. But England followed this course safeguarded by the United States. If we continue on our present course, there is no greater power to shield us. The future, in the most literal sense, depends upon our recovery from the disease that grips us." Buckley, on the lecture circuit, would normally cover a variety of unrelated subjects, titling his speech "Reflections on the Current Contentions." For the fall of 1971, his standard speech was a comprehensive examination of the President's domestic and foreign policies, titled "Reflections on the Nixon Administration."

Two weeks *before* the August 15 bombshell, a dozen leading conservatives had met at 73rd Street and hammered out "A Declaration." Buckley, Burnham, Meyer, and Rusher for *National Review*, Tom Winter and Allan Ryskind for *Human Events*, Jeffrey Bell and John Jones for the American Conservative Union, Anthony Harrigan for the Southern States Industrial Council, Dan Mahoney for the New York Conservative Party, Neil McCaffrey for the Conservative Book Club, and Randal Teague for YAF "resolved to suspend our support of the Administration." Citing mostly the dereliction in military preparedness and the turns toward Moscow and Peking, they wrote, "We consider that our defection is an act of loyalty to the Nixon we supported in 1968."

Then in December, Ohio congressman John Ashbrook decided to mount a primary challenge to Nixon. Ashbrook was a card-carrying conservative: an old YR buddy of Bill Rusher's, a member of the Draft Goldwater Committee, a former chairman of the American Conservative Union. There was a lot of back-and-forthing behind the scenes before Ashbrook declared. Goldwater, Reagan, and Tower— and freshman senator Jim Buckley—had already pledged their support to Nixon. Bill Buckley was reluctant to oppose them, and also worried about what message it would send if Ashbrook ran and did poorly—not only against Nixon, which was expected, but also against California congressman Paul McCloskey, who was challenging Nixon from the left, as an antiwar Republican. But Buckley finally agreed that the challenge was worth the effort and threw the magazine's support behind it. "It would have been . . . a sad business," Burnham wrote in the endorsing editorial, "if New Hampshire voters (and voters everywhere, who will be identifying themselves with the country's lead-off primary) could have expressed their wish for a changed Republican course only by voting for Paul McCloskey. John Ashbrook has offered them a happier and more fruitful alternative."

Only 10 percent of Republican voters in the states where Ashbrook ran (New Hampshire, Florida, and California) chose that alternative, many of the others doubtless reasoning that Nixon was going to be the nominee in any case. Buckley withdrew his (and *NR*'s) support of Ashbrook after New Hampshire, to Rusher's chagrin. But the magazine did, in an editorial just before New Hampshire (again by Burnham), maintain the usefulness of the exercise: "The primary vote will not measure [the] objective validity [of certain fundamental conservative principles]. Nor, because of the practical circumstances of the primary campaigns and this critical election year, will it reflect at all accurately the degree to which Republican voters still cherish these beliefs. But John Ashbrook has raised them on his banner, so that the nation is able to look at them at least once more."

Both the Buckleys and the Taylors had always had dogs, and Bill says he can't remember a time in the course of their marriage when he and Pat didn't have at least one. For a while they had a poodle, and Christopher's first dog was a gentle little cocker spaniel.

Then one year an English friend came to visit them in Rougemont, bringing as a hostess gift a puppy: a Cavalier King Charles spaniel. He had long silky fur, white and chestnut, and Bill named him Rowley, the nickname of King Charles II. From that time forth, Bill and Pat have never had anything but Cavalier King Charleses—with the one exception of Foo, "horrible Foo," as Bill called him, a bad-tempered Pekinese who was a gift to Pat from their old friend Marvin Liebman ("the only person who could be forgiven such a gift").

Thenceforward the dogs—there might be one, two, or three at any given time—would come with the Buckleys to Rougemont each winter. At first, this was easy: Bill and Pat just brought the dogs with them on the plane. But then, presumably as the result of some fracas, Swissair tightened up its rules: no more than one dog per cabin, even if the dogs in question were members of the same household. There was at least one trip when Pat rode in first class with one dog, Bill in business with another, and a maid—who was coming with them to the château anyway—in coach with the third.

Back home, Rowley adored above all else riding in the car with Jerry. Whenever Jerry shuttled between Stamford and New York City, with or without Bill or Pat, Rowley would come along. Bill's then-brother-in-law Ray Learsy (Carol's husband) recalled one sweltering

Pat and Rowley at
Wallacks Point.

summer day when, standing in a non-air-conditioned Lexington Avenue bus, he watched the car inch past them through the traffic with Rowley looking cool and comfortable on the back window ledge, the sole passenger.

On June 13, 1971, the *New York Times* published the first installment of the Pentagon Papers, seven thousand pages of classified documents leaked to it (and to the *Washington Post*) by former RAND Corporation employee Daniel Ellsberg. One month later *National Review* stunned its readers, the nation's press corps, and its publisher—who was traveling in Europe and did not learn of the project until he saw the report in his morning newspaper—by publishing fourteen thousand words of additional Pentagon Papers. The cover read: "The **SECRET PAPERS** They Didn't Publish," and the inside subtitle read: "Strategy and counterstrategy from highly classified documents not published by the *New York Times* and the *Washington Post*, leaked to *National Review*." The editors announced on the contents page that they believed publishing these documents was in the national interest, for "they thrust into an appropriate context the fragments published by the *New York Times*."

In fact, as Buckley announced the day after the formal press release—which is to say, after twenty-four hours of media uproar—

the "secret papers" had been concocted by *National Review.* The idea was to demonstrate that "forged documents would be widely accepted as genuine provided their content was inherently plausible. (This, as I note, we demonstrated far beyond our own expectations.) We have proved that it was inherently plausible that back before the Vietnam war erupted in 1965, American strategic consultants made a few basic recommendations," leading to the conclusion that "the U.S. military and intelligence did not fail us during the crucial years. The failure was a failure of will: a political failure."

William Randolph Hearst Jr. began his column that week: "One of the most sensationally successful spoofs in the history of American journalism was staged this week—a put-on which deserves special attention here both because of its delightful novelty and because of various valuable lessons it should teach." Hearst went on: "It was a devastating indictment, and one which should be heeded by editors who gave so much space to the antiwar propaganda recently distilled from the Pentagon Papers and presented as news by the liberal press."

That was indeed the reason why the hoax was done—but it was also a heck of a lot of fun. The junior editors just worked at getting the rest of the magazine out while the seniors produced the papers. Most of the writing was done by Jim Burnham and, of all people, Gerhart Niemeyer. Our surprise at Niemeyer's involvement didn't reflect any lack of regard for his geopolitical knowledge. On the contrary. It's just that he had never struck us as the sort of chap to be involved in a hoax—even a hoax of high purpose. But he was as good at it as Jim, and young Jim Burnham (as we referred to Jim's son), just out of naval intelligence, provided details that added to the verisimilitude. One document, for example, was headed:

```
FROM:  CINCPAC
TO:    JCS
SUBJ:  LIGHTNING
A. YOUR 2110114Z
B. CINCPAC 211002Z (GENSER)
C. OPPLAN 65-34K
```

The day of the press release, Priscilla received several phone calls from an old friend at the *Washington Post.* He was able to slip out to a pay phone at intervals to report on his colleagues' progress: they had their raw copies of the Pentagon Papers for the relevant years spread out on a huge table, and were desperately trying to see if ours could be genuine. Eventually the *Post*'s editors decided that our papers were the real thing.

The *New York Times* was more savvy. One of the present authors was startled when she met a friend for dinner that evening. "It's a hoax, isn't it?" said the friend.

"What do you mean, a hoax?" the writer exclaimed.

"Well, the *Times* doesn't believe your papers are real." The Newspaper of Record didn't say that straight out, but to someone accustomed to deciphering its code words, the message was clear.

Angry as Buckley was about Nixon's turn toward Red China—and the expected concomitant turning away from our ally Taiwan—he was not about to forgo the chance to witness this momentous visit. He put in his bid for one of the eighty-five slots reserved for journalists—and later quoted his old friend Teddy White as saying, "Buckley, if you are on that plane and I am not, I will never talk to you again." In fact, Buckley and White were seated together on the way over, trading clippings from their respective stacks of research.*

Buckley's reporting from that trip is a mixture of careful, detailed observation, savage irony, and occasional black humor. A sample:

> I watched [Nixon] through binoculars, after his remarks, raising his glass to toast Chou En-lai and the three or four Chinese officials seated at his table. Then—to the astonishment of everyone and the consternation of the Secret Service—he strode purposefully one by one to the three surrounding tables and greeted Chinese official after Chinese official, his face red with the sweat of quite genuine idealism, bowing, smiling radiantly, touching each individual glass. He looked altogether noble, flushed with the righteousness of great purpose, and the two dozen Chinese—old generals, commissars, politicians—were quite visibly startled, first at being approached at all, then at being wooed so ardently.

---

*One of the most moving exchanges on *Firing Line* was with White, as he recounted his adventures in China during World War II. White told of the wonderful camaraderie among the Chinese Communists in the years before they came to power, when they were fighting the Japanese. "You sound like John Reed," said Buckley, to which White replied: "But John Reed died too soon to see what happened later, to see Stalin knock off Trotsky, and knock off Bukharin and knock off Zinoviev. I have lived to see these comrades in arms . . . poisoned with power, shoot each other down, exile each other. It's a terrible thing. I think ours is the only revolution in all history where the revolutionaries did not kill each other off."

Kindly make no mistake about the moral courage all this required. It is unreasonable to suppose that anywhere in history have a few dozen men congregated who have been responsible for greater human mayhem than the hosts at this gathering and their spiritual colleagues, instruments all of Mao Tse-tung. The effect was as if Sir Hartley Shawcross had suddenly risen from the prosecutor's stand at Nuremberg and descended to embrace Goering and Goebbels and Doenitz and Hess, begging them to join with him in the making of a better world.

In December 1971 Priscilla started to worry about Frank Meyer. At first it was little more than an in-house joke: many days Frank was calling her as early as 3:00 P.M.—a sure sign, in him, of insomnia. Then his voice, always husky from his interminable cigarettes, grew huskier, and he eventually confided that he was suffering pain in the chest area. It took the doctors a while to make their diagnosis; in mid-February, when Bill called Frank from Peking, he said, "I never guessed I would sit here hoping I had tuberculosis." He didn't have tuberculosis. But even if the doctors had moved faster, the cancer was probably already inoperable by the time Frank first acknowledged the pain.

The big question for Bill and others of Frank's friends was whether he would join the Church before he died. He had been drawn to Catholicism as long as Bill had known him, going back to the early 1950s. But he had reservations, principally concerning the Church's "collectivism," to which the Communist Party had given him a violent allergy. "The emphasis of Vatican II on collegiality," Bill wrote, "set Frank back ten years." Other stumbling blocks were the Church's position on suicide, and the antagonism, through so much of two millennia, between Catholics and Jews.

Finally, on March 31, Bill drove up to Woodstock. "I arrived the afternoon of Good Friday, tense with the pain of knowing that never before had I visited with someone when the lifesaving dissimulations ('The doctor says you'll be fine in just a couple of weeks') were simply out of the question, but his instinctive consideration saved me." Frank told Bill that the Bozells had come to see him on Tuesday, and that as a result of their conversation Monsignor Eugene Clark—known as the unofficial chaplain of the New York conservative movement—had driven up the next day. So far, however, Frank was still holding back. "Frank," Bill wrote, "was not going to give up arguing merely to expedite death." The next day, Holy Saturday, "he was worse, much worse. That afternoon he saw Father Clark, and made the great submission, and a few hours later I was called to the telephone. It was his son Gene. I told him the truth, that his father was a great man, and hung up."

The following week Bill went to Vancouver to give a lecture to the annual luncheon of the Red Cross Association, taking advantage of the occasion to speak about his spirited mother-in-law. Austin Taylor had died six years earlier, but Babe, although suffering badly from arthritis, was still active in Vancouver affairs. In his introduction to his formal remarks, Bill described her as

> a pillar of reliability not only in community relations but also in family relations, where her authority is absolute, except when her sense of humor is provoked—and inasmuch as her sense of humor is more easily touched off than Bob Hope's, her family usually manages to navigate around her sense of order and rectitude by the simple expedient of making her laugh.
>
> I know of only one occasion when this failed. Her late husband, the formidable Austin C. Taylor, was a taciturn man, particularly respecting his business affairs, concerning which his family notoriously knew nothing. On one occasion, many years ago, Babe came home bursting with organizational pride, and launched at lunchtime into an extended account of her prowess in her capacity as chairman of the Vancouver Ladies Society in shepherding the society away from, let us call it, the Brighton Hotel, where for years it had had its headquarters at considerable profit to the Brighton Hotel, on over to, let us call it, the Piccadilly Hotel. Babe bubbled on about how she had finally won the fight, and had just that morning signed a ten-year lease in behalf of the ladies club with the Piccadilly Hotel. Austin Taylor had been stirring his coffee wordlessly throughout the extended account. At this point he spoke up. "You know something, Baby?"—as he called her. "You own the Piccadilly Hotel."
>
> It is recorded that she did not speak to him for two weeks, and did so then only after forcing him to sell the hotel, preferably at a loss.

It was well that Bill took this occasion to give his toast, for five months later Babe Taylor unexpectedly died, deeply mourned. Christopher later wrote to his other grandmother, Aloïse Buckley: "You know, Mimi, when Gran died, I felt terribly cheated by God for not giving us any notice." And decades later, Pat told an interviewer, "My mother's the person, outside of my husband and my son, I love most in this world. When she died, I went into a slump for a year."

*   *   *

In the issue of *National Review* that carried the remembrances of Frank Meyer, the cover story was James Jackson Kilpatrick's report on the candidacy of Hubert Humphrey for the Democratic presidential nomination. HHH had pulled ahead of Ed Muskie, whose campaign had dissolved in his tears in New Hampshire over an insult to his wife. But George McGovern was moving up fast on Humphrey's left—his far left. And it was McGovern who won the nomination in Miami.

This was a huge gift to Nixon in terms of bringing disaffected conservatives back into his tent. Humphrey was a devotee of the welfare state, but Nixon had not exactly proved to be an enemy of it. And Humphrey was not prepared to turn his back on Vietnam. Despite having lost to Nixon in 1968, Humphrey might have been a formidable opponent. McGovern, however, was an avowed antiwar candidate, and some of his rhetoric was of the variety Jeane Kirkpatrick would later tag "Blame America first." On domestic policy he made one proposal after another (most famously, an annual grant of $1,000 to every man, woman, and child in America—but with most of it taxed away the following April), and backed down from each one when someone calmly did the arithmetic. From the time of the conventions on, it was primarily a matter of Vice President Agnew rubbing it in from coast to coast. Agnew functioned as the administration's chief campaigner, which he did primarily by giving variations on a speech ("McGovern's Consistent Inconsistencies") written by one of the authors of this book, who traveled with him.

In *National Review*, Burnham went so far editorially, with Buckley's approval, as to describe the McGovern campaign as not merely an "opponent" but an "enemy." And so *National Review*, over Bill Rusher's strenuous objections, endorsed a Richard Nixon who was, from *NR*'s point of view, much worse than the Richard Nixon with whom it had declined to associate the conservative movement back in 1960. But then the state of the country was also much worse, and the potential consequences of electing McGovern appeared worse yet.

Meanwhile, there was a cloud no bigger than a man's hand on the horizon. Back in June, it was reported in the press that five men were arrested inside Democratic National Headquarters in the Watergate Hotel. They had cameras and various items of bugging equipment on them, and they all had ties to anti-Castro Cuban exiles in Miami.

President Nixon immediately denied any knowledge of their activities, they all pleaded guilty and clammed up, and Nixon won reelection by one of the greatest landslides ever recorded: 60.83 percent of the vote; 49 states to 1 (and the one was not even McGovern's home state of South Dakota, but rather Massachusetts), plus the District of Columbia.

Nixon, however, had no coattails. This was partly because that huge landslide was less *for* Richard Nixon than it was *against* McGovern and the Sixties radicals. It was also partly because of the way Nixon's campaign was structured. The election strategy was framed and implemented not by the Republican Party apparatus, but by the Committee for the Reelection of the President—CREEP, as it appropriately became known—under the careful supervision of Haldeman and Ehrlichman. Despite his huge lead in the polls, Nixon looked only to his own reelection and did not spend time campaigning for other Republicans. Whether he would have helped or hurt them is another question, but in any case there was a net loss of two senators and one governor, and a gain of only thirteen seats in the House. In his memoirs, Nixon maintained that the 1972 results represented a New Majority landslide. However, for conservatives like Rusher, that New Majority was a majority of one.

Buckley, as we've seen again and again, believes in encouraging younger conservatives, and he has always been willing to listen to them—to a fault, some of his colleagues would say. One of these occasions occurred in late 1972. A young libertarian named Richard Cowan (Yale '60 and a charter member of YAF) pressed on Bill an article drastically challenging the traditional position on marijuana. Over the objections of his colleagues—including, this time, Jim Burnham—Bill decided to run Cowan's article as a cover story, although he did turn it into a symposium, printing Burnham's and Hart's objections, and then his own explanation of why "I for one find [Cowan's] arguments not merely plausible, but overwhelming."

Cowan began by making nine assertions about marijuana and its use that, he said, "are of course contrary to what most agencies of the government have been telling us for the past forty years. (*National Review* has frequently ventilated the official line on marijuana.)" He then adds, "I ask you: If you are a young person who has found by experience—yours and your friends'—that virtually everything you have been told about marijuana is totally untrue—wouldn't you question what they tell you about LSD, heroin, speed?"

Buckley, in his reply, stresses that he himself is in favor not of "legalization" but of "decriminalization": "the President's Commission did not advocate a distinction that is purely idle when it recommended that pushers should be illegal, but consumers not so. Thus it was, mostly, under prohibition. Thus it is, by and large, with prostitution and even with gambling."

Many conservatives, then and on later occasions when Buckley returned to the subject, were dismayed by what they saw as "softness" on drug addicts. Some speculated that he had had word that some of his nephews and nieces, perhaps even his own son, had used marijuana and that this had inclined him toward leniency. In any case, he has frequently reverted to the subject, even testifying before the New York City Bar Association in 1995. And whatever one's own policy recommendations, it is hard to disagree with the title he gave that testimony: "The Drug War Is Not Working."

On January 11, 1973, Senate Majority Leader Mike Mansfield announced that Senator Sam Ervin would head a probe of the Watergate affair. On January 20, Richard M. Nixon took the oath of office for his second term as President of the United States. On January 23, the Paris Peace Accords were announced with great fanfare by President Nixon. To *National Review* conservatives these accords embodied the worst fears the magazine had been voicing editorially: abandonment of South Vietnam couched as statesmanship.

Meanwhile, there was Watergate. In February, before the scandal had significant legs, *National Review* published a strongly worded editorial (written by Jim Burnham) that concluded: "This Watergate affair, under its suffocating cover, has acquired a sour, rotting quality that can only be cleaned up by the truth, or at least enough of the truth to provide an adequate and intellectually acceptable account of what happened and why. We believe it is in the interest of the nation, and most particularly of the conservative community and the Nixon Administration, that such an accounting should be made, and that the Administration should purge itself of any person of whatever level whose relation to the Watergate affair was legally or morally culpable."

Buckley was already in Switzerland when this editorial was written, but he would not have discussed the matter in any case. His colleagues had subliminally noticed over the previous several months that whenever the subject of the burglary came up, he did not join in the speculation. Then, at the beginning of the editorial quoted above, he officially recused himself, saying, "The editor of *NR*, an old friend of Howard Hunt and the late Mrs. Hunt, was recently named as trustee of their children. Accordingly I have removed myself from editorial discussion involving the Watergate affair." Only after it was all over did we learn that Hunt had burdened Buckley with the story as far as he knew it. His knowledge was only partial, but still difficult enough for a working journalist to live with.

Sorrows, said King Claudius, come not single spies, but in battalions, and there were more to come for Bill that winter. He and Pat had scarcely arrived in Rougemont when the château caught fire. Not a modest kitchen fire with a bit of smoke damage, but a serious, destroying fire. There was no loss of human or canine life, but the château was virtually gutted. Pat managed to save her glorious full-length mink and some jewelry. Bill literally had to be pulled away by firemen as he tossed books out the study window into the snow in hopes of saving them. (Some left-wing New York publishing types, told about this, said it was the first good thing they had ever heard about Buckley.) The culprit, investigators decided, had been the wife of the elder Ed Tuck. Paranoid about the sturdiness of old construction, she had had additional beams put in here and there. One of these, alas, had apparently breached a chimney, and the beam had finally reached the critical temperature and caught fire. The exterior stone walls, though old, proved sturdy indeed, and Tuck was able to rebuild within them—he, the insurance company, and the Canton of Vaud each putting up a third of the money. But for the time being the Buckleys were scrambling.

Pat managed to find a chalet they could rent, and her designer friends rallied around and speeded up the production of some clothes she had already ordered; Priscilla was deputed to bring "the purple outfit" when she and Jane flew over. Raymond de Botton did a haunting painting of the fire—a little splotch of red on a black field—that still hangs at 73rd Street.

Then, near the end of February, Bill flew to London to tape some *Firing Line*s. He fell asleep on the return flight without having removed his contact lenses. The lenses were constantly giving him trouble anyway—something about the shape of his eyes, the doctors said—but this was serious. He needed medical treatment over there, and when he was able to travel he and Pat cut short their trip and returned to New York. He missed a week of columns—unheard of even when he was laid up with the worst bronchitis—and he failed to complete the draft of that year's book. It wasn't until July that he was able to carve out the time from his schedule to finish writing *Four Reforms*, a little book that is not as well known as it deserves to be. It is a serious analysis of structural problems in four areas—welfare, taxation, education, and criminal justice—with proposals for concrete reforms in each area. But it doesn't read like a white paper from a think tank—it reads like Bill Buckley. ("Turning the murder of Robert Kennedy into a whodunit is testimony to the total ascendancy of ritual in American jurisprudence.") The other reason why it should be brought out and reread is a sad one. It is that in the intervening thirty years only one of the problems surveyed has been corrected at all (welfare), and several of them have gotten worse.

On January 22, 1973, the Supreme Court stunned the legal community with its 7 to 2 decision in *Roe v. Wade*. Over the previous decade, the country had been moving toward looser abortion laws. In the mid-1960s thalidomide had tipped sympathies toward allowing abortions in hard cases, and New York state had legalized abortion in 1970. But no one was prepared for the comprehensiveness of the High Court's ruling, which, although it carefully segmented pregnancies into trimesters, laid the groundwork for permitting abortion up to the moment of birth. Nor was anyone prepared for the bizarre, far-from-constitutional grounds on which the decision, written by Nixon's accidental appointee, Harry Blackmun, was based. To create a "right of privacy" for the woman that would trump any claims on behalf of her child, Blackmun drew on one of the most outrageous decisions of the Warren Court, William O. Douglas's discovery, in *Griswold v. Connecticut,* of "emanations" from "penumbras" surrounding the Fourteenth Amendment. The Douglas decision, and now the Blackmun one, were intellectually indefensible, but that doesn't matter if you have a majority. The Court had taken one more step toward reifying future chief justice Charles Evans Hughes's boast, "The Constitution is what the judges say it is." As Professor John P. Noonan put it in *NR* at the time, this was an exercise in "raw judicial power."

The decision had one positive effect: it drove Jim McFadden to take action. With Buckley's blessing, McFadden, a devout Catholic, founded the Human Life Foundation and the *Human Life Review.* These enterprises have not succeeded in getting *Roe* repealed, but they have raised the intellectual level of discussion of the whole range of "life issues"—abortion, euthanasia, assisted suicide—and have given aid and comfort to those doing practical work on the ground, such as crisis-pregnancy centers. At about the same time, McFadden added yet another hat to his collection, starting the National Committee of Catholic Laymen and producing the pun-laden (McFadden's weakness) monthly newsletter, *Catholic Eye.*

By late March, Bill had mostly recovered, and in April he wrote a column, reprinted in the magazine as the lead editorial (but signed), which began: "I do not believe that President Nixon knew about the impending Watergate operation, let alone that he commissioned it. . . . Even those who decline to believe that Mr. Nixon had foreknowledge of the affair believe—many of them—that Nixon's supervision of the Watergate investigation was at best self-serving, at worst criminal."

Then, in the June 8 issue, Jeff Hart wrote an editorial entitled "President Agnew."

"Richard Nixon may be forced to resign," Hart wrote.

> That possibility is no longer merely in the realm of abstract theory. So far, to be sure, no direct testimony has connected the President with either the original break-in or the subsequent cover-up, though the President's claim that he did indeed limit the investigation in some respects in order to protect "national security" will doubtless now come under examination. So far, only hearsay and inference connect the President with culpable activities.
>
> Nevertheless, in the White House pyramid of power, direct testimony implicates the level just below the top. . . . The waves lap just below the President, and may inundate him.
>
> In cold political terms an incoming Agnew Administration could be in a strong position. "After all," writes syndicated columnist Kevin Phillips, "Agnew is not remotely implicated in the Watergate syndrome; he should be no more affected by its fallout than Calvin Coolidge was by the scandalous odor attached to the Admin-

istration of Warren G. Harding. . . . Similar success could await Agnew. If Richard Nixon were to leave office within the next year, then Vice President-turned-President Agnew would have nearly three years to gain or lose the nation's trust, affection, and respect. One thing is certain: He would run a very different White House. . . . If the President serves out his remaining four-year term, the Democrats are likely to win in 1976. But if Agnew takes over as Chief Executive in 1973 or 1974, then another set of precedents comes into play. . . . And seven years (1973–1980) of Spiro T. Agnew in the White House could hardly help but have a decisive impact on the future of American politics."

A strong statement indeed. But then, as if to demonstrate just how diverse and idiosyncratic the conservative movement can be, in this same June 8 issue there was a column by *National Review*'s new Washington correspondent, George F. Will, a gimlet-eyed young high Tory from Illinois with degrees in political science from Princeton and Oxford. After a couple of years of teaching at the University of Toronto, Will had gone to work for conservative senator Gordon Allott of Colorado; he had also started writing occasionally for *National Review*, mostly book reviews. Senator Allott was one of the casualties of the 1972 election, and Will partly blamed Nixon for this.

The word in Washington at the time was that Will, although he had briefly been associated with Jesse Helms, was more a Scoop Jackson Republican (an ancestral pre-neocon designation, Senator Jackson being the leader in the 1970s of the pro-defense, anti-détente wing of the Democratic Party). Will had pretty well let it be known that he scorned the sitting vice president and was firmly in the camp of those who wanted to replace Agnew with John Connally, the erstwhile Texas Democrat who had switched parties and was a favorite of President Nixon.

The column, entitled "The Snicker Factor," began by rehearsing the various elements that might be involved in the president's removal, voluntary or otherwise. Then Will came to the vice president.

> But at this point it must be said that the controversial vice president is a major inhibition on those, Republicans and Democrats alike, who might otherwise be glad to be shed of Mr. Nixon.
>
> For nearly five years now, since Mr. Nixon chose Mr. Agnew to be his running mate in 1968, it has been a standard piece of gallows humor to refer to Mr. Agnew as Mr. Nixon's "insurance policy." The point of the joke has been that no one will assassinate Mr. Nixon as long as Mr. Agnew is where he is. Today, as the possibility

of Mr. Nixon resigning becomes greater, such jokes aren't funny to
Nixon's enemies.

Mr. Agnew has been Mr. Nixon's Nixon, the spear-point of Republican partisanship, the instrument of "positive polarization." He
is not the ideal instrument for healing a troubled nation. In addition, there are those who believe that Mr. Agnew has certain of the
same character traits that brought Mr. Nixon low. Like Nixon, they
will tell you, Agnew has displayed at times in the past a certain mor-
bid hypersensitivity, feelings of insecurity and inferiority regarding
the press, the academic community, and the establishment generally.

Agnew's admirers smile and say there is a pleasant surprise, a
Harry Truman, buried in Spiro Agnew, yearning to breathe free.
But the feeling here is that a maimed, tainted, impotent Mr. Nixon
is preferable to Mr. Agnew.

That was indeed the kind of thing that many of Spiro Agnew's
admirers were saying. As a matter of fact, five years earlier, Bill Buckley—although we can't know whether he was smiling—wrote exactly
that. (Interestingly enough, the life insurance reference is also
included.) "Let's face it," Buckley had said in his column of October
22, 1968, "Mr. Agnew is the only spontaneous thing in town, and I
like that. His instincts are gloriously unprogrammed, and I like that
too. There are those who believe that Mr. Nixon appointed Mr.
Agnew as a sort of personal life insurance. No one, they reason, will
pop off President Nixon while Vice President Agnew is around.
There is a view, and I share it, that in Mr. Agnew, Nixon found a high
deposit of some of the best American ore lying around: toughness,
sincerity, decent-mindedness, decisiveness—much of which went into
making Harry Truman a relatively happy national memory."

It was also pretty much what one of the writers of this book said
when, soon after "The Snicker Factor" appeared, Will visited him and
Aram Bakshian, a fellow *NR* contributor and one of Nixon's speechwriters. (Bakshian would later become Ronald Reagan's director of
speechwriting.) Will was an honest man with strong opinions, looking for sufficient reasons to modify his opinion of Agnew—something, apparently, that he'd been instructed by Bill Rusher to attend
to. But we discovered that the Truman analogy cut no ice with Will,
even though we no doubt offered it smilingly.

At *NR*, "The Snicker Factor" set off a firestorm. Bill Rusher
described it in a memo to Bill Buckley as "another blast by the fast-
dwindling Connally clique for which Will works as a Stakhanovite
spokesman. . . . We must not permit Will to open an unbridgeable

gap between *National Review* and Agnew." Nor did the Agnew staff want that gap—especially this writer, who felt loyalty to both camps, and David Keene, Agnew's chief political aide, former head of Young Americans for Freedom (and today the able head of the American Conservative Union). Keene was working to mobilize conservative opinion against Will in Washington, as Rusher was in New York.

Despite their best efforts, however, Buckley refused to fire Will, although he did issue a mild reprimand. At the time, the vice president's staff—and conservative activists in general—found this hard to understand. But in retrospect, it seems almost simple. For one thing, Will was—and is—a wonderfully clever and precise writer, every word just right and in place, sharp and witty, yet analytic and thoughtful. In short, like Buckley himself, Will is both polemicist and artist. For another, since the earliest days of *National Review*, Buckley had managed an enterprise in which warring voices representing every shade of conservative opinion fought to be heard. That's something unique in American journals of opinion, and something in which Buckley can take great pride. And in that respect, Will's anti-Agnew column, appearing in the same issue that editorially endorsed Agnew for president, was a throwback to some of the magazine's greatest and most contentious days.

The battle over Agnew was to rage for several months. But then, on a warm day in early October 1973, it all became academic. The scene was a conference room in the Old Executive Office Building, where General Mike Dunn, Agnew's military aide, had called the staff together. (It was Dunn who, some months earlier, had told one of the writers of this book that his phone, like the phones of all the Agnew staff, was tapped.)

"Our leader is today resigning his high office," said Dunn. "He has asked me to thank you all."

There was a brief silence. Then Keene slapped the table. "Don't you think he owes it to thank us himself?" he snapped. Several of the women began to cry. And that was that.

Earlier, the writer had made two phone calls (from an untapped phone) warning of the impending resignation. One was to an old friend and supporter of Agnew's from California, Senator S. I. Hayakawa ("I still think the world of him," said Hayakawa). The other was to *National Review*. A similar call would be placed to *NR*, again from an untapped phone, a little less than a year later, when Richard Nixon,

who by then employed the writer on his personal staff, also decided
to resign. At least, the writer thought, half the loyalties are intact, and
the record is consistent.

Later that day, in a courtroom in Baltimore, the vice president of
the United States pleaded nolo contendere to one count of failing to file
taxes on money he had received from contractors while governor of
Maryland. And so, when all the dust from high drama and the fall of
princes had settled, it seemed that Agnew's problems, hitting with light-
ning suddenness and apparently blindsiding an already shell-shocked
administration, had nothing whatsoever to do with the Watergate concerns that so preoccupied the White House. Nixon, still thinking he
could save his presidency, chose a popular longtime congressman to succeed Agnew, House Minority Leader Gerald Ford of Michigan.

There were those, Bill Rusher among them, who refused to buy
the whole scenario, seeing it instead as yet another maneuver by a corrupt White House to save the president's bacon—this time, in collusion
with Nixon's liberal enemies. "After all," as Rusher put it in *Rise of
the Right*, "it would scarcely do, from the liberals' standpoint, if their
ancient bête noire were to be toppled from his presidency only to be
replaced by a successor now far more genuinely conservative than he.
Several Maryland business felons were found who, in return for
reductions or total remissions of the penalties for tax evasion and
other crimes, were willing to testify that Agnew, when governor of
Maryland, had accepted cash contributions from them in return for
state contracts and even continued the practice when he became vice
president. At least some of these charges may well have been true, for
such contributions were standard practice in both parties in Maryland
for many years ... But their precise location on the spectrum of
American political misbehavior is hardly the point, for their significance ..., as the Watergate scandal moiled on, was simply that by
forcing the resignation of Agnew as vice president, they cleared the
way for the final assault on Nixon."

At *NR* editorial conferences and other discussions for months
afterward, whenever someone mentioned Agnew's guilt, Rusher
would doggedly point out that his plea had not been guilty, but
rather nolo contendere. His colleagues admired Rusher's loyalty but
saw this as a distinction without a difference.

Buckley took a different tack in his speech to the New York Conservative Party's annual dinner just five days after Agnew's resignation. The speech was called "The Terrible Sadness of Spiro Agnew,"

and in it Buckley carefully distinguished between our principles and the fallible men who embody them:

> A year ago our guest of honor was Spiro Agnew. I gather, from listening to the president's speech the other night, that Mr. Agnew's name will not again cross presidential lips. This is what Mr. Nixon must mean when he deplores what he calls our "obsession" with the past.
>
> One wishes that his instinct—to treat Spiro Agnew as an unperson—were an act of chivalry. One fears it is something other than that. My own feeling is that it is unkindness to Mr. Agnew to proceed as if he had never existed. . . . There is much to learn from the tragic career of Spiro Agnew. We go to such lengths in identifying positions with people that we find it hard to detach those people from those positions when we would like to do so. So comprehensively did Agnew emerge on the political scene as the incarnation of law, order, probity, and inflexible ethics, now that he has fallen, we are made to feel that the case for law, order, probity, and inflexible ethics has somehow fallen too: that ethics is itself subject to bribe and delinquency. This tendency to anthropomorphize our ideals is an American habit that can get us, indeed has just now gotten us, into deep trouble. . . .
>
> I do not see that it is a part of our creed to suggest that no one who affirms our creed could ever succumb to temptation. Rather our political creed is substantially built upon the need to advertise the lures of temptation: government, we believe, is presumptively guilty of self-enhancement at the expense of the people's liberty. . . .
>
> It is the highest tribute to Mr. Agnew to take his ideals so seriously as to apply them to Mr. Agnew himself. To say that the guilty should be removed from power, however great the sacrifice to those of us who are bereft; that we are mature enough to make moral decisions and abide by the consequences; that we are so gravely committed to high standards of behavior that we are willing to renounce those who stray from those high standards even if they are our friends and our heroes. . . .

When Buckley gave that speech, he was midway through an assignment unlike anything else he had ever done: serving as a delegate to the 28th General Assembly of the United Nations, a body that he had excoriated regularly for his entire public life. Specifically, Ambassador John Scali, whom he liked and admired, had asked him to be U.S. Representative on the Human Rights Committee for the three-month-long session starting in mid-September. "You'd occupy the same chair Eleanor Roosevelt occupied," Scali told him, smiling, "and Daniel Patrick Moynihan, two years ago." Conquering his impulse to, as he put it in his book *United Nations Journal*, "laugh, stand up, and depart the room," Buckley asked a few questions, though still assuming he would decline. "In the fifteen blocks between the Waldorf-Astoria and my office I changed my mind, and I do not think I concealed the reasoning even from myself. It was, I think, the only experience I ever had in pure, undiluted Walter Mittyism. I saw myself there, in the center of the great assembly at the UN (which I had never visited in my twenty years in New York), holding the delegates spellbound as I read to them from Solzhenitsyn, as I described the latest account of concentration camps in Mainland China, as I pleaded the case of the ballet dancer Panov. I would cajole, wheedle, parry, thrust, mesmerize, dismay, seduce, intimidate."

In fact, on the one occasion when he went so far as to compose a speech giving an honest account of the state of human rights in the world, "I was advised, most gracefully and warmly, that my short analysis, its great philosophical merits to the contrary notwithstanding, was inconsistent with détente: and, accordingly, pleading the urgency of business elsewhere, I arranged for an aide to read a speech recalling in copious detail the exalted oratory that had celebrated the promulgation of the United Nations Declaration [of Human Rights] twenty-five years ago."

One of the reasons Buckley had almost refused the assignment was the complete lack of newsworthiness of the United Nations. But a sharp-eyed *New York Times* reporter, James F. Clarity, lamenting that most of the delegates had abandoned their native costumes, happily noted that Buckley had retained his: "Gone . . . were the colorful raiments of the Bhutanese and the flowing robes of the African delegates. There was hardly a fez in view. A notable exception was William F. Buckley, Jr. . . . who wore a dark suit, rep tie, and button-down shirt."

One Wednesday evening the following February, Frances Bronson burst into the conference room as editorial drinks were in progress. She fixed Priscilla with an exasperated stare and said, in her emphatic English accent, "Your brother is driving me bonkers." What Bill had done this time was call Frances from Switzerland, interrupting her in the middle of complicated schedule work on his spring speaking tour, to say, "Ahhh, Frances, do you by any chance have a tuning fork?"

She quoted herself as replying, "William. You are in the country where tuning forks come from." She didn't hang up on him with the *crash-bang* that other callers sometimes received, but she let it be known that this conversation was at an end.

By Wednesday of magazine week the staff tends to be a little punchy, and someone wondered if retaliation wouldn't be in order. From out of our collective unconscious grew the idea. Bill has always been very sensitive about what Burnham called "tone," and about maintaining distinctions between *NR* and "the fever swamps." He is also allergic to what he calls "ungraceful Buckley references"—dragging in quotations from Chairman Bill to no purpose except to mention his name. (The one exception he would make, though with gritted teeth, was in promotional material that might benefit the magazine.) How about—the idea emerged—if we concocted a page of editorial paragraphs that contained as many of Bill's bêtes noires as we could stuff in? Not for publication, obviously: but somehow inserted into the two copies of the magazine that were delivered to him, by one courier or another, every two weeks.

In the cold light of dawn the plan sounded just as delicious as it had after a couple of Scotches. All the junior editors took part, with Priscilla serving as editor. Kevin Lynch, the self-effacing but highly competent articles editor, produced a gem about John-John Kennedy being given a souvenir pair of boxing shorts by Muhammad Ali. Good thing, wrote Kevin, because "he has an uncle who never seems to have his swimming trunks when he needs them." Carol Buckley Learsy, who had been in charge of our "Chile Watch" editorials during the Allende years, wrote a paragraph mentioning two men named López and adding "No relation!" Her paragraph concluded, "But that will take, as they say, some *tiempo*." Elsie Meyer, who had joined us as copyeditor after George Will took over the book section, threw herself into the project as joyfully as the young 'uns. She came up with OPEC's being forced to see "the oil painting on the wall, as it were!" (Did we mention that Bill hates inappropriate exclamation marks?) Joe Sobran, whom Bill had plucked from the University of Michigan a couple of years earlier and whose lyrical prose style and incisive analysis of social issues had made him a star, fractured one of Bill's favorite Latin tags—*"Quod licet Jovi non licet bovi"* (What is permitted to Jove is not permitted to a cow) became the grammatically impossible *"Quod licet Jovus non licent boves"*—and capped it with: "as Bill Buckley likes to say." Executive editor Daniel Oliver, economist Alan Reynolds, and one of the present authors added their own mischiefs, including some bizarre Russian transliterations and incomprehensible economics.

The plan was that the bogus paragraphs had to fit on a single page, which would be set by our compositor (the metal type then being melted down, as a safeguard, before the real editorial section was set in type), printed on the same paper as the magazine, and pasted into the finished copies by our obliging art director, Jimmy O'Bryan. Priscilla took off for her two weeks in Switzerland, we produced the next issue, and we sent off the doctored copies—"the Swiss Edition," we called it—timed to arrive just about when she would be returning home.

We waited for Bill's phone call, but nothing happened. He left Switzerland for South Africa and Rhodesia, where he was taping two *Firing Lines*. Could he possibly not have looked at the paragraphs? Totally unlike him.

Days passed. Then Frances warily called Priscilla: "I'm putting his memo in the dumbwaiter." It was a thunderbolt from Jove. Bill had picked up every single excrescence—plus, to our consternation, two or three things on later pages that were not part of the Swiss Edition. He gave Priscilla time to absorb the memo (he knew *she* hadn't been involved in the issue—she'd been in Switzerland at the time) and then he rang. We could hear her side of the conversation. "Bill, it's a joke. . . . A *hoax*. . . . You've got the only two copies." She later reported that he had dissolved into slightly hysterical laughter. All was well, though we did have a twinge of guilt that we had caused him two weeks of agony. On the other hand, we were a bit hurt that he hadn't at least questioned the assumption that his entire editorial staff, including presumably Jim Burnham, had gone simultaneously mad. Months later, one of the present authors asked him why he hadn't phoned earlier. He said, and his face was quite serious, "I was afraid the wires would burn up."

Meanwhile, we had kept the project from Burnham, fearing he would have pulled the plug on it. And so he might. But when he read it as a fait accompli, he laughed till tears streamed down his face. And, like Bill, he caught every single gaffe.

On March 19, 1974, Jim Buckley stood up in the Senate Caucus Room and delivered what the press almost unanimously called "a bombshell": "I propose an extraordinary act of statesmanship and courage—an act at once noble and heartbreaking. . . . That act is

Richard Nixon's own voluntary resignation as President of the United States." In twenty-five hundred tightly reasoned words, Senator Buckley rehearsed the drama so far and looked forward to the disaster that impeachment proceedings A.D. 1974 would bring: "History would come to a stop for the duration—in the country and throughout the world. The ruler of the mightiest nation on earth would be starred as the prisoner in the dock. The [Senate] Chamber would become a twentieth-century Roman Colosseum, as the performers are thrown to the electronic lions." His statement did not, he emphasized, imply a belief that Nixon was "legally guilty of any of the hundreds of charges brought against him by those sections of the media that have appointed themselves permanent grand juries and public prosecutors." Rather, he had come to believe that "In order to preserve the Presidency, Richard Nixon must resign as President." He must not leave behind him "an office that has . . . been irrevocably weakened by a long, slow, agonizing, inch-by-inch process of attrition."

Senator Buckley's declaration was not universally hailed. Governor Reagan and Senator Goldwater both stated that they thought President Nixon should stay in office unless and until he was impeached and convicted. Buckley's staff started separating his mail into three stacks—according as the writers labeled him "Judas," "Brutus," or "Benedict Arnold"—and taking bets on which stack would mount the highest. But he had the wholehearted backing of his brother Bill and of Jim Burnham, who wrote, respectively, a column and a lead editorial giving historical precedents and constitutional exegesis supporting the senator's arguments. Who knows whether the declaration had anything to do with Jim Buckley's failure, two years down the road, to win reelection? But it was something the sainted junior senator believed he had to do.

It would be another five months before Nixon finally stepped down—a most miserable period for the Republic he had sworn to serve, but one not without its shafts of dark humor. Phrases entered the American political vocabulary that are still remembered—at least by people of the present authors' ages: "The big enchilada." "What did he know and when did he know it?" "The modified limited hangout route." "Twisting slowly in the wind."

The previous summer, when word started leaking out that Nixon, with a view toward posterity, had routinely taped conversations in the

Oval Office, Burnham mused that given Nixon's savviness as a political operator, and also his deviousness, this talk of taping must be a blind. The tapes, if indeed they hadn't already been destroyed, would prove to be totally innocuous. The evidence of the President's involvement, if it existed, was elsewhere. We all agreed that Burnham must be right. No one, least of all Tricky Dick Nixon, would deliberately create evidence against himself. But then, piece by piece, it came out, and Burnham's calculation of what a rational man would have done was proved not to apply to Richard Nixon.

An incredible amount of time and cerebration was spent on the eighteen-and-a-half-minute gap—the missing portion of one of the most incriminating tapes. Could Rose Mary Woods, Nixon's longtime secretary, possibly have erased them by simple honest mistake— perhaps an urgent phone call coming in while her foot was still on the transcribing machine's pedal? Or was the gap what the *New York Times* and the *Washington Post* assumed, plain obstruction of justice?

This also became the subject of the *NR* editorial department's longest-running comic drama. Bill Rusher had for two decades stoutly and consistently opposed Richard Nixon as embodying the wrong tendency in the Republican Party. Of course, he had opposed the editorial policies of the *New York Times* and the *Washington Post* even longer. Now, in the depths of Watergate, he threw down his gauntlet—not before Nixon but before Nixon's enemies. At one editorial conference after another, he presented ever more ingenious explanations of the gap, while Burnham and Will, and to a lesser degree Buckley, said basically, "Oh, come *on*, Bill."

Finally, mercifully, the smoking gun emerged. Pat Buchanan later recounted on *Firing Line* how many hours, days of argument it took, even then, to get Nixon to admit defeat. Part of the problem was the loyalists who still thought his presidency could be saved—starting with his two splendid daughters ("A man with daughters like that can't be all bad," Norman Mailer once said of Nixon).

On August 7, Senator Goldwater went to the White House along with Senator Hugh Scott of Virginia and House Minority Leader John Rhodes of Arizona. They told the President that his support in both houses had dwindled to near zero.

On August 8, the day of the formal resignation announcement, one of the writers of this book, having called *National Review* to report that the end was at hand, sat in the office of David Gergen, head of the writing staff, waiting for the resignation speech and talking with Ben Stein and Bill Safire. A staffer went by carrying an open bottle of Scotch, and we remarked that we'd never before seen an open bottle on the premises. Ken Khachigian, Pat Buchanan's good right arm, looked in, and we joked about martial law, about asking RN's friend Brezhnev for a first strike, about arresting the White House press corps en masse for treason.

The speech writers also joked about not having to complete the final project. The idea was that three writers—those with law degrees—would sift through the stacks of impeachment material, pinpointing the legal weaknesses, and then three of us without law degrees would write speeches highlighting those weaknesses, pointing out that on the basis of such flawed evidence, impeachment would be a miscarriage of justice. The speeches would then be given to those senators and representatives sufficiently sympathetic to the President to read them. But there were no takers. A few days earlier one of us had written what proved the last pro-Nixon speech requested by a legislator. Senator Scott of Virginia, who gave that speech, had been voted by Hill staffers, no doubt unfairly, the dumbest man in the Senate. But no matter. (A couple of doors down from Gergen's office, someone continued to type. One of us walked over and patted him on the shoulder. "It's really over," we told him. He kept typing.)

We watched the resignation speech on the TV set in Gergen's office, and when it was over we agreed it was a good and dignified and profoundly sad and lonely speech. Ben Stein, who loved Nixon and had served him well, cried.* And the next day, after an emotional farewell to the staff, Richard Nixon was gone. He flew off to California, leaving Gerald Ford to pick up the pieces.

And was the Nixon presidency an unmitigated disaster? As we've said, the most important charge given to Richard Nixon was to calm the nation after the near civil war of the Sixties. He did this in his own

---

* Stein, son of the illustrious economist Herbert Stein, has made a successful career as a lawyer, an actor, an author, a television commentator, and an economic columnist for the Sunday *New York Times*. But despite his success in such cathedrals of liberaldom as the *Times* and Hollywood, he remains a highly articulate and outspoken defender of Richard Nixon and his policies—as he is of George W. Bush.

way, drawing all the high emotion and hatred of a decade into himself and his administration. And then, in the final explosion that he himself was primarily responsible for igniting, he cleared the air of a decade's worth of hatred and bad feeling. That explosion destroyed his presidency, and added miles to Bill Rusher's "long detour." But it also cleared the way for a new conservative synthesis.

There are so many mysteries in the Nixon persona. Bill Gavin, one of the first and best Nixon speech writers, says: "Richard Nixon had a heart, and I believe a large one. Much of his political energy was spent trying to hide his heart beneath the political tough-guy pose he thought he had to wear. In my view, he was not a true tough guy—he only played one on TV. That was his strength (he was, after all, a better man than he thought he was) and his weakness (he wanted to be somebody else). In reading the notorious White House transcripts from the Watergate era, I found Nixon's cold, callous approach to the cover-up less a disclosure of what the real Nixon was like than an insight into a man who has always wanted others to see him as tough, someone who would not let others put one over on him, as the Kennedys had—an operative, a tough old pro who could sling around the barracks-room tough-guy words with the best, or the worst, of them."

That would account, in large part, for those awful, strained Haldeman/Ehrlichman conversations with Nixon, where he mouthed words and phrases that one suspects made him uncomfortable to mouth, words and phrases that he used to prove himself to those two, who brought out the very worst in him. He wanted so much to be one of the boys, and they let him think he was.

For *National Review* personally, so to speak—that is, aside from what all of this had done to our country—Watergate was a disaster. We had hit 100,000 circulation in 1968, 115,000 in 1972. But over the next two years, between those who were disgusted by George Will's harshness toward Nixon and those who were disgusted by lingering traces of sympathy for Nixon (mostly from Jeff Hart, who liked the tough-guy persona), we lost more than twenty thousand readers.

One piece of imperishable art emerged from this whole debacle, a deadpan review by Hugh Kenner of *The Poetry of Richard Milhous*

Nixon. A man named Jack Margolis had crafted this little book by taking excerpts from the tapes and arranging them on the page as free verse. Kenner writes:

> And how flexibly his emotions pulse against the skin of language! Once or twice a simple heartfelt lilt breaks through:
>
>> You can say I don't remember
>> You can say I can't recall.
>
>> I can't give any answer
>>   To that
>>   That I can recall.
>
> —and how subtly this evades the merely ingenious rhyme!
>
>> But more often, as in the haunting "Who Are They After?" (a profound reversal of Wyatt's "They flee from me," effected by a student of "The Hound of Heaven"), Nixon will pare away the merely formal core to leave *Angst* freestanding:
>
>> Who
>>   the hell
>>   are they after?
>> They
>>   are
>>   after
>>   us.

While Watergate was paralyzing the highest levels in Washington, it was by no means all dust and ashes within the conservative movement. On the contrary, conservative activism during the period was intense. Computer lists of people who had contributed to the Goldwater campaign were drawn up and provided to conservative candidates. Paul Weyrich established the Committee for the Survival of a Free Congress to support conservatives in congressional elections. Terry Dolan (brother of future Reagan speechwriter Tony Dolan, who at this point was engaged in investigative reporting for the *Stamford Advocate* that would win him a Pulitzer Prize) set up the National Conservative Political Action Committee to raise campaign funds for conservatives. Jay Parker founded the Lincoln Institute to work on black issues. There was Phyllis Schlafly, organizing to bring about the defeat of the Equal Rights Amendment; Barbara Keating, who set up

Consumer Alert; and Dr. Elizabeth Whelan, who established the American Council on Science and Health. The American Conservative Union had been founded back in 1964, one month after the Goldwater defeat, to monitor congressmen's voting records; now, in 1973, it started hosting CPAC (the Conservative Political Action Conference), a huge annual gathering of conservative activists. In the realm of foreign policy, there were John Fisher's American Security Council, Frank Barnett's National Strategy Information Center, and Midge Decter's Committee for the Free World. And on the campuses, the long-established ISI and YAF were joined by Irving Kristol's Institute for Educational Affairs.

Most important of all was the founding of the Heritage Foundation in 1973 by Paul Weyrich, Joseph Coors, and Ed Feulner, providing conservatives with a high-powered think tank for policy guidance. By the end of the decade, the Heritage Foundation and the American Enterprise Institute had become refuges and staging grounds for conservative scholars. They overshadowed older and somewhat tired liberal organizations such as the Brookings Institution, and they would provide staff and intellectual support for Republican administrations once the long detour had ended.

6

New Directions

One month after Richard Nixon went into exile in San Clemente, he received a full pardon from his former vice president, Gerald Ford, "for all offenses against the United States" that he had committed "or may have committed" while in office. It was hoped that this would put an end to the all-consuming preoccupation with Watergate that had effectively crippled the operations of the executive branch for more than a year. And much of the rancor that pardoning Nixon could have engendered seemed to be forestalled when Ford went to his old colleagues on the Hill to explain his reasons for doing so, thereby becoming the first president ever to testify before a committee of Congress.

But after a sure start, marked by a graceful swearing-in speech ("Our long national nightmare is over," it began, memorably), the wheels on Ford's wagon soon began to loosen. Politically, when he chose Nelson Rockefeller for his vice president, "the conservative movement," as Bill Rusher puts it, "could only feel that it had been deliberately slapped in the face by the new president." To the further distress of some conservatives, Ford retained Nixon's foreign policy staff, headed by Henry Kissinger, and fully embraced the China initiative, new overtures to Cuba, and détente with Moscow. In September 1974, on the eve of the congressional elections, Bill Buckley put it this way: "Mr. Nixon's policies were so confusing as regards conservative priorities domestically and internationally that he has left the

165

conservative movement scattered, slightly incoherent, and perhaps even emasculated."

Emasculated, no. But scattered and slightly incoherent, yes. And this was certainly true inside the White House, where 1974 and 1975 were chaotic. One of the authors of this book, strangely enough, was still there, having remained for a time on the vice presidential staff after the resignation of Spiro Agnew, then joining the Nixon staff, and staying on after the Nixon resignation as one of President Ford's writers—meaning, as Priscilla Buckley pointed out, that in a period of less than twelve months, he worked for two vice presidents and two presidents of the United States.

Résumés aside, the operative word in the Ford White House in 1974 was confusion. The difficulty was hitting on a set of consistent and coherent principles that Ford's closest advisors—his transplanted Hill staff—would accept. As the newly minted leader of his party, and as a man of Congress, Ford felt obligated to campaign hard for Republicans across the country in the congressional elections. The problem was what to say. Finally, Aram Bakshian, who had also made the swivel from Nixon to Ford, came up with a theme for the pudding that Ford's people would buy: the need to preserve the two-party system by voting Republican.

The theme made sense, up to a point. No one wants to advocate one-party rule. But given the political climate of 1974, it wasn't easy to argue. Under one-party rule, massive abuse of power becomes possible. Therefore, to prevent abuse of power, it was necessary to send Republicans to Washington. But since it was a Republican administration that had just given us Watergate, the rhetoric had a somewhat unconvincing ring. At any rate, it didn't work. The Democrats gained forty-six seats in the House and four in the Senate, giving them their largest majorities since 1936. *National Review*'s cover line was: "The Electoral Disaster." And it wasn't only the numbers of Democrats elected, it's how far left many of them were. The "Watergate class" of 1974 included Senators Gary Hart and Patrick Leahy, and Representatives Christopher Dodd, Paul Simon, and Stephen Solarz, who would bedevil conservatives for the next two decades. However, it did also include a Republican representative from Illinois named Henry Hyde.

Complicating matters—and boding ill for the presidential election of 1976, if Ford were the candidate—was Ford's speaking style.

The holdover Nixon writers were told by the new chief speechwriter from the Hill that Ford suffered from "swimmer's breath," meaning, apparently, that he couldn't get through a long sentence without taking a gulp of air. (The Hill speechwriter's name, incidentally, was Milton Friedman, which caused a good deal of confusion. Once, several years later, he was called by Jimmy Carter to come to the White House to consult on economics. He went, but didn't stay long.)

Further, the writers were told, Ford had trouble with unfamiliar words and phrases, tending to get them tangled on his tongue. This was a problem that quickly became legendary, as when he spoke of the disease "sickle-cell Armenia," referred to the "great people of Israel" in a toast to Anwar al-Sadat, and praised the "ethnic of honest work."

Part of the problem was no doubt some personal mental quirk. But much of it was the result of a good and honest man and his bewildered advisors trying to find words, policies, and programs to deal with a set of inherited problems waiting to become disasters. Thus, caught up in a raging inflation ignited by LBJ's guns-and-butter strategy, then fueled by Nixon's NEP ("We are all Keynesians now"), Ford's advisors from the Hill came up with the slogan Whip Inflation Now (WIN). There were WIN buttons, and a "WIN Fight Song," written and sung by a quavery and cracked-voiced Meredith Willson, sadly past his prime. Then the economy turned. Inflation slowed, as had been hoped. But it didn't stop slowing, and the result was a severe recession. All WIN references were expunged from speeches and public pronouncements, the WIN buttons became instant collectors' items, and the president, at the urging of his Hill advisors, solemnly instructed his fellow citizens that we should "take all we want, but eat all we take."

In matters of foreign policy, the situation became especially bleak in 1975. In March, President Ford ordered the airlift of some 250,000 South Vietnamese loyalists from Da Nang and Saigon. Images from the television footage, graphically capturing the tragedy of our first lost war, imprinted themselves indelibly on the consciousness of America. The defeat was crushing. And it was political. In 1977, writing about David Frost's interviews of Nixon, Buckley put it this way: "We are all supposed to know the official story: The Gulf of Tonkin Resolution was repealed, the President was stripped of authority to carry out aggressive missions in defense of the terms of the treaty,

Congress turned niggardly in supplying South Vietnam with arms, no one seemed to care that the North was indifferent to the obligations of the Treaty. The political reality was—Watergate."

Watergate was in no way the fault of Gerald Ford, of course. But Saigon fell, that footage was aired on his watch, and what Buckley called "the long reach of Watergate" inevitably—and unfairly— tainted the administration of the man who pardoned Richard Nixon.

Samuel Vaughan, the amiable, imaginative president of Doubleday, had been an admirer and friendly acquaintance of Buckley's for years and had been trying to come up with a book project that wouldn't be ruled out by WFB's contract with Putnam's. In October 1974, Vaughan invited Buckley to lunch, bringing along three Doubleday colleagues to help him move the ball along. The breakthrough came when Vaughan asked Buckley what he'd found interesting in his recent reading, and Buckley mentioned *The Day of the Jackal*. As Buckley recounts the conversation, " 'Why don't you,' Sam said smiling, 'write a novel?'

" 'Why don't you,' I replied with that wit for which I am famous, 'play a trumpet concerto?' " The lunch came to a genial close, and the next morning Frances Bronson informed Bill that a contract for a novel had arrived from Doubleday.

Bill was apprehensive about his ability to write something that different from anything he had ever done, and so he asked his agent, the immensely capable, no-nonsense Lois Wallace (who had been introduced to Bill by her then husband, Tom Wallace of Putnam's), to negotiate a clause that would hold off payment of the bulk of the advance and would leave Bill free to decide at any point, no hard feelings, that this was not going to work.

As he headed off for Switzerland in January 1975 he told his colleagues what he was going to be attempting, and we were very much in awe. The kind of novel he and Vaughan had agreed on was a spy thriller, and that meant it had to have not only characters and atmosphere but also a sharply defined plot. Especially for those of us whose academic training was on the literary side, the question was whether someone who was a brilliant writer but who had never felt compelled to create an alternative world could do this on command, at age forty-nine.

The reports from Switzerland—via Frances and, when she returned from her two weeks there, Priscilla—were encouraging, and we could hardly wait to see the result.

One name not on the ballot in the midterm elections of 1974 was that of Ronald Reagan. He had decided back in 1970, he tells us in his autobiography, to run for a second term as governor—"but *only* one more term." And so, on January 3, 1975, Ronald Reagan became a private citizen once more. But most conservatives earnestly hoped he would not remain one for long.

NR led off 1975 with an eleven-thousand-word cover story (about three times as long as our normal cover stories) by one Charles D. Hobbs, exploring in depth "How Ronald Reagan Governed California." Hobbs points to two areas that Reagan failed to address: K–12 education and, to a lesser degree, land use. But for Hobbs the bottom line was this: "Clearly California and Reagan are parting friends, and the consensus, except at the raveled fringes of the political fabric, is that both have profited, but the state more so, from their eight-year association." Hobbs cites a dozen fields where the Reagan administration had achieved serious reform, among them: energy and water supply systems, welfare, quality of air and water, the transportation system, property tax relief, a streamlining of state government, and "a public university system in which teaching, learning, and research have replaced violent confrontation and preparation for armed revolution." All this, plus a $500-million budget surplus "to buffer California against the coming hard times."

To illustrate how Reagan achieved what he did, Hobbs narrates in detail the welfare reform effort of 1969–1971. Reagan started by appointing a small task force to make independent recommendations (a strategy that he would use again, to excellent effect, in areas like crime and tax reduction). When the legislative battle began, he went to the public for support, and he held on even when members of his own administration turned against him. It was a masterly campaign, and, says Hobbs, "the entire set of reforms had been designed and implemented, against overwhelming odds, by fewer than ten people, including the Governor."

As 1975 rumbled on and conservatives became more and more disgruntled with President Ford, there was no doubt at *NR* who was our man. Buckley wrote a column in August headed "Reagan for Challenger." That same month, an *NR* editorial was titled simply, "Reagan Must Run."

On the last Monday in April 1975, Priscilla seemed uncharacteristically subdued when she arrived for work. A few minutes later she called the entire editorial department into her office—something she never did. She came straight to the point: the day before, Elsie Meyer had committed suicide.

We were shocked and not shocked. On the one hand, Elsie was interested in everything, had become friends with all her colleagues, and had two sons whom she adored—the elder, John, a chess grand master, working in a government job in Washington (as he put it, "You can't cede the entire bureaucracy to the liberals"); the younger, Gene, a senior at Yale.

On the other hand, she had made no secret of how she missed Frank. She had also filled in for us some of the background of what Frank had told Bill of his reasons for waiting so long to become a Catholic. His objecting to the Church's proscription of suicide wasn't simply out of prudential fear about the pain that might await him as his cancer progressed. Decades earlier he and Elsie and their friends had talked into the night about the ethics and imperatives of suicide. One of the closest of those friends, Eugene O'Neill Jr.—after whom their son Gene was named—had in fact shot himself to death in his home in Woodstock; it was Elsie who had found his body. (She was more considerate than he of those who would find her: she did not shoot herself inside the house, but went out into the woods in back, where no one would have to worry about cleaning up.)

Besides all the emotional background, Elsie had just had a debilitating bout of pneumonia. She despaired of ever making a complete recovery, and the steep pull up *NR*'s block ("Murray Hill" is not just a real-estate agent's designation) reminded her every day of her physical condition. At lunch that Monday—Bill scooped us all up and took us to Paone's—Bill, trying to make sense of it, wondered whether she had learned that she had cancer. Dan Oliver said, perceptively, "More likely, she learned she didn't have cancer."

This was only the first, though by far the most traumatic, of the staff changes that season. Shameless (and desperate), Priscilla and Linda actually approached Vicki Marani in the parking lot after Elsie's burial to ask whether she might become our copyeditor for a year. Vicki, a bright, feisty redhead, was one of the Yale contingent who had come up for the funeral with Gene Meyer. She had worked for *NR* two summers; we had stayed in touch and knew that she was thinking of taking a year off between Yale and law school. That day she said she might, and to our great joy and relief she did.

At some point during that year, Jim Burnham communicated to Bill that he intended to retire from his position as de facto deputy editor. He would turn seventy just two days before Bill turned fifty, and he thought it was time. He would still come to New York—but only every other week—and he would still write his column. And indeed, he had lost none of his analytical rigor or strength of purpose—or esteem in Bill's eyes—as demonstrated most vividly by the three columns in May/June 1976 titled "The Kissinger–Sonnenfeldt Doctrine" I, II, and III. The "Sonnenfeldt" in that unwieldy title was in deference to Bill's close friendship with Kissinger—Burnham was rhetorically spreading the blame. But these columns were nonetheless a devastating attack on the change in U.S. doctrine regarding the Soviet Union. The U.S. government, under Secretary of State Kissinger and his deputy, Helmut Sonnenfeldt, was abjuring the position it had taken throughout the Cold War, of regarding the Soviet government as illegitimate. It now accepted the Kremlin's control not only of the Soviet Union but also of Eastern Europe. We would no longer speak officially of "the Captive Nations," Burnham wrote, or support their "aspirations for the recovery of their freedom and independence." Burnham concluded: "In the last analysis, a foreign policy is determined by the choice of enemy. . . . The Soviet Union has no doubts about the identity of its enemy. From what Secretary Kissinger declared in Lusaka, our choice is Rhodesia."

Meanwhile, at 150 East 35th, there was an orderly changing of the guard. Jeff Hart took over the editorial section during Bill's absences, and Nicholas King, a buddy of Priscilla's from UP Paris and now head of the United States' Foreign Press Center in New York, took over some of Jim's duties on the *NR Bulletin*. Kevin Lynch, who had come to *NR* at about the same time as the present authors, took over much of the editing of the *Bulletin*. Operations hummed along nearly as smoothly as before, though we missed Jim's presence and guidance.

Then in the fall George Will announced that he had been hired away: the *Washington Post/Newsweek* consortium had made him an offer that, in terms not only of money but also of visibility, he couldn't refuse. Bill and Priscilla recruited Chilton Williamson Jr., a young editor at St. Martin's Press and a frequent contributor to the book section under George, to take his place.

Ever since Bill Buckley and Firpo Taylor acquired *The Panic*, sailing had been an integral part of Bill's life. Whenever he was home on a Friday during the season (roughly May through October), there would be the Friday evening sail: Bill and two or three guests—it might be friends his own age, like Van Galbraith; or young Yale Political Union types or *NR* editorial assistants; or anyone in between— would sail across from Stamford to Eaton's Neck Point on Long Island, swim, have dinner, play cards or Ghost and listen to music, go to bed, and sail back the next morning. Then there were the sails, lasting a week or two, up the New England coast and into New Brunswick. On many of these, especially in the early years, Pat would come along; she never hoisted a sail, but she would cook superb meals in primitive conditions. And *The Panic* took part in many day races, in New England or near Annapolis, and in four Newport– Bermuda races.

But Bermuda is only about a fifth of the way across the Atlantic, starting from the American side. By his own account, Bill had been thinking since at least 1960 of sailing all the way across. But taking a month out of your life is difficult enough for someone on a normal schedule. How ever could the editor-in-chief of *National Review*, the host of *Firing Line*, the author of a three-times-a-week column, the author of a book a year, and the popular public speaker possibly do it? Answer: By deciding to. Jim Burnham would not retire till the end of the year; he could take over the editorial section, as he did each year when Bill was in Switzerland. Normally, no article went into *National Review* unless Bill had approved it, but he knew he could trust Priscilla's judgment if something hot came along while he was incommunicado. He could stockpile a few installments of *Firing Line*, which in any case took a summer break; Universal Syndicate, which by now handled his column, was proud of offering its writers a bit of vacation time; the manuscript of his novel was in the hands of a half-dozen friends for critical reading; and the lecture circuit did not impinge on the summer—it occupied a specific few weeks in the spring and fall.

This, incidentally, raises a point the present authors would like to put on the record. Over the years many movement conservatives have said to one or the other of us, "You know, *NR* just hasn't been the same since Bill started" *x*, *y*, or *z* new activity. In fact, the magazine has had ups and downs (and different readers would have different ideas of which periods were in which category), owing to the arrivals and departures of various contributors and editors. But there was no change reasonably attributable to fluctuations in Bill's own involvement between 1959, when he signed up for the lecture circuit and then started taking six weeks in Switzerland, and 1990, when he retired as editor-in-chief. Throughout that period, he edited the editorial section about three-quarters of the time, made the final decision on all signed articles (with the exception noted above), commissioned articles, hired and fired columnists, and was available by phone and, by the late 1970s, fax if we needed to check with him on the editing of a particular piece. His was the controlling intelligence, but Priscilla and her team did most of the day-to-day work.

And so, in early 1975, the preparations for the transatlantic sail went forward—not on *The Panic*, which had been killed in a hurricane in 1961, but on *Cyrano*. There were complications. As Bill recounts in the book that resulted from this trip, *Airborne*, an integral member of the crew was to have been Peter Starr, who had started crewing for Bill as a teenager in the 1950s and who, when Bill decided that owning radio stations would be a good way to augment *NR*'s income, became the head of Starr Broadcasting. But just as preparations for "the Big One," as they started calling the crossing, were being made, Starr Broadcasting was heading for treacherous waters, and Peter had to bow out.

Then there was the Pat question. With her dramatic turn of mind, she had started preparing for "impending widowhood" way back in her Hamden pressure-cooker days. Bill's "cruising speed" schedule was a perpetual worry to her. Once at a small editorial dinner, with just a few colleagues present, Bill mentioned the recent death of a college classmate. "Ducky," Pat said sharply, "I've been telling you you need to slow down."

"Ducky," Bill replied, lifting both eyebrows, "overwork isn't what killed [Classmate X]."

But now it was not just her husband who was throwing himself into harm's way but also her only son. And then her only sister, Bill Finucane, expressed a desire to come along, even though she couldn't tell a jib from a mainsail. Pat's comments were apparently pretty fierce, but although Bill is devoted to her, he has developed ways of transcending her objections. And so he pressed forward with his plans, and at the end of May she gave in gracefully and flew with him down to Florida to see off her nearest and dearest and the rest of the crew: Van Galbraith, Reggie Stoops, and Christopher's childhood friend Danny Merritt, who had worked for Bill on *Cyrano* and on his smaller boat, *Suzy Wong*.

As it turned out, it was a very good thing that Bill Finucane was on board. She shared her mother's interest in the Red Cross and had taken serious first aid training. And so when a winch did something winches aren't supposed to do and severely gashed Van's forehead, Bill F. was able to produce a butterfly bandage and patch him up well enough that evacuation strategies weren't needed.

Thirty days after their departure, Captain Bill and his crew pulled triumphantly into Marbella, Spain, and he had the material for *Airborne*.

That same spring, despite the skepticism of most of his *NR* colleagues, Bill Rusher unveiled his plan for a third party. Although he had been active in Republican politics ever since his Princeton days, he had started talking about bolting the GOP when the Ashbrook challenge to Nixon failed in 1972. As he would put it as a guest on *Firing Line* in the summer of 1975, "I'm a bereaved member of the [Republican] party, let's put it that way. There's no doubt that the party is for any practical purposes dead. If we conservatives don't bury the Republican Party, I'm afraid the Republican Party is going to bury us."

Rusher's book *The Making of the New Majority Party* was published that spring, and a five-thousand-word excerpt ran in *NR* as a cover story. Meanwhile, he was actively working to make the Independence Party a reality. But there was a major obstacle. Robert Novak, reviewing the book for *NR*, had his crystal ball working well on every point but one: "Although Mr. Rusher stresses that the Independence Party's existence cannot depend on any one man's decision whether to run for President, the hard truth is that it *does* depend for 1976 upon Ronald Reagan. And Ronald Reagan today seems to be inching ever closer toward a final [*sic*] try for the Republican presidential nomination and away from any new party venture." Eventually the party was launched—and was promptly hijacked by Georgia governor Lester Maddox.

Bill Rusher gauges the readiness of WFB and RR to hear about his Independence Party.

However, the sad end of Rusher's party in no way vitiates his analysis of the sociopolitical landscape. "Since at least the early 1950s," he wrote, "the basic economic division in the United States has been, not between the old categories of the haves and have-nots, but between those elements at all economic levels of the society who, as the producers, still subscribe to its original basic values, and those who are converts, voluntary or otherwise, to the liberal world view; a world view that is militantly secular, heavily guilt-ridden, and perhaps even subliminally suicidal. The new division is based on a growing resistance to the all too successful attempt of a new class of liberal verbalists, centered in the federal and state bureaucracies, the principal media, the major foundations and research institutions, and the nationwide educational establishment, to run the United States for the benefit of interests (notably their own, and those of a huge welfare constituency) conformable to that world view." Add to the verbalists' camp the Hollywood types and George Soros, and you've got the blue-state constituency of 2004.

Late that summer, after many consultations with the friends who had read the whole manuscript, plus specific queries to other friends concerning particular plot elements—for instance, to Bill Rickenbacker on a question concerning fighter planes—Bill decided his novel was viable and sent it off to Sam Vaughan. Vaughan was delighted and started the editorial wheels rolling. In due course, Doubleday issued the check for the delayed advance—and Bill received it just after he had spotted an ad in the *New York Times*. As Frances Bronson recalls it, he came into her office with a big grin and a bigger idea: Why not use the advance money to take the staff on Intourist's weeklong package tour of Moscow and Leningrad?

He himself had been to the Soviet Union twice, on official USIA business. But most of the staff had not, and Bill reasoned that we ought to experience the place that occupied so much of our thoughts and our pages.

Over the previous decade Aleksandr Solzhenitsyn had emerged as a towering world figure. From the taut, economical account of *One Day in the Life of Ivan Denisovich*, published in the Soviet Union during a brief thaw in the Khrushchev era, to the expansive *Cancer Ward* and *First Circle*, published only in the West and in *samizdat*, Solzhenitsyn had become the bard of the Russian soul, which was still alive after half a century of Soviet oppression. When Solzhenitsyn was exiled in 1974, his Western admirers finally had a chance to see and hear him live, first in a television interview with Bernard Levin in Britain—which Bill acquired the right to reshow on *Firing Line*, with Levin and Malcolm Muggeridge along as commentators—then in a few other venues, before he resolutely burrowed into his new home in Vermont to continue his heroic labors on behalf of all those who were still in Gulag, or who had died there.

Andrei Sakharov did not have the métier of a novelist, but he found other ways to speak out for freedom—and the Kremlin found a different way to punish him. Presumably thinking his nuclear expertise too dangerous to send into the West, they kept him essentially under house arrest—first in Moscow, where Senator Buckley visited him in the spring of 1975, and then in "internal exile" in Gorky, a few hours' train ride away. Solzhenitsyn had refused, in 1970, to go to Stockholm to accept his Nobel Prize, lest he not be allowed to return. Sakharov was simply denied permission to go to Oslo to accept his. But he remained a thorn in the regime's side—calling for freedom of speech and of worship, denouncing oppression of believers and of ethnic minorities—until the regime started to wobble, and Gorbachev, trying desperately to hold it together, called him back to Moscow to take part in the first Congress of People's Deputies.

Early in 1972 *NR*'s editorial department had received a little volume from David Martin, one of Bill Rusher's successors as counsel to the Senate Internal Security Subcommittee. It was formally titled *The Abuse of Psychiatry for Political Persecution in the Soviet Union*, but it quickly became known as the Bukovsky Papers, after the brave young man who had collected and sent to the West the testimonies of a dozen people who were being tortured for dissident activities. Bill and Priscilla decided it merited full treatment, and one of the present authors had the honor of producing a cover story out of excerpts from these documents, extraordinarily moving in the sufferings they recounted, and in the restraint and lack of self-pity with which they were written. Basically, the Kremlin had changed the way it punished dissidents. Under Stalin, they were condemned as traitors and shot, hanged, or sent to Gulag. Now, in a fiendish twist on the therapeutic state, it was judged that anyone who opposed the regime must be mentally ill. Dissidents were diagnosed as suffering from "schizophrenia with a paranoid development of character," or perhaps "chronic schizophrenia of paranoid type," and sent to a Special Psychiatric Hospital. There, the "treatment" included injections of drugs that caused physical agony as well as mental disorientation, and "warm damp wrapping"—wrapping the patient's body in plaited wet bed-sheets, which contracted as they dried, again with agonizing consequences. Vladimir Bukovsky gave these victims a voice, and eventually he, too, was expelled from the Soviet Union.

This was the country to which two dozen *NR* staffers and columnists would soon be going. But first we had a twentieth anniversary to think about.

Not that we hadn't been thinking about it for months. To produce an anniversary issue, three times the size of a normal issue, while getting the normal issues out every two weeks requires much advance planning and steady work. Under Priscilla's generalship, we were in good shape as summer turned to fall.

The centerpiece of the issue was a lengthy (nearly fifty thousand words) excerpt from a book called *The Conservative Intellectual Movement in America since 1945*, by a young Harvard-trained scholar named George Nash. The volume was meticulously researched and organized with magisterial skill, and its publication by Basic Books was something of a landmark. Many of the writers depicted in its pages had been vilified at one time or another as racists, extremists, ultraconservatives, the lunatic fringe. Now here they were, treated respectfully in a serious volume with ninety pages of endnotes.

Three who made a revolution: Goldwater, Reagan, and
Buckley confer before the twentieth anniversary party.

At the other end of the anniversary issue's seriousness scale was an
eleven-page parody section. It was edited by D. Keith Mano, novelist,
former pupil of Jeff Hart, and author for *NR* of the superbly eccentric "Gimlet Eye" column. The parody section spoofed everything
from "For the Record" to our regular columnists to Marcia Burnham's real estate ads on the Classified page. Among the present
authors' personal favorites: the Russell Kirk parody, beginning "Oft
meseems the night deepens round us," and ending with an account
of Kirk's forthcoming vacation in Scotland: "There we will take our
fleeting rest, far from the getting and spending and the dark, Satanick
mills where change and decay in all around I see, and be lulled by the
crash of the surf and the moans of starving crofters." And this, by
Christopher Buckley (by now a senior at Yale), parodying his editor,
Keith Mano: "What do editors know of the common man? Nothing.
You think Buckley knows what it's like to eat souvlaki, sleep with
Krishna Kids, or do deep knee bends with fat people at Overeaters'
Anonymous? I work with my feet. He has chauffeurs."

As for the anniversary party, it was a modest affair at the Plaza,
just a few hundred people in the Grand Ballroom. It was emceed by
James Jackson Kilpatrick—wearing a kilt and speaking in rhymed
couplets—and addressed by Barry Goldwater, Jim Buckley, Ronald
Reagan, and Bills Rusher and Buckley. Of one of our speakers, WFB

said that evening: "Ronald Reagan is about to engage in a great enterprise—indeed this occasion is at once his last, and unlikeliest, chance to back out." Two weeks later Reagan officially declared his candidacy for the Republican presidential nomination.

For the Russian trip, it was Frances Bronson who was assigned to make the "couple of phone calls," a process that threatened to send her, as she put it, "up the pole." The visas alone consumed more hours than all her other tasks put together. But a few seconds before the drop-dead hour, she had it all in order.

Most of those who were invited on the trip accepted eagerly, even if with a bit of trepidation. But several of the senior people declined, mostly in characteristic ways. Bill Rusher drawled, "I'll go to Moscow when I can ride over the radioactive ruins in a Sherman tank." Jeff Hart shrugged and said, "No après-ski." Jim McFadden said somewhat sharply that a man with five children could hardly go away a week before Christmas (something in that—but it's also true that Mac was petrified of flying). The surprising one was Jim Burnham. Jim was not normally given to self-dramatization, and while his words were understated enough, the message was not: "Well, there just might be someone over there who would want to ask me some questions that I wouldn't want to answer." Was it remotely credible that, ten years into the Brezhnev regime, in the midst of détente, anyone in the Kremlin would care what James Burnham had done forty years ago on behalf of Trotsky, or thirty years ago on behalf of the CIA?

We'll never know whether the KGB would actually have pounced on him. But one of the present authors had an eerie reminder that Communists have long memories. In the course of the trip she sent two dozen postcards to family and friends. Amazingly—given what we knew about Soviet efficiency in every field except the military—all but two of them arrived. One of the ones that did not arrive was addressed to a woman whose father had been condemned to death in absentia under Stalin for his anti-Communist activities. The other was addressed to—Mr. James Burnham.

The trip itself was a microcosm of life with Fearless Leader. He brought with him staffers and friends of all sorts and conditions: the whole editorial department, from Priscilla to our newest member, Vicki Marani; on the business side, Ed Capano (and wife Margie) and ad director Rob Sennott; on Bill's own staff, Frances, research director

Robin Wu, researchers Henry Fasciani and Jim Manzi, and Bill's sister Jane, who handled much of his correspondence; our crusty receptionist, Helen Puwalski; columnists Keith Mano (and wife Jo) and Nika Hazelton (and husband Harold); and, to keep the company amused, Marvin Liebman.

Marvin was only partially successful when it came to keeping Pat amused. She was genuinely worried that one of our young blades would do something that would require Bill to put his prestige on the line to prevent an international incident. It was scarcely reassuring when, on our first full day in Moscow, three of our guys, all old enough to know better, spotted the changing of the guard at Lenin's tomb and went racing across the street to photograph it—oblivious to the official Lada cars that at that moment had started pouring out of the Kremlin gate. Fortunately, the traffic cop just yelled at them and didn't have them hauled off to the Lubyanka.

The weather and the food also didn't help. Pat was quoted in the press after our return as saying, "I would have killed for celery." When asked how the trip was, she replied, "Bleak. I was bleak, the Russians were bleak, the weather was bleak. Bleak, bleak, bleak."

For the rest of us, though, it was a tremendous adventure. We didn't learn anything substantive about Soviet Communism that we didn't already know, but we accumulated a wealth of images that haven't faded to this day: Red Square with St. Basil's Cathedral at night, lit up like the set of *Boris Godunov*; the pickled corpse of V. I. Lenin, evil incarnate, and the goose-stepping soldiers guarding him; the lighted New Year's decorations over the streets in Leningrad, in lieu of the forbidden Christmas decorations; the old babushkas half-heartedly sweeping the streets; and, wherever there were shops, the interminable lines of would-be purchasers. There was the museum in Kaliningrad, where the guide invited Bill to play something on the piano; he chose "Old Black Joe," and we weren't sure whether he was thinking only of Stephen Foster's politically incorrect character or also of Stalin. There was the evening in Leningrad, on our way back from a genuinely good meal at a restaurant not run by Intourist (that is, semi-independent of government control), when Marvin Liebman stood up next to the bus driver and gave a hilarious parody of a tour guide. There was Bill's request to our elegant, Westernized Moscow guide, Lyra, that the bus swing round by the Lubyanka; and his insistence, over the indignant objections of our unreconstructed Leningrad guide, Ludmila, that we make a detour in Tsarskoe Selo so that he could show us where Nicholas and Alexandra and their five children had lived before being sent off to be shot. (In *Last Call for Blackford Oakes* Bill has the guard actually permit Ursina and her school chum to go inside the tsar's palace.) Ludmila asked angrily what we would say if *she* came to *our* country and asked to see the Bowery; she seemed nonplussed when we said we'd gladly take her there, it was just a few blocks from the office.

And, for one of the present authors, there was a little vignette on the train from Kaliningrad to Leningrad. Vodka was cheap in the dollar stores, the December weather was frigid, and the gents in our party had been taking turns buying a bottle to hand around whenever we returned to our bus (we each had our little plastic glass, carefully husbanded). But some had evidently bought extra vodka for themselves, and the train ride was five or six hours long. We occasionally caught disapproving looks on the faces of our KGB minders, sitting at the end of the car facing the rest of us. Suddenly Louise Oliver came over to Linda. The KGB men had gone out to the platform at the end of the car where the lavatory was. Louise was dying to know what they were saying to each other, but she didn't dare send her husband to eavesdrop, sure that they would know he was a Monterey language-school graduate. Would Linda see if she could understand them? Linda's three semesters of nonintensive Russian were rusty indeed, but she said she'd try. And she was rewarded by a sentence of simple vocabulary, and of breathtaking irony coming from a Russian in the eleventh year of Chairman Brezhnev's reign. "These people," said one KGB man to the other, "drink too much."

We returned to the States on December 23 (the flight had been delayed a full day because of an ice storm; we were pretty sure runway-clearing devices would have been found had we been at a military airport) and dispersed to our various Christmas celebrations. Two weeks later, a new sensation burst onto the scene: Blackford Oakes.

When Bill Buckley set out eleven months earlier to write a spy thriller, he did so, he has written, "with only a single idea in mind. And that idea was to commit literary iconoclasm. I would write a book in which the good guys and the bad guys were actually distinguishable from one another. I took a deep breath and further resolved that the good guys would be—the Americans."

Furthermore, the novel he proposed to write would leave no doubt "that the CIA, whatever its failures, seeks to advance the honorable alternative in the struggle for the world."

Needless to say, this wasn't the view of the CIA being peddled in the popular culture of the 1970s. As a typical example of what we were being offered, he singles out a Robert Redford movie, "the point of which is that the CIA is a corrupt and bloody-minded secret instrument of an amoral government." Reinforcing this view were "novels by Graham Greene, and John le Carré, and Len Deighton . . . their point being, really, that there is little to choose between the KGB and the CIA."

"Both organizations," he continues, "it is fashionable to believe, are defined by their practices." But there's this distinction to be made: "I said to Johnny Carson, when on his program he raised the question, that to say that the CIA and the KGB engage in similar practices is the equivalent of saying that the man who pushes an old lady into the path of a hurtling bus is not to be distinguished from the man who pushes an old lady out of the path of a hurtling bus: on the grounds that, after all, in both cases someone is pushing old ladies around."

This, however, was a meaningless distinction for those "ideological egalitarians" who write novels with titles like *The Ugly American* and, to drive their point home, create CIA protagonists with "appropriately disfiguring personal characteristics . . . late-middle-aged, a paunchy alcoholic, a cuckold who ruminates late at night when well along into the booze that—after all—who is to answer so indecipherable a question as whether the United States is all that much better than the Soviet Union?"

And so, to correct the record, Bill Buckley created Blackford Oakes—a protagonist "distinctively American." A primary characteristic of "the distinctively American male," writes Buckley, "is spontaneity. A kind of freshness born out of curiosity and enterprise and native wit." Freshness, curiosity, enterprise—and there was *Saving the Queen*, with the young, handsome, distinctively American CIA agent in bed with the queen of England. "There is something distinctively, wonderfully American, it struck me, about bedding down a British queen," Buckley writes, "a kind of arrant but lovable presumption."

It's this arrant presumption, and consequent entrée to the queen's bedchamber, that allows Oakes to uncover a KGB plot to steal American H-bomb secrets, supposedly known only to the queen and her prime minister. Perhaps the most striking novelistic feature of *Saving the Queen* is the author's ability to personify the complex moral issues that shape the theme. Boris Bolgin, head of the KGB in London, is well drawn and curiously sympathetic, as is the villain, Viscount Peregrine Kirk, who has the decency to die well. As for the delicious Queen Caroline, physically she resembles the young Grace Kelly, but in her manner of speech Bill appears to have been drawing from someone rather closer to him. "Queen Caroline was awake, but did not ring for her tea, toast, marmalade, and one sausage. ('I said *one* sausage, Emily, one-one-one-one sausage,' she had exploded almost two years ago. 'Do I have to pass a royal decree to make that clear?')"

And, of course, there is the characterization of the newly born literary protagonist, the distinctively American Oakes himself. "I remember with delight reading a review of that first novel," says Buckley, "published in *The Kansas City Star*, written by a professor of English from the University of Missouri. . . . I had never heard of the gentleman, but he made it quite clear that he had spent a considerable part of his adult life abominating me and my works and my opinions. He was manifestly distressed at not quite disliking my first novel, which he proceeded to describe. He salved his conscience by concluding, 'The hero of *Saving the Queen*, Mr. Blackford Oakes, is tall, handsome, witty, agreeable, compassionate and likeable, from which at least we can take comfort in knowing that the book is not autobiographical.'"

Certainly there is no correspondence between Buckley's own boyhood and the sudden disruption of Blackford's home life by his parents' divorce, his mother's remarriage, his own removal to England, and his lonely growth from boyhood to young manhood and extraordinary self-sufficiency. The fact that it is entirely fictional makes all the more remarkable this sometimes wrenching depiction of the making of a young man—a distinctive, individualistic, independent young American man.

Saving the Queen quickly put Buckley back on the bestseller list, from which he had been absent since *Cruising Speed*.

The second Blackford Oakes novel, *Stained Glass* (1978), won the American Book Award as the best suspense novel of the year. The plot is complex, the theme profound, involving "the central question of counterintelligence and espionage as conducted by a free society."

The decision has been made in Washington to assassinate a charismatic West German political leader. Count Axel Wintergrin is a hero of the resistance to Hitler who now, seven years after the Nazis were replaced by the Communists in the eastern half of his country, believes in the reunification of Germany. Wintergrin's rapid political rise and candidacy for chancellor brings a threat from the Soviets to go to war if he is not stopped. To avert a third world war, the CIA agrees to cooperate with the KGB. Oakes is given the assignment of working his way into Wintergrin's inner circle and supervising the plan to electrocute Wintergrin. Although he cannot bring himself personally to push the button, the plan succeeds. And so a right-thinking young German politician, who might successfully have challenged the Soviet hegemony, is executed by our intelligence service.

But from Wintergrin's death grows legend, so that every year, in the family chapel—which Blackford Oakes had helped to reconstruct—more and more Germans gather to commemorate the anniversary of his death. On the tenth anniversary, Oakes goes to the chapel and sees retired CIA director Allen Dulles also there, traveling incognito. Dulles is the man who ten years before gave the order for the execution—an execution, time has shown, that was totally unnecessary, since it was now clear that Stalin was bluffing.

In a memorable scene that dramatizes the nature of the moral choices lying at the heart of all the Oakes novels—and indeed, at the heart of the Cold War—Oakes confronts Dulles, who is about to drive away:

> He waited until the old man had unlocked the door on the driver's side and entered. He knocked on the window opposite. Surprised, but without hesitation, the old man reached over and tripped open the door handle. Blackford opened the door, got in, and closed it. Sitting with his hands on the steering wheel, Dulles turned his head.
>
> Blackford did not extend his hand. He said simply, "I am Blackford Oakes."
>
> "I see." Allen Dulles did not go through the formality of introducing himself.
>
> There was a pause.
>
> "Well, Mr. Dulles, did we do the right thing in 1952?"
>
> "Mr. Oakes, the question you ask I do not permit myself. Not under *any* circumstances."
>
> "Why not?"
>
> "Because in this world, if you let them, the ambiguists will kill you."
>
> "The ambiguists, as you call them, were dead right about Count Wintergrin."
>
> "You are asking me to break my rule."
>
> "Excuse me, sir, but is your goddamned rule more important than Wintergrin and his cause?"
>
> "Actually," said Dulles, "it is. Or, if you prefer, put it this way, Oakes: I have no alternative than to believe it is more important. And I hope you will understand, because if you do it will be easier.

If you do not, you are still too inexperienced to discuss these matters with me."

"I don't want it to be easier for me." Oakes turned now to look directly at the man whose will had governed Blackford's own for ten years. He found himself raising his voice, something he never did. "*Wintergrin was the great hope for the West. The great opportunity. The incarnation of Western hope. You made me ...*" He stopped, already ashamed of a formulation that stripped him of his manhood. Nobody had *forced* Blackford to lead Axel to the execution chamber. He changed, as quickly as possible, the arrangement of his thought. "You lost the great chance."

Dulles was now aroused. He lit his pipe with jagged movements of his hands.

"I believe you are right. I believe Wintergrin was right. The Russians—I believe—would not in fact have moved. But do you want to know something I *don't* believe, Oakes?" His voice was strained.

Blackford was silent.

"I *don't* believe the lesson to draw is that we *must not* act, because, in acting, we may *prove* to be wrong. And *I* know"—his eyes turned to meet Blackford's—"*that you know that Axel Wintergrin thought so too.*" ...

There was nothing more to say. Impulsively, Blackford extended his hand, and Dulles took it.

A passage worthy of the very best novelists of manners—showing, not telling about, deep and intense emotion, and through simple dialogue and gesture giving us all the nuance and complexity involved in a matter of honor, duty, and moral choice. And this is true of all the Oakes novels, written, as all novels are, for entertainment, but also written, as Buckley puts it, "to make the point, so difficult for many Westerners to comprehend, that counterintelligence and espionage, conducted under Western auspices, weren't exercises in conventional political geometry. They were—they are—a moral art."

During the worst of the raging Sixties, as governor of California, Ronald Reagan seemed the only politician around who was willing to stand against the irrational excesses sweeping much of the country. Nor was it just conservative Republicans who felt this way. In 1966, in a two-to-one Democratic state, he won election by a landslide.

In 1976, it was against the backdrop of the violent unrest of Sixties California that Americans best remembered him. However, this vividly remembered backdrop also raised questions about his viability as a presidential candidate in a very different time. First, he'd have to win the Republican nomination by campaigning against a sitting president of his own party, admittedly unelected, but perceived by most voters as a decent and honest man. Could Reagan, who had made his bones by battling and beating the radical left, campaign effectively without a radical left to score against? His forte was attack. If he were unable to attack, would he be ineffectual, a man out of his time in a post-Watergate world?

In the early days of the 1976 primary campaign, it seemed so. One of the authors of this book, having finally run out his White House string, was asked by *National Review* to write articles on Carter and Reagan. He joined the Reagan campaign as a reporter in Florida, just after Reagan had lost the New Hampshire primary to Ford. The loss had been a crushing one, especially because of the high expectations in the Reagan camp. Reagan's own staff, and most of the national media, had taken a win for granted. A poll conducted a week before the voting had given him an eight-point lead, and despite a large uncommitted vote, the Reagan high command, led by John Sears, was sufficiently confident to leave New Hampshire two days before the voting in order to campaign in Illinois.

Meanwhile, on primary eve, the Ford camp was so sunk in despair that Stuart Spencer, Ford's professional campaign manager, went to the unprofessional length of publicly blaming Ford's anticipated poor showing on a conspiracy between Richard Nixon and John Connally.

The day after the voting, both the Ford and the Reagan people were stunned. Ford had beaten Reagan by 1,300 votes out of 108,000 cast, a margin of 50.6 to 49.4 percent. A post–New Hampshire cartoon summed it up. A dazed Ford-like sheriff dressed in white grins down uncertainly at a smoking six-shooter held unsteadily in both hands. Sprawled in the dust is a lean Reaganesque gunfighter in black, his two drawn guns beside him. Says the Ford figure: "Well, I'll be darned!"

By prevailing political standards, Reagan's narrow loss to an incumbent president in New Hampshire could have been considered a moral victory, as was Eugene McCarthy's when he lost to Lyndon Johnson by some seven percentage points. But because Reagan had appeared to outorganize and outcampaign a seemingly ineffectual and frequently confused Ford, and because all the accepted indicators predicted a Reagan win in a conservative state, Ford was widely perceived as the underdog, and his victory therefore a genuine upset.

This threw the whole Reagan game plan into doubt. Sears et al. had reasoned that the unelected Ford was presiding over a Nixonless Nixon administration that lacked purpose, direction, and philosophical underpinning, all ingredients that Reagan could promise to provide in spades. And judging from past performance, Ford could be embarrassingly weak on the stump. But as the occupant of the White House, Ford also had considerable strengths to draw on: the vast resources of the executive branch to provide position papers, speeches, and campaign personnel; the power to make or change national policy instantly; and the active support of most of the important party leaders and prominent establishment Republicans.

It had been essential, therefore, for Reagan to strike quickly and take Ford out in New Hampshire and in Florida. Victories there, it was believed, would have a snowball effect, pushing Reagan over the top in Illinois and encouraging conservative Republicans to defect from Ford en masse. Thus the Reaganites believed they'd have a clear field by April.

But it didn't work, and when this author joined the campaign in early March, the candidate was a Reagan his admirers from the raging Sixties had never seen—both on the stump and in his meetings with the press, he was tentative, indecisive, defensive. This, too, was partly the fault of John Sears, a former Nixon advance man who, as Bill Rusher put it, was "a reasonably competent political technician" but "not in any serious sense a conservative." Not taking Ford with the seriousness he deserved, Sears shaped a campaign strategy based on the premise that for Reagan to run well in the general election, he'd have to start early to defuse the predictable charge of right-wing extremism. So, accepting the script written by Sears, Reagan muted the conservative trumpet. And as the tone became uncertain, Reagan, who had been running well ahead in the Florida polls, found himself sitting on a melting landslide. Those of his conservative aides who hadn't been purged by Sears knew he'd have to go on the attack to survive into the Western primaries. The problem was, attack what?

Meanwhile, Ford had suddenly stopped bumbling and mumbling and bumping into things and came roaring into Florida, having discovered just what uses the incumbency could be put to. He promised Orlando that it would host an International Chamber of Commerce Convention, offered Bay Pines a new veterans' hospital, promised Miami a whole new mass transit system, and then, with the huge Dade County Latino audience in mind, branded Fidel Castro "an international outlaw" and, no doubt much to the distress of the exile in San Clemente and Henry Kissinger in Washington, announced: "I don't use the word détente any more."

"We've got the momentum," Ford would shout in his Florida stump speech, "and we're going to move and move and move." And for a time, that's just what he did. He took Florida, then Illinois, by widening margins, and the presidential steamroller seemed to be picking up speed, carrying Ford toward the Kansas City convention and a first-ballot nomination by acclamation, and leaving Ronald Reagan's political corpse flattened along the campaign trail.

North Carolina was where the knockout punch was to be delivered. During the week this writer traveled with the Carter campaign, our stay in a Winston-Salem hotel briefly overlapped with a stay by the Reagan entourage. The mood among the Reaganites was extremely low. One of them, a former associate of the writer's, said it was all over. He and several others were already negotiating for new jobs, as the word had spread that after Reagan lost in North Carolina he would withdraw.

The polls showed Ford running well ahead, and local reporters assured this writer that the polls were right. They also told him that the North Carolina contest had meaning at more than one level. It was a power struggle, they said, between Governor James Holshauser and Senator Jesse Helms. Holshauser, self-identified as a moderate Republican, had reportedly been promised a high post in a second Ford administration and was solidly in the President's corner. Helms was a rock-hard conservative for whom Spiro Agnew had enthusiastically campaigned in 1972. He was one of the few Republicans swept into office with the Nixon-Agnew landslide, becoming the first Republican to be elected to the Senate from North Carolina in the twentieth century. Helms was a fervent supporter of Reagan—one of the very few in the U.S. Senate, and one of the very few politicians standing who believed that Ronald Reagan still had a chance. But Helms also believed that Reagan had that chance only if he reverted to the form that had electrified crowds during the Goldwater campaign in 1964 and had carried Reagan to the governor's mansion in 1966.

Few of the political experts agreed with Helms. The Ford/Holshauser versus Reagan/Helms confrontation was a microcosm of the civil war raging nationally within the Republican Party, and they believed the trend was toward Ford. The Reagan right, which had flourished in the 1960s, was dead or dying, the experts believed—a belief shared by much of the Reagan staff, especially John Sears.

Sears had built the Reagan strategy on the premise that the 1976 campaign would be one of images and personalities rather than issues. But the idea of Reagan playing image politics was a dubious one. His core constituency, ideologically committed *National Review*-style conservatives, was perhaps the single most issue-oriented constituency in the country. These conservatives had been dismayed by Reagan's performance in New Hampshire, Florida, and Illinois. Things seemed no better in North Carolina, where Reagan was still trying to be statesmanlike, still trying to avoid anything that could be construed as an attack on Gerald Ford.

For conservative voters, Ford was vulnerable on many issues, foreign and domestic. But those issues were precisely what the Sears approach would not address. The soft-sell image campaign left voters pondering the fact that Ford was a decent man with conservative instincts, and he already had the job. Why turn him out?

Thus, North Carolina seemed to spell the end. But then Senator Helms persuaded Reagan, over Sears's objections, to buy statewide television time to show the film of a speech in which Reagan tore into détente with all the eloquence and fervor his supporters remembered. Helms proved right. That speech turned it around, and Reagan's come-from-behind victory in North Carolina was even more of a stunner than Ford's upset in New Hampshire. (In 1984, Reagan would return the favor by strongly supporting Jesse Helms in his extremely tight race against Governor Jim Hunt.)

From then on, the gloves were off. The money began to pour in again, and Reagan roared through Texas, Indiana, and Nebraska, and for a time seemed on the verge of upsetting Ford in his home state of Michigan. North Carolina had convinced Reagan that the Republican Party was more conservative than the experts believed, and from that moment on his primary campaign became a campaign of issues—détente, deficit spending, arms-control agreements with the Soviets, (above all, SALT—the Strategic Arms Limitation Treaty), and, especially potent, the Panama Canal. This issue became for Reagan what reporters called his "Golden Kazoo"—an emotional issue that transcends logical analysis, turning normally well-behaved audiences into shouting, purse-swinging mobs.

No one had imagined at the beginning of the campaign that the Panama Canal would become such an issue. In fact, when Reagan first began mentioning it, the crowd response so startled him that he twice referred to it as the "Canama Panal." But by the end of the campaign it had become a staple of his stump speech, bringing audiences to their feet with the extraordinarily effective rhetorical formulation he had developed (and he may have been more the master of this sort of memorable formulation than any other American political figure): "We built it. We paid for it. It's ours!"

In the end, partly because of his disastrous start in the early primaries, and partly because of the defection of the Mississippi delegation at the Kansas City convention, Reagan narrowly lost what had become a dramatic race for the nomination. But it was Reagan, at the end of the race, who clearly had the momentum.

The Democratic primaries had started out wide open. The old guard—Humphrey, Muskie, McGovern—had spent themselves in the Vietnam years. Ted Kennedy had been expected to follow his elder brothers on the road toward the White House, but after Chappaquiddick he was held by many to be fortunate to be still sitting in the Senate; he had the prudence not, just yet, to try for the presidency. So in the run-up to the formal campaign, the field was crowded with more than a dozen senators and governors (and former senators and former governors) of every stripe. Among the more serious candidates: Senator Scoop Jackson of Washington, not too far left on domestic issues and a hero to many conservatives for his hard-charging opposition to the Soviet Union and to détente; Senator Frank Church of Idaho, the implacable foe of the CIA; former governor George Wallace of Alabama, campaigning from a wheelchair but unbowed, with observers still arguing as to where he stood on the right-left spectrum; Mo Udall, the witty left-wing conservationist congressman from Arizona; and James Earl Carter, former governor of Georgia, campaigning as a centrist—and as a born-again Christian.

"In 1967," said Governor Carter during the 1976 campaign, "I had a profound religious experience that changed my life. I accepted Christ into my life."

"That," wrote Bill Buckley, "really, is a terrifying statement. And I do not doubt that it is the source of the awe and horror some people are feeling as Carter heads for the nomination. When Jonathan Edwards preached to a generation of deists at Yale, the historian records, 'infidelity skulked its head.' The prospect of a President who would attempt to rule according to the Word is not only anti-cosmopolitan, it is in the nature of heresy against the commandments of the secular state."

However, Buckley continued presciently, "It is likelier that the system will break him, than that he should break the system." As to Carter's reputation as a centrist, Buckley added, "It has been calculated that, while governor, the whole of his administrative indulgences was equal to more than the sum of its parsimonious parts. Promise them simplicity and a decent austerity, and give them Macy's window."

And that would be pretty much it with the Carter administration—a string of unfortunate images reflected in that Macy's window, a breakdown of discipline, and some very bad luck, which led certain cynics to conclude that the Lord just might be pulling for the other team.

In the spring of 1976, however, the other team was still choking on the detritus of Watergate, demoralized by the rout in the congressional elections of 1974, factionalized, splintered, and feuding. To many on the right, a Southern governor who seemed to espouse conservative principles—and who not only walked with Him but claimed, for goodness sake, to talk with Him—exercised a very real appeal. Even Jim Burnham, who was not drawn by Carter's Southern Baptist manner, found other aspects of his persona attractive. Of course, Burnham enjoyed the role of contrarian. Once the contest had narrowed to Carter versus Ford, Jim addressed the group at an editorial lunch. He listed some of Carter's policies, and mentioned the fact that he had served in the Navy and was a working farmer. In other words, on Bill Rusher's and Kevin Phillips's model, he was a producer, not a verbalist. "How about it, ladies and gentlemen?" Burnham finished his summation. "If this man were a Republican, wouldn't we see him as nearly the ideal candidate?"

Although intrigued by Burnham's iconoclasm, *NR* went with Ford after his agonizingly close defeat of Reagan in Kansas City. Indeed, Buckley observed, "having adopted the Reagan line" at the convention, "Jerry Ford appears to have been transformed by the experience of Kansas City. He succeeded, with plain but heroic prose, in dissipating some of the hallucinations so painstakingly constructed by Jimmy Carter and the party of everything for everybody paid for by nobody."

All the fluffs and malapropisms seemed finally to be things of the past. Jerry Ford was again perceived, as he had been perceived at his swearing-in, as an honest, plain-spoken straight shooter. But then came the first mistake. Ford was running behind because of that slight but unshakable Watergate taint, and because of questions about his judgment and competence raised by his handling of the *Mayagüez* affair, in which forty-one Americans were killed and fifty others wounded in the course of freeing a cargo ship captured by Communist Cambodians. And so Ford decided to accept the challenge by Jimmy Carter to debate. He was the first incumbent president to accept such a challenge—and by so doing he was giving his still largely unknown opponent a nationally televised forum.

Then came the second mistake—in the opinion of many, all that was needed. In challenging Carter's rather routine description of Soviet power, Ford declared, "There is no Soviet domination of Eastern Europe." And then—as he himself might have put it, just to dot the *t*—he added, "I don't believe that the Poles consider themselves dominated by the Soviet Union."

"There is simply no accounting for this," Buckley wrote. "The notion that what Mr. Ford intended to say was not that Poland was autonomous and independent, but that the United States does not recognize the satellization of Poland by the Soviet Union as a permanent arrangement, is simply not validated by what Mr. Ford in fact said in answer to Mr. Frankel's chivalrous question designed to straighten Mr. Ford out. President Ford said, 'Each of those countries [Yugoslavia, Romania, Poland] *is* independent, autonomous; it has its own territorial integrity, and the United States does not concede that those countries *are* under the domination of the Soviet Union.' . . .

"Those who desire the truth must settle for a kind of trans-literal confidence. Mr. Ford is not a specialist in verbal precision or rhetorical inflection, and is certainly not at home with the subjunctive mood. One is required to conclude that he meant to convey something else—he is, after all, a bright man. But he faces difficulties now, yet again, of a very broad character, which afflictions he was successfully pulling away from before he committed the ultimate Polish joke."

But he couldn't pull away. And so, after the first half of the 1970s, which gave us Watergate, presidential and vice-presidential resignations, neo-Keynesian economics, WIN buttons, and the fall of Saigon, we were embarked on the second half, with an administration that would give us unwhipped and flourishing inflation, a new and novel energy crisis, a response that was officially labeled the Moral Equivalent of War (soon to be summed up in the acronym MEOW),

Billy Beer, and hostages. In short, it was a decade in which American prestige in the world and self-confidence at home hit all-time lows, a decade when we seemed unable to manage our national affairs on the most basic levels, and when we were increasingly condescended to by our remaining friends and reviled by a growing number of enemies. The Soviets were on the move on nearly every continent in the world, ruling Eastern Europe with an iron hand, making inroads into Africa and the Middle East, and increasingly threatening to control the shipping lanes for our petroleum supplies.

President Carter's response? To complain about the "malaise" gripping his fellow citizens, and to instruct us that we had to jettison our "inordinate fear of Communism."

7

Time to Regroup

F or political journalists it can be exhilarating to be in opposition. But as Americans, the *NR* crew could not enjoy the Carter slough of despond.

We also had our own problems to worry about. We had hoped that *NR*'s circulation would rebound during the election campaign, but by the fall of 1976 it was still at ninety-five thousand. Then our beloved Jim Buckley lost his bid for reelection. He might have lost in any case: he didn't trouble about "constituent services" as much as many of his colleagues did, or perhaps as much as he should have—no one would ever have dubbed him "Senator Pothole." But when the Democrats rejected the far-left Bella Abzug and instead nominated the relatively centrist Daniel Patrick Moynihan—whose invigorating performance as UN ambassador had made him a hero to many (including *NR*'s editors, who had declared him Man of the Year)—Jim's fate was pretty well sealed. Meanwhile, Bill was in the midst of a long-drawn-out battle with the Securities and Exchange Commission.

This was a painful and costly episode. At some point in the course of it, Bill wrote, in white heat, a little book about the whole thing. To a man, his friends and advisors told him: *You must not publish this.* The SEC is an 800-pound gorilla, they said in effect, and since you haven't prevailed against it so far, the last thing you want to do is provoke it to defend itself by nailing you even harder. Their good counsel prevailed, and this remains one of the very few pieces of writing Bill has ever started without bringing to fruition.

The present authors have no intention of rushing in where Bill was persuaded not to tread. So we'll confine ourselves to the noncontroverted parts of the story.

Back in the mid-1950s, before the fund appeal idea had coalesced, Bill was looking for ways to help support his fledgling magazine. He noticed the success other media figures had had with radio stations and decided to buy one. It didn't flourish under his care until young Peter Starr, the Stamford boy who had crewed on *The Panic*, became its ad salesman. Suddenly KOWH, Omaha, took off, and after a few months Bill put Peter in charge of the enterprise. They bought more stations, and in 1969 they took the company public in order to acquire additional capitalization. In *Cruising Speed*, which was drafted in February/March 1971, Bill wrote: "I feel for Peter that special affection I reserve for anyone who has made me a million dollars."

However, at about the same time, some ancillary real estate speculations were going wrong. In attempting to recoup, Starr Broadcasting bought these properties from the satellite company—which would have been no problem, except that Starr was now a publicly traded company, and the transactions weren't properly reported on its 10-Ks. Since Bill was the chairman of Starr Broadcasting, he was technically responsible. Nowadays, with Sarbanes-Oxley, this may seem more than obvious, but the rules about directors' responsibilities have been shifting and changing ever since the Great Crash, and Bill hadn't kept up with the changes since his father's day.

Eventually the SEC accepted a payment of moneys to be distributed to the shareholders and banned Bill from serving as a director of a public company for five years. Bill's friends kept reminding him that it could have been much worse. The SEC was being extremely aggressive in that season, as the bad economic climate was sending many companies into deep trouble, and people were actually going to prison for what seemed to the general public to be fairly arcane infractions. But the whole thing left a very bad taste—especially when the SEC took out after Bill's brother John for actions taken by Catawba. The one consolation: since Bill was not directly involved in the Catawba fight, he was able to write about it without doing any harm.

While the SEC cloud hung over the horizon and the Carter malaise deepened, there were plenty of bright spots nearer by. One of the brightest of these was the development of a new generation of conservative thinkers and writers.

Bill Buckley, Priscilla Buckley, and Bill Rusher, all in their early to mid-fifties, were far from ready to pack it in. But for people who prize a continuity of generations—what the Church calls "the communion of saints," and what Chesterton called "the democracy of the dead"—encouraging the next generation is not simply a good thing, it is a necessity. John Leo, who counts himself as one of the recipients of this encouragement, remarked to one of the present authors that it's far more common for established journalists to regard up-and-comers as competition. But developing young writers was an ongoing fact of life at *National Review*, where the position of summer editorial assistant was used to scout for emerging talent. In 1976 Richard Brookhiser, a junior at Yale, finally applied for the post.

We say "finally" because Rick had first come to our attention in the fall of 1969, when he was a freshman at Irondequoit High School in Rochester, New York. He had written a letter to his brother, who was away at Yale, telling him about the anti-Nixon Moratorium at his school. The brother, Robert, thought enough of the piece to send it along to *NR*, and it was published as a cover story, with virtually no editing. We had heard from Rick from time to time over the intervening years, and now he was our summer assistant.

As with Linda Bridges seven years before, the understanding was that if everything worked out, Rick would return after graduation, and so he did. He was made our chief reporter and then—partly to persuade him to stay at *NR* instead of going to law school—our youngest-ever senior editor. One of his first big contributions was a masterly, depressing two-part piece entitled "Why You Can't Fight City Hall in Washington, D.C." This was an exploration of how the dynamics of pork-barrel politics—what Erik von Kuehnelt-Leddihn called "the Santa Claus state"—make it so very difficult for Congress or the president to resist new spending measures, and even more difficult to repeal them once they're in. Starting in 1980, Brookhiser would be our reporter on the presidential campaign trail, successor to Jack Kilpatrick and John Coyne, and he would help shape *NR*'s understanding of the politics of the 1980s.

The year before Brookhiser, our summer assistant was Daniel Ritchie, who has since become one of the nation's leading Burke scholars. The year after, it was Charles Kesler, who would become a disciple of Straussian political economist Harry Jaffa; Kesler is now the director of the Henry Salvatori Center at Claremont University and the editor of the *Claremont Review of Books*. Also in 1977, Paul Gigot, a protégé of Jeff Hart's at Dartmouth, joined the staff as an editorial assistant; he would go on to a stint at the *Wall Street Journal, Asia*, and now is Bob Bartley's successor as editor of the *Wall Street Journal*'s editorial page. Later staffers who would go on to stellar careers include Mona Charen, Maggie Gallagher, and David Brooks. (Not all of these careers are in politics or journalism, however. Lacey Washington became a thoracic radiologist, Will Dunbar a venture capitalist, and Vicki Marani an appeals lawyer at the Department of Justice.)

But while there were plenty of young conservatives, there were not many new conservative periodicals. Perhaps would-be publishers were deterred by *NR*'s perpetually "indigent" state (Bill's word). Several not-for-profit organizations had journals, some of them very fine—Heritage's *Policy Review*, ISI's *Intercollegiate Review*, the Educational Reviewer's *University Bookman* (founded under *NR* auspices and edited by Russell Kirk). But on the popular front, one of the few survivors among new publications was *The American Spectator*, founded by R. Emmett Tyrrell Jr. and some fellow University of Indiana students in 1967. The magazine was originally titled *The Alternative*—that is, it was an alternative to the radicalism of the raging Sixties. But by the mid-1970s, as Tyrrell put it, "the word 'alternative' had come to be associated almost exclusively" with those self-same radicals and their successors, and so he changed the name.*

---

* If memory serves, in 1969 or perhaps 1970, a couple of years after *The Alternative*'s founding, Bob Tyrrell, Baron Von Kannon, and several other Indiana conservatives came to *National Review* to get Bill Buckley's blessing. (In those days, just as devout Catholics traveling through Rome hoped to receive the papal blessing, smart young conservatives traveling through New York made pilgrimages to 150 East 35th Street.) As one of the present writers recalls it, Tyrrell and company had brought along with them a very young and even younger-looking Harvard undergrad whom they addressed as Billy. To celebrate receiving the blessing, Tyrrell invited this writer to accompany his troop to McSorley's Old Ale House—at that time, still a men-only hangout—where we feasted on crackers and cheese and onions, washed down with large quantities of beer and ale. The young man called Billy became, as the poets say, somewhat green around the gills. As it turned out—or so at least this writer was told—this was Bill Kristol's first experience with beer.

Meanwhile, successors to Hayek and Voegelin and Kirk were making their way in the academy. Ellis Sandoz in Louisiana and Dante Germino in Virginia were making Eric Voegelin's abstrusities accessible to a wider audience. George Nash's volume on the conservative intellectual movement had been a landmark; he was now beginning his definitive research on Herbert Hoover. Forrest McDonald was emerging as one of the leading American historians, with a particular concentration on Alexander Hamilton. In economics, Gordon Tullock, James M. Buchanan, and Vernon Smith were working on public choice theory at George Mason University; Smith and three others would win the Nobel Prize for economics in 2002. Robert Conquest—British by birth, but about to take up permanent residence at the Hoover Institution—had produced his magisterial *The Great Terror*, about Stalin's purge trials and his deliberate starvation of Ukraine. For those who haven't made the time to read this six-hundred-page book, the multifaceted Mr. Conquest distilled its message into an amazing limerick:

> There was a great Marxist named Lenin,
> Who did more than six million men in.
>   That's a lot to have done in,
>   But where he did one in
> That great Marxist Stalin did ten in.

The Panama Canal—Ronald Reagan's Golden Kazoo—remained one of the hottest topics on the American political scene long after President Carter and Panamanian president Omar Torrijos signed the treaties on September 7, 1977.

Buckley, who was initially opposed to the Canal treaties, changed his mind after a five-day visit to Panama in September 1976. He made his new position known in a series of columns and in *National Review*, much to the distress of many hard-line conservatives—including Ronald Reagan. As Buckley tells it, "Ronald Reagan and I would from time to time genially disagree on the subject, in public and in private. Late in 1977 I thought to ask him, in a telephone conversation, whether he would debate the subject on a special two-hour *Firing Line*. At first he was reluctant ('Why should I want to debate with *you?*'). But a few days later, after he had contemplated my proposed format, he said yes." This was, by the way, the first of some fifty

Firing Line debates. Some of these brought more heat than light, but most were illuminating as well as good theater.

The debate, called by the *Washington Post* "the Super Bowl of the right," was held in January 1978 at the University of South Carolina. The topic: "Resolved, the Senate should ratify the Panama Canal Treaties." Each of the principals was joined by two debating partners and one military expert. The main treaty negotiator, Ellsworth Bunker, was there to answer technical questions, and the moderator was former senator Sam Ervin, who as Buckley put it, "had presided over the liquidation of Richard Nixon."

On the Buckley team were James Burnham and George Will as debaters and Admiral Elmo Zumwalt, former chief of naval operations, as military expert. On the Reagan team were Pat Buchanan, former assistant to President Nixon and future assistant to President Reagan; Roger Fontaine, a Latin American scholar; and Admiral John McCain, commander of our forces in the Pacific during the Vietnam War and the father of a future presidential candidate.

The debate disappointed no one, from the opening questions to the rebuttals. Reagan began with this: "Well, Bill, my first question is why haven't you already rushed across the room here to tell me that you've seen the light?"

Buckley's response: "I'm afraid that if I came any closer to you the force of my illumination would blind you."

Reagan was relaxed throughout, very much in command of his material, and aware of 1980 and the political implications of his performance. He spoke to national pride: "The Panama Canal is just one facet of our foreign policy, and with this treaty, what do we do to ourselves in the eyes of the world, and to our allies? Will they, as Mr. Buckley says, see that as the magnanimous gesture of a great and powerful nation? I don't think so, not in view of our recent history, not in view of our bug-out in Vietnam, not in view of an administration that is hinting that we're going to throw aside an ally named Taiwan. I think the world would see it as, once again, Uncle Sam putting his tail between his legs and creeping away rather than face trouble."

Buckley, arguing both from magnanimity and from hard political realities, put it this way: "I think that Governor Reagan put his finger on it when he said the reason this treaty is so unpopular is because we're tired of being pushed around. We were pushed out of Vietnam because we didn't have the guts to go in there and do it right. . . . We're prepared, as it was said, to desert Taiwan because three and a half Harvard professors think that we ought to normalize our relations with Red China. We are prepared to allow sixteen semisavage countries to cartelize the oil that is indispensable to the industrial might of the West because we don't have a diplomacy that's firm enough to do something about it. And therefore, how do we get our kicks? How do we get our kicks? By saying no to the people of Panama. . . .

"Let's listen to reason. Let's recognize . . . that [for military and strategic reasons] we need the Panama Canal with a people who are residents of Panama, who understand themselves as joined with us in a common enterprise, because when they look at the leaders of the United States they can recognize that, not as a result of our attempt to curry favor with anybody, but as a result of our concern for our own self-esteem, we were big enough to grant little people what we ourselves fought for two hundred years ago."

It's no doubt unfair, looking at the debate nearly three decades later, to say that history has validated the Buckley position. But it is fair to say that both sides won that night. Buckley won the debate rhetorically and intellectually. Reagan won it emotionally and politically.

As Buckley would later point out, "Reagan's conspicuous position on the treaty, combined with the treaty's ratification by the Senate, made possible his election as president. . . . My thesis is that if he had favored the treaty, he'd have lost his hard initial conservative support (Senator Howard Baker suffered crucially for his support of the treaty). But—I speculated—if the treaty had *not* passed the Senate, which it might not have done if the conservative opposition to it had been hegemonic, uprisings in Central America during the 1980 presidential campaign might have frustrated Reagan's hopes."

At the time, although the flak Buckley caught from several quarters on the right was intense, the national reaction to the debate was positive. True, there were some in the press, always eager to take shots at Buckley, who tried to find nits to pick. For instance, Ward Sinclair, writing in the *Washington Post*, took Buckley to task for historical inaccuracy: "He [Buckley] says Cortez crossed Panama and was the first to espy the Pacific Ocean. It was Vasco Nuñez."

Here is Buckley's response, in a letter to the *Post*: "What I said in my speech was, 'If there is a full-scale atomic war, the Panama Canal will revert to a land mass, and the first survivor who makes his way across the isthmus will relive a historical experience like stout Cortez when, with eagle eyes, he stared at the Pacific and all his men looked at each other with a wild surmise, silent upon a peak in Darien.'

"The lines are from John Keats. His sonnet 'On First Looking into Chapman's Homer.' I felt presumptuous enough correcting Ronald Reagan's foreign policy without straightening out Keats's historical solecism. But tell Mr. Sinclair not to worry: It happens all the time, people's inability to tell where I leave off and Keats begins."

Jim Burnham, who had made very few public appearances in recent years, nonetheless performed very well and clearly enjoyed the whole debate. But then as he was flying home from South Carolina, disaster struck. For a couple of years his eyesight had been weakening; the problem was diagnosed as a leakage in the capillaries feeding his retinas. Suddenly, in the course of the flight, the sight in his left eye virtually disappeared. The doctor warned him that the same thing could happen to his right eye.

Jim coped—Jim always coped. He acquired magnifying glasses and special reading lights, and informed himself about recorded books and magazines. He missed one column for the magazine, but then was back at the old stand, writing about Somalia and Rhodesia, Italian terrorism (this was the period of the Red Brigades), and "normalization" of our relations with Peking. In October, he and Marcia took off, as they did every election year, for a leisurely driving tour around the eastern states—though this time Marcia had to do all the driving. The column recording his impressions, "Autumn Miscellany," appeared in the November 10 issue of NR. It was the last thing he wrote for publication. A few days after it went to press he had a massive stroke. The doctors weren't sure that he would live. Priscilla called us into her office, as she had done three years earlier when Elsie died. The newest editorial staffers scarcely knew Jim except as a byline, but for the veterans—Kevin Lynch and Linda Bridges, Joe Sobran and Rick Brookhiser—who had been taught by him the craft of editorial writing, had listened to his tales of playing baccarat on the French-Spanish border or making maple syrup at his home in Kent, Connecticut, and had witnessed his verbal combat with Bill Rusher, this was like losing a favorite grandfather. For Priscilla, it meant losing one of her closest friends and comrades-in-arms. For Bill, who took

Jim and the elegant Marcia, with Priscilla at the twentieth anniversary party.

us to a subdued lunch in Paone's dark little back room, as he had after Elsie's death, it meant losing the man who had made it possible for him to have the extraordinary career he had. Officially, the magazine announced simply that Mr. Burnham was seriously ill and had to suspend his column, and that for the next few issues Brian Crozier would be writing in Burnham's space. (Crozier, a major anti-Communist figure in Britain and a longtime admirer of Burnham's, would wind up taking over the column permanently.)

In fact, Jim survived, and his paralysis receded, unlike Will Buckley's twenty years earlier. But that formidable brain that Willmoore Kendall had made the crack about was irrevocably damaged. Jim could no longer absorb new information and synthesize it with the old. His personality remained intact, however, and when he came to town for an editorial dinner there was enough of the old Jim there to make the occasion bearable, even pleasant. But how we missed his weekly presence!

Nor could we take much relief from the surrounding landscape. At home, Americans were still living with crippling "stagflation"—simultaneous high inflation and high unemployment. In 1976, campaigning against Jerry Ford, Jimmy Carter had unveiled the "Misery Index"—the sum of the inflation rate and the unemployment rate. No one, he said, who had allowed the Misery Index to rise as high as Ford had (it was then 13.75) had a right to sit in the Oval Office. As of November 1978, the Misery Index was at 14.79 percent, unemployment having fallen slightly but inflation having increased. Even so, the Republicans made only slight gains in the midterm elections, and the Democrats remained solidly entrenched in both houses of Congress. *NR* writers were dispiritedly predicting a permanent Democratic majority.

Britain under Labour prime minister James Callaghan was in even worse shape. The labor unions, having knocked Ted Heath's Conservative government out of power, were ungovernable, and analysts were wondering how long a country could survive double-digit inflation. On the Continent, the Red Brigades were terrorizing Italy—in May 1978 they actually kidnapped and killed the prime minister, Aldo Moro—and France was bedeviled by strikes. The one bright spot was the collapse, in West Germany, of the Baader-Meinhof gang after its leaders committed suicide in prison.

In the Middle East much was happening, much of it because of American involvement, and with seismic aftershocks that continue to this day. President Carter, as a born-again Christian, felt a particular obligation toward the Holy Land. This was one of the reasons he worked so hard to bring about the Camp David Accords between Israel and Egypt, negotiated in September 1978 and signed in January 1979. At the time, these seemed a great achievement. As *NR* put it (in an editorial written by Norman B. Hannah, who succeeded Burnham as our foreign policy editorialist), "Carter deserves all the credit he gets." But the accords led to the assassination of President Sadat, which surely was a factor in the ascendancy of Saddam Hussein within the Muslim world. Meanwhile, the shah of Iran had been working to modernize his country and make it less theocratic. Many observers—even ones who basically approved of the shah's aims—wondered if he was doing too much too fast, and if he was too out of touch with his own people to notice how his reforms were being received. In this already dangerous situation, Carter began putting heavy pressure on the shah to do more, faster. In January 1979 the shah and his empress were forced into exile; two weeks later Ayatollah Khomeini returned from his own exile in Paris. In October, the Carter administration permitted the shah to come to the United States for treatment of his cancer. In protest, Iranian student radicals invaded the American embassy in Teheran and took sixty-six Americans hostage, creating the defining background to the 1980 American elections.

Around the world, Communism was on the march. Bill Buckley was chosen to give the commencement address at Notre Dame that year, and he began by quoting the previous year's commencement speaker, President Carter, who had told the graduating class that, "being confident of our own future, we are now free of that inordinate fear of Communism which led us to embrace any dictator who joined us in our fear." Buckley then catalogued some recent occurrences by which to measure the ordinacy of our fear of Communism. (1) In the Soviet Union, Yuri Orlov was sentenced to seven years in prison followed by five years in Siberia. His crime? Monitoring Soviet compliance with the Helsinki Accords, which, on paper, guaranteed the free movement of people and ideas. "May we suppose," Buckley asked the graduating seniors, "that Yuri Orlov's fear of Communism has not proved to be inordinate?" (2) In Cambodia, "there have been aggravated shortages. Of the usual things—food, fuel, shelter, medicine—to be sure. But most pressing, it appears, has been the shortage of ammunition with which to kill Cambodian civilians." And so Cambodian men and women suspected of imperialist tendencies, tens of thousands of them, were tied up and clubbed to death. "Pol Pot," Buckley went on, "does not devote the whole of his time to overseeing this enterprise in population control. He is otherwise engaged— for instance, as guest of honor recently in Peking at a banquet tendered by the rulers of the People's Republic of China, who, now that we have got over our inordinate fear of Communism and our corollary addiction to dictators, we are finally ready to embrace." (3) We did nothing to stop the march of Cuban soldiers as Soviet surrogates in Angola, Mozambique, and Ethiopia. "And we have given concrete form to our contempt for anti-Communist dictators by embracing the democratic leaders of Poland, Romania, and Yugoslavia, and hailing our purposes in common."

A final straw, it seemed, for Catholics and for others who value the Church as an institution, was the tumult in the Vatican. In August 1978, Pope Paul VI had finally been gathered home after a long and painful illness, and the Synod quickly elected the little-known Albino Cardinal Luciani to succeed him—only to have that new pope, John Paul I, die after one month in office.

Then came the first glimmer of hope. While Vaticanologists' heads spun, the Synod elected not another Italian, and not any of the

Germans whose names were regularly mentioned, but a Pole. It wasn't that Karol Wojtyla was unknown. Far from it. As the cardinal-archbishop of Krakow he was a leading churchman in the only country behind the Iron Curtain to have a flourishing church; and he, along with his primate, Stefan Cardinal Wyszynski, had been a major behind-the-scenes player in the Synod that elected John Paul I. But he had been on nobody's short list—except, presumably, Wyszynski's and the Holy Spirit's.

Soon we started to learn more. Malachi Martin, the brilliant, charming, fanciful defrocked Jesuit who had become *NR*'s religion editor, quickly wrote a column on Wojtyla's background that suggested he might be a very good thing. Throughout World War II he had been an active member of the *Armia Krajowa* (Home Army), the Polish Resistance. Besides the perilous day-to-day activities of distributing underground literature and helping those who were fleeing the Nazis, the young Wojtyla was part of the group that obtained information for the Allies about the Nazis' experiments with V-1 bombs and V-2 rockets, which were being done using Polish slave labor. Once the Soviets took Poland from the Nazis (as Joe Sobran put it in an editorial about the new pope, "World War II was precipitated by the barbarian attack on Poland, and the war ended with its conquest by the surviving power in the barbarian partnership"), Wojtyla worked closely with his mentor, Wyszynski, defying Stalinism and keeping the Church alive. Martin presciently concluded his column: "Everything in Wojtyla's background and mentality points up his conviction that the only way Marxism and materialism can be defeated is through the form of Catholicism and of Christianity which has successfully flourished behind the Iron Curtain, and specifically in Communist Poland. Given the total lack of American leadership, as Europeans today see it, and given Wojtyla's deftness in dealing with the Stalinist mind, we can look forward—with trepidation or enthusiasm—to a time in the near future when a change of policy may well be forced on both the USSR and the U.S.A. by the Polish clergyman now become Bishop of Rome."

In his column written the day after the Panama Canal debate, Buckley made an early declaration for Reagan in 1980. After analyzing President Carter's difficulties and the difficulties facing a hypothetical Democratic challenger, he turned to the Republican side. "Gerald

Ford is the titular leader of the Republican Party," he wrote, "and that will get you a ham sandwich, if you have some ham, and if somebody comes along with the bread." Ford just had not, Buckley went on, "developed the political skills that take you to the mountaintops of New Hampshire. . . . Reagan, on the other hand, has." The public perception of his governorship of California was steadily rising, and he "maintains his ability to inspire a crowd. . . . He suffers the single presumptive disability of being thought too old."

Whereupon Buckley told a memorable little story. A year earlier, in November 1976, Ron and Nancy Reagan were in Connecticut. Ron Jr. had announced that he wanted to drop out of Yale and become a dancer, and his parents had flown East to try to dissuade him. Thanksgiving was approaching, and Bill invited the three Reagans to come to Sharon for the Buckley family's traditional gathering on that day. "Lunch," Bill writes, "is always followed by a touch football game, and I asked Reagan if he would consent to referee it. 'What's the matter?' he asked with genuine surprise and just a touch of indignation. 'Can't I play?'

"He did, and was indistinguishable in his energy, and very nearly indistinguishable in his skills, from his 18-year-old son. 'What's the matter? Can't I play?' I can hear that said, implicitly, in New Hampshire, and, unless there is between now and then a galloping decrepitude, the voters, looking at him, are quite possibly going to answer, 'Why not?'"

It would not be until November 1979 that Reagan formally declared—as Buckley explained in another column that season, modern election laws regulating finances, television time, and so on discourage early formal declarations—but he was far from idle. Besides staying in the public eye through speaking engagements, his radio show, and his newspaper column, Reagan set about shoring up his knowledge of the world scene. Taking with him a few companions, he first went, in April 1978, to the Far East—Japan, Taiwan, and Hong Kong. The Japanese, according to one of those companions, Reagan's future national security advisor, Richard V. Allen, were rather cool to him, but the Taiwanese were enthusiastic, as was he about them.

The second trip was supposed to have been to the Soviet Union that summer—but, according to Allen, John Sears leaked to the press the fact that the trip was being planned. The plans were immediately cancelled—before, as Allen puts it, "misunderstanding among the governor's natural constituency could run out of control."

So the second trip Reagan actually took was to Western Europe, in November 1978. The French, like the Japanese, were standoffish. In Britain, Prime Minister Callaghan would not meet with him, but the Conservative Party leader, a two-time *Firing Line* guest named Margaret Thatcher, eagerly did. (Nine years earlier Governor Reagan had given a major address to an audience of high-powered business-men at Albert Hall. Denis Thatcher had come home that evening and reported to his wife how impressive Reagan had been, both in con-tent and in style.) "It was in Berlin, however," Allen writes, "that Reagan experienced a powerful first-hand encounter with the face of Communism. Approaching the Berlin Wall, his countenance dark-ened, and he stood before it in silence for several minutes before turning to Peter Hannaford and me, saying, 'We have got to find a way to knock this thing down.'"

Christopher Buckley recently recalled an evening back in the 1960s when, at the end of dinner, his father announced that he had to go back to his study and finish an article for *Playboy* that was due the next day. "'Never become a writer,'" Chris remembers Bill as saying. Chris adds, "I was never very good at following instructions."

In his first book, *Steaming to Bamboola*, he recalled his principal means of asserting some independence at that rather strict boarding school Portsmouth Abbey (strict by American standards, he hastened to add, not by the standards of the British schools his father and uncles attended—let alone the Greyburn Academy of Blackford Oakes and Count Wintergrin). The abbey is located right on Narra-gansett Bay in Rhode Island, a few miles north of Newport. In the winter, young Christopher would walk out on the ice as far as it was safe and watch the boats going through the channel. But at that time of year the vessels weren't sailboats, they were commercial ships, most of them freighters. He conceived a powerful desire to join them, and that's what he did for half a year immediately after graduating from Portsmouth Abbey. He shipped out as a deckhand on a Norwegian freighter, coming back with a ton of memories and, to his mother's dismay, two large tattoos (one of them later expunged).

He duly went to Yale (class of '75), and after graduating was hired by *Esquire* as a junior writer and editor. Soon afterward Clay Felker was hired as editor-in-chief. Felker liked the young man's work and before long had promoted him to managing editor. But *Esquire*

Buckley *père et fils*, aboard *Suzy Wong*, with tattoo front and center.

was losing money, the owners sold, Felker was out, and Chris decided to turn to something quite different. In the spring of 1979 he shipped out again on a tramp freighter—but this time with the specific intention of writing about his experiences. The book would not appear till 1982 ("I don't work like my father," he once said. "He writes in a week what takes me a year to produce"), but it would truly launch his career.

As Chris Buckley and the semifictionalized *Columbianna*'s crew of misfits were steaming across the Atlantic ("The ship, the people, and the events are real," he writes. "The names of the ship and her crew were changed"), the Republican hopefuls were jostling their way toward the starting gate: ex-President Gerald Ford, Senators Bob Dole and Howard Baker, Representatives Phil Crane and Jack Kemp, CIA head George Bush, and—first in the early polls and in the hearts of *National Review* and its editor-in-chief—Ronald Reagan.

Meanwhile, there was momentous news from Britain. The first week in May 1979, the Conservative Party won control of Parliament, and Margaret Thatcher was the new prime minister. As Bill

Buckley pointed out in his ebullient column titled "Margaret Is My Darling," she had a right mess to clean up: "We had in Great Britain a government which had turned over effective power to a few militants who dominated a single institution, the trades unions. . . . Under the government of Mr. Callaghan, postal workers were permitted to refuse to deliver the mail to a small industry being struck. That was bad enough as political pusillanimity. That it was defended in serious journals was intolerable. The only thing worse than a Hitler on the loose is someone who defends Hitler using the vocabulary of reason." Buckley then quotes a remarkable passage from Mrs. Thatcher: "'It seems to me that our Christian tradition has bequeathed to politics two great and permanently important ideas, and that almost the whole of political wisdom consists in getting these ideas into the right relationship with each other. The first is defined as the notion that we are all members of one another, and from it the importance of interdependence is learned; the second and equally important Christian contribution to political thinking is that the individual is an end in himself, a responsible moral being endowed with the ability to choose between good and evil.'" Buckley concludes his column: "Evelyn Waugh complained that the trouble with our century is that we never succeeded in turning the clock back a single second. The voters may now have proved him wrong."

In contemporary American politics it was Jimmy Carter who first ushered God onto the scene, enter stage left, but soon other actors were clamoring to be written into the script, enter stage right. As Bill Rusher put it, "The off-year elections of 1978 saw the religious right organized for political action for the first time since Prohibition." By 1980, "the religious right had been brought fully on line as a member of the political coalition sustaining the conservative movement. It is far from representing politically, in and of itself, a 'majority' of the American electorate, despite the claim implicit in the catchy title of Jerry Falwell's organization. [Later, perhaps in response to misgivings such as Rusher's, Moral Majority's name was changed to Liberty Federation.] But it is a new, distinct, and powerful force on the national political scene and will unquestionably continue to make its influence felt in both local and national elections henceforth."

Indeed it has. But where did it come from? As Rusher points out, the religious right grew to a great extent out of Jimmy Carter's demonstration in 1976 that, just as ethnic Catholics were an important constituency in the Northeast, so there were Protestant and evangelical groups in the South and elsewhere that could be mobilized into effective voting blocs.

No doubt in part the result of a national reaction to Watergate and the apparent collapse of morality in Washington, there were unprecedented stirrings throughout the country in those days. According to the direct mail genius Richard Viguerie, the first stirrings occurred among Christians concerned about the taxation of private schools and what was widely perceived as court-sanctioned immorality. Those stirrings intensified with the Carter demonstration and with the rise of some of the most effective young organizers of the self-styled New Right, among them Viguerie, who pioneered the political use of direct mail; Howard Phillips, later chairman of the Conservative Caucus; and Terry Dolan of the National Conservative Political Action Committee. The term "New Right" had sometimes been used back in the 1950s to distinguish *National Review*–style conservatives from the prewar isolationist Old Right. But for the new New Right, the emphasis was on building a new conservative political majority with populist and religious overtones. Largely as a result of their efforts, Christian voters turned out in droves in the elections of 1978 and 1980 to help elect several new senators—and a new president.

Bill Buckley's capacity for friendship is frequently remarked. Less often, his material generosity, if only because, like his father, he doesn't talk about it himself; and because recipients, understandably, don't say much in public about their having been in need. But remarked least often of all is his kindness. In fact, when it comes to Buckley's public persona, most people would agree with Michael Kinsley: "If you had seen William Buckley on a lot of *Firing Lines*, kind and gentle are not the words that arrive."

But in the sense of readily forgiving those who have made costly but unintentional mistakes, Bill is supremely kind. He has written of the time the eighteen-year-old Danny Merritt, filling in for the regular captain, was taking *Cyrano* from Manhattan back to Stamford. At two in the morning Bill's phone rang. It was Danny, saying, "Something terrible has happened." No, no one was hurt, he assured Bill. But *Cyrano* was completely demasted; Danny had misjudged the height of the mast vis-à-vis the Queensborough Bridge, and had no room to maneuver by the time he realized his error. "I told him never mind," Bill writes, "these things happen, try to get some sleep, I'd be around in the morning." (Bill hadn't connected this, until reminded by a colleague, with an incident early in his life when he was the recipient of exactly the same benison. He had got special permission, when a schoolboy in England, to attend the Grand National. His headmaster had asked him to place a small bet for him; the headmaster's horse won—but Billy had forgotten to place the bet. Returning to the school that night, he told Father Sharkey of his dereliction. Father Sharkey's "dismay was acute. Then, suddenly, he smiled. 'Those things happen. Now get to bed.'")

One of the present authors had a similar experience, though the error was on a smaller scale. Bill had been invited to sail from Santo Domingo to New York on the three-masted tall ship of the Dominican Republic's navy. Owing to other commitments, he would need to write his next day's column on the plane and dictate it from Santo Domingo; the next morning, he would be on the ship, incommunicado.

Frances, Dorothy, and Tony Savage, Bill's amanuensis, all had things planned for the evening. Linda, hearing of their distress, volunteered to stay and man the tape recorder. Bill called as scheduled, dictated the column, and said good night. Linda thought to check that the dictation had come through all right—and found, horror-struck, that the tape contained nothing at all. She had failed to depress the record button. And she didn't know how to reach Bill.

After a few minutes of panic, she did what she should have done initially: tested the machine four times over to make *sure* she knew how to work it. She then, with fear and trembling, called the overseas operator and explained that she needed to find her boss, who was staying in Santo Domingo, surely at one of the top hotels, and could the operator possibly ask her opposite number down there to help track him down? Of course, she had to give her boss's name, and the operator, already friendly, was delighted: she was a big Buckley fan, and her husband was a cop who had had the privilege of guarding Jim Buckley during his second campaign. She said she'd give it a try.

The operator at the other end proved helpful and knowledgeable. She guessed the right hotel on the first try. Linda then—knowing that Bill *hates* double work—had to break it to him that he would have to read his column all over again. But he just said, "That's all right—but you're sure the machine works now?" And all was well.

* * *

As of February 1980, Ronald Reagan's presidential campaign was not off to a good start. Despite John Sears's poor performance in 1976, Reagan had reengaged him for the new campaign. And despite the results of his poor performance then, Sears seemed determined to follow the same game plan this time: have the candidate stick to generalities and never criticize an opponent. Forget about flesh-pressing and stump-speaking in the states where the first primaries would be held; instead, send the candidate on a speaking tour in major cities around the country. Above all, never let the candidate be spontaneous.

The strategy worked brilliantly in the Iowa caucuses—if the real objective was to get George Bush nominated. As *NR* observed editorially, "Reagan spent 41 hours there; George Bush practically lived there." Bush won in Iowa with 32 percent to Reagan's 29, and it was looking like 1976 all over again.

This time, however, stung by the Iowa loss, Reagan came roaring into New Hampshire, much as he had come roaring out of North Carolina in 1976, when Jesse Helms had persuaded him to let Reagan be Reagan. And this time, in New Hampshire, where people supported him on such basic issues as the Panama Canal treaty and SALT II, Reagan became Reagan with a vengeance. He crisscrossed the state, feeding rhetorical red meat to hungry conservatives. He participated in a debate in Manchester with the other primary candidates, whom he had avoided in Iowa, and more than held his own. And then on February 23 he went to Nashua for the debate in a high school auditorium that made presidential campaign history.

The debate was sponsored by the *Nashua Telegraph*, but the idea for it had originated with Bush's people. They held, and Sears agreed, that Bush and Reagan were so clearly the front-runners that they should go head to head, excluding the other five candidates: John Anderson, Howard Baker, John Connally, Phil Crane, and Bob Dole. However, Dole complained to the Federal Election Commission that if he and the others were excluded this sponsorship would constitute an illegal campaign contribution. The commission agreed, and the Reagan and Bush teams discussed picking up the tab for the debate. However, Hugh Gregg, Bush's New Hampshire campaign manager, vetoed splitting the costs. And so the Reagan campaign decided, while leaving the *Telegraph* in charge of the logistical arrangements, to pay the entire cost of the debate. And since they were paying for it, the

Reaganites also decided to invite the five other candidates. Anderson, Baker, Crane, and Dole accepted; Connally was campaigning in South Carolina.

On the evening of the debate, told that the four were there, waiting to come onstage, Bush refused to alter the one-on-one format. Reagan then took matters in hand. He led the excluded four onto the platform and took his seat with the four standing awkwardly behind him. While Bush sat off to the side, staring straight ahead, Reagan attempted to explain to the cheering and applauding crowd why the four should participate.

Then came the moment. First, the *Telegraph*'s publisher (a friend of Hugh Gregg) tried over a rising chorus of boos to quiet the crowd. Then his editor turned to a technician and said, audibly: "Turn Mr. Reagan's microphone off." Responding with what one reporter called "controlled fury," Reagan said, loudly and clearly: "I am paying for this microphone, Mr. Breen."

And that was that. A debate ensued, but it was almost ritualistic. With those eight words, just eight words out of the millions spewed out across the country during the 1980 primary season, Ronald Reagan had locked up his party's nomination. A *Boston Globe* subhead summarized the event: "At a high school in Nashua, the Gipper grabbed the brass ring."

On Tuesday, February 26, Reagan took 51 percent of the vote; Bush finished second with 22 percent. Reagan then fired John Sears, something conservatives had long hoped for, and replaced him with William Casey—the same William Casey who had drawn up the incorporation papers for *National Review*, and who would later head the CIA.

With Sears finally disposed of, Reagan roared through the remaining primaries, dispelling any lingering doubts about age or intellectual dexterity with his resounding win in Illinois on March 18. For admirers of Reagan's way with words, the Illinois debate was a treat. After Crane and Bush had pushed Anderson into saying he'd prefer Teddy Kennedy to Ronald Reagan as president, Reagan turned to Anderson and asked, in mock astonishment, "John, would you *really* find Teddy Kennedy preferable to me?"

Later in the debate, Reagan pointed out that wage and price controls had failed throughout history, even in ancient Rome, when the emperor Diocletian had tried to impose them. "And," he added, again bringing down the house, "I'm one of the few persons old enough to remember that."

Reagan won the debate handily, and when the ballots were counted he had won the primary with 48 percent of the vote, capturing an impressive number of Democratic crossovers, and in the process demolishing the candidacies of Anderson and Crane, two highly respected Illinois politicians. After Illinois, only Bush continued to soldier on. By the time he finally dropped out in May, he had won only four of the thirty-three primaries in which he'd run against Reagan.

Despite reservations in the Reagan camp, which comments like "voodoo economics" did nothing to dispel, Bush's gritty no-quit performance won him a good deal of admiration in party circles and, ultimately, among the Reaganites themselves. As a result, after a strained kabuki dance involving Gerald Ford and peculiar talk of a co-presidency, Bush, reservations and all, was the only real choice for vice president.

Bill Rusher spoke for most conservatives when he wrote: "I was perfectly comfortable with the idea of Bush as vice president. A balanced ticket seemed to me desirable if the party was to be united for the campaign, and I certainly didn't consider Bush very far to the left."

It was fortunate for Bill Buckley's journalistic reputation that Reagan wrapped up the nomination in May—because Bill's second quinquennial transatlantic sail was going to begin May 29, no matter what might have been happening in the California primary campaign. Actually, by this time technology had advanced to the point where Bill would be able to write and transmit his columns during the first leg of the trip. It would be just the last two weeks of June that he would be incommunicado. In his column for June 12, he advised his readers of his impending silence: "It is horrifying to meditate what enormity the White House will execute, I having advertised my isolation. On the other hand, if President Carter is determined to make me a boat people, I am splendidly well ahead of the game: I need only to sail on.

"But sail on to where? Ah, there's the rub, as the poet intuited four hundred years ago. Where can we go, if distress should come to America? There is only Switzerland: but nature so arranged it all that you cannot sail to Switzerland, and this would not be the season to rely on U.S. naval helicopters to pick up my boat and ferry it onto Lake Geneva." (Desert One, the operation to rescue the U.S. hostages in Teheran, had been attempted six weeks before, and had disastrously failed.) "Accordingly, I adjure my Lords, secular and spiritual, not to be too licentious while I am gone."

In this sequel to the Big One, the cast of characters was not identical. Reggie Stoops and Danny Merritt had signed up for the whole trip, but Dick Clurman was getting off at Bermuda, Van Galbraith at the Azores. Christopher was back at *Esquire* and struggling with his book about his very different sort of Atlantic crossing, on the tramp steamer. Bill Finucane's husband, John, was seriously ill and she could not think of taking a month at sea. Filling in for the missing sailors were Tony Leggett, a young lawyer; Tom Wendel, a historian roughly Bill's age; and Christopher Little, a young photographer. And the boat was not *Cyrano*. Not long after the Big One, Bill had finally acknowledged that his plan of chartering *Cyrano* out to pay for her upkeep wasn't working. He couldn't afford both *Cyrano* and *National Review*, and fortunately for the Republic (as the present authors see it) he chose to keep the latter. And so, this time out, he would be sailing not his own boat but a chartered one, the *Sealestial* ("iron rule," Bill wrote in a pre-sail memo to his crew: "pronounced Celestial by anybody who intends to board and stay aboard"). Once again, the sail would yield a book. (Naturally. It's hard to think of anything Bill has ever done that he hasn't written about in one way or another, though sometimes in the guise of fiction.) *Atlantic High* would follow the same pattern as *Airborne*: recollections of past sails, excerpts from the journals kept by Bill's sailing companions, and musings on this or that sailing topic (the rules for ocean racing, for instance, or Hugh Kenner's wonderful invention for celestial navigation, WhatStar). The photos in *Airborne* were homemade, but for *Atlantic High* Bill had engaged Christopher Little, who would become and remain a close friend.

These books have high drama and warm camaraderie. They also have some of Bill's funniest storytelling. His account (in *Airborne*) of the maiden voyage of *Cyrano* under his captaincy is a classic. By the time the *second* outboard motor has become an overboard motor, and the *second* fire has started (all in the course of what should have been an easy four-hour sail), the reader's eyes are likely to be filled with tears of laughter. "'You know,'" Bill quotes the electrician brought on board to fix the initial problem, "'I've been doing marine electrical work for years, but this is the first trip I've ever taken except on my fishing dinghy. Is it always like this?'

"I knew she would be the first to speak, even though I'm fast at the draw. . . . 'Yes,' said Pat, calm as Ethel Barrymore. 'Oh, yes. In fact, tonight was one of the more *peaceful* sails we've ever *had*.'"

George Will, in town in August 1980 to cover the Democratic convention, dropped by the *NR* offices. "What do you think of Reagan's chances?" one of us asked him.

"I'm not sure," George replied. "But I'm worried about the country's chances if he's *not* elected."

Carter had easily beaten off a halfhearted challenge from Teddy Kennedy. But that was about the only thing that had gone right for him that year. The campaign had been conducted against an appalling backdrop. Internationally, American prestige was plummeting. There were the hostages in Iran, with every day bringing fresh reports of failed administration efforts to free them. The most disastrous of these was Desert One, which, somewhat unfairly, Carter was given no credit whatsoever for attempting. As Bill Buckley put it, "One can have no objections whatever to President Carter's mission, restricting our criticism to the maladroitness of its execution and the inefficiency of contingency planning." Domestically, Carter's administration was hounded by a hard and growing energy crisis, galloping inflation and unemployment, and flat economic growth. As Reagan put it, "I'm told I can't use the word depression. Well, I'll tell you the definition. Recession is when your neighbor loses his job. Depression is when you lose your job. Recovery is when Jimmy Carter loses his."

The temptation is to feel sorry for Carter. There was his brother Billy, marketing Billy Beer and urinating in the bushes while escorting a group of Libyan businessmen. Jimmy himself was attacked by the "killer rabbit" while fishing; the photograph on the front page of the *New York Times* showed him wearing a ferocious frown, with his line tangled in trees and all over his body. There was President Carter sitting in front of a White House fireplace (calling up for some of us memories of Richard Nixon, who liked blazing fires with the air conditioning turned up full blast), wearing a too-large old cardigan and giving his "malaise" speech. In the end, these and other images evoke something very much like pity. Carter was a professing Christian who had served his country well and took his duties as a family man seriously. But perhaps he was just not the man for the job. Or perhaps, as Michael Corleone said of Moe Green, he was just unlucky.

That having been said, there was something about Carter that was almost schoolmarmish, a fussiness and an ill temper that had increasingly contributed to the perception of his campaign as a negative one. And whatever the reasons, Ronald Reagan seemed to exacerbate this peevishness, as if Carter were playing the small, intense, studious type who knew he was worlds smarter than that big, easygoing cowboy who was forever saying shucks, beating the bad guys, and getting the girl without really seeming to try.

Carter had not wanted a debate with Reagan, but finally he could no longer duck it. The debate would take place on October 28 in Cleveland.

For most of us at *NR*, Reagan wasn't just the best available candidate. He was *our guy*, the way Barry Goldwater had been. We hadn't forgotten Bill's warning after the fall of Spiro Agnew: "This tendency to anthropomorphize our ideals is an American habit that can get us, indeed has just now gotten us, into deep trouble." But in Reagan's case, as *NR* put it editorially, "He has been our favorite politician for roughly as long as we have been his favorite magazine." On October 28, Priscilla invited the whole editorial staff to her apartment to have dinner and watch the debate together. We were as nervous as parents whose son had been chosen class valedictorian.

The debate started slowly, with neither candidate taking an advantage—although Carter's tendency to pop his eyes angrily, under two bushy caterpillar-like eyebrows that appeared to have a ferocious life of their own, seemed to give the edge to the challenger.

Then, late in the proceedings, came four words that had the same effect as those eight words in New Hampshire. Carter had launched into a scolding attack on Reagan's record on health care, charging that Reagan "began his political career campaigning around this nation against Medicare."

Reagan responded, with a sorrowful shake of the head: "There you go again."

The audience laughed, and Carter's eyebrows danced with fury. The group assembled in Priscilla's living room burst into sustained laughter. Someone—probably Priscilla herself, the most politically astute of us—said, "I think that did it."

She was right. With those four words, Reagan had summed it all up. That was precisely what was wrong with Carter. The audience in Cleveland knew it, and so did the nation. With those four words, Reagan won the debate in October and the election in November. And in the process, he added a new phrase to the lexicon of political legend.

There were a couple of other sentences that stayed in the mind. When Carter made his twelve-year-old daughter his chief defense advisor, he seemed finally to demolish any hope he and his followers had for redemption. "I had a discussion with my daughter Amy the other day before I came here," Carter said, "to ask her what the most important issue was. She said she thought nuclear weaponry and the control of nuclear arms." The well-behaved audience groaned, the comedians had a field day, and ASK AMY signs became staples at Republican rallies.

Just to finish it all off, Reagan concluded with eleven more words, spoken in the form of a rhetorical question, that also have a place in that legendary lexicon: "Are you better off today than you were four years ago?" The answer, delivered in November, was quite clearly no. (Four years later, in 1984, it would be a resounding yes.)

The importance of the debate can't be overstated. In *Rise of the Right*, Bill Rusher described its effects: "The impact was almost seismic. A vast television audience had at last watched Reagan under obvious pressure and liked very much what they saw: not a wild man, or a bumbler, but a warm, thoughtful, and manifestly self-possessed human being with a gift of gentle humor."

That fall, as the election loomed, *NR* was once again preparing for an anniversary, our twenty-fifth. And some of the mainstream media were taking notice—friendly notice. Morley Safer did a segment on Bill and his magazine for *60 Minutes*. The *New York Times* and *Washington Post* each sent around a reporter, Deirdre Carmody and Henry Allen, respectively, and each did a piece that we enjoyed unabashedly. Allen, interviewing one of the present authors, noticed a bumper sticker on her office door: MARGARET THATCHER FOR PRESIDENT. Oh, said the writer, I put that up *before* Reagan announced. (A few years later, the writer was on assignment in South Africa. At lunch with a local journalist in Pretoria, she described herself as representing an American conservative magazine. "Stop!" he said. "In the South African context 'conservative' means only one thing: in favor of apartheid. If that's *not* what you mean to say, you must find another formulation." The writer thought for a moment, then said, "How about Reaganite–Thatcherite? Will people get that?" "Perfect," said the South African.)

Meanwhile, we were sweating our way toward the completion of the anniversary issue. That January, *NR* had finally gone the route of so many other publications: we had dropped our old compositor, with its wonderful team of Linotypists and proofreaders, and started do-it-yourself typesetting on a pair of huge, recalcitrant computers that Priscilla dubbed Oscar and Wilde. We had been more than dubious when assured how much *easier* this would make our lives: "You can make changes at the touch of a button!" one helpful soul had assured us. Yes, and you can also lose an entire article at the touch of a button, and instead of sending the packet out with the printer's messenger at 5:30 Wednesday in the serene assurance that you would find your proofs waiting for you at 9:00 the next morning, you might find yourself coming back down after editorial drinks and working until 10:00. But while not easier, it was a whole lot cheaper, and employees of "indigent enterprises," as Bill puts it, can't be choosers.

November 4. Again, most of us are nervous. The polls have been showing Reagan and Carter running neck and neck. Rick Brookhiser, who has been tirelessly covering the campaign, is more confident than most of us, but not much. He predicts Reagan in a squeaker. Priscilla says, No, I think a lot of people will vote for Reagan but won't tell a pollster they're voting for him. Rick and Priscilla make a bet: each picks the number of electoral votes Reagan will get, and whichever is closer will collect from the other a dollar for every vote between what the loser picked and the actual number.

On election night, an old friend—Jim Buckley's former office manager, Liz Doyle—invited one of the present authors to watch the returns at Reagan's Manhattan headquarters. Expecting a long night, the writer and another friend went to an Italian restaurant across the street for a fortifying dinner. The waiter, sensing and sharing our sympathies ("I like Reagan," he said. "He's old, but he's wise."), brought reports from his radio each time he came by our table. We skipped coffee to get back to headquarters before it was all over.

As we returned, the television was showing a map of the United States as a sea of blue (this was before the colors inexplicably got reversed). A few minutes later, President Carter was conceding and President-elect Reagan was congratulating him on a hard-fought race. At Reagan headquarters, pandemonium broke out. A young television reporter was trying to send in her story, but she was visibly struggling to hear herself think, let alone speak comprehensibly into her microphone.

The networks doubtless were wrong to make their projections so early, before the polls had closed in the Western states, but as far as the presidential tally went it wouldn't have made any difference. Reagan had taken 51 percent of the vote, to Carter's 41 and Anderson's 7. (Anderson, dubbed on *NR*'s cover "Doonesbury's Candidate," had garnered only thirty-seven delegates, out of about two thousand, in the Republican primaries. After the convention he stayed in the race as an independent, running on a "National Unity Platform.") Reagan took 489 electoral votes to Carter's 49.

Alone among *National Review*'s editors, Priscilla had correctly predicted a landslide. She took pity on her young colleague and let Rick take her to a really nice lunch instead of forking over the $210 she had won.

When the congressional tallies came in, the significance of Reagan's victory assumed even greater proportions. Bill Rusher quotes the highly respected liberal commentator Max Lerner:

> "No greater upheaval in American politics has occurred for a half-century, since Franklin Roosevelt's victory over Herbert Hoover in 1932," wrote Lerner. "The reach and the depth of the Reagan sweep belie the current wisdom that it came only as a protest vote against Jimmy Carter and inflation. . . .
>
> "This wasn't a tremor. It was an earthquake. . . . Something like a class revolution has been taking place. Since the violent 1960s, the middle-middle and lower-middle classes have been seething with social resentment over the runaway changes in the culture. They too were part of the American dream—they had worked and scrimped, fashioned a trade or a small business, built a house, raised a family. They felt threatened by the forces that seemed intent on taking this away from them."

These were the Buckley Democrats, the Silent Majority. They would come to be called Reagan Republicans. The scrupulously nonideological *Facts on File* summed it up this way: "The sweeping Republican vote that ousted the Carter Administration and brought the GOP into control of the Senate stunned the Democratic Party. Its revered coalition of support since Franklin Delano Roosevelt's day lay in ruins. The blue-collar vote, the ethnic vote, Roman Catholics, Jews, and the South all deserted to Reagan."

Not only did Republicans take the Senate, but there were some notable names among the winners and losers. Departing were a half-dozen leading left-liberals, including George McGovern, Birch Bayh, and Frank Church. Arriving were a crew who would become some of the strongest conservative voices of the 1980s: Jeremiah Denton, John East, Robert Kasten, Mack Mattingly, Don Nickels, Dan Quayle, and Steve Symms.

Joy was unconfined at 150 East 35th Street—until we learned that the president-elect's civilian calendar, so to speak, had been tossed aside by the transition team. He had agreed, a year or so earlier, to be the principal speaker at our twenty-fifth anniversary celebration. But by the time, postelection, that Bill again mentioned the party to his old friend, something else had been scheduled for December 5, something the cancellation of which would have had severe repercussions. It was acutely disappointing for us all, but especially for Bill. There are downsides, we learned, to having your friends elected president of the United States.

8

The Reagan Years

A few years ago the town of Chatham, Cape Cod, suffered a break in a sandbar, allowing waves to threaten some oceanfront houses. When residents demanded that the town *do something*, an official said, "The Chatham Board of Selectmen is a very powerful body, but it's not as powerful as the Atlantic Ocean."

Ronald Reagan was now the leader of the free world, and in the judgment of Bill Buckley and *National Review* he was one tough hombre. But he faced a sea of problems not significantly smaller than the Atlantic Ocean.

One problem that had darkened Carter's last year in office had been resolved: the very day Reagan was inaugurated, the ayatollahs released the American hostages. The present authors have read the conspiracy theories and the refutations of them. We believe the latter, but we have no special inside knowledge. In any case, whatever the ayatollahs' reason for their timing, the fifty-two hostages not previously released were on their way home, after 444 days in captivity.

But most of the problems of the late 1970s remained. Domestically, in Carter's last two years in office, the Misery Index had risen spectacularly—to 19.29 in 1979 and 21.98 in 1980. Gerald Ford doesn't strike one as the sort of man to hold a grudge, but he might legitimately have felt a certain Schadenfreude when he recalled what Carter had said in 1976 about who is fit to occupy the Oval Office. The Leviathan State was out of control, as programs put in place by Johnson and, yes, Nixon bred new regulations like bunny rabbits; the *Federal Register*, which lists all regulations, was expanding so fast that young lawyers working in Washington, D.C., were advised, before completing a brief, to call Dial-a-Reg for any new regulations that might have sprung up overnight. And the "social indicators"—illegitimacy rate, length of time spent on welfare, crime—were dispiriting.

Abroad, Mrs. Thatcher was making a start, but she too faced ocean-sized problems. The most quantifiable were the economic problems, and those were the ones she tackled first—to howls not only from the Labourites, but also from the "wets," the softliners, in her own party. At the 1980 Conservative Party conference in Brighton, her predecessor as Conservative Party leader, Ted Heath, "was assuring his party," as *NR* put it editorially, "that it wasn't too late to perform a life-saving U-turn." Mrs. T., already known as the Iron Lady, told her fellow Tories: "You turn if you want to. The lady's not for turning." In fact, as *NR* went on to point out, she hadn't yet accomplished much. Taxes were still ruinous, the British Misery Index was at 26, and nothing had been done to tame the labor unions. But the prime minister knew what needed to be done. It was particularly reassuring, as our longtime London correspondent, Anthony Lejeune, reported, when she appointed Alan Walters, an "unswerving monetarist," as her personal economic advisor. Time would tell, but, as Reagan later put it, "From our first meeting we'd been on the same wavelength." The Special Relationship between Britain and the United States, which had languished during the unhappy 1960s and 1970s, was back in business.

In Western Europe the social scene was much calmer than it had been from 1968 through most of the 1970s. French students weren't pouring into the streets, and Baader-Meinhof was dead, though the Red Brigades were still active in Italy. But except for Switzerland, the economies were suffering as much as Britain's and America's from the heavy hand of government, and the term "worldwide recession" was commonly used.

In Central Europe there were stirrings of hope. In 1977, a few Czechoslovakians had circulated a document called Charter 77. It called on the government to observe the human rights listed in the Helsinki Accords, which Czechoslovakia had signed. The government promptly arrested the men who drafted the charter, but the document itself continued to circulate underground and to pick up signatures as it went.

In June 1979, the leader of the Catholic Church visited his native Poland, an event unprecedented since the Soviets had squatted down on Central Europe in the late 1940s. After John Paul's tumultuous nine-day visit, the Communists were still firmly in control of the Polish government, but citizens were emboldened to demand more political freedom and less government control of the economy. The event that made the headlines worldwide was the strike at the Gdansk shipyard that began on August 14, 1980—as it happens, the last day of the Democratic convention in New York. The strike was led by an unemployed electrician named Lech Walesa. Three weeks later, the regime recognized Walesa's union, Solidarity.

But elsewhere in the world the Soviets and their surrogates were on the march. The Cubans were still fighting in Angola and Ethiopia; they were no longer fighting in Mozambique only because they had won, installing a Marxist government under President Samora Machel. In 1978, Moscow-backed Vietnam invaded Peking-backed Cambodia; for the next several years China would conduct retaliatory raids across the Vietnamese border. On December 27, 1979, the Red Army itself invaded Afghanistan, called in by puppet president Babrak Karmal to give fraternal aid to the progressive government in Kabul. In Nicaragua, the "Government of National Unity" that had succeeded strongman Anastasio Somoza was turning into a one-party government, and that party, the Sandinistas, was increasingly letting its Marxism show.

The Cold War was hot in many places, and it was now Reagan's problem.

The mix-up that kept the Reagans away from *NR*'s twenty-fifth anniversary party—whether it was a genuine mix-up or, as some have speculated, deliberate sabotage by someone on the White House staff who wanted to distance the President from "the Buckleyites"—had no effect on the Reagans' friendship with the Buckleys. Bill and Pat each spoke regularly on the phone with Nancy; less often with Ron, given the demands of his office. In the spring of 1982 the two couples traveled together to Barbados to spend Easter weekend at Claudette Colbert's beachfront house. And Bill and Ron regularly exchanged notes, always making some reference to Bill's covert role in the administration. As Buckley tells the story, he wrote to Reagan around August 1980, saying that he did not expect and indeed did not want a job in a Reagan administration, his plate being quite full as it was. Reagan wrote back to say that was a pity, because he knew exactly what job he wanted Buckley to take: ambassador to Afghanistan. From the inauguration on, the running theme in their communications was that Buckley was in fact operating from Kabul. As he later put it, "With Ronald Reagan, the show must go on"—but of course that's equally true of Bill Buckley, who, as he has amply documented, has some particular ritual with most of his friends. Even the not very ritualistic Jim Burnham happily went along with Bill's picking him up to ride to the office together on "CIA time." As Bill explains in *Saving the Queen*, if you arrange to meet someone at 9:15 or 9:30, your opposite number is likely to take that as an approximation; for covert agents, having to wait around for twenty minutes at a rendezvous point could be dangerous, indeed fatal. So, instead, you specify an exact and offbeat time: 9:22, let's say. It sounds weird to the uninitiated, but it saves grief—or, in this case, impatience.

Meanwhile, old friends and acquaintances were filling the administration—Aram Bakshian and Tony Dolan in the speechwriting office, Dan Oliver as general counsel to the Education Department, Van Galbraith as ambassador to France, Jim Buckley as undersecretary of state for security assistance, Bill Casey (who had taken over the 1980 campaign when John Sears was finally, belatedly, tossed into the snows of New Hampshire) as director of central intelligence, Ed Meese as counselor to the President. *NR* staffers mock-complained about how much time we were spending with the FBI as they did their background checks. One of the present authors was sorely tempted, when the FBI agent got to the routine question about Daniel Oliver's loyalty to the United States of America, to say that Mr. Oliver's family had had their doubts at one point, but that he himself was a loyal citizen. (His great-great-great-great-grandfather, Peter Oliver, had been run out of Boston on a rail along with his brother-in-law, Thomas Hutchinson, the last British governor of Massachusetts.) The writer restrained herself, fearing that FBI agents weren't allowed to have senses of humor. She had forgotten Bill Rusher's great line, when Bill Buckley was being screened for his United Nations post. Rusher asked the FBI man why they needed to go through all this, since Buckley had been cleared for the USIA position just four years before. Well, said the agent, has Mr. Buckley done anything in the last four years to embarrass President Nixon?

"No," said Rusher, "but President Nixon has done a great deal to embarrass Mr. Buckley."

Another old friend, the Heritage Foundation, came into its own: it produced a huge document, solemnly presented by Ed Feulner to Ed Meese, to guide the new President in his goal, stated in his first inaugural address, of "get[ting] government back within its means." As Rick Brookhiser characterized it, "At 3,082 pages, the Heritage document runs twice as long as *War and Peace*. Tolstoy, of course, was only chronicling the rise and fall of Napoleon. The Heritage Foundation offers an Owner's Manual for the Federal Government."

And Christopher Buckley joined the administration, as a speech-writer for George Bush. He liked the work, he liked his boss. But, as he later put it, "All my hard work on speeches didn't matter because nobody cares what a Vice President says" (unless—Chris did not add—the vice president is Spiro Agnew). So after a year and a half, Chris left to go back to journalism and book writing. But while he was still with the administration, *Steaming to Bamboola* came out, and his parents gave a book party for him at a favorite restaurant of Pat's set, Mortimer's. Bill's calendar entry for May 11, 1982, is piquant:

"Party at Mortimer's for Christopher's book

"Then dinner for King of Greece"

In that first inaugural address, Ronald Reagan spelled it all out, drawing on the great promise of America's past to outline his program for America's future:

> These United States are confronted with an economic affliction of great proportions. In the present crisis, government is not the solution, government is the problem. . . . It is time to reawaken this industrial giant, to get government back within its means, and to lighten our punitive tax burden. . . .
>
> "We the people," this breed called Americans, [are] special among the nations of the earth . . . and as we renew ourselves here in our own land, we will be seen as having greater strength throughout the world. We will again be the exemplar of freedom and a beacon of hope for those who do not now have freedom. . . .
>
> It is time to realize we are too great a nation to limit ourselves to small dreams. We're not, as some would have us believe, doomed to an inevitable decline. I do not believe in a fate that will fall on us

no matter what we do. . . . So with all the creative energy at our command let us renew our determination, our courage, and our strength.

It was an eloquent address, written in large part by Ken Khachigian, Reagan's chief writer through the campaign. Khachigian had earned his bones as one of Richard Nixon's toughest and most dependable writers. He worked closely with Pat Buchanan during the Nixon years, and was called by some of his fellow writers, admiringly, Buchanan's Buchanan.

Khachigian preferred not to move to Washington with Reagan, returning instead to California, where he is still sought out by politicians smart enough to realize the value of well-crafted speeches. Nonetheless, Reagan was extremely well served by his White House writing staff, chief among them Aram Bakshian and Tony Dolan, both with strong *National Review* connections.

This is in no way to suggest that Reagan was one of those politicians who need gifted writers to put words into their mouths. He wasn't. Primary documents such as letters, columns, essays, and worked-over speech drafts demonstrate that Reagan was heavily involved at all levels in writing and working through his thoughts. As Bakshian pointed out in *National Review*, Reagan was a speechwriter's delight because he himself was a man of words.

Nor was Reagan's facility limited to programmed occasions. We saw this in the 1980 campaign—*"I am paying for this microphone." "There you go again"*—and we would see it at one of the gravest moments of his career, when he took a bullet fired by a deranged would-be assassin that lodged within an inch of his heart. His words to Nancy—"Honey, I forgot to duck"—echoed throughout the nation, five words that carried a comforting reassurance that even at one of the darkest moments in our country's history, we were in good and steady hands.

Like Margaret Thatcher, Ronald Reagan saw his first task as rebuilding the economy—or, rather, getting the government out of the way so that the people could rebuild the economy. The supply-siders, led academically by Arthur Laffer and politically by Jack Kemp, gave Reagan's program a name. But he maintains that they taught him nothing that he hadn't learned in Hollywood. "At the peak of my career at

Warner Bros.," he wrote in his autobiography, "I was in the ninety-four percent tax bracket. . . . When you have to give up such a large percentage of your income in taxes, incentive to work goes down. You don't say, 'I've got to do more pictures,' you say, 'I'm not gonna work for six cents on the dollar.' . . .

"The same principle that affected my thinking applied to people in all tax brackets: . . . What coal miner or assembly-line worker jumps at the offer of overtime when he knows Uncle Sam is going to take sixty percent or more of his extra pay? . . .

"A few economists call this principle supply-side economics. I just call it common sense."

Like Thatcher, Reagan knew that reversing long-entrenched practices and assumptions would not be the work of one season. By concerted pressure on Congress—exercised in part by going directly to the American people via television and, as he put it, "ask[ing] their help to persuade the legislators to vote as *they* wanted, not in the way special-interest groups did"—he got his first tax cut passed in 1981. That September, *NR* reported: "Although rate reductions on personal income tax will not come into effect in any significant magnitude until July 1982, the President's economic program is already being declared a failure. On August 31, the *Los Angeles Times* editorialized that 'it would be far less painful' to reverse course now and to raise taxes before the President's economic program gnaws away much longer at the economy and the American people." Shades of Ted Heath's "U-turn"!

The other part of the plan was reducing spending. Conservatives had high hopes that a significant part of Heritage's program would be put into play. Why *not* abolish the Energy Department and drastically cut the Education Department? What do they *do*? But one thing they do is provide jobs for many, and those many found it far more appealing to lobby their congressmen than to contemplate productive employment. The Reaganites had to fight for every cut in every regulatory agency, board, or program, and they didn't get nearly as many as they wanted.

Reagan later recalled that the 1983 G-7 economic summit, which he hosted in Colonial Williamsburg, took place "just as the economic turnaround in the United States was beginning to gain a strong head of steam." The Misery Index had dropped from 19.33 in January 1981 to 11.86 in July 1983. At dinner the first evening of the summit, Helmut Kohl, the new (and quite conservative) chancellor of

West Germany, spoke up: "Tell us about the American miracle." So Reagan did, talking of cutting tax rates, "eliminating unnecessary regulations and interference in the free market," and turning functions government had usurped back to the private sector. The other heads of state listened, and "It wasn't long after that that I began reading about a wave of tax cutting in several of their countries." Even Thatcher, who had preceded him and who eventually was able to carry her reforms much further, frequently told Reagan that, as he put it, "her ability to point to the success of our policies in the United States had made it easier for her to convince Britons the policies had merit."

As the Reagan years were beginning, so was a campus phenomenon that would have far-reaching consequences. By the 1980s, the men and women who had been student radicals in the 1960s were making their way in their careers, many of them as university professors or administrators. To a much higher degree than had been true when Buckley wrote *God and Man*, even formerly conservative universities with fairly conservative trustees were being dragged left, and "political correctness" (thus dubbed by a young campus cartoonist, who picked up the old Marxist phrase and turned it ironic) was being imposed relentlessly. One of the oddball specifics was that any mascot or symbol having to do with American Indians was deemed not friendly but demeaning. And so the Dartmouth Indian came under heavy-handed attack.

Dartmouth professor Jeffrey Hart had various venues outside Dartmouth to express his contempt for the newly PC university administration, chiefly *National Review* and his syndicated column. There was really not much Dartmouth could do to him. He was tenured and, unlike Willmoore Kendall at Yale, was not continually asking for leaves of absence. Colleagues could haze him, but Jeff thrives on controversy—his favorite stance, like Kendall's, is *contra mundum*. Jeff picked up numerous allies and admirers among the Dartmouth students, and in 1981 the *Dartmouth Review* was founded, with Jeffrey Hart as its faculty patron. Soon conservative newspapers were being founded on many other campuses, with the backing of venerable conservative organizations like ISI, headed now by Vic Milione, and newer ones like the Smith Richardson Foundation, headed by Les Lenkowsky.

The *Dartmouth Review* claimed to be modeling itself, at least in its political stance, on *National Review.* This was flattering, except that the *Dartmouth Review* frequently went further in one direction or another than *NR* was happy about. Still, the paper has given aid and comfort to Dartmouth conservatives for twenty-five years now, has confounded the ungodly in the faculty and administration, and has produced a satisfying number of professional journalists and policy experts. Dartmouth grad and *NR* alumnus Paul Gigot is not one of these, only because he was born too soon: when the *Review* was founded, he expressed his intense regret that it hadn't come along ten years earlier. But the list includes Dinesh D'Souza, Laura Ingraham, Peter Robinson (who has now fought his way onto the Dartmouth board of trustees), Ben Hart (Jeff's eldest son), James Panero, Alston Ramsay (who put in two years at *NR* before going to the Defense Department), and Joseph Rago (of the *Wall Street Journal*). Chris Baldwin was suspended from Dartmouth at one point, for his role in demolishing some "shantytowns" (symbolizing opposition to the South African government) on the Dartmouth green. He spent his months of exile at *NR*, where he served as financial manager for BuckPAC.

BuckPAC was one of Bill and Priscilla's many great jokes with a serious point: it was a PAC founded by the Buckley family to defeat one of the few human beings this side of Stalin in whom Bill can find no good, Lowell Weicker. (This campaign, scrupulously independent of the official campaign run by Democrat Joseph Lieberman, succeeded, and Weicker was removed from the Senate.)

The *Dartmouth Review* still gets under the skin of campus leftists, faculty and students alike, but it's almost hard to recall how acrimonious some of the early battles were. The most incredible yielded the headline: ADMINISTRATOR BITES STUDENT. Ben Hart was trying to distribute copies of the *Review*, and the associate director of the Alumni Fund, Samuel Stewart, was trying to stop him; Stewart started hitting Hart, Hart got him in a headlock, and Stewart literally bit Hart in the side, deeply enough to send him to the hospital for bandaging and a tetanus shot.

William P. Clark, Reagan's second national security advisor (Dick Allen had been driven from office on charges concerning—incredible as it may sound in these post-Clinton days—a gift of cuff links), recalls a meeting with the President near the end of his first year in

Washington. "At the end of 1981 he called us into the Oval Office and said, 'Gentlemen, our concentration has been on domestic matters this year, and I want to roll the sleeves up now and get to foreign policy, defense, and intelligence.'"

This would doubtless have been Reagan's agenda anyway. He had already asserted his determination to rebuild America's badly neglected military, symbolized by the Desert One helicopter that crashed and burned, killing all its occupants; he had issued to Chairman Brezhnev his first "zero option" challenge on intermediate-range nuclear forces in Europe; and he had charged Bill Casey with finding some way to help the opposition to the Sandinistas in Nicaragua. But the agenda was given special urgency by the imposition of martial law in Poland on December 13, after a heady year and a half of escalating action by Solidarity.

In that Oval Office meeting Reagan added, "By the way, lean on our experience in Sacramento. Take a leaf from our book out there"— namely, the task forces that had proved so effective. Thus were born the National Security Decision Directives, studying the Soviet Union and our relations with it. The most important of these would be NSDD-75, completed in December 1982. As Clark recalls, "My covering memo stated that U.S. policy towards the Soviet Union would consist of three elements: first, external resistance to Soviet imperialism; second, internal pressure on the USSR to weaken the sources of Soviet imperialism; and third, negotiations to eliminate, on the basis of strict reciprocity, outstanding disagreements."

The first element would include assistance to the Nicaraguan opposition (later called the Contras) and to Jonas Savimbi in Angola, and Stinger missiles to the mujahedin in Afghanistan (no doubt brokered by Ambassador Buckley?). The third would include the START talks, successor to SALT, with the goal of strategic arms *reduction* replacing the goal of strategic arms *limitation*. The second was the really radical element. As Clark puts it, "Internal pressure on the USSR represented a new objective of U.S. policy." It would include ceasing to subsidize the Soviet Union through trade; communicating directly with the Soviet people through three new Liberty radio stations; and pushing the Soviets beyond their economy's capacity to match our own military buildup. Above all, it included rejecting the theory adopted back in the 1960s by Robert McNamara and his whiz kids at the Pentagon, which American presidents had followed ever since: deterrence of nuclear war through Mutual Assured Destruction.

This theory, Reagan and *National Review* had long believed, was, as its acronym suggested, quite MAD. But *National Review* could only argue against it. Reagan could do something about it, and he did. To a public reaction that mostly ranged from scoffing to outrage, he proposed the Strategic Defense Initiative—dubbed by its friends the Space Shield, and by its foes Star Wars. Among its greatest friends were Bill Buckley and *National Review*. Buckley engaged physicist Robert Jastrow to write a regular feature in the editorial section, "SDI Watch," reporting on advances (and setbacks) in the development of SDI and attacks on it in the media. Its greatest foes were in the Kremlin. They decried it as an offensive weapon. This was manifestly untrue in the literal sense: the weapons envisioned could not have blown up a single Soviet citizen or city. But in another sense it was profoundly true. In line with NSDD-75, by forcing the Kremlin to expend resources to counter it, SDI was a powerful force in the eventual dissolution of the Soviet empire.

February 23, 1983, was a great day for *NR* old-timers. On that day President Reagan conferred the Presidential Medal of Freedom on James Burnham. The only sadness was that Marcia wasn't there: to everyone's shock, and Jim's deep bereavement, she had died the previous August, after a brief respiratory illness that at first looked entirely treatable, but then quickly worsened.

But Jim clearly enjoyed the ceremony, which, with his characteristic understatement, he later described as "a bit of all right." With his three children and Priscilla Buckley in attendance, he heard the President read out his formal citation: "As a scholar, writer, historian and philosopher, James Burnham has profoundly affected the way America views itself and the world. Since the 1930s, Mr. Burnham has shaped the thinking of world leaders. His observations have changed society and his writings have become guiding lights in mankind's quest for truth. Freedom, reason and decency have had few greater champions in this century than James Burnham." Then, as Priscilla reported in *NR*, "The President's face crinkles in a smile. 'I owe him a personal debt,' he tells the audience, 'because'—turning to Burnham—'throughout the years traveling the mashed-potato circuit I have quoted you widely.'"

Nine other Americans (including Bill's old friend and frequent *NR* contributor Clare Boothe Luce) received their country's highest civilian honor that day. But two days before, Reagan had graced a strictly *National Review* celebration. The occasion: the opening of *NR*'s first official Washington office.

NR had had a Washington presence from the beginning, starting with senior editor Brent Bozell and columnist Sam Jones. But Buckley had always resisted pressures from various sources to move our principal office to D.C. There was, first, the obvious reason: as he told that interviewer, where he wants to live is "Where I live," and Washington would be a heck of a commute from Stamford. But there is also the nature of Washington, D.C. It is a company town with a vengeance, and that company is the federal government. Washington tends to suck its denizens, however conservative they may be, into believing that what the government does is the most important thing on earth. *National Review* was founded in opposition to that notion, and it's easier, Buckley reasoned, to keep that in mind from somewhere else.

However, having a satellite office inside the Beltway made a lot of sense, particularly when we acquired a new Washington editor who needed a base of operations. John McLaughlin was our second defrocked Jesuit (though the two did not serve at *NR* simultaneously: Malachi Martin had long since gone off to other pursuits and had been replaced as religion editor by the former-leftist-turned-traditionalist Michael Novak). It was Tony Dolan who brought McLaughlin to Buckley's attention. Buckley liked his work and hired him, and now here we were in a ballroom at the Madison Hotel with scores of conservative writers, activists, congressmen, and administration members, all assembled to hear our own senior editors welcome the President, and the President welcome our higher Washington profile.

One of the present authors was standing with Tony Dolan and Aram Bakshian as the President made his remarks, in which he repeated that statement we love to hear: "I think you know that *National Review* is my favorite magazine." As Reagan gently roasted Bills Rusher and Buckley, Bakshian, who had drafted the speech, interjected occasional sotto voce comments: "Oh good—he kept that line. . . . Ahh, that's one of his. . . . That's his. . . . He changed that a bit." This writer doesn't now remember which of the following were Bakshian's lines and which the President's own, but whoever wrote them, they went over like hotcakes with a very happy bunch of conservatives: "There's a problem, though, Bill, that I think you should

"Let Buckley be Buckley."
Looking on (from left to right):
Rick Brookhiser, Priscilla
Buckley, Joe Sobran, Jeff Hart.

know about. It's all the talk about your being aloof and insensitive and an out-of-touch editor. People are saying that you spend too much time away from New York. They're also saying you're being pushed around by your staff. And I understand there's a new button on the market, 'Let Buckley be Buckley.'"

In 1979, in the tiny Caribbean island of Grenada, a group of indigenous Communists, with heavy Cuban and Soviet backing, ousted the government of Eric Gairy and installed one of their own, Maurice Bishop, as prime minister. There followed four tumultuous years, during which Bishop called in Cubans to build a new "international airport" that observers found suspiciously large. Over that period, the Grenadian economy worsened drastically, and Bishop's New Jewel Movement split into factions. Then in October 1983 some of the hardest-liners in New Jewel killed Bishop, took over the government, and gave every indication of intending to turn Grenada into a fortress state. On October 21 the Organization of Eastern Caribbean States asked the U.S. government to intervene and depose the new strongman, Bernard Coard. As Reagan later recalled the OECS's communication, "Unless [the Communists] were stopped, the Caribbean neighbors said, it was just a matter of time before the Grenadians and Castro moved on *their* countries."

Meanwhile, in the Middle East, Syrian-dominated Lebanon had given refuge to Yassir Arafat's Palestine Liberation Organization, and the PLO was using its encampments in southern Lebanon as bases for conducting raids into northern Israel. The PLO attacks and the Israeli retaliations both escalated, until finally Prime Minister Menachem Begin authorized General Ariel Sharon to launch a heavy bombardment of Beirut. Sharon did not spare civilian neighborhoods, and President Reagan, in his note to Begin, quite deliberately described the bombardment as a "holocaust." In an attempt to restore order, Reagan agreed to send a detachment of marines to Lebanon as part of an international peacekeeping force.

The invasion of Grenada was being prepared in strictest secrecy, lest a leak endanger (a) the mission and (b) the eight hundred Americans attending medical school in Grenada. The night before it was to be launched, President Reagan was awakened with the horrendous news that a suicide bomber had rammed a truck filled with dynamite into the marine barracks in Lebanon, killing all 241 marines stationed there. (The same night, a similar truck bomb was driven into a French barracks, killing 58 French soldiers.)

Despite the grief and shock over the Lebanon disaster—and despite an eleventh-hour phone call from Margaret Thatcher, who had somehow learned of the Grenada operation and was furious that her friend would invade a Commonwealth country without even notifying her—Reagan nonetheless went ahead with Grenada. The invasion proved a stunning success. It turned out, among other things, that the Cuban "construction crews" included seven hundred crack troops, fully armed. Relieved of Bishop and New Jewel, Grenada recovered and became once again a true jewel of the Caribbean.

NR editorially criticized Reagan for having put the marines in harm's way in Lebanon when it was not at all clear what their mission was, or what mission could have been accomplished by so few men. Grenada was another matter. Brian Crozier spoke for the magazine when he wrote about "the lesson of Grenada." Under the Brezhnev Doctrine, Soviet gains were regarded as irreversible. But now, Crozier wrote, "The irreversible has been reversed. Soviet imperial power has been rolled back, if only to the extent of 100,000 people and 133 square miles. Not much? It is enormous in significance."

Bill Buckley has often enough spotted storm warnings ahead, pulled down his cap, and sailed straight on. This was so with his first three books, as also with innumerable positions taken on *Firing Line*, in

"On the Right," and in *National Review*. But it never occurred to him that he was sailing into treacherous seas when he wrote *Overdrive*, a second week-in-the-life book, sequel to *Cruising Speed*. Different reviewers had liked *Cruising Speed* to different degrees, but few who bothered to write about it disliked it. *Overdrive* was another matter. Critics went apoplectic—not, mostly, about Buckley's political statements, but about his descriptions of what they would call his "lifestyle."

Among other things, he wrote about his limousine and how he had had it customized, so that he and Jerry could exercise separate preferences about temperature, for instance, and music. He wrote also about the wonderful work his friend the painter and sculptor Robert Goodnough had done in decorating the indoor swimming pool at Wallacks Point. Bill had written about these things in deference to the craftsmen who had performed the work; his critics saw these passages as evidence of grotesque self-indulgence and self-regard.

And the critics weren't just leftists disposed to dislike Buckley. One of the present authors knows two couples, close friends who spend a lot of time together. All four of these people are thoughtful conservatives and Buckley fans. When the excerpt from *Overdrive* came out in *The New Yorker*, all four read it immediately. Both husbands found it delightful; both wives were embarrassed and disappointed.

But good did come out of the whole episode. One of the critics, an undergraduate at the University of Chicago, had couched his complaints in a satire that tickled Bill's funny bone. For example: "Buckley spent most of his infancy working on his memoirs. By the time he had learned how to talk he had finished three volumes: *The World Before Buckley*, which traced the history of the world prior to his conception; *The Seeds of Utopia*, which outlined his effect on world events during the nine months of his gestation; and *The Glorious Dawn*, which described the profound ramifications of his birth on the social order." The next time *NR* had an appropriate opening, Bill hired the satirist, David Brooks, and thereby launched his adult career.

Honoring James Burnham had taken some courage, but in 1984 Reagan took an even bigger plunge: he gave the Medal of Freedom posthumously to Whittaker Chambers. And oh! what a fuss that stirred up. As Bill tells it,

The conversation went something like this:

> Q *(over the telephone):* Mr. Buckley, we are doing a story on the decision of President Reagan to give the Medal of Freedom to Whittaker Chambers. Do you know why Chambers is being given the award this year?
>
> A: No, I don't.
>
> Q: You mean, you don't think he should be given the award this year?
>
> A: No, I mean I don't know why he wasn't given the award last year. Or the year before that, as far as that goes.
>
> Q: Oh. Well, you know, there has been a considerable amount of controversy about giving the Medal of Freedom Award to someone who lied under oath.
>
> A: Whittaker Chambers did a lot worse than lie under oath. He engaged in treasonable activities against the United States.
>
> Q: Well then, you think it's all right, just the same, to give a confessed perjurer the Medal of Freedom?
>
> A: It seems to me the settled Christian position on such questions is that we view a man's work with attention to where he arrived, rather than where he came from. Otherwise it would be hard to have a high opinion of St. Paul.
>
> Q: But St. Paul didn't lie under oath, did he?
>
> A: I don't know. But he tortured and killed and persecuted a lot of people.

We didn't, as one can quickly gather, get very far. Friends of Whittaker Chambers, indeed friends of freedom, knew that the decision by Ronald Reagan, easily the most arresting, courageous, and admirable choice for a Freedom Medal winner made in our time, would rouse the old fever-swamp denizens to furies of ignorance and philistinism. The cartoonist Sanders of the *Milwaukee Journal* pictures Reagan, the medal in hand, laying it on a wreath of Whittaker Chambers, with the citation: "For your outstanding contribution to the McCarthy era." The cartoonist evidently is unaware that Chambers opposed Senator McCarthy, and that there is a difference between identifying someone who was (and may still be) a Communist, like Alger Hiss, and someone who wasn't, or wasn't proved to be one (like Dorothy Kenyon). . . .

To speak of Chambers as the man who fingered Hiss and hid the documents in a pumpkin and who earlier on lied to a congressional committee (in an attempt to save Hiss from more severe treatment) is—there is no other word for it—sheer philistinism.

*   *   *

From a policy viewpoint, Reagan's 1984 campaign was a no-brainer. It was, as the ads put it, morning in America: "It's morning again in America. Today more men and women will go to work than ever before in our country's history. With interest rates and inflation down more people are buying new homes. And our new families can have confidence in the future. America today is prouder and stronger and better. Why would we want to return to where we were less than four short years ago?"

Why indeed? The economy had made a dramatic recovery that was seen as a direct result of tax cuts. Inflation was down, as were unemployment and the nation's poverty rate; jobs and wages were up; and the GNP was growing. As for foreign policy, Reagan was the first world leader to write the obituary for Communism. In 1983, he put it this way: "I believe that Communism is another sad, bizarre chapter in human history whose last pages even now are being written." And he, with strong editorial assistance from Margaret Thatcher, had authored several of those pages.

With all this brightness and optimism, the Reaganites could be forgiven for feeling extremely confident. The nomination in Dallas was in effect a coronation, and that summer Reagan, in Los Angeles, became the first president to open an Olympics, which American athletes proceeded to dominate.

It was, indeed, morning in America, and the Reagan campaign's prospects brightened even more at the Democratic convention, when Walter Mondale, a gray ghost from crises past, received the nomination and immediately promised to raise taxes.

So positive were the omens that Reagan accepted his advisors' game plan and ran a leisurely modified Rose Garden campaign, counting on surrogates and TV ads to do most of the heavy lifting through the summer and into early autumn. But then, on October 7, the first debate was held in Louisville, and suddenly the clouds rolled in. Reagan stumbled repeatedly in exchanges, lost track of his thoughts, seemed to be reciting unrelated facts and figures, and at one point said to the moderator, Barbara Walters, "I'm all confused now."

Stunningly, the man who had demolished Jimmy Carter with four words—the Great Communicator—seemed overnight to have lost his ability to think and talk. For the next two weeks, with the second debate scheduled for October 21 in Kansas City, policy questions took a back seat to the resurrected issue of Reagan's age.

In his splendid book on the 1984 election, *The Outside Story: How Democrats and Republicans Reelected Reagan*, Rick Brookhiser put it this way:

> Questions of health and age had dogged Reagan through the early phase of his 1980 campaign. . . . Reagan, if elected, would become the oldest man to be inaugurated; the oldest up till that time, William Henry Harrison, had died thirty days after taking the oath of office, a not very auspicious precedent. Concern over Reagan's age coincided with the enervation of his campaign. After New Hampshire, it had vanished; after Hinckley's bullets, it had seemed like a joke. Now it all came flooding back. *The Wall Street Journal*, the morning after the debate, ran a long health story, obviously prepared in advance in case some loss of physical or mental edge occurred, and made timely with the reaction of "experts." "I am very concerned," said one, "as a psychologist." Another helpfully suggested a few simple senility tests that Reagan might take, such as counting backwards from 100 by sevens. . . . The potential problem was not fantastic. Twice already in this century—in Reagan's lifetime, if not in anyone else's—the country had had incapacitated leaders. Woodrow Wilson, after a series of strokes, spent his last two years in office a non-functioning wreck. Franklin D. Roosevelt began deteriorating physically as early as 1940; by 1944, he was in bed eighteen hours a day.

Thus, for the second debate in Kansas City, the issue was joined: not the arms race, not the deficit, not taxation or supply-side economics, but Reagan's age, pure and simple. The subject dominated the election coverage. The networks ran and reran the clips of Reagan dozing off at the Vatican and various verbal fluffs and stumbles that up until that moment hadn't been thought worth airing. For those two weeks between the debates, the race seemed on among the media to see who could most effectively portray the President as someone's senile Uncle Dudley.

Finally, the evening of the debate arrived, and after some unremarkable rhetoric on both sides, the *Baltimore Sun*'s Henry Trewhitt raised the issue: "Mr. President, you already are the oldest president in history, and some of your staff say you were tired after your most recent encounter with Mr. Mondale. I recall that President Kennedy had to go for days on end with very little sleep during the Cuban missile crisis. Is there any doubt in your mind that you would be able to function in such circumstances?"

Reagan: "Not at all, Mr. Trewhitt. And I want you to know that also I will not make age an issue of this campaign. I am not going to exploit for political purposes my opponent's youth and inexperience."

That was it. A home run, with the bases loaded. Just to make it official, Trewhitt responded: "Mr. President, I would like to head for the fence and catch that one before it goes over."

But go over it did. To his eternal credit, Mondale, instead of gnashing his teeth, started to laugh. And it was pretty much his last laugh of the campaign. With those thirty-seven words, Reagan was judged to have won the debate. His lead in the polls resumed widening, and in November he defeated Mondale—and old-line establishment liberalism—by historic margins. Reagan became the first presidential candidate to receive more than fifty million votes, won the most electoral votes ever recorded, and in the process completely reversed the debacle of 1964. He marked the twentieth anniversary of Goldwater's defeat by registering a popular-vote margin against Mondale larger than the margin Johnson had run up against Goldwater.

Bill Buckley and his brothers had all married in their twenties, but times and mores had changed, and Christopher was still single at thirty. Finally, in 1984, he became engaged to Lucy Gregg, younger daughter of Vice President Bush's old friend Donald Gregg and his wife, Margaret. Lucy, a lovely and rather shy young woman, a Phi Beta Kappa from Williams College, was working at the State Department when she and Chris met. The wedding took place in Washington, D.C., on December 8, 1984.

Some observers remarked that Pat seemed rather grim throughout the celebrations and assumed that she was unhappy with her only son's choice. In fact, she was in physical agony. She had inherited her mother's propensity to arthritis, and in the spring of 1979, just before Christopher went sailing to Bamboola, she had had a hip replacement. The technology has since improved, but at that time Pat was younger than doctors liked to do hip replacement, for fear of having to do it again in fifteen or twenty years when the artificial joint wore out. But the pain and lack of mobility were seriously interfering with one of her great joys, gardening, and she went ahead. Now, not fifteen or twenty but just five years later, something had gone badly wrong.

It turned out that the prosthesis would have to be replaced. And this was the season when HIV had been found in some blood supplies, and patients needing nonemergency surgery were advised to stockpile their own blood in advance of the operation. So Pat stayed home that winter, methodically giving blood, while Bill went to Switzerland to write his next Blackford Oakes novel, *High Jinx*. The one upside: when Christopher brought his bride to Rougemont that winter, Lucy had to acclimate only to her formidable but mostly cheerful father-in-law, and not simultaneously to her equally formidable and frequently caustic mother-in-law.

Aloïse Buckley had always seemed a bit scatterbrained—although reading about her, one gets more the impression that when her mind made the leap from one thing to another she simply didn't slow down to fill in the connection for her interlocutor. In any case, she did truly start becoming vague after a cataract operation in the 1970s. The family's privately published memoir about her is full of hilarious accounts of confusions. (Hilarious but also sad. However, she retained her personality even as she lost her memory, and people found it hard to feel sad around her.) There was the time she was trying to telephone an old friend of her late husband's, and as she was dialing directory assistance her son John reminded her that the man she wanted to talk with was dead. Undeterred, she placed her call: "Hello, operator. . . . Yes, I need to speak to Caracas, Venezuela. . . . I need to know the number for a Mr. Warren Smith, oh, and operator, he's dead." Or the time she introduced her son Jim to a woman named Ann, saying what a lovely couple they would make—as indeed they had been doing for twenty-five years.

Gradually her physical health started to fail as well, and the family found a fine nursing home in the neighborhood of Sharon and Lakeville, where John Buckley lived. Then on December 1, 1984, John died of complications of alcoholism. As Bill wrote in his obituary of his mother:

> She was by then in a comfortable retirement home, totally absent-minded; she knew us all, but was vague about when last she had seen us, or where, and was given to making references, every now and then, to her husband, "Will," and the trip they planned next week to Paris, or Mexico.

But [when John died] she sensed what had happened, and instructed her nurse . . . to drive her to the cemetery, and there, unknown to us until later that afternoon, she saw from her car, at the edge of an assembly of cars, her oldest son lowered into the earth. He had been visiting her every day, often taking her to a local restaurant for lunch, and her grief was, by her standards, convulsive; but she did not break her record—she never broke it—which was never, ever to complain, because, she explained, she could never repay God the favors He had done her, no matter what tribulations she might need to suffer.

In February 1985 she started slipping away. As Priscilla quoted the doctors, it was nothing specific, just the whole system winding down. She died two weeks later. All her surviving children and their spouses, and most of her fifty grandchildren and *their* spouses and children, came to the requiem Mass in Sharon, as did much of the *National Review* staff. ("Fifty grandchildren" is a precise number, not a rounding off: number 50 was John Alois Buckley, son of Reid with his lovely second wife, Tasa.) The gathering at Great Elm afterward was not at all gloomy. Even those who were not of Aloïse's faith felt some of it rub off onto them. The next day, Bill chartered a plane, and he and his siblings, along with a few friends, flew with Aloïse's body down to Camden for a memorial service and her burial there, next to her beloved Will.

That same spring Bill's sixth novel was published—one of his best (and also the biggest seller of the Oakes series), *See You Later Alligator*. The colloquies between Blackford and Che Guevara are scintillating and entirely believable, and the action is gripping, as Blackford, his fearless colleague Cecilio Velasco, and the interpreter with whom Blackford has an affair that is more than merely fleshly, Catalina Urrutia, learn the truth about the Soviet missiles in Cuba and have to find a way to get the word back to President Kennedy.

Mentioning Cecilio Velasco brings up an added attraction of the novels for people who are part of Bill's (extremely wide) circle. As we started reading each new novel, we would wonder which real-life friend or associate would lend something to a character in this one. Mixing observed elements with things read about and things purely imagined is presumably the way most novelists work. (Ross Hoffman was a highly regarded American historian, but, as he confided in a letter to the editor published in an early *NR*, his proudest boast was that he was Evelyn Waugh's model for Mr. Scott-King in *Scott-King's Modern Europe*.) But as we read Bill's novels we could actually see part of the mixture taking shape. Bill's character Velasco took his name and his personal mannerisms from Will Buckley's friend and colleague—but the real-life Velasco was never a Communist, was born in Mexico, not Spain, and did not see his fiancée die in an intra-Soviet rivalry. Michael Bolgiano in *Marco Polo if You Can* looks and speaks like Bill's Yale classmate Dino Pionzio, and shares Dino's generously accommodating friendship; but Dino's father was not a Communist, and Dino lived to retire from the CIA. Dimitri Chadinoff in *Stained Glass* takes his name from another associate of Will Buckley's, but in personality Dimitri and his wife, Anna, are basically Vladimir and Vera Nabokov; however, the Chadinoffs' daughter, Erika, bears no resemblance to the Nabokovs' son, Dmitri, a skiing friend of Bill's. Anthony Trust, Blackford's oldest friend, doesn't look like Van Galbraith, but in style of humor and ability to take the edge off an uncomfortable situation they are as one.

As for Bill himself, that reviewer of *Saving the Queen* was quite right that Blackford is not Bill's alter ego. But, Bill's admirers would maintain, the reviewer was right for the wrong reasons. The principal ways in which Blackford does *not* resemble Bill are their respective career paths and an important part of their personal behavior (as Taki Theodoracopulos has said of Bill, he's "so good-looking and yet so monogamous"). However, Bill does give Blackford some of his own characteristics—his impatience, mounting to agony, if deprived of reading matter when alone; his hatred of obsequiousness; his "slouchy informality."

Partly because of the administration in power, partly because of seeds sown long before in various institutions, suddenly, in the early 1980s, the right was the place to be. In the 1970s a young man named George Gilder had written two books that were acclaimed by conservatives and reviled by liberals: *Sexual Suicide* and *Naked Nomads*. Now, in 1982, he wrote *Wealth and Poverty*; it became a bestseller, and he went from being regarded as a quirky antifeminist to being a respected public figure.

Another new star, Jude Wanniski, was a friend and supporter of Arthur Laffer, whose Curve illustrated Reagan's perception that increased tax rates bring in increased revenues only up to a point, after which point taxpayers, being sentient creatures, stop working so hard or find some way to shelter their earnings. The Laffer Curve had given Representative Jack Kemp and Senator William Roth the idea for their tax-cutting bill—the first Reagan tax cut, signed into law in August 1981. It also gave Wanniski the idea for his big book, *The Way the World Works*, which brought him nationwide prominence.

Many academic or quasi-academic writers were making a big mark. Thomas Sowell, based at the Hoover Institution, was writing his down-to-earth social commentary. Walter Williams, at George Mason University, was popularizing his academic work on economic topics such as labor policy and taxation. At the University of Chicago, Gary Becker was applying his "rational choice" economics to a whole range of topics more usually the purview of sociologists: family size, crime deterrence, racial discrimination. Also at Chicago, Ronald Coase was working on "law and economics"—reconciling competing interests through monetary payments rather than outright government prohibitions. Coase won the Nobel Prize in 1991, and gave a brilliant keynote address to the Philadelphia Society (of which he was a member) the following year. Becker won the Nobel Prize in 1992.

Tom Wolfe was already a very big deal, but in 1987 he published his first novel, *Bonfire of the Vanities*, and became a household word. Even people who have never read the novel know the general shape of the plot, and some of Wolfe's phrases ("master of the universe," "social X-ray") have entered our everyday language.

Also not a new face, but new to *National Review*'s circles, was John P. Roche. He had been a chairman of Americans for Democratic Action in the 1950s and had served in both the Kennedy and Johnson administrations. But as Reagan put it, first in speaking of himself and then in wooing Democratic voters, "You haven't left the Democratic Party—the Democratic Party left you." In the 1950s Roche earned a place in Buckley's hall of fame with his reply to a question about the McCarthy Reign of Terror. "Well," said Roche, "I rank McCarthy as 26th on my list of fears. He comes in just after #25, my fear of university presidents, and just before #27, my fear of being eaten alive by piranha fish." In the late 1960s Roche was a university administrator who didn't give in to The Kids and who didn't retire in trauma. In the 1970s he was appalled by the left turn of so many prominent Democrats. He started writing a syndicated column, mostly on foreign affairs, titled "A Word Edgewise from an

Old Liberal Cold Warrior." In 1981, Buckley started running it in *NR*. Roche had a wealth of stories and pungent one-liners. He liked to say, "I knew Henry Kissinger before he had a German accent," and he told the story of going to visit Averell Harriman on some Democratic mission. "The Governor is looking awfully well," he said to Pamela Harriman when her husband stepped out of the room. "You'd look awfully well too," said Pamela, "if you'd done nothing till you were thirty except play polo and f—.") But the comment one of the present authors treasures most has a direct bearing on some of the taxonomical questions we have explored in this book. This writer was talking on the phone with Roche about some point of domestic policy, and she said to him, "Why, John! You sound like a Disraeli Tory."

"No!" he thundered, with an audible thump of fist on desk. "A Catholic syndicalist." But in this case, the two points of view converged.

Leonid Brezhnev had died in November 1982 and been succeeded by Yuri Andropov. Westerners were eager for something new after the dour Brezhnev and the shoe-banging Khrushchev, and Andropov seemed to fit the bill. Unlike any of his predecessors, he wore well-tailored Western-style suits, and it soon was learned that he loved American jazz and drank Scotch instead of vodka. He was also, however, a longtime head of the KGB, and while he knew the Soviet economy needed serious reform, he had no intention of loosening the Kremlin's reins. Markus Wolf, the fabled head of the foreign division of East Germany's Stasi, thought Andropov might have been able to bring it off—energizing the economy without giving personal liberty to the people. We doubt it, for the reasons cited by Hayek and Mises and Friedman and Hazlitt: Central planning boards are a blunt instrument; they can't replicate the millions of bits of information supplied by the free workings of the market. But Andropov didn't have much time to try: already ailing when he took office, he died of kidney failure in February 1984, aged only sixty-nine.

He was succeeded by an undistinguished apparatchik named Konstantin Chernenko, three years his senior and also ailing. John O'Sullivan tells the story about Margaret Thatcher going to Andropov's funeral. As the car is leaving 10 Downing Street, an aide thinks to ask

Mrs. Thatcher whether she has snow boots with her; he insists she will need them. She grumbles, but directs the car to detour via Marks & Spencer, where she buys a pair. She grumbles more about the cost of an item she will probably never need a second time. On the return journey, however, she congratulates the aide on his perspicacity. Having seen Chernenko, she tells him, she's quite sure they'll be going back to Moscow before long.

Exactly thirteen months later, on March 10, 1985, Chernenko died. This time the successor really did seem to be different. Mikhail Gorbachev was also an apparatchik, but he was twenty years younger than Chernenko—he was, in fact, the first Soviet general secretary to have been born after the Revolution. He had some Western tastes, and his wife, Raisa, bore no resemblance at all to poor old Nina Khrushchev or Viktoria Brezhnev. Conservatives wondered if the Iron Lady was going soft when she welcomed his accession: "I like Mr. Gorbachev—we can do business together." But we watched with skeptical fascination as he introduced his *perestroika* and *glasnost*.

December 1985. It's *NR* anniversary time again, and for once we can't complain about the traffic tie-ups. Manhattan goes into gridlock when the President comes to town, and normally the *NR* crew grumbles along with everyone else. But this time it was *our* President coming to *our* party.

We didn't even grumble at the security checks slowing our passage to the Plaza's Grand Ballroom. When a Secret Service man with a German shepherd hesitated to squeeze into an elevator full of people in evening dress, one man said jovially, "Come on in. You're among friends."

Bill himself had done the seating for the head tables, as he always does for major *NR* events. He placed Priscilla at Reagan's right, Clare Luce at his left. He placed himself at Nancy Reagan's left, George Will at her right. Pat had Jack Kemp and Charlton Heston as her dinner partners. Heston was the MC (Bill had ghostwritten his script), and Bill's favorite jazz pianist, Dick Wellstood, handled the interludes. A bittersweet part of the evening was that Priscilla Buckley had announced her retirement as managing editor (she would continue to work halftime as a senior editor). She was given a rousing sendoff by a graduate, summa cum laude, of "the Priscilla Buckley School of Journalistic Craftsmanship," George Will. Her reply to George's toast

The First Lady, flanked by admirers GFW and WFB, with Norman Podhoretz in foreground.

began: "As is well known to my friends and colleagues, I rarely speak in public. But both times I have been forced to speak, the President of the United States has been in the audience. Now I'm getting the hang of it. The Pope of Rome had better watch out."

After Priscilla came the one we had been waiting for ever since our disappointment at the twenty-fifth anniversary, El Presidente. He gave us a substantial, meaty speech about the advances of freedom around the world and the role American conservatives had played in fostering those advances. But he spoke, too, about how we were gathered to "celebrate thirty years of witty, civilized pages from our beloved *National Review* and the damage, the terminal damage, those pages have done to modern statism and its unrelenting grimness." He paid the tribute to "our clipboard-bearing Galahad" quoted in the prelude to this book, and then closed (try to imagine Richard Nixon speaking these words): "So, Bill, one last word to you. We thank you for your friendship. You are, of course, a great man. And so we thank you also for *National Review*, for setting loose so much good in the world. And, Bill—thanks, too, for all the fun.

"God bless you."

There were stirrings back at 150 East 35th Street. Our beloved Reagan administration had acted like a cuckoo in the nest and taken Kevin Lynch away from us, to work for Voice of America. He had been succeeded by a young man whom Rick Brookhiser knew from the Party of the Right at Yale, Richard Vigilante. Someone—maybe Jeff Hart, maybe Joe Sobran—noted the piquancy of an editor named Lynch being succeeded by one named Vigilante. Now Priscilla's semi-retirement led Bill to appoint Rick managing editor, with a view to his eventually succeeding Bill as editor. Rick, Rich, and Linda formed a sort of troika (we're not feminists but we are aspiring Latinists, and you can't say "triumvirate" when one of the three is a woman) in charge of the article section. However, Bill still had the final say on what ran and, on occasion, when it ran. A memorable instance involved an essay on Harold Macmillan by Alistair Horne, Bill's old friend and Macmillan's official biographer. Horne had accepted Macmillan's condition that no part of the biography would go into print during Macmillan's lifetime. Horne had given Bill the essay—actually an excerpt from the book—around 1980, and as of 1986 we were still holding it. Then in December 1986 Macmillan died—on the weekend before "magazine week," that is, near the end of our fortnightly publication cycle. In principle, the article section was supposed to be more or less final by the Friday preceding magazine week. In this case, it was less: Put in the Horne piece, Bill told Linda on Monday morning. Rich was shocked when he got the word—surely someone who had been out of the public eye as long as Macmillan could wait another fortnight to be memorialized? But Bill was adamant, and the section was torn up to accommodate Horne's superb essay.

Mostly, though, things went smoothly, and Vigilante brought in some good, mostly young writers whom we hadn't used before—libertarian Wally Olson, for example, just starting to make his mark as a tireless exposer of scientific and economic shams; and Maggie Gallagher, who would become a leading traditionalist concentrating on marriage and the family. On another front, though, life was anything but smooth. In April 1985, word got out that in the course of an upcoming trip to Germany, President Reagan would be visiting a military cemetery in the company of Chancellor Helmut Kohl, to commemorate the fortieth anniversary of the end of World War II and celebrate forty years of friendship between the United States and West Germany. The name of the cemetery—Bitburg—became all too famous, because among the two thousand or so soldiers buried there were four dozen SS men. Jewish spokesmen, here and in Europe, went apoplectic. Reagan later recorded that he wished his advance team had found out earlier about the SS men and spoken quietly to Kohl's people, but at this point he didn't want to put Kohl in a bad position. He wrote in his diary, "I still think we were right. Yes. The German soldiers were the enemy and part of the whole Nazi hate era. But we won and we killed those soldiers. What is wrong with saying, 'Let's never be enemies again'? Would Helmut be wrong if he visited Arlington Cemetery on one of his U.S. visits?"

NR agreed with Reagan and defended him stoutly. But the incident was a turning point for Joe Sobran. He had a syndicated column by now, and he, too, defended Reagan. He correctly, from his colleagues' point of view, pointed out that no one gets mad when American presidents shake hands with live Communist leaders, all of whom, including the urbane Gorbachev in his earlier years, had done their share of persecuting Jews. So why should visiting a cemetery that incidentally contains some dead Nazis be the end of the world? But when Jewish writers then attacked Sobran, instead of calmly continuing to defend Reagan, he started to counterattack. As Buckley put it when he finally wrote his memo entitled "In Re Joe Sobran and Anti-Semitism," published in *NR* in July 1986:

> Complaints have reached us concerning a series of columns written by my colleague Joseph Sobran under the aegis of his newspaper syndicate. It is charged that these columns constitute anti-Semitism. In the columns, Mr. Sobran, among other things, has declared that Israel is not an ally to be trusted [the Jonathan Pollard case had just broken]; surmised that the *New York Times* endorsed the military strike against Libya only because it served its Zionist editorial line; and ruminated that the visit of the Pope to a synagogue had the effect of muting historical persecutions of Christians by Jews.

Buckley continued: "What needs to be said first is that those who know him know that Sobran is not anti-Semitic." And yet,

> Any person who, given the knowledge of the reigning protocols, read and agonized over the half-dozen columns by Joe Sobran might reasonably conclude that those columns were written by a writer inclined to anti-Semitism. . . .
>
> We know him not to be what he is thought by some to have become; but what they suspect is not, under the circumstances, unreasonable. Accordingly, I here dissociate myself and my colleagues from what we view as the obstinate tendentiousness of Joe Sobran's recent columns. We are confident that in the weeks and months to come, he will charitably and rationally acknowledge the right reason behind the crystallization of the present structure of

taboos, and that he will accordingly argue his positions in such fashion as to avoid affronting our natural allies.

Many *NR* readers wrote in to take issue with Buckley. They said, in summary, that if what Sobran wrote was anti-Semitic, he should not remain on our masthead; but if it was not anti-Semitic, but only violated certain "taboos," then it was wrong to kowtow to the critics and publicly chastise him. Most readers, though, understood and accepted the point, convoluted though Buckley's expression of it was. (On the rare occasions when Bill's writing is really opaque, that's a sure sign that he's embarrassed by whatever controversy he has been caught in the middle of.) The point in this case was that Sobran's arguments about the relative evil of Nazis and Communists could have been made without offending Jewish anti-Communists. And Sobran's constantly attacking Israel when there were, in many conservatives' view, so many riper targets was starting to seem like what Buckley later called it, an "obsession."

In the middle of the Bitburg year, Joe had produced a brilliantly thought-out, limpidly written meditation on a whole range of social and moral issues. This long essay, which Bill titled "Pensées," formed the centerpiece of the anniversary issue. A rabbi, agreeing with Buckley that Sobran should not write about Jews or Israel until he became willing to find more temperate expressions, also reported that he had found in "Pensées" the inspiration for many sermons.

For the time being there was no breach. Joe agreed that he would not write about Jews or Israel in the magazine, and that he would submit to Bill any syndicated column on those subjects before publishing it. He turned his formidable mind to cultural matters, and his colleagues breathed a sigh of relief.

Meanwhile, an inter-Buckley rivalry was shaping up—but one that gave great joy to both participants and the nearest spectator, Pat. In the spring of 1986 she saw her son join his father on the bestseller list—and then remain on when Bill dropped off. Buckley *père et fils* were a dual selection of the Literary Guild in April.

Bill's book—his seventh consecutive bestselling novel—was *High Jinx*. It begins with four teams of British and American commandos parachuting into Albania. They land successfully but are immediately captured, having been betrayed by men loosely based on the Cambridge spies: Philby, Burgess, Maclean, and the long-undiscovered fourth man, Anthony Blunt. In this novel Bill gives to Blackford's old-est friend, Anthony Trust, a meditation that's basically what Sobran *should* have said about the Nazis and the Communists: "When my spir-its flag," Anthony tells Blackford, "I pick up one of those books [about life under Communism]. I'll give you just four or five titles—you know them all. *I Speak for the Silent. The Captive Mind. I Chose Freedom. Darkness at Noon.* Tchernavin, Milosz, Kravchenko, Koestler, and twenty-five more. Then I reach out and I pick up *The Diary of Anne Frank*, but I say to myself: 'The people who did that to her are dead or in prison. We managed that! We finally reduced the Thousand-Year Reich to one bunker and an automatic pistol, and Hitler took it from there. The remaining bastards we dithered over at Nuremberg before hanging them (should just have shot 'em, Black, and then hanged them). There is no such thing any more as a Nazi threat. But the *other* bastards are doing it all the time. Every year there is another book I add to that shelf.'"

Chris's novel was *The White House Mess.* Back when he took the job of speechwriter to George Bush, he signed an agreement saying that he would not write a memoir upon leaving the administration—tell-all memoirs had become all the rage post-Watergate. However, that did not bar him from writing a fictional recollection of a very dif-ferent administration. And so he gives us the memoirs of Herbert Wadlough, an aide to democratic president Tommy Nelson Tucker, Ronald Reagan's successor (but based loosely—very loosely—on his predecessor, Jimmy Carter). We follow Wadlough in his hilarious bat-tles with his archrival, Chief of Staff Bamford Lleland IV, who tries to deny Wadlough access not only to the president but to his own park-ing space. Meanwhile the First Hamster disappears, and Wadlough is deputed to find him; Tucker contemplates an invasion of Bermuda; and finally Wadlough has to try to achieve reelection for arguably the worst president ever.

Chris had already shown the makings of a fine comic writer in his Yale days, as witness his contributions to *NR*'s twentieth anniversary issue. Now he had come into his own, and he has remained there ever since. An outside observer remarked, early in his career, that it was a pity his calling wasn't to be a neurosurgeon, say, or a concert cellist—something totally outside the shadow of his superfamous father. But as things turned out, if he had to be a writer, his style is so different from Bill's as not to invite invidious comparisons.

*   *   *

Normally, the Philadelphia society is a pretty amiable group. The founding documents specified that it would be a forum for many different varieties of thought: "We shall seek understanding, not conformity." And the society tries to adhere to the original intentions of its founders. The 1986 meeting was the rare exception. Jeff Hart, *NR*'s designated reporter at that meeting, accurately titled his article "Gang Warfare in Chicago."

The background was second-term Reagan appointments. M. E. Bradford had been on the short list for head of the National Endowment for the Humanities. He was undeniably a distinguished American historian. However, some influential right-wingers—some though not all of them identified as neocons—strongly opposed his nomination. They held that in praising the good parts of the Old South—the parts that Weaver and the first-generation Agrarians had praised—he was altogether too unconcerned about the "peculiar institution." Bradford had the backing of his old friend and adversary Harry Jaffa. Jaffa would argue to the death with Bradford the merits of Abraham Lincoln—whom Jaffa elevated to the rank of last of the Founding Fathers, and whom Bradford excoriated as the great "centralizer"—but Jaffa thought Bradford deserved the NEH post. However, Jaffa's voice did not prevail. It never came to a Senate fight: the battle was conducted within the administration, and William Bennett was the (successfully confirmed) nominee.

Bradford was bitter, and Bradford was now the president of the Philadelphia Society. The society's presidents serve for one year, and by longstanding tradition the president has a lot to say about the topic for the annual meeting. In Bradford's year, it was neocons versus paleocons.

Even at that, there was no advance warning of how acrimonious the weekend would be. As one neocon put it on the Saturday afternoon, "We were set up." The most inflammatory remarks were by Stephen Tonsor, professor of history at the University of Michigan. He basically read the neocons out of the conservative movement. There was some very good intellectual history in his speech, but there was also—well, let him speak for himself:

> The Right that is born of modernity is a radical, a revolutionary Right, which cannot in any important degree be distinguished from the revolutionary Left.

Now it is a matter of fact that most of those who describe themselves as neoconservatives are or have been cultural modernists.
They have been, to use Peter Berger's telling phrase, baptized in the
"fiery brook." (He was making an elegant pun on the name of Ludwig Feuerbach, the Left Hegelian inspiration of Marx and the
Church Father of alienation theory.) We Conservatives have been
baptized in the Jordan, and there is a vast difference between the
Jordan and the fiery brook.

It has always struck me as odd, even perverse, that former
Marxists have been permitted, yes invited, to play such a leading
role in the Conservative movement of the twentieth century. It is
splendid when the town whore gets religion and joins the church.
Now and then she makes a good choir director, but when she
begins to tell the minister what he ought to say in his Sunday ser-
mon, matters have been carried too far.

At the question period, Arnold Beichman—a former leftist not
normally associated with the neocons, and a frequent contributor to
NR—rose to ask, with some passion, whether Tonsor was rejecting
James Burnham, Whittaker Chambers, Frank Meyer, George Orwell,
Arthur Koestler, and Paul Johnson. With maddening calm, Tonsor
replied, "Would you accept an ex-Nazi?"

Whatever one thinks about Tonsor's idea of conservatism, it wasn't
National Review's idea. His River Jordan comment would seem to
rule out not only secular modernists, but also observant Jews. On
the contrary, Buckley had found nothing odd in a Catholic editor's
choosing a Jew, Will Herberg, as the first religion editor of his non-
sectarian magazine. And Buckley's point about St. Paul is as apposite
an answer to Tonsor as it was to the journalist asking about Whittaker Chambers. God didn't call St. Paul to be the new Church's
choirmaster—He called him to be its first theologian.

Subsequent panels that weekend in Chicago were more than a little heated; in one of them, Bob Tyrrell nearly dissolved into tears.
Finally Stan Evans—who had taken over the post of most irenic available presence from the mostly retired John Chamberlain—spoke
words that brought a temporary peace.

But the underlying tensions were still there, fueled, as long as a
Republican occupied the White House, by the neocons' eagerness to
take jobs that many movement conservatives had disdained on the
grounds that getting involved with government would entail unac-
ceptable compromises.

*   *   *

Just days before the 1986 midterm elections, word got out in the media of something that would come to be called "Iran-Contra." As the story murkily unfolded, *NR* was entirely sympathetic with the Contra part—as Brookhiser put it, you can't conduct a coherent foreign policy with Congress changing the rules every few months. The Iran part we weren't so sure of. American foreign policy in the Middle East had been badly hampered for decades by lack of hard intelligence and by conflicts among various agencies of the permanent government in Washington. In the present case, Reagan was told by his advisors that the people they were dealing with in Iran were moderates who had a chance of succeeding Ayatollah Khomeini.

Whatever the full truth of the matter, Iran-Contra never descended into a second Watergate. In the first place, there was no question of self-interest for Reagan or anyone close to him. In the second place, Reagan stuck to his story that he had told his subordinates to do as much as they could to help the Contras *within the law*, and that he had then left the details to them. Still, there was unedifying confusion, including Oliver North and Fawn Hall being caught shredding documents, and the attempted suicide of former National Security Advisor Bud McFarlane. And the Republicans lost control of the Senate in the 1986 elections, with the Democrats taking a 55–45 majority.

This was a great disappointment in and of itself: 1980 had been the first time the Republicans had taken the Senate since the Eisenhower years, and holding it for six years had enabled Reagan to do much, though only a fraction of what he, and the conservative movement, had hoped. Now that was gone.

More specifically, though no one knew it in November 1986, Supreme Court Justice Lewis Powell would retire the following June. Back in 1981, when Justice Potter Stewart retired, conservatives had hoped Reagan would nominate as his successor Robert Bork, a brilliant constitutional scholar then teaching at the Yale Law School. Instead—Nixon Goes to China stuff—Reagan nominated the first female justice, Sandra Day O'Connor. Bork's admirers were reminded consolingly that several other justices were quite old, and there would surely be another opening during Reagan's tenure. In the fall of 1981, Reagan nominated Bork to the D.C. Circuit Court of Appeals (where, four years later, he was joined by Jim Buckley).

In April 1987, the Philadelphia Society meeting was on the theme "Constitutional Government: The Design, the Reality, the Prospect." The leadoff speaker was Robert Bork. One of the present authors, reporting on the meeting, wrote, "I can't imagine there were many people in that room who will be glad to see Robert Bork leave the crucial D.C. Circuit Court. But, equally, I can't imagine there were many who weren't hoping, that April weekend, that a Supreme Court slot would soon open up." The writer went on to paraphrase Bork's own address: "Fifty years ago there was nothing labeled an 'interpretivist' school of legal thought. The very term would have been seen as redundant: How could you practice constitutional law *except* by interpreting the Constitution? By the time the term was coined, however, it was almost to taxonomize an extinct species. Judge Bork related a conversation that took place a year or two ago: 'I made the argument I just made'—that the Constitution is law—'and an eminent constitutional theorist at a *very* major law school said to me, "Your notion that the Constitution is law must rest upon some obscure philosophical principle with which I am not familiar.'"

Powell retired two months later, and Reagan promptly nominated Bork. But by that time the Senate Democrats had tasted blood with Ollie North.

For a decade, Priscilla had kept a small portable television in her file cabinet (a going-away gift from two departing staffers, Vicki Marani and Barbara Devlin). In 1987 this little TV got constant use, whenever someone could take a few minutes to look at the Iran-Contra hearings or the Bork confirmation hearings. Low points of the latter that stick in the memory include Senator Howell Heflin declaring that Robert Bork did not have the judicial temperament because one summer, while on sabbatical, he had grown a beard. And we had Senator Edward M. Kennedy questioning Bork's understanding of the Constitution, while—or so it looked on the screen—Kennedy himself was so incapable of formulating a constitutional question that he was simply repeating the words fed to him by an aide standing behind him, virtually ventriloquizing. On October 23, 1987, all but two Democrats (David Boren and Fritz Hollings) voted the party line, and six Republicans jumped ship to join them. One of the finest jurisprudential minds in America went down to defeat, 58 to 42, and in the eyes of movement conservatives, Senators John Chafee, Bob Packwood, Arlen Specter, Robert Stafford,

John Warner, and Lowell Weicker had added a very large black mark to their already blotted copybooks.

In the spring of 1987 we thought our President himself had gone out of his mind, when he permitted Secretary of State George Shultz to go to Moscow and negotiate the Intermediate-Range Nuclear Forces treaty with the Soviets. Reagan and Thatcher had spent so much political capital and leaned so hard on our allies, especially West Germany, to get the Pershing II and cruise missiles installed in Europe, and now Reagan was throwing it away.

Bill got on the phone to commission articles, and he put *NR*'s research director, Dorothy McCartney, to work finding published commentary. This time Bill's juniors were happy to tear up an issue. "Reagan's Suicide Pact," the dramatic new cover read, and the section included articles by John Roche and Van Galbraith, and a commentary published in the *Los Angeles Times* by Richard Nixon and Henry Kissinger.

The principal argument being made in favor of the treaty was that Gorbachev was a reformer and he needed "a deal" with the United States in order to shore up his position at home. The gravamen of *NR*'s criticism was that this treaty would deeply destabilize Western Europe and leave it at the mercy of the Soviet Union.

Roche: "Ever since Jimmy Carter sandbagged Helmut Schmidt on the neutron bomb, responsible Germans have been looking nervously over their shoulders at Washington. Yet the Christian Democrat–Free Democrat coalition bravely went to bat for the installation of the Pershing IIs, essentially putting their political future at the mercy of American collegiality. For them to be left twisting in the wind by a great-power agreement would create an extremely dangerous vacuum in the heart of Europe."

Galbraith: "Perhaps [Shultz] and President Reagan both feel this pact with the Soviets will entitle them to a revered page in history. They are wrong. The umbrella of nuclear deterrence is being exchanged for the umbrella of Munich."

Eight years later, and four years after the collapse of Soviet Communism, Buckley gave Reagan the last word, in his novel *A Very Private Plot*. "I love my conservative friends," the fictional Reagan muses, alone in the Oval Office, "and they've been good and faithful to me, but dammit sometimes they don't see the important things and some of the important things I can't very well remind them of, at least not publicly. It isn't going to help us pull Gorbachev in the direction we're trying to pull him to say, Look, gang! What that fool is giving up is five times as many missiles as . . . we're giving up. . . .

"And anyway, Gorbachev isn't giving away anything he isn't prepared to give away. He doesn't know how much I know about how much he's hurting. Wasteland, the Soviet economy."

In June 1987, Reagan returned to Berlin. It was the 750th anniversary of the city's founding, and he had been invited to speak at a huge outdoor ceremony in the shadow of the Brandenburg Gate. As Buckley put it in his little book about the Berlin Wall, "Some European commentators observed that Berlin was a young city, when compared with Rome, Paris, London, Madrid, Berne, and a dozen others. Reagan failed to make a joke on the question whether he or Berlin had been born first, but he did better."

Peter Robinson, a *Dartmouth Review* alumnus who had been Buckley's research assistant for his book *On the Firing Line*, was by now a Reagan speechwriter, and he is widely credited with providing one of the most famous lines of Reagan's presidency. However, as Tony Dolan recalls it, one day in the Oval Office, months before the Berlin event, he asked the President whether he had any preliminary thoughts. "Well," said Reagan, "tear down the wall." And that certainly squares with what Reagan had said to Dick Allen and Peter Hannaford nine years earlier: "We've got to find a way of knocking this thing down."

In any case, as Buckley recounts, it was a near-run thing: "It was much later that historians learned how close some members of the Administration had come to suppressing those electric lines, the most renowned of Reagan's presidency. The draft of the speech had come out of the speechwriting shop and was sent routinely to the State Department and the National Security Council for vetting. Red flags shot up. The President must not speak those words. They would harm Gorbachev and get in the way of continuing Soviet reforms. And if Reagan used such language, it would harm *him*. Any demand so importunate, so outrageous and inflammatory, was among other things 'not presidential.' But one or two of the President's aides made the point that it was up to him to decide whether those words were presidential. Reagan's decision lives in history, in Berlin of course, and worldwide."

That same season Bill and Pat had taken a boat trip very different from anything they had done on *The Panic* or *Cyrano*: a passage across the South Pacific, from Tahiti to Easter Island, aboard a 360-foot three-masted brigantine bark that had belonged to Marjorie Merriweather Post. This was not a long-planned trip, like the crossings on which Bill and his friends formed the crew. As Bill wrote about a different impulsively agreed-to trip, "I'm sure it has happened to you, the special invitation—however conveyed—to a trip, perhaps even to an adventure. You stare at it for a little while, then pull up an Uzi and blast away at your calendar, leaving not one living trace of what had been commitments trivial and solemn, some of them months old." In this case, Bill had to shoehorn the two weeks on the *Sea Cloud* in with all his normal duties, plus a special *Firing Line* debate among the Republican candidates for the 1988 nomination; and Pat, as Bill put it, was coming off "(we like to think) the most hectic social/civic week of her career in New York City."

Bill wrote about the trip, lyrically, for *Condé Nast Traveler*. But before *Traveler* ran the piece, someone—probably editor Harold Evans, who knows the Buckleys personally—had the brilliant idea of asking Pat to write *her* account, which was published along with Bill's under the heading "A mate's mutinous thoughts." It begins:

> Sometime last June I am crawling around the rose garden murdering Japanese beetles when I espy, loping across the lawn at a depressingly sprightly clip, my husband.
>
> "Guess what, ducky?"
>
> After thirty-seven years I do not need a guru to interpret this phrase of his.
>
> "Guess what, ducky?" means horror and lurking death are just around the corner. As in:
>
> "Guess what, ducky? I'm taking up ski gliding."
>
> "Guess what, ducky? I'm diving down to the *Titanic*."
>
> This time, "G.W.D.?" means fifteen days on board the *Sea Cloud*, stopping only at the two most remote inhabited places in the world: fabled Pitcairn Island and fabled Easter Island.

After a hair-raising landing on Easter Island (the boatman miscalculated a wave and several passengers were injured), Pat would never again consent to go ashore in a Zodiac landing craft. But she did admit that the Pitcairn Islanders were enchanting.

In August 1987 Jim Burnham died. Unlike the news, a decade earlier, of his near-blindness and then his stroke, this came less as a shock than as a blessed release. He had been suffering from cancer, and Priscilla had been reporting that each time she stopped in at Kent to see him, on her way between Sharon and New York, he had seemed thinner and frailer, though still courtly, still himself. ("You're looking remarkably well," he would always say to Priscilla, who suffered at being unable to say the same in return.) Now Bill planned a big send-off, a full article section devoted to reminiscences by colleagues, friends, pupils, family—with those categories often overlapping.

To one of the present writers, the most remarkable thing about the contributions to that issue is how varied they were. When people told stories about Willmoore Kendall or Willi Schlamm—or even Frank Meyer—the stories tended to be essentially similar. But people who thought they had known Jim fairly well learned from other writers in that issue many things they had never known. There was nothing incongruent in the different views. It was just that Jim, although a strong personality in his own right, seemed more than some other strong personalities to bend his immediate response to his interlocutor. We were all reminded how much we had learned from him, not merely in the crafting of editorials but in life.

The cast of characters at *NR* was changing yet again. Rick Brookhiser had found that the administrative side of editorship didn't appeal to him at all, and so he told Bill he would be stepping down as managing editor and as heir apparent as of December 1987. Dealing with the first part of the problem was easy: Bill put one of the present authors, who had served as assistant managing editor for a dozen years, into the m.e. slot. The hard part was rethinking the succession. He had already decided (though he had not announced, except, we later learned, to Priscilla) that he would follow his father's example and hand over the reins at age sixty-five, though remaining connected to the enterprise. He sought the advice of several old friends and collaborators, and the name that kept coming up was that of John O'Sullivan.

Jim McFadden, John O'Sullivan, and WFB in the Pompeii room at Paone's restaurant; JO'S has just been named heir apparent to Buckley as editor.

O'Sullivan was born in Liverpool, the son of an Irishman who served as purser on the ferry between Liverpool and Dun Laoghaire and an Englishwoman whose parents had been Liverpool pubkeepers. John recounted that he had become actively conservative at age fourteen, when he watched on television the Soviet tanks invading Hungary. He had studied classics at London University and gone into newspaper and radio journalism; before long he was the *Daily Telegraph*'s parliamentary diarist. When Rupert Murdoch went big-time international he hired O'Sullivan away from the *Telegraph* and sent him to New York to run the editorial page of the *New York Post*, which is when several *NR* staffers first got to know him. O'Sullivan then shuttled back and forth a couple of times between the United States and England, serving among other things as editor of the Heritage Foundation's prestigious quarterly, *Policy Review*. At the time Ernest van den Haag and others mentioned him to Buckley as a candidate for editor, he was working as a special advisor to Prime Minister Thatcher.

O'Sullivan accepted Buckley's offer in November 1987 but explained that he would be unable to disengage from Downing Street for several months. Meanwhile, Rusher told Buckley of his own intention of retiring in December 1988.

Back in the early 1970s, a young man named Wick Allison wanted to start a magazine in Dallas along the lines of *New York* magazine, and he came to *NR* for advice on how to do it. Given our perpetual insolvency, one might have suggested he seek another model, but *D* nonetheless got off the ground and prospered. Allison eventually sold *D* and came to New York as publisher of *Arts and Antiques*. Having reestablished the acquaintance, he had approached Buckley about the possibility of his buying *National Review*. Buckley decided to find out what Allison could do by bringing him in as Bill Rusher's successor. The changing of the guard was scheduled to take place on January 1, 1989. But when WAR's doctors told him he needed a heart bypass operation, and the sooner the better, the date was pulled forward to September.

Buckley took a sort of revenge on Rusher for his longstanding resistance to holding editorial dinners on Buckley's boat by planning the retirement party for—a boat. But this was not a sailboat, not a craft requiring an inclinometer. It was a stately vessel that, on our cruise anyway, never ventured more than a mile from the edge of Manhattan. The timing was arranged so that we sailed by Lady Liberty just as Rusher was being toasted by his old friend the longtime chairman of *NR*'s board, Roger Allan Moore—"no relation!" as our Swiss edition would have put it, to Bill's skiing friend, the actor Roger Moore.

9

New World Order

In January 1989, having tamed the town and restored hope, pride, and law & order, Ronald Reagan turned in his star, hung up his guns, and, with his lady at his side, rode off into the Western sunset. His legacy was the remarkable restoration of a strong and regnant conservatism, with few serious ideological challenges on the national or international horizon.

This is how John Micklethwait and Adrian Wooldridge, two reporters for *The Economist,* sum it up in *The Right Nation: Conservative Power in America*: "By the end of Reagan's term all the pieces on the Right seemed to be in place. Republicans had a lock on California and the West. The South was now Republican territory—undoubtedly in presidential elections and increasingly in congressional ones. ... Between 1972 and 1986 the average rating for Republican House members from the American Conservative Union increased from 63 percent to 75 percent. The Religious Right was on the march. White ethnics in the North were ceasing to think of themselves as Democrats (one of Reagan's slogans for reelection in 1984 was 'You haven't left the Democratic Party, the Democratic Party left you'). The American people seemed to be fully committed to small government. The Right had won the great foreign-policy argument of the Cold War."

For conservatives, morning in America had become high noon, with no discernible clouds in sight.

263

When the 1988 campaign began, George Bush had spent seven years as Reagan's loyal vice president. He had suppressed any hints of the old criticisms (most famously, from the 1980 campaign, "voodoo economics") and had performed his ceremonial duties without complaint, chief among them overseas diplomatic trips and state funerals. ("I'm George Bush," he once quipped. "You die, I fly.") Even among many movement conservatives, Bush was considered the rightful heir to Reagan. He stumbled out of the starting gate, losing the Iowa caucuses to Bob Dole and Pat Robertson, and down the line he faced serious challenges from voodoo economists Jack Kemp and Pete du Pont. However, with the organizational and fundraising apparatus that Bush largely inherited from Reagan, and enlisting the efforts of Lee Atwater, the Republican strategist whom later operatives like Karl Rove emulate, George Bush carried the day and was nominated by unanimous roll-call vote at the Republican convention in New Orleans. He chose as his running mate Senator Dan Quayle of Indiana.

Quayle was conservative and boyishly appealing. The press jumped on him as unintelligent, although we at *NR* quickly got a differing opinion. Bill had gone down to Washington the week before the convention at the invitation of Jeane Kirkpatrick, to discuss national security matters with a group of senators, including Quayle. The next editorial Tuesday, Bill told us: "If there hadn't been all this stuff in the press, I would have been reporting to you today, 'You know, I just met a very bright, well-informed young senator.'"

It was helpful that the Democrats were spending their primary campaign going through an excruciating and sometimes comic process of elimination. Front-runner Gary Hart, apparently just discovering girls, was caught by a photographer on a boat called *Monkey Business*, dandling actress Donna Rice on his knee and grinning sappily. (As Priscilla observed in summing up the Willmoore Kendall affair, "Aren't men silly?" Just so.) Senator Joe Biden, another strong candidate, actually plagiarized a speech from Neil Kinnock, a British Labour Party leader—apparently not noticing the difference between his own more prosaic accents and Kinnock's soaring Welsh diapason—and then was further accused of plagiarism while in law school (a false charge, planted by a rival campaign). After Richard Gephardt and Paul Simon knocked each other out and Pat Schroeder drifted off, Ophelia-like, the candidates left standing for the Democratic nomination were Jesse Jackson, Al Gore (then a senator from Tennessee, and even more wooden), and Michael Dukakis, the small and intensely humorless governor of Massachusetts, who acknowledged that one of his campaign aides was responsible for planting the Biden plagiarism charge, and who was probably, next to Jesse Jackson, the candidate from either party least qualified to be president of the United States.

The nomination went to Dukakis, and the presidential race was effectively over. Beginning with a substantial lead in the polls, Dukakis moved with an unerring instinct from one misstep to another. Portrayed by Atwater as a left-liberal ideologue, he proudly defended his assertion, made during the primaries, that he was a "card-carrying member of the ACLU," and "a proud liberal" to boot. In his campaign debate with George Bush, when asked whether he would support the death penalty if his wife were raped and murdered, he responded in an abstract and emotionless way that left much of the national viewing audience either cold or disconcerted. And in that famous photo op, contrived to prove that he was not soft on national defense, he was shown with his head barely sticking out of a moving tank, wearing an oversized helmet and grinning like Chuckie Chipmunk.

In the end, on November 8, Bush won easily, 426 to 111 in the electoral college, with 53.4 percent of the popular vote. However, there were warning signals. In Illinois, Bush lost downstate counties that had gone heavily for Reagan. Bush's margins were also significantly smaller than Reagan's in Midwestern states like Missouri, Kansas, and South Dakota, and Bush lost Iowa by a surprisingly large margin. Still, all in all, a satisfying result, with Bush becoming the first serving vice president to be elected president in the twentieth century.

That fall there were whispers around the *NR* offices that something was wrong between Bill and Christo (as Bill calls his son). It wasn't until two years later that Bill told about the episode. In the last of his sailing books, *WindFall*, he divulged that he and Christo had been estranged for nine months—completely out of communication, despite Pat's best efforts to bring them together. Bill writes analytically about it, with all the remembered pain and self-reproach kept tautly just below the surface.

The background is technological. Back in 1982 Bill had become one of the first writers to switch from typewriter to PC, with his primitive Kaypro. Soon afterward he acquired MCI Mail, an early form of e-mail. He proselytized Christo, who joined him in the computer age, and from then on father and son communicated regularly and copiously via MCI. In September 1988, when Christo returned to his Washington, D.C., home from a summer in northern New England, which he had spent working on his new novel, he told his father by phone that he was not reconnecting his MCI Mail, on the grounds that he found it too "intrusive." Father unleashes the biting wit he has been practicing in the public arena for forty years, and the rest is silence.

As Bill analyzes it in retrospect, there were a number of strands that led to this confrontation. Christo was now not only a husband but also a father, his daughter, Caitlin, having been born that spring. "My bereavement" Bill writes, "reflected primarily my failure to begin to comprehend, let alone fully to do so, that evolution of loyalties that accompanies marriage—and should do so. . . . Day-to-day closeness of the kind we had had was becoming a drain, distracting to the primary emotional and psychological demands he was feeling."

Then there was Reggie Stoops. Reggie was an old, old friend, one of the survivors of that first ski trip to Pico back in 1956. He had frequently been part of the crew when Bill and Firpo were racing *The Panic*, and he had been on all three transoceanic sails—the Atlantic in 1975 and 1980, and the Pacific (also on the *Sealestial*) in 1985. Early in 1988 Reggie was diagnosed with lung cancer. He was engaged to be married, and he and his fiancée decided to go through with their wedding plans. They married in June; Bill gave the couple a party and broke down at the end of his toast. He did not want to subject Reggie—or himself—to a renewal of such a display, and so he did not once go to visit Reggie in person. However, he did speak with him two or three times a week, finding the emotional traps easier to negotiate over the phone. Christo, meanwhile, was driving from Maine to Rhode Island at least once a week to spend hours at Reggie's bedside, and, his father writes, he "intimated his dismay at my own deportment."

Bill cites additional irritants, but whatever the complexity of reasons, the silence lasted nine months. Then in May 1989 the phone rang in Bill's study at Wallacks Point. Christo was making the first move. Bill accepted, and, as he puts it, "We conjugated our reunion." In 1990 Christo was on board *Sealestial* for the fourth (and last) ocean crossing.

While all this was going on at home, amazing things were happening in Eastern Europe, things that some of us younger than Bill had not expected to see in our lifetime. As he wrote in *The Fall of the Berlin Wall*, "A generation had elapsed between 'Ich bin ein Berliner' and 'Mr. Gorbachev, tear down this wall.' One year and a half after Reagan made his mythogenic plea, he left office, and the wall was still standing. The day before George H. W. Bush's inauguration, Erich Honecker reaffirmed his commitment to the wall. Outgoing Secretary of State George Shultz had designated the wall as the 'acid test' of Eastern Europe's progress toward human rights. Honecker defiantly replied: 'It will stand in fifty or a hundred years.'"

But, Bill went on, "Bravado notwithstanding, the Iron Curtain was fraying." In Hungary and Poland there were stirrings. In the Soviet Union, Gorbachev had tried to reform the economy without giving up state control. He introduced the ideas of *perestroika* (restructuring) and *glasnost* (openness), though not much of the reality of either. Then in June 1988, at the All-Union Conference of the Soviet Communist Party, Gorbachev called for a radical restructuring of the government in Moscow. There would be a Congress of People's Deputies, some of whom would actually be chosen by the people in contested elections. As Bill quoted him in the Berlin book, Gorbachev declared: "The people demand total democracy, full-blooded democracy with no reservations. There can be no compromise." Well, maybe *some* compromise. Only one party would be permitted to compete in the elections—the Communist Party. "A multiparty system," said Gorbachev "—two parties, three parties—it is all rubbish. At first [it is] one or two parties on class grounds, then 120 on national grounds, then international. All that is thrown at us by irresponsible people." Still, Gorbachev had mounted the tiger, and the whole world watched.

One year later, in June 1989, Poland held parliamentary elections, and Solidarity won a victory almost as unanimous as the old Communist victories—except that these elections were free, the first free elections in Poland since 1935. But, as Buckley would write, "There remained the heart-stopping question: Would Gorbachev assert the Brezhnev Doctrine?" One of Gorbachev's aides, Yevgeny Primakov, delivered the Kremlin's answer: Poland's future was "entirely a matter to be decided by Poland." Poland was alive, and the Brezhnev Doctrine was dead.

The most dramatic moment was yet to come. East Germany had been one of the most heavily repressed of the Soviet satellites—right up there with Romania and Bulgaria. But now it started to awaken. Once Hungary opened its border with Austria, East Germans started "vacationing" there by the thousands, with no intention of going back. Then, in September, the marches started: protest marches led by an organization called the New Forum, born in the Lutheran churches. Week by week the marches grew, and they spread to nearly every city in East Germany. The Honecker regime made plans to crack down on the next big march—but the crackdown never happened.

When Buckley was going through his research material for the Berlin Wall book, he was enchanted to read that Kurt Masur, director of the Leipzig Gewandhaus Orchestra, had been instrumental in persuading the East German army not to go through with the intended massacre in his city. "*Our* Kurt Masur?" he asked happily. Yes, came the answer: one and the same. That Leipzig march was on October 9. One month later to the day, Günther Schabowski, the Party chief for East Berlin, was holding a televised press conference. He was nearly finished when someone asked one final question. Schabowski replied: "Permanent emigration is henceforth allowed across all border crossing points between East Germany and West Germany and West Berlin." That was at 9:00 P.M. Before the night was out, Berlin was undivided, and East Germany was free.

Buckley had a column due the next day, and he made the most of it. "When the news came in, President Bush sat quietly in his large chair in the Oval Office and said in grave tones that we must not overreact. He is absolutely right about this. JINGLE BELLS! JINGLE BELLS! JINGLE ALL THE WAYYYY! It is proper to deem it a historical development, but its significance must not affect our judgment. OH WHAT A BEAUTIFUL MORNING! OH WHAT A BEAU-TI-FUL DAY!!! After all, there is tomorrow to think about in Germany GERMANY?!?! WHAT DO YOU MEAN, 'GERMANY'? YOU MEAN WEST GERMANY OR YOU MEAN EAST GERMANY? and the score allows for many variations. Calmness is in order."

As these real-world developments were beginning, Buckley was back in the might-have-been Germany of his second novel, *Stained Glass*. In late 1987 the Actors Theatre of Louisville had approached him about crafting a play based on the novel, and he had agreed. In Switzerland that winter, he interleaved work on the play with work on his book about *Firing Line*.

It would take another year, with occasional trips to Louisville for readings and rehearsals, but finally the opening was scheduled for

March 1989. On (of all days) Good Friday, a chartered plane left La Guardia with Bill and Pat and three dozen friends and colleagues. Priscilla and Jane were there, John O'Sullivan and Wick Allison, Frances Bronson, Linda Bridges, and Dorothy McCartney, Sam and Jo Vaughan, and Van and Bootsie Galbraith. To the delight of his fellow travelers Van had appointed himself Director of Refreshments: he was then on the board of Moët & Chandon, and he supplied a case of bubbly.

Actors Theatre is a repertory group, and so the actors didn't necessarily look like one's idea of the characters. The Axel Wintergrin, for example, was short and bald, which the "real" Axel Wintergrin was not. But the story took hold, and it was a happy group that flew back to New York the next day. Without, however, our Fearless Leader: while we returned home, he flew to Richmond, Virginia, for a speech.

Nor was writing a play Buckley's only new trick in that season. The director of the Phoenix Symphony Orchestra had approached him with an invitation to play a harpsichord concerto, and after many misgivings, and many consultations with his several keyboard teachers, he agreed. In an essay for *The New Yorker*, republished as the introduction to his collection of speeches, *Let Us Talk of Many Things*, he says casually of stage fright, "I don't get this." Quite true in approaching a lectern; not at all true in approaching a keyboard instrument in front of hundreds of people. Still, he performed well enough to be asked to do the same by several other music directors. But it didn't get any easier. One of the present authors witnessed two later performances, at each of which Bill approached the harpsichord stiff-legged and with an expression suitable for going to the gallows. After eight or nine of these, enough was enough. He would henceforth play only for himself and, diffidently (except when it came to playing accompaniments for the singing of old songs), his friends.

In August 1990, Saddam Hussein's Iraq invaded Kuwait, foreseen by almost no one. (Notable exceptions: Gregory Copley, cofounder with his mentor, the master strategist Stefan Possony, of the International Strategic Studies Association; and the crown prince of Qatar, Sheik Hamad bin Khalifa al-Thani.) President Bush decided that action was necessary, but that the United States mustn't go it alone: a coalition was needed. Bush and his team spent weeks lobbying the UN and Congress to get the authorizations they wanted.

Even though Iraq had just come out of the debilitating ten-year-long war with Iran, it had formidable military reserves. And in that war with Iran—and in attacks on Kurdish rebels in his own country—Saddam had shown himself ruthlessly willing to use any weapon available, including chemical and biological weapons. Any counteraction by the United States would be serious business. Still, there appears to be something symbolic in the contrast between Reagan's swift, silent invasion of Grenada and the noisy, agonizingly slow-motion windup to Desert Storm.

National Review could not, however, complain about one side effect of that protracted windup, known as Desert Shield. Earlier in the summer Wick Allison had made a cooperative advertising deal with C-SPAN: *NR* advertised without paying up front; the network then got a percentage of receipts on any new subscriptions the ads brought in. C-SPAN had warned Wick that this probably couldn't continue once fall programming started, but in the event, it was so successful that C-SPAN was happy to continue it. The Reagan years had already pulled our circulation out of the Watergate/Carter doldrums. By 1984 it was back to better than pre-Watergate, at 119,400; by 1988, up to 124,800. Now it soared: 137,600 in 1990, 153,100 in 1991.

On another front, though, Desert Shield had a devastating effect. The impending war infuriated many conservatives who had already been critical of the United States' relations with Israel, including our longtime friend Pat Buchanan and our own Joe Sobran. Sobran had for a while abided by his deal with Buckley about avoiding the topic of Israel. (Instead, he drove his colleagues crazy by taking up with equal tenacity the cause of the Earl of Oxford as the real author of the works of Shakespeare.) But now he started writing again about Israel. Buchanan, meanwhile, had taken up the cause of one John Demjanjuk, put on trial by Israel on charges of having been a particularly vicious Nazi concentration camp guard. To those who remained skeptical, Buchanan's ingenious refutations of every new allegation started to seem strained. And now Buchanan joined Sobran in the antiwar brigade.

Neocon Norman Podhoretz, by now a friend of Buckley's, was relentless in seeking Sobran's and Buchanan's excommunication. This, Buckley would not give. However, in a lengthy essay titled "In Search of Anti-Semitism" (it took up nearly a whole issue of the magazine and later formed the core of a short book by the same name), he explored the two men's writings, alongside many others', and came to much the same conclusion he had come to about Sobran five years earlier: Sobran and Buchanan were not anti-Semitic in any normal sense of the word. However, they were anti-Israel, and they allowed their feelings about that country to color their perceptions about other things. And they both enjoyed provocative formulations. Buchanan famously said, in regard to the Gulf War: "There are only two groups that are beating the drums for war in the Middle East—the Israeli Defense Ministry and its amen corner in the United States." Buckley comments: "Unless Mr. Buchanan was prepared to define the 'amen corner' of Israel as comprising approximately 75 percent of the American people—that was the number the polls then told us were supporting Administration policies—he was deluding himself, or his listeners, or both. . . . Inevitably, when an intelligent person makes an assertion that is manifestly absurd, he arouses suspicions."

Sobran was understandably not happy about Buckley's rebuke, though most of their colleagues believed it was both justified and necessary. During at least two editorial dinners over the next two years, Bill said something on the order of "Now, come on, Joe," and Joe replied explosively and left the table, not returning that evening. John O'Sullivan tried to smooth things over, but finally the rupture came. Joe by now had a column in *The Wanderer*, a traditionalist Catholic newspaper. One week he devoted his column to an attack on Bill, saying among other things that by discussing his father's country-club anti-Semitism he was committing "parricide." (The rest of us had all read that passage as saying: *If so good a man as my father shared this view, it was truly part of the prevailing American culture—and it had nothing whatever to do with what Adolf Hitler was cooking up in Germany.*) That was it. Bill regarded that column as Joe's letter of resignation from the magazine. Some mutual friends have tried over the years to effect a reconciliation, but nothing seemed to have come of it. However, just recently Joe wrote a lovely column in response to a column of Bill's, and Bill gratefully replied.

NR's thirty-fifth anniversary coincided with Bill's sixty-fifth birthday, and Bill did what he had long planned: announced his retirement as editor-in-chief and turned over the reins to John O'Sullivan. (His innermost circle—plus those at the magazine most immediately involved, particularly John O'Sullivan and Wick Allison—knew he would be making the announcement that evening. But it came as quite a surprise to most of his colleagues, not to mention most of the guests at the celebration.) What this meant in practice was that Bill would no longer routinely lead the editorial meetings and edit "The Week," and he would no longer vet every article proposed for publication. However, except when in mid-Atlantic, he would be available for consultation, and he would let John and Wick know if there was anything he disliked. The one running battle—which Bill always won, if only because, after all, it was his football—was over length. John was, in the best sense, always greedy: he always wanted to put in one more article, one more editorial, and he thought the increased circulation justified increasing the number of pages. Bill believed that one of the ways *NR* differed from ordinary magazines was that subscribers should want to read it from cover to cover, and that even a busy man or woman should be able to finish each issue before the next one came out. When John and Wick did, at one point, increase the page count, Bill started hearing from siblings and old friends that there was now too much to read. The page count went down again. This may sound quaint in these days of the Internet; now, National Review Online has enough material to keep an Evelyn Wood speed reader busy. But at the time it was a serious bone of contention.

But it was the only such bone. John's editorship was in some ways very different from Bill's, in other ways very similar. Both men are interested in practically everything; each has a tremendously wide circle of friends and friendly acquaintances. As to the differences, working with John helped illuminate Bill's modus operandi. John's toast at Bill's big, splashy eightieth birthday party in November 2005 touched on this point. "How," John asked, "can you possibly convince potential employers, girlfriends, mothers even, that the job you do is a difficult, responsible, and demanding one when Bill edited *National Review* for thirty-five years while writing a thrice-weekly column, conducting a weekly television interview show, . . . [and on through a paragraph full of accomplishments]?" How Bill was able to do this, as we have seen, is that once the magazine was fairly launched, he was happy to delegate most of the day-to-day work to trusted deputies, whereas John was very hands-on, even a bit of a control freak. On the other hand, John liked working collaboratively: often he would sit across the desk from one of his colleagues—it might be the managing editor, or the articles editor, or the book editor—each with a galley proof, each calling out proposed changes as we went. Bill was dumbfounded when he heard about this—the *time* it must have taken!—but it worked very well. In fact, in one of our more exciting moments, an editorial was written from scratch in that way. It was the day in 1996 that Colin Powell was going to announce whether he was running for president. It was press day, and we had no one in Powell's circle to make the sort of phone call one of the present authors had made concerning Agnew and then Nixon. We had gotten permission from the printing plant to send one last page not by 1:00 P.M. but by 4:00 P.M., and the announcement was scheduled for 3:00. We sat in front of the television in John's office and listened to the announcement. John and Rick Brookhiser quickly hashed out the line we would take, each scribbled a few notes, Dorothy McCartney was dispatched to find a couple of elusive facts, and then John and Rick started, by turns, dictating to Linda, who typed their words into the computer, offering editorial changes as she went. In about fifteen minutes it was finished; another five for the three of us to reread it; and then into the typesetting room to have Michael Ashton turn it into a page proof. That one we never even printed out. We read over Michael's shoulder, making small cuts to fit, and off it went by modem. As Michael was sending it, John said happily, "That's *journalism.*"

Another way in which Bill preferred to delegate and John did not was by using regular columnists. From the magazine's inception, Bill's idea was to have men and women whose writing he liked and whose judgment (at least in one particular field) he trusted, and then let them decide what was important to write about that week. John preferred to discuss potential topics even with those, like our new man in Washington, Bill McGurn, who wrote in every issue. And he believed some of the columnists he had inherited were out of touch with changes in, say, the British political scene or the direction of NATO. Many of those whose columns he discontinued, he later commissioned to write specific pieces. Still, there were hurt feelings, understandably, and a period of adjustment.

There were also grumblings, here and there, about the oddity of having a Brit as editor of an American magazine with "National" in its name. Now, no one could claim that John has become indistinguishable from a native-born American. Then again, as Christopher Buckley put it at his father's eightieth, "Until I was three, I thought we were British." And John certainly loves this country, and knows it. He had his first test in the 1988 election, when he had been with us only three months, and he earned an A+. One of the present authors remembers that there were minutiae having to do with pivotal districts in Illinois and Iowa where John accurately predicted both what the voters would do and what the network commentators would (inaccurately) predict. Of our editorial crew, only Priscilla and Rick could match him on partisan politics. (Bill, as he is the first to admit, isn't in the running.)

And no one quibbled with the writers John brought in, or used more regularly. To name just a few, foreign correspondents Radek Sikorski, Noel Malcolm, and Mark Almond; social critics Barbara Amiel and Lisa Schiffren; defense expert Eliot Cohen; foreign policy expert Elliott Abrams; economists Larry Kudlow and John Dizard; analyst Peter Brimelow; philosopher Hadley Arkes; and last but certainly not least, professional curmudgeon Florence King.

Chilton Williamson had done Frank Meyer one better in the editor-in-absentia sweepstakes. He had gone out to Wyoming on a vacation, fallen in love with the place and decided to write a book about oil wildcatters, and wound up living there full-time. Technology had made huge advances since Frank's day, and with the help of an assistant back in New York, Chilton was able to manage the book section from Kemmerer, Wyoming, coming back roughly once a quarter to meet with colleagues and outside writers and to attend the editors' Agony. That suited Bill, but it didn't suit John, who wanted more advance discussion of the book section. At first Chilton tried flying back once a month, but that proved too onerous, and he resigned.

Wick had a candidate to replace him, and also to start a new project, National Review Books. Brad Miner was, like Wick, a Catholic convert; he was also an experienced, though young, book publisher and a solid traditionalist. *NR* published several books under Brad's guidance, notably his own *NR College Guide* (coauthored with Charles Sykes) and *The Art of Persuasion: A National Review Rhetoric for Writers*, by Bill Rickenbacker and one of the present authors. These weren't runaway bestsellers, but they did very well.

During the 1988 campaign, George Bush had courted both social and economic conservatives assiduously, hitting all the right notes on gun control, welfare, crime (Willie Horton), defense, taxes, and federal spending. Movement conservatives still felt some residual unease over what they viewed, despite the Texas transplant, as an almost instinctive hereditary Northeastern liberalism. Nor was this unease assuaged by some of the lines in his acceptance speech at the New Orleans convention, notably his call for "a kinder, gentler America"—heard by many, among them Bill Buckley, as disparagement of Ronald Reagan—or "a thousand points of light." Some hard-boiled conservatives were suspicious of the fact that Bush seemed most comfortable with a female speechwriter, Peggy Noonan. Then again, it was a woman of a very different sort, Margaret Thatcher, who put it all into words just before the invasion of Kuwait when she warned, "You're not going to go all wobbly on me now, George."

Whether he went wobbly in not following through in Iraq and ousting Saddam Hussein remains an open question. On domestic matters, however, "wobbly" is an understatement. The "environmental president" greatly expanded federal intrusion into the private sector and into the lives of individual Americans, going along with Democratic initiatives such as the Clean Air Act and the Americans with Disabilities Act. He closed down the Public Liaison Office created by Reagan to deal with conservative groups; he chose nonconservative, anti-supply-side economic advisors like Richard Darman, a Harvard Business School M.B.A. who had held various positions in the Ford and Reagan administrations; and he allowed John Sununu to purge Reaganites from the White House staff and replace them with pragmatic party regulars. (Sununu inspired one of our favorite contributions by *NR*'s house poet, Bill von Dreele: "Deck the halls for John Sununu, fa-la-la-la-la la-la-la-la. He's the bull they all say moo to, fa-la-la-la-la la-la-la-la.")

In the same acceptance speech that sent up warning signals with "kinder, gentler," Bush had made the emphatic pledge that warmed conservatives' hearts: *"Read my lips: No new taxes."*

In 1990, however, he allowed Darman to convince him that the only real problem with the economy was the deficit, and the only solution to that problem was to raise taxes—what Robert Novak, in an *NR* article during the 1980 campaign, had called the "root-canal school" of Republican economics.

To that end, Darman bypassed House Republicans and undertook a series of negotiations with the Democratic leadership in Congress. These resulted in a proposed deficit reduction program that included large tax increases. Conservative House members, energized and united under the leadership of the charismatic new Whip, Newt Gingrich, sent a letter to the President telling him they would vote against the proposal. Caught between what he (or more likely Darman) thought of as conservative intransigence and liberal insistence that the tax bite cut deeper, Bush decided to go with the liberal Democrats, and allowed Darman to propose bigger increases in order to pass the legislation.

Thus, in one fell swoop, Bush allowed Darman to undo the Reagan administration's supply-side achievements and reinstate Keynesian principles as the economic law of the land. In the process, he not only alienated congressional conservatives but violated one of the most basic promises made to conservative constituents during the campaign. They had read his lips. And he hadn't kept his word.

Over the last few months of 1991 unfolded the final act in the Evil Empire's breakup: the end of the Soviet Union itself. It was gradual, beginning in August with the attempted coup against Gorbachev by Kremlin hardliners. We sat in John O'Sullivan's office, glued to CNN. When ordinary Russians started pulling up paving stones to use as weapons against tanks, John and Linda had a frisson: Hungary 1956. We were the only ones present who had watched the Hungarian uprising on television at the time, and for whom it had been a formative experience. But this time the military officers refused to obey the hardliners' orders. Before long, a large white-haired man was standing on top of a tank addressing a crowd. Boris Yeltsin was in charge, the coup was over, and by the end of the year so was the Soviet Union.

Buckley's reaction is for the ages. "I was nineteen years old at the time the Yalta conference was held," he told an audience at Vanderbilt University in September. "Soon after that came Potsdam, and the West lost Eastern Europe to the Communists. The Cold War had begun. On the last day of August, one month ago, the Communist Party was banned in the Soviet Union. Coincidentally, I am sixty-five years old. I passed from teenage to senior citizenship, coinciding with the duration of the Cold War.

"We can sleep better for knowing that our cousins have regained their freedom. But we can't bring back those who lost their lives, nor bring back lifetimes in freedom to those who spent theirs without it."

When, a decade later, he wrote *The Fall of the Berlin Wall*, some liberal reviewers expressed pleased surprise that he did not give all the credit for the end of Communism to Ronald Reagan—or perhaps to Reagan, Margaret Thatcher, and John Paul II. But those reviewers hadn't been paying attention. Buckley had always taken pleasure in giving the President, the Prime Minister, and the Pope due credit for their encouragement of the dissidents and their practical actions to undermine the Communist regimes (notably Reagan's NSDD-75). But he had also always given credit to the men and women behind the Iron Curtain who risked far worse than political defeat in opposing their countries' regimes. As he put it in a speech in 1990, "The 1980s are most certainly the decade in which Communism ceased to be a creed, surviving only as a threat. And Ronald Reagan had more to do with this than any other statesman in the world.

"Reagan is not Solzhenitsyn. It was Solzhenitsyn who emerged as the Homer of anti-Communism. After the publication of *Gulag*, the European intellectual class could no longer—believe. . . .

"The great heroes of the decade—Walesa, Solzhenitsyn, Sakharov— have earned their place in freedom's House of Lords; but the political leader was Ronald Reagan."

How was retirement suiting Bill Buckley? One day in Gstaad, four months after his surprise announcement at the anniversary dinner, Bill went off to the men's room at the end of lunch. The Buckleys' Swiss friend Nina Schneller said in wonderment to the rest of the party: "He really must be retired. He let us finish our coffee!"

Still, Bill's wasn't what most people would call retirement. He was still doing his full ration of *Firing Line*—although, three years before, he had reduced the shows from a full hour to a half hour. He was still writing his column three times a week. (In 1994 he would reduce it to twice a week.) He was still actively riding the lecture circuit. And he was still producing a book a year (sometimes two, if you count the collections of his columns and other journalism).

He was also still actively encouraging the next generations—as he still is a decade and a half later. There was an illuminating vignette around the time of his retirement. Henry and Nancy Kissinger wanted to give him a sixty-fifth birthday party. Their assumption had been that they would invite their glamorous mutual friends from the social circuit. Bill happily accepted the offer, but asked the Kissingers instead to invite younger journalists. And so in January 1991, between Bill's return from his fourth, and last, ocean crossing and his departure for Gstaad, some three dozen young and youngish conservatives assembled in the Kissingers' splendid apartment in River House to toast their leader.

The year was capped when, in November, Bill received the Presidential Medal of Freedom from his old friend George Bush. The citation read: "William F. Buckley Jr. has long served this Nation as a prolific author and as a thoughtful and insightful commentator on public affairs. His columns, books, novels, and television programs have enlightened and entertained millions with a style marked by grace, an irrepressible wit, and vibrant energy. The magazine he founded, *National Review*, is one of America's leading journals of opinion and has greatly contributed to the intellectual foundation of the American conservative movement. The United States honors a man who has given much to this country, a tireless worker in the vineyards of liberty."

At the end of the Gulf War, President Bush's polling numbers were stratospheric—91 percent approval ratings—and he was exultantly talking of a New World Order. But the economy was limping and the Darman betrayal had backfired, leaving the deficit higher than ever. By the runup to the 1992 campaign, Bush's numbers had plummeted and Pat Buchanan was considering a challenge in New Hampshire. *NR* summed up the Bush record in a major editorial, "Fortune Favors the Brave" (written by John O'Sullivan):

> Until the last few months, President Bush's record might—with charity—have been described as mixed. True, he had broken his pledge to hold down taxes in order to reduce a deficit that promptly rose by another $100 billion. Admittedly, the major reason for that deficit was that domestic federal spending had been increasing by 10 per cent annually in the Bush years—a faster rate than under any other postwar President. To be sure, the revival of regulation, enshrined in legislation like the Clean Air Act, had piled burdens onto an already staggering U.S. industry. But there were some positive achievements on the other side of the ledger: his record of conservative judicial appointments culminating in Clarence Thomas; his principled opposition to abortion; his repeated use of the veto; his opposition to the Democrats' quota policies; and, above all, his

skilled and courageous prosecution of the Gulf War. All these persuaded conservatives to give Mr. Bush the benefit of the doubt
when reaching an overall verdict on this Administration.

That doubt has dissolved in recent days, and not to the President's benefit. His decision to endorse the quota bill, his echoing of
the Democrats' analysis of the November [1990] elections as a call
for more of the same in national health insurance, his flip-flopping
on credit-card interest rates, his collapse before liberal criticism of a
White House attempt to reform federal rules on racial and sexual
quotas, and his fiscal paralysis have revealed a vacuum where his
principles are supposed to be.

In fact Buchanan did run in New Hampshire and several other
early primaries, while conservative stalwarts Jack Kemp, Pete du Pont,
and William Bennett chose not to challenge a sitting president. But
Buchanan did badly, not winning more than a third of the vote in any
state where he campaigned. And although he did, in *NR*'s judgment,
succeed in pulling Bush back toward the right, "he failed to articulate
an attractive and coherent conservatism for the post-Reagan era."
Specifically, he failed to assuage conservative doubts about his apparent isolationism and protectionism, and he did not propose serious
spending cuts. Nor did he take the opportunity to back down from
any of his provocative remarks about Israel, Jews, or neocons.

The Democratic nominee turned out to be the garrulous young governor of Arkansas, Bill Clinton, who had positioned himself as a centrist New Democrat, in the process laying to rest the stigma of
McGovernism. Darman's budget deal gave Clinton ammunition for a
double-barreled assault on Bush's tax proposals, attacking the tax
increases themselves and Bush's apparent dishonesty. The charges
stung, aimed as they were at Bush's strong suit, his integrity. Nor was
Bush's position helped by the fact that a recession was well under
way, and many of those losing their jobs were, for the first time,
white-collar workers who normally voted Republican.

Also, there was the personal dimension. Although the differences
were profound, Clinton shared certain strengths with Reagan. Both
were articulate, both telegenic, and both could convince voters that
they cared. When Clinton told voters concerned about the economy
that he could feel their pain, they believed him. When Bush was questioned about the economy, he looked at his watch.

True, he was a man with impeccable credentials, and he had overseen an impressive military operation, driving the Iraqi army out of Kuwait. But with the larger threat of the Cold War gone, there was little taste for foreign adventures. Although Bush's poll ratings had shot up in the immediate aftermath of the war, they dropped precipitously as election day approached. As James Carville was fond of saying, "It's the economy, stupid." And as Pat Buchanan accurately pointed out, it would become increasingly difficult to find voters who really cared whether Iraq did or didn't occupy Kuwait.

By election day, through a combination of perceived overemphasis on foreign policy, the reinstatement of Keynesianism, personal aloofness, and coolness to social issues, Bush had lost much of the old-line conservative constituency. In previously strong Republican states like Illinois, conservatives didn't vote for Clinton, but they didn't work for the Bush ticket with any enthusiasm, and a significant number voted for wild card Ross Perot, running as an independent. There's no consensus about the effect that Perot had on the outcome of the 1992 race. Some say Bush would have won had Perot not run; others say that's not the case. The numbers can be interpreted either way, just as they can in reruns of Gore, Nader, and Bush the Younger in the 2000 election.

But one thing Perot's strange quasi-candidacy did was to lay bare old fissures running through the conservative movement that had been taped over by common opposition to Communism and apparently exorcised by the strong and unifying presence of Ronald Reagan. These were the fissures that would split the conservative movement back into factions—neocons versus paleocons, supply-siders versus root-canalers, internationalists versus America Firsters.

Ski and travel writers who keep a chip on their shoulder love to sneer at Gstaad. One guidebook in the 1980s said, "There's lots of nightlife in Gstaad, but don't expect to see any of it unless you're Roger Moore's houseguest or staying at the Palace Hotel." An article in a ski magazine began, "Gstaad is a town where everyone sounds like William F. Buckley Jr., and usually is." (Actually, only one man ever was.)

In fact, while the valley is full of the rich and famous, the locals have managed to keep much of the atmosphere traditional and down-to-earth. True, one of the most expensive (and best) French-style restaurants in Switzerland, the Chesery, sits at the center of Gstaad. But right across the courtyard is the traditional Posthotel Rössli (a favorite of Ernest Hemingway's). At Rössli's informal restaurant, the Stübli, visitors with designer outfits and high-toned accents sit cheek by jowl with locals in work clothes speaking Schweizerdeutsch (as opposed to school-learned high German). One of the hardest places to get a reservation is the Café du Cerf in Rougemont, where until very recently the menu listed only cured meat and melted cheese (in the form of raclette and fondue), and the music was piano, accordion, and saw. (Yes, an ordinary carpenter's saw—not twanged, as in our Appalachians, but played with a violin bow; it has an unearthly beauty, like the voice of a boy soprano.) The Cerf has recently added two or three cooked dishes, and Walter, the saw player, has died. But the tone hasn't changed.

Admittedly, down-to-earth isn't the term for the Eagle Club, in any sense. Geographically, it's up at the top of the Wasserngrat chair-lift, and, at least according to Taki Theodoracopulos, the members can get a bit raucous. It was one of David Niven's favorite lunch places, and Bill has been less inclined to go there since Niven died. But oh! the memory of that buffet, with its dazzling array of salamis and smoked fish and pâtés and salads and cheese. One day Bill was eating on the terrace with a couple of skiing companions when who should turn up but Pat. (She hasn't skied since that accident in 1965, but the chairlift is entirely accessible to pedestrians.) She was meeting a large party of skiers, who were running a bit late. Presently they swooped out to the terrace, led by Roger Moore and Nan Kempner, each resplendent in a white jumpsuit, and led Pat away on skirls of laughter, while Bill's party headed out to the slopes.

One of his guests remarked that the Wasserngrat is her favorite mountain in the area, even though parts of it are a bit of a stretch for her. Bill replied, "That's interesting—it used to be Pat's favorite, too. But then, she took lessons and practiced beautiful turns." Bill himself would rather go fast down the Videmanette, the long cruising trail that ends a few hundred feet from the château. But even though he never took the time to cultivate a beautiful form, he could handle any slope, and he was quite distinctive, by the time one of the present writers skied with him, in his brimmed sailing cap and long red jacket; the thought of him in a white jumpsuit was quite simply unthinkable.

On the slopes at Gstaad; center: Taki Theodoracopulos, resplendent in jumpsuit; WFB, unmistakable in sailing cap.

*   *   *

In April 1994 Richard Nixon died quietly in California. But the aftermath was anything but quiet, as commentators left, right, and center tried once again to make sense of what Bill Rusher called this "strange, stubborn, and ambiguous man."

Perhaps one of the most remarkable things about Richard Nixon was that beyond the usual set of preconceived opinions, no one really seemed to know who he was, and those who thought they knew him best often came to feel they didn't know him at all. Of his last meeting with Nixon in March 1960, Whittaker Chambers wrote to Bill Buckley: "I came away with a most unhappy feeling. I suppose the sum of it was: we really had nothing to say to each other."

The following year, in a letter in which he urged Nixon to make the race for governor of California, Chambers told Nixon that there was in him "some quality, deep-going, difficult to identify in the world's glib way, but good, and meaningful for you and multitudes of others." Chambers, a man of great sensibility and understanding, had reason to know Nixon well. But Nixon has baffled generations of analysts now, and that indefinable "deep-going" quality is as close as anyone has come.

After his death, of all the analyses and all the discussions, the single most telling and poignant may be Bill Buckley's obituary, written for *National Review*:

Clare Boothe Luce once remarked that all public figures come to be associated with a single achievement, never mind how complex their career. And, true, we can say about Lincoln that he won the Civil War, about Edison that he harnessed electricity, about FDR that he created the New Deal. But with what achievement will Richard Nixon be associated, a generation from now? A negative achievement: he is the only American President in history to be kicked out of office. Even so, in America and in much of the world, he was the dominant political figure. It can happen only to a man who takes very large strides in history, that he could win re-election with a runaway majority, and in less than two years leave the White House in greater ignominy than was ever before suffered by a departing American President.

His excommunication from public life was so decisive, his subsequent return has to be credited to him alone, the most spectacular reopening in contemporary political history. Remarkable not only because he came back, so to speak, into power, but that he did so notwithstanding the implacability of those who were hostile to him. In the darkest days of August 1974, it looked unlikely that a single member of the press corps could be persuaded to be civil to Richard Nixon. Ten years later, after he addressed their convention in Washington, he was given a standing ovation.

Of Nixon's life postpresidency, Buckley wrote:

Retirement suited him singularly well. Henry Kissinger, in his own memoirs, remarked on how little Nixon actually enjoyed the life he had struggled so hard to achieve in the White House. He hated meeting with the press, hated state functions. He engaged in much that chiefs of state engage in with a visible detestation of ceremony and light talk.

That now was all gone, and he had only his tiny staff, his yellow pads, and the publishers, waiting for book after book. He resumed those travels he did enjoy—briefing foreigners, being briefed by them; renewing the company of men and women he had met when he was sun-king.

Buckley concluded:

In the final analysis, he was a heroic, intensely personal figure, whose life was lived on the public stage. He was at once the weakest of men, and the strongest; a master of self-abuse, and of self-recovery.

Stained by worldliness, and driven by the hunger to serve. For Americans under seventy, there never was a world without Richard Nixon. Not many people can pitch whole generations into loneliness, as he has now done, R.I.P.

Surely, one of the truest and most perceptive analyses of Richard Nixon ever written—or ever to be written.

Bill's friend Sir Arnold Lunn—English conservative polemicist, Catholic convert and apologist, and inventor of the slalom—once titled a collection of his essays *Unkilled for So Long*. The phrase came from a Swiss friend who yanked him back to the sidewalk when he had absentmindedly stepped out into oncoming traffic. "How," the Swiss asked indignantly, "have you remained unkilled for so long?"

Friends have often wondered this about Bill. It's not just the big things—sailing on instead of pulling into port when there's a storm ahead; taking off, alone, in his single-engine plane when he was dead tired from cramming for exams (granted, the plane episode occurred when he was at Yale, and twenty-one-year-olds notoriously think they're immortal). It's also little things like walking from the office to Paone's and back again. Numerous colleagues, trotting to keep up with him across Third Avenue as the light was changing, have wondered whether he was about to lead the *National Review* branch of the conservative movement into oblivion.

When it comes to cars, Bill is an excellent driver when he keeps his mind on it. But Elsie Meyer recalled one trip on the lovely, winding Merritt Parkway in Connecticut. Frank had just made some important concession about the Catholic Church. Bill, surprised and delighted, slewed around to look him in the eye while saying, "That's awfully big of you, old man!"—just as they were approaching one of the Merritt's tighter curves. But one of Bill's oceangoing companions could top that, and did. In *WindFall*, Bill writes: "Dick Clurman obviously went to such extravagant pains to indite his slanders, I have no chivalric alternative than to reproduce his journal entry." It chronicles a drive down a mountain road in the Azores. Clurman writes:

> The two-hour, steep climb brakes his Le Mans driving proclivities. So the ride up, with Bill at the wheel, is relatively tame.
>
> The steep ride down is another matter. Bill is winding and weaving at never less than fifty—up to sixty—miles an hour. I am in the passenger seat on the right, my seatbelt fastened (as, foolishly, I

never do when driving with anyone else). Bill slows down not one whit as he pulls his crew-necked cashmere sweater over his head. "Grab the wheel," Danny shouts to me from the back seat. Good thinking, because Bill's sweater is snagged, covering his face and eyes. "Pull on my sleeve," Bill says calmly, as I hastily reach with my right hand to oblige. My left hand is clutched to the wheel. Bill's foot is still on the accelerator. The sweater maneuver completed, he resumed his conversation in midsentence where he left off, never deigning to mention his murderous and suicidal auto-gymnastic undressing.

His skiing friends have their own stories. Van Galbraith's first ski lesson almost was his last, as Bill had forgotten to explain to him, in the lift on the way up, that you must stand with your skis at a right angle to the fall line until you're ready to go. As Bill himself tells it, the resulting scene might have come from a Marx Brothers film, *A Day on the Mountain*. Through native athleticism and nerve, Van survived, and he eventually became a superb skier. There are also accounts of nephews being led off piste and across fenceposts (if the bottoms of the skis got ripped out, Uncle Bill would ante up for a new pair), and nieces being ordered by Aunts Jane and Priscilla to stick with them instead of listening to their captivating uncle. But the best story is told by Bill's old friend Anita Matti. A group of Buckleys and friends had traveled from Gstaad to Mürren to visit Sir Arnold Lunn. The rule in group skiing is *Follow your leader*, but Bill shot past Anita, around a blind corner—and there was a fallen skier, right where Bill's next turn would have been. He swerved and found himself going off the groomed trail into thick crud (for non-skiers, that's not slang, it's a technical term for wet, gluey ungroomed snow). By the time he came to a stop he was twenty feet away, his skis and his legs up to the boottops buried immovably in crud. Anita had to flag down eight or ten teachers and get them to form a human chain to pull him gently back to civilization.

To a great extent, the "conservative revolution" of the 1990s was all about Newt. From 1979, when he first entered Congress, Newt Gingrich had been setting the table, preparing for the day when the Republicans would retake Congress. In 1988, Gingrich was instrumental in having ethics charges brought against Democratic Speaker of the House Jim Wright, who had used a book deal to circumvent campaign-finance laws. Wright was forced to resign, and within the Republican caucus Gingrich was given great credit for his downfall. In 1989, when the minority whip, Dick Cheney, was tapped by President Bush to be secretary of defense, he was succeeded by Gingrich, who immediately went on the attack against the Democrats for corrupt practices in the House, which they had controlled for forty years. The House banking and post office scandals were exposed as typical examples of institutional corruption.

In the election campaign of 1994, Gingrich finally got his chance. In order to counter the Democrats' agenda and pull the various ideological strands of the Republican Party back into something like Reaganite unity, Gingrich offered his colleagues and the nation the Contract with America—a list of ten ambitious policy proposals that included term limits, tax cuts, welfare reform, tougher criminal penalties, and a balanced budget law. More than three hundred GOP candidates signed on to the Contract, which ended with the adjuration: "If we break this contract, throw us out."

And it worked. The Contract with America, writes Lee Edwards, "was the tip of a giant conservative iceberg that tore into the seemingly permanent Democratic majority in Congress and sank it faster than the *Titanic*.

"In the November 1994 elections, Republicans gained fifty-two seats and assumed a majority in the House of Representatives for the first time since 1953, when Dwight Eisenhower was president. And they recaptured control of the U.S. Senate. The *New York Times* called the Republican-conservative triumph 'a political upheaval of historic proportions.' "

Conservatives had already defeated the Clinton health care proposal—with some help from liberal legislators who would have preferred a Canadian-style system to Hillarycare's mandated employer-provided HMOs. *National Review*, *Human Events*, and the *Wall Street Journal* all did as thorough a job as we could of covering the issue, with John Goodman's National Center for Policy Analysis in Houston doing a lot of the heavy lifting. The NCPA provided research material and writers, and with their help we were soon all talking knowledgeably about medical savings accounts and "portability" of health insurance—ideas that Bush the Younger has taken some steps toward implementing.

In any case, the 1994 election was a political triumph for conservatives, and a personal triumph for Newt Gingrich. House Minority Leader Bob Michel of Illinois, a great legislator and a gentleman of the old school, did not run for reelection in 1994, leaving the way open for Gingrich to become Speaker. Under his direction, during the first hundred days of the session, the 104th Congress voted on all ten of the Contract's proposals. Not all the provisions became law, and some were weakened considerably. Nevertheless, Congress had taken a decisive turn in terms of goals and priorities.

That summer John O'Sullivan wrote about the fortunes of America post-Reagan and Britain post-Thatcher. (Margaret Thatcher had been unseated by a revolt within her own party over the question of what Britain should do about the tightening stranglehold of the European Union.) "How did it come to this?" O'Sullivan asked.

> After the Reagan-Thatcher heroic age, both Republicans and Tories reverted to unheroic leaders steeped in establishment respectability and conventional unwisdom.
>
> Mr. Bush and Mr. Major duly set about squandering their legacies. They raised taxes, let spending rip, and dropped broad hints that they would retreat from their predecessors' bolder conservative approaches—Mr. Bush promised "a kinder, gentler America," Mr. Major "a nation at ease with itself" and a "classless society."
>
> Both roads led to nemesis, but by different timetables. The GOP was fortunate enough to lose the 1992 election, freeing Reagan's children, pre-eminently Newt Gingrich, from the bonds of loyalty to failed policies. They revamped Reaganism for the Nineties in the Contract with America.
>
> In Britain, however, Mr. Major did not abandon Thatcherism until after his 1992 election victory. So Thatcher's children were restrained from criticism by the golden chains of high office as conservatism deconstructed itself.

The Contract with America and the hundred days were, as Lee Edwards rightly points out, a historic achievement, and Gingrich could be forgiven certain triumphal assertions. But there were also some cooler heads, striking a note of caution. In the summer of 1995, the Heritage Foundation's quarterly, *Policy Review*, asked nine respected observers of national politics to comment on Gingrich's comparison of the First Hundred Days of the 104th Congress with the First Hundred Days of the presidency of Franklin Delano Roosevelt, and to point to any serious errors that Gingrich and the House leadership might have made.

One of the commentators was Bill Rusher, who summed it up in this way:

The First Hundred Days of the new House Republican leaders will deserve that well worn adjective "historic" even if relatively few of the measures listed in their Contract with America ever become law in a form they would recognize. For the central achievement of the First Hundred Days was to change the whole terrain and direction of American politics. . . . Whether the First Hundred Days of this House will ultimately deserve comparison to the First Hundred Days of Franklin Roosevelt's presidency depends upon how success- ful the Republicans are in setting their initiatives in concrete, as the New Dealers managed to set theirs. . . .

Any major mistakes? Yes, one: The failure to anticipate and pre- pare for the Democrats' counterattack, based on the tired old charge that Republicans want to starve America's children and stuff the money into the pockets of the rich. . . . A big enough lie will be believed, by a small but often crucial percentage of voters, if it isn't nailed promptly and repeatedly by spokesmen whom the media can- not ignore. (Note how disastrously the Bush administration let the liberals rewrite the whole history of the 1980s.) We may yet pay dearly for the Republican party's sloth in this regard.

Pay we did, when the Republicans flunked the first big test, administered by the voters in 1996. As Edwards puts it, "[T]he year that began with such shining promise ended in bitter disappointment. The Republican House watched its public approval sink from 52 per- cent to the upper 20s in January 1996, while speaker Gingrich received a perilous disapproval rating of 51 percent.

"Republicans grossly underestimated President Clinton's political skills, especially his use of the veto, and they failed to respond force- fully enough to the Democrats' propaganda"—precisely as Rusher had predicted. "And they overestimated the ability of Congress to govern. In the age of mass media, presidential power is too great and congressional power is too diffuse for Congress to prevail over the President for long."

Whether, as Micklethwait and Wooldridge believe, Gingrich came to think of himself as an American prime minister and coruler, there's no doubt that the election of 1996 was too much about Newt.

The wheels had begun to come off early in 1996 as a result of the budget fight between House Republicans and Clinton. Gingrich did not have the votes to override a veto, and yet he refused to submit a revised budget. This meant allowing appropriations to expire and effectively shutting down parts of the federal government. The shut- down was inevitable, he argued, because the President would not agree to a balanced budget. The Democrats, in turn, trotted out all the arguments Bill Rusher had predicted they would make—cuts in school lunches, Medicare, Medicaid—with the President taking every public opportunity, visibly and emotionally, to share the pain of the least among us.

Gradually, with that intense media focus that Edwards cited, sentiment began to turn. As Micklethwait and Wooldridge put it, "After twelve months of unrelenting government bashing by Gingrich, most Americans blamed the omnipresent House Speaker. Clinton's political sonar—his ability to say roughly what the American people wanted to hear—was returning. . . . Whatever political sonar Gingrich had possessed was now turned off. In November he complained to the press that he had been put in the back of Air Force One on the way back from Yitzhak Rabin's funeral, so the New York *Daily News* ran a cover with him as a crybaby."

Obviously, too much about Newt. But the fact remains that he was an innovative and imaginative thinker, and until the 2006 elections, the House of Representatives remained a conservative institution, at times the primary keeper of the conservative flame.

This is how he is viewed by a former House Republican aide and old friend of *National Review*, who worked closely with the leadership during the Gingrich period:

> As to Newt the Revolutionary, before the revolution, he had a great talent for what I call "a demagoguery of information," a gift for grabbing and using any new idea or fad—"futurology" or "the information highway"—that came to hand and developing it to suit a preconceived political end. But he liked talking about ideas more than he did implementing them.
>
> His problem, as a revolutionary, was that he was more Trotsky than Lenin or Stalin. He was "brilliant" (in the worst sense of the word) rather than solid. He made a revolution, but didn't know what to do with it. He had a genius for a strange kind of genial invective. He could call the Dems the most awful things—"corrupt" was his favorite word—but he'd never get angry or raise his voice, just speak in that professorial let-me-explain-the-facts-and-you'll-agree-with-me tone of voice.
>
> He also had a talent for getting under the skin of Democrats. (Tip O'Neill got so mad at him one day that he questioned Newt's integrity and, under House rules, had to leave the floor. And it was Tip's floor!) Like Trotsky, Newt wanted "continuing revolution," but it was never clear what for. In leadership meetings he'd dish out

four or five "ideas." Three would be too silly to consider. One would be interesting. The last, if pursued, might have been useful. But he had no follow-through. None.

Let me put it this way: without Newt the Republicans would not have won a majority in 1994. But without Clinton, Newt would not have been able to seize the day. If Newt was Trotsky, Clinton was the Czar he needed.

I should also say this. Newt drove us crazy. But there was something about him in those days, a vitality, a kind of boyish enthusiasm for ideas that made him hard to dislike and impossible to ignore.

Bill Rusher, quoted in Lee Edwards's *The Conservative Revolution*, adds one important point: "I also question whether he is a 'movement conservative,' in the way that Reagan was. He is a conservative on most subjects, certainly, but his mind is too restless to seek—or find—comfort in simply cleaving to certain bedrock principles."

And Edwards adds this philosophical codicil: "Conservatives believe that cleaving to principle and even being willing to lose on principle—not always but sometimes—are what conservatism is all about. Sometimes, as Taft, Goldwater, and Reagan all demonstrated, you win by losing."

Ronald Reagan had made occasional appearances on the public scene since his departure from Washington. In October 1990 he taped two installments of *Firing Line*, under the title "Two Friends Talk: Ronald Reagan and Wm. F. Buckley Jr." There were no fireworks in these shows—nothing like the Panama Canal debate. But there was broad and deep discussion of world affairs. Reagan at one point recalled a conversation with Gorbachev, one of the many times the latter tried to dissuade him from going ahead with SDI. "I used the example of World War I," Reagan told Buckley and the viewers. "I said all the nations of World War I met and outlawed poison gas, but we all kept our gas masks. I said, Who can say that down the way somewhere there won't be another Hitler, there won't be another madman that could use the knowledge of how to make weapons and blackmail the earth?"

The dedication of Reagan's presidential library in November 1991 was a grand occasion. John O'Sullivan took the trouble to fly out to California for it and was well rewarded. "Every schoolboy knows," he wrote, "—as Macaulay used to say in happier times when schoolboys did know such things—that there were four crowned heads (and five lesser monarchs) at Queen Victoria's funeral.

"Well there were five presidents—Reagan, Bush, Carter, Ford, and Nixon—(and six First Ladies) at the dedication of the Ronald Reagan presidential library in the Simi Valley. It was, in short, a historic occasion."

O'Sullivan quoted Richard Nixon: "Thirty-two years ago in Moscow, Soviet Premier Nikita Khrushchev jabbed his finger into my chest and said, 'Your grandchildren will live under Communism.' I replied, 'Your grandchildren will live in freedom.'

"At the time, I was sure he was wrong. I was not sure I was right. Now we know.

"Thanks in great part to . . . Ronald Reagan, Khrushchev's grandchildren now live in freedom."

Reagan's next big appearance was at the Republican Convention in Houston in 1992. Rick Brookhiser was on the scene for *NR*. "It was an autumnal performance," Brookhiser wrote of Reagan's speech, "and he ended by bidding the delegates 'good-bye.' Yet the text was all youth and hope, quoting—and believing—Emerson, on America as 'the country of tomorrow.'" Bill Buckley, watching it all on television in Stamford, summed up: "[Reagan] has been around a very long time—after all, he reminded us, he and Thomas Jefferson were friends, and Clinton is no Thomas Jefferson. He has addressed six conventions, and the laws of probability suggested that this would be his final appearance, and he wished to leave his fingerprint indelibly in the memory of his flock: America is unique. America was born to be exceptionalist."

The following January, one of George Bush's last acts as President was to bestow the Presidential Medal of Freedom on his predecessor. With Nancy and Barbara looking on (Nancy in her trademark red, Barbara in her trademark royal blue), Bush said:

Today we honor the American life of an American original. . . . I consider him my friend and mentor, and so he is. And he's also a true American hero. . . .

Ronald Reagan didn't just make the world believe in America; he made Americans believe in themselves. And I remember Inauguration Day in 1981 and how the clouds—maybe you remember it— of a gloomy morning gave way as he began his speech. He turned that winter of discontent into a springtime of possibility.

President Reagan believed in the American people, so he helped the private sector create 19 million new jobs. He knew that government was too big and spent too much, and so he lowered taxes and spending, cut red tape, and began a peacetime boom, the longest in American history.

Some men reflect their times. Ronald Reagan changed his times. And nowhere was that more true than abroad, where he championed the holy grail of liberty. Mr. President, you helped make ours not only a safer but a far better world in which to live. And you yourself said it best. In fact, you saw it coming. We recall your stirring words to the British Parliament . . . : "the march of freedom and democracy . . . will leave Marxist-Leninism on the ash-heap of history."

Two years later, Reagan made one of the most graceful and touching exits from public life in history. His age had been his running joke ever since the second Mondale debate. But when age finally did overtake him, he was the first to admit it. In a handwritten letter released by his Los Angeles office in November 1994, he told the American people that he was suffering from Alzheimer's disease and that he would not be addressing us again. He had begun, he wrote, "the journey that will lead me into the sunset of my life."

Buckley's 1994 book-writing trip to Switzerland brought two changes. The first had to do with living arrangements. Ed Tuck had sold the château, and the new owner wished to occupy it in the winter. So Pat went house-hunting again and found a chalet high up in Rougemont—the first of several they would occupy over the next few years before finding the right one, on the Wispile side of Gstaad. That first chalet directly overlooked the château, and Bill would amuse his guests by hauling out, after dinner, a pair of infrared binoculars through which to view his old home.

The second change was in the type of book he would write. The last two Blackford Oakes novels, *Tucker's Last Stand* and *A Very Private Plot*, had not sold nearly as well as their predecessors. Although the Soviet Union was still in existence when *Tucker* was published, the Cold War was effectively over, and it seemed that readers didn't want to be reminded of it. And so Bill decided to try non–Blackford Oakes novels. The first one, *Brothers No More*, has a gripping plot but a bitter taste. In shape, it is what we were taught, while studying Henry James in college, to call a chiasmus: one of the protagonists starts out a coward and forces himself to become strong; the other starts out brave and resourceful and gradually digs deeper and deeper into moral weakness, becoming, finally, not quite evil, perhaps, but criminally amoral. *Brothers* didn't hit the bestseller list, but it sold well enough to encourage Bill in this line. There were people and events he had long wanted to write about, but he didn't relish the constraints of formal scholarship. But in a fictional mode he could mix a less rigorous form of research with his own recollections and write about Joe McCarthy (*The Redhunter*); James Jesus Angleton (*Spytime*); Ayn Rand, the John Birch Society, and the early days of *National Review* (*Getting It Right*); the Nuremberg trials (*Nuremberg: The Reckoning*); and, most surprisingly, Elvis Presley (*Elvis in the Morning*). (We were aware that Bill knew Angleton personally, but it was only after Angleton's death that Bill revealed how often, in the months after Angleton's dismissal as head of counterintelligence, he had called Bill from pay phones to whisper his latest thoughts on the mole he was convinced was undermining the CIA.) And in 1997 Bill finally completed what he had been calling "my Catholic book," *Nearer, My God*, which he had been working on sporadically for years. The delay had one serendipitous effect: he was able to include a luminous chapter about the ordination of his nephew Michael Bozell, who had years earlier become a monk at the great French Benedictine house of Solesmes, and who now accepted his vocation as priest.

A profusion of younger, very bright conservative senators and governors had emerged during the Reagan and early Bush years, and despite the loss of the White House in 1992 and the close-down-the-government debacle of 1995, conservatives had high hopes that one of them would surge forward and make Bill Clinton a one-term President. But Bill Armstrong, a riveting speaker and highly telegenic, meant what he said about being a citizen legislator: after two Senate terms he went back to Denver to make some money for his family. Senator Malcolm Wallop of Wyoming, Governor Tommy Thompson of Wisconsin, and Governor John Engler of Michigan all decided for their own reasons not to make the run. And so vying for the conservative vote in 1996 were Pat Buchanan, magazine publisher Steve Forbes (a very bright man but not an exhilarating speaker), Senator Phil Gramm of Texas (endorsed by *National Review* and no one else), and Alan Keyes (who had written splendidly on restoring a sense of community to inner-city neighborhoods, but who as a candidate veered uneasily between policy wonk and old-time Southern preacher). Bob Dole was the man whose turn it was to represent establishment Republicanism. Rounding out the primary field was Lamar Alexander, who ran an offbeat quasi-populist campaign, based mainly on his unusual name (his bumper stickers and campaign placards said merely: "Lamar!") and his plaid shirts.

So strong and audacious was Buchanan's guerrilla candidacy that he very nearly unhorsed Dole by winning the New Hampshire and Louisiana primaries. He might well have had a clear shot at the nomination had he been able to upset Dole in South Carolina.

As Ramesh Ponnuru pointed out in a powerful *National Review* article, "Reagan's Spoiled Children," published in May 1996, "in the absence of a unifying candidate, the Reagan coalition split, with economic conservatives backing Steve Forbes and social conservatives going to Buchanan. . . . [T]he Beltway Right inadvertently helped Buchanan to exploit fissures in the coalition by blithely ignoring the sentiments of social conservatives. A steady drumbeat from D.C. had signaled that social issues, notably abortion, had to be pushed to the back burner. Washington conservatives' blind spot on the familial and moral principles that animate the grassroots caused them to underestimate Buchanan's political potential."

"Social and economic conservatives," Ponnuru concludes, "signed a suicide pact." Forbes drew the supply-side, antitax vote, and Buchanan took the pro-life voters. "When he was going strong, Buchanan simply isolated religious conservatives from the rest of the party." As a result, Dole owed very little to either economic or social conservatives, or they to him.

Thus, in the general election, the conservative base failed to rally to Dole in sufficiently enthusiastic numbers. Part of the problem was the candidate himself. Dole was an honored WWII veteran and a great pragmatic deal-making senator of the old school (and the consensus is that he should never have given up his Senate seat). But he was showing his age, especially when contrasted with Bill Clinton's aw-shucks, Peck's Bad Boy youthfulness. Also, Clinton, like Gingrich, is a nonstop-talking polymath, which came in marked contrast to Dole's acerbic terseness. At one point Dole referred to a game played by the Brooklyn Dodgers as if he hadn't heard the team had moved; at another he pitched headfirst from a speaker's stand into an audience (a dive surpassed only by Gary Bauer's backflip off a stage in the 2000 campaign while trying to flip a flapjack).

And so what Hillary Clinton would later call the Vast Right-Wing Conspiracy fell over each other's feet while her husband waltzed to reelection. Reagan had been dubbed "the Teflon President," but the Clinton administration was redefining the meaning of Teflon, as neither Hillary's financial improprieties, Bill's sexual improprieties, the campaign's improper and probably illegal dealings with Chinese bagmen, nor Bill's stirring up the Middle East for the sake of his "legacy" managed to deny him a second term.

Near the end of the 1996 campaign, Spiro Agnew died unexpectedly, just hours after being diagnosed with advanced leukemia. A year earlier, in June 1995, he had finally been able to tie up one loose end.

It is the custom of the U.S. Senate to install in the Capitol a bust of each outgoing vice president—since one of the VP's official duties, under the Constitution, is to serve as president of the Senate. But Spiro Agnew, leaving town in disgrace in 1973, was denied this routine commemoration.

In 1991, Matthew Scully, who had succeeded Brad Miner as *NR*'s Books, Arts & Manners Editor (retitled by O'Sullivan "Literary Editor"), went to work for Vice President Dan Quayle. Looking around the Capitol, he was astonished and then angered to discover that there was no Agnew bust. He started a campaign, which his former employer was delighted to join. As Scully later put it: "*National Review* took up Agnew's cause four years ago after learning that he, alone among Vice Presidents, had been excluded from the Capitol's pantheon, apparently the old Senate leadership's idea of a moral point. Under the new leadership it has all been resolved satisfactorily: not only is there a bust, the thing stares right out at the main entrance to the Senate chamber (a reminder to Democrats of which party's in charge, and to Republicans of which magazine not to cross)." Agnew gave a brief and dignified speech at the unveiling ceremony. "I am not blind or deaf to the fact," he said, "that there are critics who feel this is a ceremony that should not take place. I would remind these people that regardless of their personal view of me, this ceremony has less to do with Spiro Agnew than with the office conferred upon me."

One of the present authors was asked to write Agnew's obituary for *National Review*. It concluded:

> Spiro Agnew was his own man, sometimes very nearly to the point of eccentricity. And generally, he was perceived as tough. ("The only way you can put a tough crust on a marshmallow is to roast it.") But there was something else. Richard Nixon is said to have observed wonderingly, "The Vice President is a soft man."
>
> And in his own way, he was. During the weeks of emotional shellshock following his resignation, he worked hard to ensure that all his staffers had jobs. And though his dislikes were strong, he was never vindictive. In April 1994, he wrote me: "Judy and I will attend the Nixon funeral tomorrow. I have never fully been able to forgive the abandonment in 1973, but I have enormous respect for his accomplishments. Moreover, both Judy and I loved Pat, and we think Tricia and Julie are first rate."
>
> To which I'd like to add on my own: So were you, Mr. Vice President. In your own way, so were you.

One of *NR*'s finest hours came in the spring of 1997. We had no idea, when it started, that we were running any risks, any more than Bill had when he wrote *Overdrive*. Rich Lowry, one of our gifted young Washington writers, had produced an article on Bill and Hillary Clinton's and Al Gore's illicit fundraising among the Chinese, including Gore's visit to the Buddhist temple in southern California and the White House's dealings with John Huang. By this time *NR*'s art director was a young Russian émigrée, Luba Kolomytseva, and she had brought on board the brilliant caricaturist Roman Genn, a fellow émigré. For Lowry's cover story, O'Sullivan commissioned Genn to put the Clintons and Gore in Chinese dress—Bill Clinton in a coolie hat, Hillary in a Red Guard uniform, and Gore in Buddhist robes with a begging bowl—to go with the title "The Manchurian Candidates."

Genn's caricature was brilliant, we thought. The professionally aggrieved Asian lobby did not. We got first a trickle, then a deluge of letters from Asian Americans hurt, outraged, disgusted by these caricatures. One phrase imprinted itself in the memory, since it was repeated by nearly every one of the supposedly spontaneous letter writers: "grotesque buckteeth and stereotypical garb."

One day there were even picketers marching outside our building. This had happened only once before, a dozen years earlier. In that case, the offense had been Buckley's column in which, attempting to come to grips with the AIDS epidemic, he had suggested that sufferers should be tattooed as a warning to those to whom they might spread the disease—on the buttocks for active homosexuals; on the upper arm for users of intravenous drugs. Well. Most of the critics started by invoking Hitler and went on from there. When the picketers came, they had placards and chants prepared: "Homophobes ain't got no class; Buckley wants to brand your a——." There were police on hand to keep order, and a few television and radio reporters. The apartment building across the street had a high percentage of retirees, and several of these brought folding chairs out onto the sidewalk to watch the show. Our editorial assistant, the free-spirited Steve Weeks, went down and chatted with the cops. The rest of us watched from our second-floor windows, or from Bill's third-floor balcony.

By the time of "The Manchurian Candidates" we had moved offices. Our old landlord on 35th Street, Mr. Scholem, had died, and his son had sold the building to a developer who wanted to turn it back into residential apartments. And so at the end of 1996 we had packed up our lares and penates, thirty-nine years' worth of memories, and moved to a conventional office building a few blocks away. We learned there how much of America is forced to work—paper-thin walls, where there are walls at all and not mere partitions; an uncontrollable heating and cooling system; no privacy except for a handful of high-ranking or lucky staffers; no windows except for ditto. As Willi Schlamm suggested way back when, corporate America has a lot to answer for.

In any case, we were now on the fifth floor—not as good for observing a demonstration. Then again, after what happened to John O'Sullivan a few weeks later, we felt perhaps it was just as well. John had a long-standing engagement to speak at Yale. As he reported in the magazine, "At Yale last week I was assaulted by a howling mob of honors students who pulled at my clothes, struck the odd blow (no cause for concern—not even my pride was hurt), waved placards, and shouted loudly a few inches from my face: 'We demand respect.'" The Yale demonstrators and many letter-writers, some of them representing one Asian American organization or another, demanded that John apologize. This he would not do. But he would explain: "The cover *was* an attack—but not on Asians. It was a political joke at the expense of the President, the Vice President, and Mrs. Clinton in the context of the Asian fundraising scandal . . . It showed them in various Asian guises, each appropriate to his personality and/or part in the scandal: Mr. Gore was a Buddhist monk soliciting donations from the faithful; Mrs. Clinton was Madame Mao—the more fanatically ideological partner of the Great Helmsman; and the President himself, all things to all men, took on the features, Zelig-like, of the Asian businessmen to whom he was serving coffee in the Oval Office."

Roman Genn also calmly defended his work. Confronted by a reporter, Genn said philosophically: "Their job is to get ticked off at cartoons. My job is to draw them. We're all doing our jobs."

We were overjoyed when the brilliant left-liberal cartoonist Pat Oliphant weighed in: "It's a wonderful fact that there is still a publication that will run these politically incorrect things."

The final act of this drama came when a local television station sent a crew over without an appointment to talk to one of our editorial staff. It was the day before press day, and there was only one writer who had time to talk to the reporter. When the latter saw the unmistakably Asian (though not, granted, Chinese) face of Ramesh Ponnuru, he said out loud: "Leave it to Buckley to have a f——ing ace up his sleeve."

Alas, John's finest hour was one of his last with *NR*. Whatever the problem was—neither John nor Bill talks about it, as far as the present authors know—John stepped down from the editorship at the end of the year. He had been with us longer, much longer, than with any previous employer, and he continues, as an editor-at-large (the same title Bill took upon semiretirement), to write regularly for the magazine and take part in events such as *National Review* cruises. After a brief but intensive search, Bill promoted from within, elevating Rich Lowry from National Political Reporter to Editor.

John had done much to raise the magazine's profile and (along with, first, Wick Allison and then Ed Capano, who had apprenticed under Jim McFadden and who took over as publisher when Wick returned to Dallas) to bring our operations into the late twentieth century. He and Wick greatly expanded our Washington presence, hiring Kate O'Beirne away from the Heritage Foundation and installing the gifted young writers Rich Lowry and, later, Ramesh Ponnuru as reporters. (Both Rich and Ramesh had come to our attention through the first—and last—annual Young Writers Contest.

The contest was a great idea, but reading all the entries while putting out the magazine nearly killed John, Linda, and Brad.) Not least, John reinvigorated *NR*'s social life. In the early days, there were frequently guests at editorial lunches. But then, after Bill and Pat acquired the 73rd Street apartment, lunches mostly became quasi-working affairs, and the guests were invited to editorial dinners instead. The only problem there was that from the magazine's side, only senior editors were normally invited.

So John started editorial lunches at which the younger editors would also get to meet the outside guests. Some of the guests were stellar, a few bombed, most were somewhere in between. One of the present authors went a bit weak-kneed at actually meeting the heroic Vladimir Bukovsky, who proved as impressive in conversation as he is in his writing. Others who performed brilliantly at these lunches are too numerous to name; it's pure luck of the draw that we mention William Bratton, former New York City police chief, who built on the George Kelling/James Q. Wilson broken-window theory to develop the quality-of-life policing that made New York City a much safer, more pleasant place; Patricia Woodworth, who had straightened out Michigan's finances for Governor Engler and would have done the same for New York's if Governor Pataki had had the guts to back her up; David Gelernter, Unabomber victim, beautiful writer, father concerned about his children's schooling; and John Cardinal O'Connor. (Of the un-stellar performers, the one that sticks in the mind is Senator Al D'Amato. Besides bobbing and weaving in his chair like a punch-drunk ex-fighter and finding it difficult to speak in complete sentences, he repeatedly attacked Van Galbraith, who, perhaps quixotically, was running for the 1994 New York Republican gubernatorial nomination against D'Amato's boy, Pataki. D'Amato hadn't done enough homework to know that Van was a friend of many of the people around the table. He also didn't know how ridiculous was his charge that Van had been born "with a silver spoon in his mouth." His doctor father died when Van was a teenager, during the Depression, leaving the family quite badly off. All the cosmopolitan polish Van had acquired had been by his own efforts.)

John also started organizing conferences. The first one was held in D.C. in January 1993, just before Bill Clinton's inauguration. (John, less prescient than usual, denominated this as not the end of the Reagan-Bush years but the midpoint of the Bush-Clinton years.) The conference, called "The Conservative Summit," was buoyant in spirit—"surprisingly cheerful," as the polymathic observer Tom Bethell would put it in his report for *NR*, "considering that 'Team Billary' had taken up residence at 1600 Pennsylvania Avenue." Speakers included Elliott Abrams and Caspar Weinberger, both survivors of Lawrence Walsh's interminable Iran-Contra investigation; traditionalists Maggie Gallagher, Mona Charen, and Hadley Arkes debating gay marriage with Andrew Sullivan; New Democrat Ben Wattenberg debating U.S. immigration policy with *NR*'s (and *Forbes*'s) Peter Brimelow; two members of Hollywood's conservative community, one long associated with *National Review* (Charlton Heston), the other a recent discovery of John's (Lionel Chetwynd); Bruce Herschensohn, a conservative hero from the 1970s for his refusal, while at the USIA, to kowtow to Senator Fulbright; L. Brent Bozell III, Brent and Trish's third son and the head of the very effective Media Research Council; and (here we are again with what Bill calls the *inclusio unius est exclusio alterius* problem) dozens of other high-powered conservatives, and a few friendly nonconservatives.

Approaching the 1998 elections, the Republicans went wobbly on the economic issues and permitted the Democrats to pass a budget with no tax cuts and billions in "emergency" spending. Nor did the party as a whole (there were many individual exceptions) campaign hard on issues like school choice and Social Security privatization. Instead, it concentrated with almost lascivious glee on Bill Clinton's personal behavior and the eagerly anticipated impeachment.

NR warned repeatedly that this was bad policy (the issues *do* matter) and bad politics (putting all your eggs in one basket is a poor idea). And *NR* was right. In August 1998 a judge threw out Paula Jones's sexual harassment suit against Clinton. In November the voters left House Republicans with a paper-thin majority. And in February 1999 the Senate failed to convict Mr. Clinton of high crimes and misdemeanors. There was considerable recrimination among the Vast Right-Wing Conspiracy as to how we had let him get away. Too often, conservative commentators had looked like a batter swinging for the fences, missing the ball entirely, and falling flat on his face.

Bill Buckley's standard speech that season worried the bone of why the public had not been more outraged by behavior that was characterized by Clinton's most eloquent *defender*, former senator Dale Bumpers, as "indefensible, outrageous, unforgivable, and shameless."

"America," said Buckley,

is correctly proud of its capacity to forgive, but also we are aware that forgiveness is a joint exercise.

Forgiveness presupposes contrition.

There is something continuingly provocative in Mr. Clinton's personal appearance. He doesn't—ever—look guilty. When he gave his State of the Union speech last week his expressions recalled the face of Winston Churchill on V-E Day. His manner was as triumphant as if he had single-handedly accomplished the rape of all the Sabine women. Good old Tricky Dick Nixon never let the public down in these matters. He *always* looked guilty, never more so than when he was facing the public and averring his innocence. His face was a polygraph. Clinton's face is that of the freshly minted altar boy. He is Oscar Wilde's Dorian Gray. We have looked at that face through the corrosive mists of Gennifer Flowers, draft evasion, platonic experiences with marijuana, through Vincent Foster, Webster Hubbell, the Lincoln Bedroom, through Huang, FBI files, Mrs. Willey on *60 Minutes*, and what we see is something in the nature of incredulity. For that reason, a convincing apology from him is as inconceivable as a sex change. Bill Clinton couldn't bring it off.

Buckley did not wait until the round-numbered millennial year to take his next steps into retirement. In December 1999, he brought *Firing Line* to a close with a couple of slam-bang roundup shows. The first began with excerpts from *Firing Line*s past, with guests ranging from Jesse Jackson to Ronald Reagan, from Allen Ginsberg to Mother Teresa; the second ended with excerpts from Bill's appearances on other shows, notably *Laugh-In*, and imitations of him by various comedians, notably David Frye and Robin Williams. In between was a spirited discussion with six guests: Michael Kinsley and Mark Green, who had both served on *Firing Line* as the liberal counterweight; *NR*'s Rich Lowry and Rick Brookhiser; Bill Kristol, founding editor of *The Weekly Standard*, the new kid on the conservative block; and Peter Robinson, the researcher for Bill's book *On the Firing Line* and himself the host of the television show *Uncommon Knowledge*.

Firing Line holds the record as the longest-running public affairs show with a single host. It also maintained over thirty-three years a level of discussion matched only by some more specialized shows, like Brian Lamb's *Booknotes*. As Brookhiser put it on this farewell installment, "How often does anyone with an intelligent opinion get an hour of television? We've just finished three series of presidential debates. We have men who want to be the most powerful man in the world having to utter haiku and slip them into forty-five-second slots, and that's the level of discourse."

That same season, Bill announced his retirement from the lecture circuit. He would continue to speak on special occasions, to organizations with which he has a long-standing connection—the Philadelphia Society, ISI, the Bradley Foundation, and of course *National Review*. But he took himself off the college and business meeting roster.

The following spring, his collected speeches were published, under the imprint of the Forum series (a collaboration between Prima Publishing and *National Review*). Bill's researcher and in-house editor on that book was one of the present authors. When Rich Lowry came in as editor in 1998, he wanted his own editorial team. He chose Jay Nordlinger as managing editor, and Linda Bridges became a senior editor, working as Bill's literary assistant. Finding and cataloguing the speeches for him to choose and arrange was her first effort for him. The resulting book, *Let Us Talk of Many Things*, is in effect a collection of snapshots from his entire career. (The only one of the blurb writers who caught—or at least, the only one who had fun with—the allusion to Lewis Carroll in the title was John Kenneth Galbraith: "William Buckley does indeed talk here of many things, with deft mention of the many cabbages and kings that he has addressed politically over these years.") The book starts with his Class Day speech from 1950 and concludes with his address on receiving the Heritage Foundation's Clare Boothe Luce Award in October 1999. In between are the high points (or many of them: we could have picked up a second book of equal length, and nearly equal quality, from the cutting-room floor) of a lifetime spent in the public eye.

10

Passing the Torch

One notable feature of that Heritage Foundation award dinner was the identity of Bill's introducer. Ed Feulner had asked Christopher Buckley to do the honors, and he did so with his usual wit and panache. Chris concluded his remarks about his father: "I've watched the President of the United States hang a medal around his neck and call him a hero. I've listened as Cardinal O'Connor . . . addressed him in a room crowded with important prelates and called him 'the jewel in the crown of American Catholicism.' And I have heard my mother say one thousand times, 'Your father is impossible.'

"And you know, they were *all* right."

Chris has made his own considerable mark in the world of letters, though, like his father and his uncle Reid, he is equally at home behind the lectern. In fact, among the many hats he wears, he serves as one of several "consulting faculty" of Reid's extremely effective Buckley School of Public Speaking in Camden.

Back in 1990 Malcolm Forbes had tapped Chris to be the founding editor of a new high-end spinoff magazine, *Forbes FYI* (lately renamed *ForbesLife*). Chris made the new magazine as stylish as Forbes could have hoped, attracting writers like Joseph Heller, P. J. O'Rourke—and Wm. F. Buckley Jr. Two of the essays Bill rated highly enough to include in his autobiographical anthology, *Miles Gone By*, were written at his son's behest: "1001 Days on the Orient Express," about a fascinating, infuriating trip across Siberia; and "Ten Friends," commissioned for *FYI*'s tenth anniversary issue. It is interesting, and appropriate, that friendship is what Chris thought to ask his father to write about.

Meanwhile, Chris's first bestselling novel was no fluke. His flair for zany plotting and perfect descriptive prose has carried him to the bestseller list another half-dozen times—most recently with *Florence of Arabia*, about an American State Department official determined to liberate the women of "Wasabia" (a fictionalized Saudi Arabia). More than one reviewer has described him as the finest satirical novelist in America today. He has also, finally, reached the big screen, with the film, released in 2006, of his hilarious *Thank You for Smoking*, in which he makes a brief Hitchcock-like appearance. Add his frequent satires for *The New Yorker* and other magazines (including *National Review*), and his articles for his own magazine—usually about some high adventure, though it might equally be about the summer he spent crewing on *Suzy Wong*, or the lost art of writing telegrams, or managing the Christmas hints of one's children (though Caitlin and Conor usually appear in his writing in fictionalized form)—and you have a splendid oeuvre, still in the making.

Coming into the 2000 election cycle after Dole's loss in 1996, the Republican field was wide open. Dole himself, unable to generate enthusiasm or funds for a repeat run, dropped out early, as did Lamar

The grandchildren: Caitlin (at age fourteen) and Conor (at age ten).

Alexander, his plaid shirt now badly frayed, and Dan Quayle, who never mastered his potato problem. Steve Forbes, still struggling with the spontaneity thing, paid his own way and remained in the race, with his integrity intact. Still standing, in addition to Forbes, were Alan Keyes—still eccentric and still without a constituency—George W. Bush, and John McCain.

Bush, with his pedigree, his positive record as governor of Texas, his strong support from the Christian right, and his equally strong support from the regular conservative Republican ranks, was listed as the early favorite. McCain, with his background as a war hero, an individualist from Arizona who revered Barry Goldwater, and a maverick in the Senate, attracted the support of independents, students, Republicans tired of the regular-party old bulls, and some conservatives, notably the editors of *The Weekly Standard*.

McCain scored early and impressive primary victories in New Hampshire, several other New England states, and Michigan. In his speeches and debates with Bush he seemed the more formidable candidate, building his party support and increasing his backing in the press. Indeed, he enjoyed the sort of honeymoon with the media usually reserved for maverick Democrats like Eugene McCarthy. But during the campaign, Bush displayed a characteristic that would come to mark his progress through the general election campaign and eventually his presidency. No matter how bad the initial performance, he would put his head down and keep pushing straight ahead, confronting those words, thoughts, ideas, policies until he got them right—improving incrementally, but steadily.

Then came South Carolina, which so often decides presidential primary fortunes. Bush beat McCain decisively, and in the process solidified his strength within the party, which had never wholeheartedly supported McCain. The key datum was that South Carolina was the first primary in which only registered Republicans could vote. Without the support of disaffected Democrats and independents, the McCain candidacy lacked legs. Bush rolled through the remaining primaries, winning most by comfortable margins, and accepted the Republican nomination in Philadelphia at what Pat Buchanan called the "We Are the World Convention." Meanwhile, one very positive effect of Steve Forbes's remaining in the race was that his flat-tax message was sufficiently resonant to prod Bush into sharpening his own economic message and promising massive tax cuts—a promise he and his team eventually delivered on.

As for Buchanan, he won the nomination of an oddly restructured version of Ross Perot's Reform Party, fending off challenges from, among others, Donald Trump and John Anderson.

On the Democratic side, Bill Clinton's almost psychopathic behavior with a young intern, which in a better age would have brought the girl's father to Washington, horsewhip in hand, threw a somewhat soiled and musty blanket over the candidacy of his chosen successor. That odor was mitigated, however, by the economic record Al Gore inherited: job creation up; a balanced budget (something every Republican politician in the nation had been demanding for decades); and, although we were starting to slide into a recession, the longest economic expansion in America's history.

Gore himself was a moral and upstanding family man. He initially seemed to take the right stance on the budget, government spending, and welfare, thereby satisfying the moderates in the Democratic Leadership Council, while carving out his own issue, global warming, which won him support on the Naderite left. Had he stuck with these general parameters, many commentators believe, he would have continued what *The Economist*'s Micklethwait and Wooldridge call the "conservatism lite" of Bill Clinton, and would probably have won the election.

But he didn't. Instead he ran a campaign that seemed to veer left, then right, then left again, as Gore, in search of himself, lurched from position to position, phase to phase. There was the "earth tone" clothes phase, initiated by a spacy female consultant; the odd, prolonged clinch with Tipper at the convention; and the sudden assumption of a William Jennings Bryan populist persona, resulting in a series of shouted speeches in defense of the working man—this from a man born into the Washington aristocracy as "Prince Al," and perhaps the only Democrat in the world who could claim as a boy to have sat on Vice President Nixon's lap while Nixon presided over the Senate (and who else in the world would want to claim that?). Finally there was that strange moment during the presidential debates when he suddenly adopted a Frankenstein's monster persona, lurching unexpectedly toward a seated George W. Bush and hovering awkwardly over him. Bush, looking up and doing a modified W. C. Fields double take, may have won the election at that moment.

And through all of Gore's campaign, there ran a studied, almost insulting avoidance of the man who had chosen him as vice president—not to mention Gore's own choice of running mate: Joe

Lieberman, who had been the first Democratic senator to take to the floor to denounce Bill Clinton's immoral behavior.

After the campaign, after the debates, came the great Florida foul-up, still the source of much argument and no doubt the subject of hundreds of future dissertations. However, according to nearly all the postelection aftercounts and studies, Bush did win, if only by an eyelash.

At any rate, when the dust settled, and by a margin of just one more vote in the Electoral College than was needed, America once again had a president who called himself a conservative, albeit a compassionate one. At *National Review*, the support for Bush was real but cautious. As Bill Buckley put it, "He's conservative, but not *a* conservative." As with Nixon, the question remained: Was he conservative enough?

On this question, there was unease, still there today, growing out of Bush's willingness to allow himself to be described as a big-government conservative.

Interestingly, writing in *The Weekly Standard* in December 2004, Andrew Ferguson, an occasional *National Review* contributor and a writer of great talent and wit, refers to "the nonsensical neologism 'big government conservatism.'" Interesting, because if memory serves, it was the executive editor of *The Weekly Standard*, Fred Barnes, who introduced that "nonsensical neologism" to describe Bush's philosophy, and is proud of having done so.

Family squabbles aside, there seemed to be little philosophical certainty about the new President Bush. Writing in 2003, Lee Edwards described the early days of the Bush administration this way: "No U.S. President was as coolly welcomed as Republican George W. Bush was in January 2001. . . . Widely described—and not only by partisan Democrats—as the man who 'stole' the 2000 election, a cautious Bush began his presidency by focusing on taxes and education reform as a reflection of his 'compassionate' conservatism. His major accomplishment in the first six months was a monumental tax cut of $1.6 trillion, a move in keeping with the supply-side economic philosophy of Ronald Reagan, not his father. . . . But the president seemed detached and even uncomfortable in the job, and Democrats began laying plans for an aggressive presidential campaign and a retaking of the White House in 2004."

Then came September 11, 2001, and the script changed utterly—and so did the nation and the President. As Edwards puts it: "The nation was no longer divided between blue Gore states and red Bush states but was united in red, white, and blue. The once passive President became an activist chief executive, asking for the authority to fight a protracted conflict against terrorists, help industries hit hard by terrorism, and rejuvenate a stalled economy. . . . Bush's approval ratings skyrocketed until they topped 90 percent—as high a level as any president since the advent of polling.

"Inevitably," Edwards continued, "President Bush's popularity has leveled off. . . . But America will not return to its pre-September 11 way of life. The terrorist attacks were a defining moment in modern American history. Americans are prepared to fight terrorism as long as they did the Cold War, which occupied us for some four decades."

That's the way it was in late 2003, heading into the election year of 2004. Bush's popularity had begun to level off, and questions were being asked more frequently about those weapons of mass destruction, as well as about the ways in which the administration had justified the Iraq war to the American people. (For some answers, see Greg Copley's *Defense & Foreign Affairs* publications. Copley and his team do not have much good to say about either U.S. intelligence efforts in the Middle East or the Bush administration's presentation of its case. However, they provide convincing evidence that the WMDs were no chimera and that Saddam's alliance with Muammar al-Qaddafi permitted research to continue even as UN inspectors wasted their time in the Iraqi desert.) But despite such questions, Edwards wrote, as of 2003 "the majority of Americans still believe the war of liberation against Saddam Hussein was justified, and they have not forgotten how quickly the United States removed the extremist Taliban regime in Afghanistan."

Bill Buckley's friends and admirers should have been warned by his closing down of *Firing Line* and his farewell to the speaking circuit. Still, many of us were startled and shaken when he began categorically giving up one activity after another—skiing, the harpsichord, the Bohemian Grove. Then in 2003 he sold his sailboat, and in 2004 he divested himself of his stock in *National Review.* Some wondered why he had to be so categorical: Why not just ski less often, one friend wrote to him, and only in perfect weather? And keeping your Grove membership doesn't require you to attend every year, if it seems too much effort.

The present authors tend to agree, and yet this sort of decisiveness is part of what has enabled Bill to do as much as he has done over the last sixty years, starting with the Yale *Daily News*. Again, the contrast with John O'Sullivan is instructive. Once Bill had put an editorial section together, he entrusted it to his colleagues, who would do any final adjusting while he went on to the next thing on his calendar. John, on the other hand, would keep fiddling, trying to squeeze one more item in, to find just the perfect combination. Usually he succeeded, though his colleagues sometimes grew desperate as the clock ticked away. Or take the simple matter of restaurants. John might spend an hour with Zagat, trying to find an exciting new place, whereas Bill is almost like the Bostonian lady in the cartoon: "Where do I *get* my hats? I *have* my hats." Bill has a half-dozen restaurants and clubs that he sticks with. If a friend introduces him to a new one and he likes it, great—it goes on his list. But he won't take the time to hunt for new places. And Bill is of the school that holds that in most matters, a good decision now is better than the best decision maybe three days from now. In the matter of his "terminal thoughts"—as he calls his various farewells—he has said, "It's a good idea, when a terminal thought arrives, to resist all reservations after one makes such a resolution; a good idea to turn one's mind to other things."

However, the decision, while categorical, is not necessarily sundering. For example, Bill used to invite his friends to sail with him; when he sold his last boat, *Patito*, it was to a consortium of three of these friends, who started inviting *him* to sail with *them*. And he continues to host *NR* functions and to meet with the editors and the directors. He also continues to write his column and to turn out books. In 2004 alone—the year he divested himself of his *NR* stock— *The Fall of the Berlin Wall* was published by John Wiley & Sons, *Miles Gone By* (composed of previously published essays, but chosen, arranged, and newly edited by WFB) was published by Regnery, and the manuscript of *Last Call for Blackford Oakes* was sent to Harcourt for publication the following spring.

The "majority of Americans" who, as Lee Edwards phrased it, "still believe[d] the war of liberation against Saddam Hussein was justified" did not include all elements of the intellectual right. As Bush pursued the War on Terrorism, the long-running rift between so-called paleocons and neocons became a chasm. We say "so-called" because the terms have shifted oddly over the years. "Neocons" originally referred to a group of Jewish intellectuals—most prominently, Norman Podhoretz and Midge Decter, and Irving Kristol and Gertrude Himmelfarb—who had been on the left and came over to the right, pushed by the excesses of the 1960s and early 1970s: the student and black violence, McGovernism, the metastasizing of the Great Society under Nixon, an increasingly militant feminism. As Kristol famously put it, "A neoconservative is a liberal mugged by reality." By not too great a stretch, Christians who made that same leap were also labeled neocons: Michael Novak, Richard John Neuhaus, Peter and Brigitte Berger. But then the term started to be used for people who were friends or indeed offspring of the above, but who had themselves been conservative all along: John O'Sullivan, Bill Bennett, Bill Kristol, Elliott Abrams, John Podhoretz. And by 2003, in the left's Internet fever swamps, members of the Christian right were being called neocons—because they supported President Bush on Iraq.

By the same token, at that Philadelphia Society meeting back in 1986, "paleocon" was used to mean, basically, "traditionalist conservative." And many of the people who started calling themselves paleocons as we left the Cold War behind and entered the twenty-first century did indeed have their roots in the traditionalism of the 1950s: Pat Buchanan, co-founder (with Taki Theodoracopulos) of *The American Conservative*; Thomas Fleming, editor of *Chronicles* and proponent of "heartland conservatism"; Allan Carlson, former president of the Rockford Institute, which publishes *Chronicles*; Chilton Williamson, books editor and columnist for *Chronicles* as well as a prolific author of fiction and nonfiction. But they have been joined by, for example, Lew Rockwell and Justin Raimondo, whose pedigrees are in the anarcho-libertarianism of Karl Hess and Murray Rothbard. What has united people of these disparate backgrounds is their view of America's role in the world. They advocate a return to the pre–World War II America First mind-set, and they oppose what they see as the uninformed Wilsonian/Theo Rooseveltian adventurism of the Bush foreign policy. Many of them strenuously oppose NAFTA, free trade as it exists today, and the whole concept of globalization. This position is perhaps best summed up in the title of one of Pat Buchanan's books: *The Great Betrayal: How American Sovereignty and Social Justice Are Being Sacrificed to the Gods of the Global Economy.*

On many of those issues conservatives of different stripes had argued peaceably over the years, as during Pat Buchanan's 1992 and 1996 runs for the presidency. But when President Bush declared the War on Terrorism, and especially when he ordered the invasions of Afghanistan and Iraq, the sides hardened. The paleocons, almost as a matter of definition, opposed the war, and opposed it harshly. A loose coalition of neocons and *National Review*-type conservatives favored the war—though many of the latter were uneasy from the start with statements by Bush and by British prime minister Tony Blair to the effect that democracy was a natural human instinct and that as soon as the Iraqis were given a chance they would flock to its banner.

In April 2003 David Frum, a former speechwriter for President Bush and the author of an admiring book about him, *The Right Man*, wrote a blockbuster piece for *NR* entitled "Unpatriotic Conservatives," in which he assembled and dissected the views of what he called the "antiwar conservatives." And some of these are provocative indeed. Buchanan: "9/11 was a direct consequence of the United States meddling in an area of the world where we do not belong and where we are not wanted." Raimondo: "[There will be] a high price to pay for 'victory' [in Iraq]—so high that patriots might almost be forgiven if they pine for defeat." Rockwell: "How horrible to realize, ten years after the Cold War, that the real evil empire is not some foreign regime, but the U.S. military state." George Szamuely, son of the great Hungarian political philosopher and anti-Communist Tibor Szamuely: "It is clear that neither laws nor any sense of fair play will stop this rampant U.S. arrogance. The time may soon come when we will have to call for the return of the spirit of the man who terrified the United States like no one else ever has. Come back Stalin—(almost) all is forgiven."

However, the paleos have no monopoly on provocation. What Frum attempted in his essay is a comprehensive indictment, in which opposition to the wars against the Taliban and Saddam Hussein is linked to anti-Semitism, white supremacy, and xenophobia. Frum did impressive research in digging up outrageous quotes on these subjects from some people who call themselves paleos. But, of course, that by no means demonstrates that everyone who calls himself a paleo shares those views. And it certainly doesn't demonstrate that someone who opposes the war but does *not* call himself a paleo—notably Robert Novak—shares any of them.

Perhaps Frum's biggest reach is when he writes, "I happen to have been in the room when 'paleoconservatism' first declared itself as a self-conscious political movement," and then proceeds to write about the 1986 Philadelphia Society meeting. Frum is implying that the current paleo antiwar movement grew directly out of Stephen Tonsor's remarks at that meeting. In fact, Tonsor was talking about modernism versus traditionalism—Nietzsche versus Burke. He said nothing about the distinctive marks of Buchananite paleoconservatism: antiglobalism, isolationism, protectionism. And since Tonsor is still around, he was able to point out, in the symposium on Frum's article that appeared three issues later, "Moreover I have supported both President Bushes and I have been an ardent supporter of the war against Saddam Hussein."

In that symposium, many writers approved of much of what Frum said, but some argued persuasively against the phrase "unpatriotic conservatives." As our elder statesman, Bill Rusher, eloquently wrote: "These people are not unpatriotic. It is true, as Frum says, that 'They began by hating the neoconservatives. They came to hate their party and this president.' But they do not hate America. They are simply, desperately, wrong."

"The days of our years are three score years and ten; and if by reason of strength they be four score years." Bill Buckley has friends young enough to be his grandchildren, but many of his closest friends are his own age or older. And so, sadly but not surprisingly, the rate at which he has received death notices has accelerated in recent years. (Sad and very surprising were the deaths, both in 2003, of two people in their fifties: longtime amanuensis Tony Savage and niece Lee Buckley, John's elder daughter, both of complications of alcoholism.) Bill concludes the acknowledgments in *Last Call for Blackford Oakes* by saying, "I did not send the manuscript for comments to the benefactors I have relied on in the past, primarily, as I pause to think about it, because two of my liveliest and keenest friends have died in the interval since my last novel. I remember Tom Wendel and Sophie Wilkins, with everlasting affection." The list goes on—Jim McFadden, Firpo Taylor, Herb Kenny, Hugh Kenner, Charles Wallen, Harold Berliner, Marjorie Otis Gifford (Old Lady), Henry Grunwald, Nicola Paone, John Kenneth Galbraith, Abe Rosenthal, Milton Friedman.

The funeral of one of Bill's friends was a world-historical event. There were as many presidents and first ladies at the National Cathedral on June 11, 2004, as there had been at the Reagan Presidential Library twelve years earlier. There were also world leaders, past and present, notably Mikhail Gorbachev, Brian Mulroney, Tony Blair, Gerhard Schröder, Silvio Berlusconi, King Abdullah of Jordan, and Prince Charles (representing his mother, with whom Reagan had several times ridden horseback while he was visiting Britain or she the United States). Senator John Danforth, who is also an Episcopal priest, conducted the brief nondenominational service and spoke beautifully of the late president. "If we have ever known a child of light," Danforth said, "it was Ronald Reagan." (And Episcopalians, so regularly battered these days by internal conflicts, could take pleasure in how beautifully the ecclesiastical discipline in the ceremony meshed with the military discipline of the honor guard.) Mulroney and Bush the Elder recalled some of Reagan's wisecracks, bringing laughter even to Nancy Reagan and her daughter, Patti. But for many of us the most moving presence was that of Reagan's old comrade-in-arms—Lady Thatcher, as she now is.

Herself ailing, having suffered a series of small strokes, and a widow for less than a year, she gamely traveled not only to Washington, D.C., for the funeral but also all the way to California for the interment. Some months earlier, for fear that when the time came her health would prevent her from speaking in public, she had recorded her eulogy of Reagan. The vast congregation in the cathedral, and millions of Americans watching on television, saw Thatcher on the screen, dressed in the same elegant black outfit she wore to the funeral, and heard her sum up the career of her friend. "In his lifetime," she said, "Ronald Reagan was such a cheerful and invigorating presence that it was easy to forget what daunting historic tasks he set himself. He sought to mend America's wounded spirit, to restore the strength of the free world, and to free the slaves of communism."

The official publication date of *Miles Gone By: A Literary Autobiography* was one week after Bill's divestiture of his *National Review* stock, and the resulting lovefest in the press was quite impressive. There were a few sour notes, mostly from some of the paleocons examined by David Frum in "Unpatriotic Conservatives." But for the most part, writers across a wide range of the political spectrum took the opportunity to express long-felt love and admiration and to do a provisional summing-up of a career that has spanned the postwar period.

Miles even hit the *New York Times* bestseller list, unusual for a collection of previously published work—but then, *Miles* is an unusual collection. As Bill explains in the introduction, instead of gathering the best of the previous five years' columns and other journalistic writing, this book would go back through his entire public career, "with an autobiography in mind. . . . What I have attempted is in the nature of a narrative survey of my life at work and play. There are personal experiences, challenges and sorties, professional inquiries, and memories beginning in childhood." There would have been no point, he concludes, "in contriving an autobiography from scratch. Why? I have already written about the events and the people that have shaped my life; any new account would simply paraphrase these. I hope this volume will achieve the purpose, and that it will give pleasure."

It certainly does. As a literary autobiography it showcases Buckley's great versatility as a writer, and nothing gives greater pleasure than reading a first-rate writer at the top of his form. Beyond that, as the survey of a life, it captures the essential nature of the man. As Jon Meacham, the estimable managing editor of *Newsweek*, put it in a review of *Miles* in *The New York Times Book Review*, "He is a partisan combatant, a key figure in the right wing's journey from the fringes of American politics to the mainstream. . . . But agree or disagree with the conservative creed he helped shape and promulgate, Buckley is the happiest of warriors, an exuberant man of the right, a Roman Catholic who has apparently taken the reassurances of Scripture to heart. 'In the world ye shall have tribulation,' Jesus says in the Gospel of St. John, 'but be of good cheer; I have overcome the world.'"

The joy in living is always there in *Miles Gone By*. Buckley spends many pages chronicling his life as sailor, skier, adventurer. He has traveled on all seven continents and sailed, as captain or passenger, on most of the world's oceans; swum in the Caribbean with a president and skied in Gstaad with princes and kings; gone down to the ocean floor in a high-tech little submarine to view the *Titanic* and flown alone in a single-engine Ercoupe.

Always there is the ability to characterize with quick strokes—just the right metaphor, distinctive physical characteristics, a snippet of dialogue, the quirks and idiosyncrasies. This ability to make us see and hear runs through all the pieces in *Miles Gone By*, from Buckley's boyhood schooling to life on the open ocean; from his battles with the Yale authorities to his battles with those who don't like big words.

Here is one of his professors at Yale: "A tall, ruddy-faced man with crew-cut hair who wore a hearing aid. He spoke the kind of sentences John Stuart Mill wrote. Never a misplaced accent, qualifier, verb; sentence after sentence of preternatural beauty, formed as if in a magical compositors' shop, by golden artisans."

Sometimes characterization comes through action, as when he first meets Ronald Reagan. The occasion was a speech in a high school auditorium in Beverly Hills. Reagan was emcee. "His assignment was to introduce me to the assembly. . . . But entering the hall we came on a huge bump in the road: not only was the sound system not on, but the room where you turned it on was locked. . . . That's when I espied True Grit in the future president. He ascertained that the window at the end of the stage overlooked a parapet about a foot wide, which extended . . . to the window of the control room. So he climbed out the window, arms outstretched for balance, and edged his way above the roaring traffic to the critical window, broke it open with his elbow, climbed into the room, found the switch and flipped it—and the show was on."

At other times, it's a simple phrase or sentence. Of Willmoore Kendall: "Willmoore made it a practice never to be on speaking terms with more than one friend at a time." Henry Kissinger, he tells us, taught a course at Harvard in the 1950s "taken only by students who intended to become prime minister or emperor." And he writes of Whittaker Chambers's "sadworldliness" and his "link to the heavy machinery of history."

There is a fine tribute to Henry Regnery, publisher of *God and Man at Yale* and of *McCarthy and His Enemies*, a man who was important to Buckley as "a friend, a publisher, a mentor" in those "very happy days in which book publishing was something of a personal partnership between publisher and author." (In later years, Henry and Eleanor Regnery liked to reminisce with one of the authors of this book about the early days when Bill would visit them in Illinois and delight their four children with "Variations on Three Blind Mice" on the piano.)

Boundless energy and enthusiasm and joy permeate this book, just as they have informed Bill's life. But there's another quality here, an undertone, a shading, just a whiff of melancholy. It's especially evident in a piece called "Aweigh," in which he tells us why he decided to sell his boat. This is an important piece, for sailing represents for Bill much of what he has found to be good in life, both in nature and in "social pleasure." "So that," he writes, "deciding that the time has come to sell *Patito* and forfeit all that is not lightly taken, bringing to mind the step yet ahead, which is giving up life itself."

In his epilogue, in a lyrical and moving passage that approaches the spiritual, sailing provides the image for that "step yet ahead." But while the reader acknowledges its force and beauty—and, of course, the inevitability behind the poetry—the inclination is to say: Let's not rush it. There's plenty of time ahead for that final cruise. And miles still to go before you even consider sleep.

President Bush's approval ratings had begun to slip by the time the election campaign of 2004 arrived, but they were still sufficiently high to discourage any meaningful challenge within his own party. He accepted the Republican nomination in New York on September 2, again chose Dick Cheney as his running mate, and proceeded to focus his campaign on the overriding issue of national security.

On the Democratic side, early front-runner Howard Dean, former governor of Vermont and spokesman for what he called "the Democratic wing of the Democratic Party" (translation: high liberalism), had rounded into 2004 as the media favorite, leading a McCarthyite (Eugene) national children's crusade and raising millions of dollars via the Internet—the first major Internet candidate, the media were fond of calling him. His great weaknesses—one being that he wanted a resurgence of liberalism, which almost no one else did—were not at first apparent to the media, although in December 2003 *National Review* put a particularly manic-looking picture of him on its cover, with the caption, PLEASE NOMINATE THIS MAN.

But the Democrats didn't. According to the national media, the Iowa primary voters would be the first to give their votes to Dean. Instead they gave their votes to John Kerry, John Edwards, and then Dean, in that order. This meant that the Iowa voters, considered among the most judicious and well informed in the country, preferred two candidates who, as senators, had voted to authorize the strike against Iraq over the candidate who had opposed it. Also done in by the Iowans was Dick Gephardt, the congressman from Missouri, who represented the last gasp of Great Society liberalism.

After Dean lost the primary he was supposed to win, there were still plenty of primaries left to be won. But then came the post-Iowa "I gave a scream" speech, and the ball game was over. Dean stayed in the race, but the media turned on him with a vengeance. As if to make up for all the affectionate attention they had lavished on him, they ran the speech over and over throughout the primary season.

After Iowa, Edwards, who seemed to have finished second because he could talk softly and earnestly, Oprah-style, remained to challenge Kerry, and he was joined by General Wesley Clark, who despite being billed as the Kennedy candidate proceeded to run a campaign characterized by an odd, even distasteful way of discussing issues. On abortion, for instance, he championed a woman's right to choose at any point in her pregnancy, even up to "the head coming out of the womb."

In New Hampshire, Kerry won again, with Dean taking second place and Clark finishing third. Edwards won in South Carolina, finished second in Oklahoma, and, after Dean dropped out, continued to pursue Kerry from state to state, nipping at his heels. As a reward for his doggedness, Kerry chose him as running mate, much as Ronald Reagan had chosen Bush the Elder.

On July 6 in Boston, Kerry accepted his party's nomination, and in his acceptance speech promised to make his experience in Vietnam a centerpiece of his campaign. He began the speech, Mr. Pinkerton fashion, with a modified salute to the crowd and this opening line: "I'm John Kerry and I'm reporting for duty." Unfortunately for him, so were the Swift Vets and POWs for Truth, who would do his campaign incalculable damage.

Kerry was the perfect foil for Republican campaign professionals. The ultraliberal Americans for Democratic Action gave him a higher approval rating than Senator Edward Kennedy. That means, said Republican National Committee Chairman Ed Gillespie, that "Ted Kennedy is the conservative senator from Massachusetts." Kerry couldn't do anything about the degree to which he resembled the Knight of the Woeful Countenance (his face was made to order for Roman Genn, and it graced several *NR* covers over the course of the campaign). But he seemed to have no sense of how things he could control would look to Middle America, like the costume he wore to ride his bicycle. In *The Weekly Standard*, Joseph Epstein, a fine writer of the old school and a man of great good sense, wrote about riding his bicycle in Chicago: "I don't suit up for these little excursions but wear whatever I happen to have on. I'd as soon put on Spandex shorts for a bike ride as give the Charles Eliot Norton Lectures in a Speedo." Had Kerry hired Mr. Epstein as his fashion consultant he might have carried Ohio, where Spandex-wearing candidates riding European racing bikes are viewed with deep suspicion.

As for the campaign, it was pretty much a matter of pounding away at national security, with Kerry, himself having voted for the war, arguing that he could do it better and alienate fewer Europeans in the process. The warning lights in Iraq had begun to flicker on, and Bush's dramatic carrier landing and announcement that combat operations had ceased was increasingly coming to be seen as an unfortunate piece of political stagecraft.

The scenario changed suddenly and dramatically when the Swift Vets and POWs for Truth came on the scene. These were men, led by the impressive John O'Neill, who had served with Kerry in Vietnam. In May they called a press conference in Washington, D.C., to refute Kerry's charges, made first in his famous testimony before Congress in 1971, that American servicemen in Vietnam—including the Swift boat units—had committed atrocities as a matter of course. Once the Swift Vets started talking among themselves—many of them hadn't seen each other since they were demobilized—they started questioning Kerry's service record, comparing notes and concluding that his exploits in Vietnam had been exaggerated. The charges were picked up by the national media and understandably given prime-time coverage. Kerry's long delay in responding to the charges compounded the problem. ("When someone insults you directly and impugns your honor," says one ex-marine, "you give him a second to apologize. If he doesn't, you break his face immediately.")

Meanwhile, Bush was suddenly blindsided by a service problem of his own. Relying on an eccentric source, rumors, and some documents of dubious provenance, CBS News ran with a full-blown exposé, purporting to prove that Bush had failed to fulfill his National Guard obligation. The charge was led by a triumphant Dan Rather, scourge of Republican presidents, no doubt dreaming of reliving those glory days when he was young and tormenting Richard Nixon and setting new standards of rudeness for reporters at presidential news conferences. In 2004, Rather, by then old enough to be eligible for Social Security, took advantage of the hurry-up work of an ambitious producer to rush the story onto the air. But the documents were discovered to be forgeries, the whole thing blew up in his face, and CBS finally had the excuse it needed to force him out of the anchor job and offer him space at *60 Minutes*. And when that announcement was made, there are those who claim they heard a ghostly voice, deep and vibrant, saying, "Now let me say this about that," and then a peal of ghostly laughter, all sounding very much like President Nixon.

The Rather fiasco plus the unanswered Swift Vets charges helped give Bush a significant lead in the polls as he went into the first presidential debate, held in Miami in September. However, during the debate, Kerry outthought and outtalked him across the board. The consensus was that Kerry had won handily.

On October 5, Dick Cheney and John Edwards held the only scheduled vice-presidential debate, and Cheney, in the eyes of Republican viewers, calmly cleaned Edwards's clock, as he had done four years earlier with Joe Lieberman. The presidential candidates met again in St. Louis on October 8, and this time it was generally considered that Bush had done at least as well as Kerry. He was following the pattern set during the 2000 campaign, initially performing poorly, then pushing straight ahead, getting better at each succeeding stage.

The third and final debate was held in Tempe, Arizona, on October 14 and it was here, many observers believe, with fifty million viewers tuned in, that Kerry lost the election. He was sailing along, perhaps better than holding his own, when late in the debate, for no apparent reason, he introduced the name and sexual preference of Vice President Cheney's daughter into a series of remarks. It seemed to many to be totally gratuitous, an appalling breach of taste, perhaps even an offense against simple decency. There was no logical reason for it, no point to be made, and it hit many viewers hard. A friend of one of the authors, apolitical but leaning toward Kerry, said he felt like he'd been punched in the stomach when Kerry singled out Mary Cheney for discussion. And that reaction was not untypical.

In the end, Kerry lost to Bush in the popular vote, 48.3 percent to 50.7 percent, and in the Electoral College, 251 to 286. The election set several records. Bush received more votes than any other president in American history, 62 million, topping even Ronald Reagan's landslide total of 54.5 million in 1984. He became the first candidate since his father in 1988 to receive a majority of the popular vote, something that Clinton (like Carter before him) failed to do. As for the minor parties—Libertarian,

Constitution, Independence, Reform, Green—their combined vote total was the smallest since 1988.

Finally, it should be noted that the 2004 election marked the first time since Lyndon Johnson's defeat of Barry Goldwater in 1964 that a sitting president was reelected while his party increased its numbers in both the House and the Senate, and Bush was the first Republican president since William McKinley (Karl Rove's idol) in 1900 to pull it off.

All in all, for George W. Bush, an impressive accomplishment. The son rose, somewhat unexpectedly, to heights not achieved by the father. He was elected twice, the second time with historic numbers; he unified his party and helped increase and solidify majorities in both houses; he responded magnificently to the attacks on 9/11; and in the aftermath of that terrible day, he set out to finish the job he believed his father had left unfinished in the Mideast. On the outcome of that protracted conflict will probably depend his place in history.

Blackford Oakes had been absent from the public scene for eleven years when, in 2005, a new novel was published: *Last Call for Blackford Oakes*. In some ways this was yet another terminal thought, a tying-up of one more loose end. But it is also a novel full of life.

We're back in 1987–1988, Gorbachev/*glasnost* time. Blackford is a little tired now, pushing past sixty, "no longer eye-catchingly handsome, but ruggedly attractive," and sadder, having lost his wife, Sally, whom he adored. A little less arrant, but still engagingly presumptuous, and still characterized by "a certain worldliness that is neither bookish nor in any sense of the word anti-intellectual"—in short, still distinctively American.

Again, as in *A Very Private Plot*, it appears that a plot against Gorbachev is being hatched in Moscow, and both Oakes and President Reagan believe it is in the best interests of the United States to keep Gorbachev alive. Oakes persuades Reagan to send him to Moscow, where he finds the rumors overblown. However, in his cover role as Harry Doubleday, a book promoter with ties to the USIA, he is introduced to Ursina Chadinov, a medical doctor and professor at Moscow University. Ursina is an unusually lovely woman, with a quick wit and lively imagination. Doubleday/Oakes, still sufficiently presumptuous and arrant, and after the death of Sally a deeply lonely man, reacts as any normal male would. The attraction is mutual, the romantic scenes are fresh and tasteful, and the dialogue sparkles.

Ursina's best friend, Rufina, has just married an Englishman living in Moscow under the name Andrei Fyodorovich Martins. There is a party at the new couple's apartment, to which Blackford escorts Ursina. In the course of the evening he realizes that Martins is actually the British master spy and traitor Kim Philby.

From here, the plot unfolds rapidly. Philby, certain that Doubleday/Oakes is much more than a book promoter, sets in motion an operation to uncover his identity, and works with the KGB to get at Oakes through Ursina, with tragic results. Back in the United States, Oakes is devastated, retreating into a Howard Hughes–like solitude, from which he is finally jolted by gloating communiqués from Philby. He returns to action and crosses swords with Philby and the KGB, and the novel comes to a quick and explosive climax. Suffice it to say that Blackford Oakes does what we would have expected of him.

The plot of *Last Call* is intricate and well developed. But most interesting is the development of character. One particularly moving strand is Oakes's relationship with two surrogate sons—his actual stepson, Tony Morales, a splendid character in his own right (Sam Vaughan suggested, not entirely playfully, that Tony might deserve a novel of his own); and Oakes's young colleague Gus Windels. Gus starts calling Blackford "Dad" as part of their cover story; but as the dénouement unfolds, the father-son relationship has become something very deep and emotionally true.

Sharing center stage with Oakes and those close to him are Philby and his real-life friend Graham Greene. In earlier novels—with Boris Bolgin in *Saving the Queen*, Erika Chadinoff in *Stained Glass*, Cecilio Velasco in *See You Later Alligator*—we've seen how Communists are made, and the process has been described with understanding and even sympathy. But for Philby, cold and reptilian, a traitor unapologetically responsible for the death of countless freedom-seekers during the Cold War, there is no sympathy.

For Greene, Philby's—and Communism's—dupe, there is a certain tolerant regard: the sort of tolerance reserved for silly but beautiful women, drunken Irish tenors with beautiful tremolos, and hopelessly naïve writers who produce beautiful sentences. In a splendid scene, Greene, not taking notice of Philby's thinly veiled contempt, prattles on about Communism and Catholicism joining forces. The real-life Greene had, years before, written the introduction to Philby's *My Silent War*. "Writing the introduction," says the narrator, "was, for Greene, one more chapter in the lifelong book in which he tried to find a philosophical star fixed enough to warrant full-time servitude."

In the end, this is what the Blackford Oakes novels set out to show us. We have found in the ideals of the United States a fixed philosophical star, and, as Buckley puts it in his essay on the genesis of Blackford Oakes, "any failure by beneficiaries of the free world"— Graham Greene, for instance—"to recognize what we have here over against what it is they would impose on us, amounts to a moral and intellectual nihilism."

At the time of *Last Call*'s publication, *NR* was preparing to celebrate its own fiftieth anniversary and WFB's eightieth birthday. And journalists were eager to interview Buckley as he approached this milestone. One of these, Dan LeRoy of the *New York Times*, in a piece titled "The Conservative Lion in Winter," noted that "With the death of President Ronald Reagan last year, Mr. Buckley became the major living symbol of the modern conservative movement he helped found."

Age is inevitably one of the subjects covered. Young Joseph Rago, a recent *Dartmouth Review* alumnus, interviewed Buckley for the *Wall Street Journal*. "There is something out of time about lunching with William F. Buckley Jr.," he wrote. "It goes beyond the inimitable WFB style: the mannered civility, the O.E.D. vocabulary, the jaunty patrician demeanor. It is also something more than mere age. 'Well, I am one day older than I was yesterday,' he says, with rather good cheer. Yet if there's anachronism to Mr. Buckley, it is also a sense of being present at a moment of creation.

"For all his versatility as editor, essayist, critic, controversialist and bon vivant, Mr. Buckley is widely credited as the driving force behind the intellectual coalition that drew conservatism from the fringes of American life to its center, with such side-effects as the utter collapse of the Soviet empire. 'There's nothing I hoped for that wasn't reasonably achieved,' declares Mr. Buckley, who will turn 80 later this month."

Buckley writes of Blackford Oakes in *Last Call* that "he was not the limber youth he had been, so memorably, for so long." Youthfulness had been a noted characteristic of Oakes's creator as well. The press was still calling him an *enfant terrible* well into his fifties, and a friend dubbed him the eternal boy (*puer aeternus*). Even now there are flashes of that, although not long after his first semiretirement a colleague remarked that when you called him on the phone nowadays, you never knew if you'd be talking with *puer aeternus* or grumpy old man. In the years since, the grumpiness has sublimated, and he has written with great serenity of that "step yet ahead."

And yet he has not let his work ethic slip. In his self-interview about accepting the invitation to play with the Phoenix Symphony back in 1989, he wrote, "I wake up every day and, roughly speaking, work until I go to bed—there is never any time just 'left over,' let alone the kind of time it takes to attack the keyboard at a professional level." That isn't swank, and it isn't exaggeration. Even at age eighty-one and suffering from various ailments that interfere with his sleep (emphysema, sleep apnea), he is cross with himself if he's not at his desk, working, by 9:30 A.M. at the latest.

Writing in *NR*'s fiftieth anniversary issue, Peter Robinson recalled life at the château the season he spent there as a researcher. " 'Bill,' I finally said one day, 'you were born wealthy and you've been famous for thirty years. Why do you keep working so hard?'

"WFB looked at me, surprised. 'My father taught me that I owe it to my country,' he replied. 'It's how I pay my debt.' "

The one way in which Bill's age truly is showing—apart from his inability now to race upstairs or whoosh down a ski slope—is his typing. His handwriting has always been legendary. His father ordered him to learn to type at a tender age because WFB Sr. wished to be able to decipher his son's communications. Much later, there were a handful of designated handwriting decoders at *NR*—Priscilla, of course; Gertrude Vogt and then Frances Bronson; Bill Rusher; Linda Bridges. But Bill really did learn to type—not legal secretary quality, but far better than most working journalists. In fact, Frances tells the story of the awful night when a guest fell off *Cyrano* and drowned. At some very late hour there was a hastily convened meeting—Peter Starr (who had been using the boat to entertain advertisers), Bill, a lawyer or two, and Frances, awakened by phone and summoned to come up to 73rd Street and take notes. When the men had their statement ready, Frances started trying to type it, but, half asleep and distressed, couldn't cope with the little portable nonelectric Bill had brought downstairs. And so Bill took the typewriter and produced an acceptable transcription from Frances's dictation.

In recent years, however, Bill's typing has slipped drastically, as anyone who receives e-mails from him knows. The formal copy he submits to editors is still fine, but his raw e-mails put one in mind of the great Paul Gallico story *The Silent Meow*. The fictional editor in that novella is trying to read a manuscript that seems to be written in some kind of code. As he stares at the typewriter keyboard, he starts to get an idea, and sure enough: the manuscript was written by a cat, whose paws were a little too big to hit the typewriter keys cleanly. Well, that's what Bill's e-mails now look like. So we're back to designated decoders.

NR's fiftieth-anniversary year was capped by two grand celebrations, one in Washington, D.C.—the first time we have ever ventured out of town for an anniversary celebration—the other, geared toward Bill's eightieth birthday, in New York. Nearly a thousand people attended each of these, and there was tremendous good cheer, although, here again, there was a ripple of consternation at the D.C. party when Bill— completely unforeseen by all but a handful in attendance—referred to his own speech as "my terminal appearance with you."

Earlier that October day there had been a lovely event at the Old Executive Office Building. It was midwifed by Tim Goeglein, an old friend of *NR*'s who serves as President Bush's deputy director of public liaison. Seven speakers chronicled their association with Bill, ranging from five of his oldest friends, Jim Buckley, Alistair (now Sir Alistair) Horne, Henry Kissinger, Jack Kilpatrick, and Stan Evans (who would emcee the party that evening); through the middle generation, represented by George Will; to the younger generation, represented by Roger Kimball of *The New Criterion*, who is one of the new owners of *Patito*. The final speaker was President Bush himself, who then escorted Bill and Pat, along with Ed Capano and Dusty Rhodes, to a private dining room in the White House for lunch.

The occasion could have been strained—though everyone on both sides simply transcended the difficulty—by the fact that conservatives were up in arms over the President's short-lived nomination of Harriet Miers to the Supreme Court. "With this nomination," a veteran of the Reagan administration said at a small *NR* cocktail party the evening before, "he has thrown away everything we accomplished in the Reagan Justice Department in making the judicial selection process more reliable in producing constitutionalists." The story had a happy ending, with Miers's withdrawal and the nomination—and confirmation—of movement conservative Samuel Alito, but it had been a bizarre episode.

Two weeks later, Ramesh Ponnuru wrote an op-ed piece for the *New York Times* entitled "Why Conservatives Are Divided." Ponnuru started with the Miers nomination and then went on to other aspects of conservatives' relations with President Bush. "While running for president," Ponnuru wrote, "George W. Bush denounced the idea that 'if government would only get out of our way, all our problems would be solved.' The Gingrich Republicans had tried to abolish the Department of Education. Mr. Bush said he would give it new responsibilities."

Ponnuru points to other areas of conservative concern: "While most conservatives supported the invasion of Iraq, many have great doubts about the conduct of the war. Medicare has been expanded more than it has been reformed. Social Security reform appears to be dead. . . . Tax cuts may have inhibited spending . . . but they have hardly imposed anything that could fairly be called 'restraint.'"

All in all, a powerful bill of particulars—unless, of course, you're a champion of that "nonsensical neologism," big-government conservatism.

For each of the big anniversary parties, *NR*'s fiftieth and his own eightieth, Bill had spent hours, days, putting together a documentary film with the help of a junior editor at *NR*, Jason Steorts. The *NR* film was narrated in voiceover by Rush Limbaugh; the WFB one was narrated in person by Chris Buckley, at the top of his form. There were inevitable overlaps—once is not enough to play the footage of President Reagan addressing our thirtieth anniversary dinner—but the first focused on the magazine's history, the second on Bill's own public career, including clips from *Firing Line*; from *Atlantic High*, the documentary about the second transatlantic crossing; and from *Laugh-In*.

At the birthday party in New York, when the time came for Bill to speak in person, it was Priscilla who introduced him, escorted from the table where she was sitting with the O'Reillys. Gerry O'Reilly had remained close to the Buckleys after Maureen's death, and they had happily welcomed to the family his second wife, Seton, who proved a superb mother to Maureen's children as well as to a son of her own.

At the party, music was provided by the Whiffenpoofs (Bill had chosen the songs, which included a hauntingly beautiful solo of "Down by the Sally Gardens") and—for the first time at an *NR* function—the Harvard Krokodiloes. There was one rollicking number where the Whiffs pulled Nancy Kissinger up to the stage with them to ask musically "What's Your Name?"

As with most of Bill's enterprises, the list of attendees included all sorts and conditions: New York glitterati, notable conservative writers and politicians, young sailing friends, college classmates, nieces and nephews, the entire staff of the magazine, and numerous fund-appeal givers. Two of the more impressive journeys by guests: classmate Bill Draper had business commitments in California, but he had caught the 7:00 plane from San Francisco that morning to make the party, and he would catch the 7:00 A.M. back the next day; and nephew Claude Buckley (Reid's third son) had driven up from South Carolina that day and would drive back the next day.

Despite that ominous phrase "terminal appearance," Bill is still, as we write, very much on the scene, and no more constrained than he ever was by a conservative "party line." In February 2006 he dismayed many *NR* readers, and caused no little gloating among the antiwar paleos, by writing in his column, after the bombing of the Shiite mosque in Samara, "Ours is a failed mission."

This was a particularly strong statement, but Buckley had been wary all along of the administration's ambitious claims for the Iraq venture. Back in March 2003 he had written, "What Mr. Bush proposes to do is to unseat Saddam Hussein and to eliminate his investments in aggressive weaponry. We can devoutly hope that internecine tribal antagonisms will be subsumed in the fresh air of a despot removed, and that the restoration of freedom will be productive. But these concomitant developments can't be either foreseen by the United States, or implemented by us. What Mr. Bush can accomplish is the removal of a regime and its infrastructure. The Iraqi people will have to take it from there."

In the interview with Joseph Rago in November 2005 he said, "Conservatism, except when it is expressed as pure idealism, takes into account reality, and the reality of the situation is that missions abroad to effect regime change in countries without a bill of rights or democratic tradition are terribly arduous. This isn't to say the war is wrong, or that history will judge it to be wrong. But it is absolutely to say that conservatism implies a certain submission to reality."

In another interview that fall, with *New Yorker* writer Tom Reiss, Buckley applied that same reality test to Bush's "big-government conservatism": "If one acknowledged the second inaugural address of the President as marching orders, well, that would keep us busy with something to do for all eternity. It's not, in my judgment, conservatism. Because conservatism is, to a considerable extent, the acknowledgment of realities. And this is surreal." Or, as Buckley had expressed this thought earlier in his career, such-and-such would not happen until "the Committee to Abolish Original Sin brings in its final report."

There have been so many attempts to sum up the career of William F. Buckley Jr.—and that career is not yet finished.

Still, a provisional assessment can start with a list. Buckley is the author or editor of fifty-four books so far, many of them bestsellers, and of more than four thousand newspaper columns and four hundred articles and book reviews. Some of those are fun & games (how to build up a wine cellar, how and when to take a vacation), but even the nonpolitical ones forward the conservative message, which includes an understanding of the grace notes of life. Buckley brought that same message to millions of Americans through the award-winning *Firing Line*, in the process demonstrating that television could be substantive and entertaining at the same time. He spread the message in a very personal way through his miles logged on the lecture circuit, not only by the words he spoke from the lectern but also by his willingness to spend time in conversation with the students (or business leaders, or church people, or political activists) who had invited him. And perhaps most important, he founded the flagship journal of the conservative movement. In his first farewell address, at *NR*'s thirty-fifth anniversary, he concluded: "*National Review*, I like to think, will be here, enlivening right reason, for as long as there is anything left in America to celebrate."

In one of the more unusual reviews of *Miles Gone By*, written for *Commentary*, veteran journalist Dan Seligman proposed a thought experiment: Suppose the young Bill Buckley had decided to be a playboy instead of working so hard and spending so much money to found *National Review* and keep it afloat. Would there have been a conservative movement as we know it? (Our own genuine playboy friend,

Taki Theodoracopulos, e-mailed one of the present authors the day after Bill's eightieth birthday party. "When the speakers were praising Bill," Taki wrote, "I told my neighbor, Nancy Kissinger, that what I've always hated about him was that he was so good looking and yet so monogamous. Mrs. Kissinger looked puzzled. Then she laughed. She understood that people like me envy people like Bill not for their intellectual achievements, but for their ability not to be playboys.")

Seligman goes on to answer the question posed by his own "wildly counterfactual scenario." Yes, he judges, "there would have been a powerful conservative tide," because of "mass affluence and the emergence of a modernized South in the 50's and 60's. But in the world of ideas, liberalism still remained overwhelmingly dominant, and it thus made a huge difference . . . to have a beacon out there to guide a generation newly receptive to conservative thinking."

Tom Reiss, in that 2005 *New Yorker* article, compares Buckley's influence on the growth of the conservative movement with that of maverick New Conservative Peter Viereck: "Buckley, despite his rhetoric, was a reconciler and an institution builder: his goal was to see conservatism become a politically dominant mass movement. To that end, in an effort to unite libertarians, traditionalists, and anti-Communists, he founded *National Review* in 1955, encouraging contributors to attack liberals when they might have preferred to criticize each other."

"An institution builder"—not many, perhaps, think of Bill Buckley that way, but that's exactly what he is. And along the way, he has displayed managerial talents that many a CEO would envy, chief among them his ability to manage one of the most idiosyncratic, opinionated, individualistic, and argumentative staffs in organizational history. But holding it all together, always at the very center of the storm, and consistently turning out a product unique in opinion journalism, was Bill Buckley.

As Bill Rusher put it, writing of the founding of *National Review*, "But who, or what, could bring the prickly components of the conservative movement together and induce it to speak with a single journalistic voice? Who could proclaim and refine conservatism's fundamental principles, resolve or compromise disputes on internal issues, promote intellectual and political spokesmen, and lead the philosophical battle against both communism and modern liberalism? Who—to descend to more practical matters—had or could raise the necessary money, recruit the writers and editors, referee the inevitable quarrels, and bring the whole enterprise into being? Who (we now know History's answer) but William F. Buckley Jr.?"

We began this book by quoting Ronald Reagan; we'd like to let him have the last word: "And, Bill—thanks, too, for all the fun."

Appendix

Books by William F. Buckley Jr.

Books written or edited by William F. Buckley Jr., as of January 2007; asterisk indicates fiction

God and Man at Yale (Chicago: Henry Regnery Company, 1951); reissued with a new introduction by the author (Chicago: Regnery Books, 1977)

McCarthy and His Enemies: The Record and Its Meaning, coauthored with L. Brent Bozell Jr. (Chicago: Henry Regnery Company, 1954)

Up from Liberalism (New York: McDowell, Obolensky, 1959)

W.F.B.—An Appreciation by His Family and Friends, coedited with Priscilla L. Buckley (privately printed, 1959)

The Committee and Its Critics: A Calm Review of the House Committee on Un-American Activities, edited by WFB (New York: G. P. Putnam's Sons, 1962)

Rumbles Left and Right: A Book about Troublesome People and Ideas (New York: Putnam's, 1963)

The Unmaking of a Mayor (New York: The Viking Press, 1966)

The Jeweler's Eye (New York: Putnam's, 1968)

Maureen Buckley O'Reilly, 1933–1964, coedited with Priscilla L. Buckley (privately printed, 1968)

Odyssey of a Friend: Letters to William F. Buckley Jr. 1954–1961, by Whittaker Chambers, edited with notes by WFB (New York: National Review, 1969; reprinted commercially: Washington, D.C.: Regnery Books, 1987)

The Governor Listeth: A Book of Inspired Political Revelations (New York: Putnam's, 1970)

Did You Ever See a Dream Walking? American Conservative Thought in the Twentieth Century, edited by WFB (Indianapolis: Bobbs-Merrill, for the American Heritage Series, 1970)

Cruising Speed—A Documentary (New York: Putnam's, 1971)

Inveighing We Will Go (New York: Putnam's, 1972)

Four Reforms—A Guide for the Seventies (New York: Putnam's, 1973)

United Nations Journal: A Delegate's Odyssey (New York: Putnam's, 1974)

Execution Eve—And Other Contemporary Ballads (New York: Putnam's, 1975)

* *Saving the Queen* (Garden City, N.Y.: Doubleday, 1976)

Airborne: A Sentimental Journey (Boston: Little, Brown, 1976)

* *Stained Glass* (Garden City, N.Y.: Doubleday, 1978)

A Hymnal: The Controversial Arts (New York: Putnam's, 1978)

* *Who's on First* (Garden City, N.Y.: Doubleday, 1980)

* *Marco Polo, If You Can* (Garden City, N.Y.: Doubleday, 1982)

Atlantic High: A Celebration (Garden City, N.Y.: Doubleday, 1982)

Overdrive: A Personal Documentary (Garden City, N.Y.: Doubleday, 1983)

* *The Story of Henri Tod* (Garden City, N.Y.: Doubleday, 1984)

* *See You Later Alligator* (Garden City, N.Y.: Doubleday, 1985)

* *The Temptation of Wilfred Malachey* (New York: Workman Publishing, 1985)

Right Reason: A Collection, edited by Richard Brookhiser (Garden City, N.Y.: Doubleday, 1985)

* *High Jinx* (Garden City, N.Y.: Doubleday, 1986)

Racing Through Paradise: A Pacific Passage (New York: Random House, 1987)

* *Mongoose, R.I.P.* (New York: Random House, 1988)

Keeping the Tablets: Modern American Conservative Thought (a revised edition of *American Conservative Thought in the Twentieth Century*), coedited with Charles R. Kesler (New York: Harper & Row, 1988)

On the Firing Line: The Public Life of Our Public Figures (New York: Random House, 1989)

Gratitude—Reflections on What We Owe to Our Country (New York: Random House, 1990)

* *Tucker's Last Stand* (New York: Random House, 1990)

WindFall: The End of the Affair (New York: Random House, 1992)

In Search of Anti-Semitism (New York: Continuum, 1992)

Happy Days Were Here Again: Reflections of a Libertarian Journalist, edited by Patricia Bozell (New York: Random House, 1993)

* *A Very Private Plot* (New York: William Morrow, 1994)

* *The Blackford Oakes Reader* (Kansas City, Mo.: Andrews and McMeel, 1995)
* *Brothers No More* (New York: Doubleday, 1995)

Buckley: The Right Word, edited by Samuel S. Vaughan (New York: Random House, 1996)

The Lexicon (New York: Harcourt Brace, 1996)

Nearer, My God: An Autobiography of Faith (New York: Doubleday, 1997)

* *The Redhunter: A Novel Based on the Life of Senator Joe McCarthy* (Boston: Little, Brown, 1999)

Let Us Talk of Many Things: The Collected Speeches, with New Commentary by the Author (Roseville, Calif.: Prima/Forum, 2000)

* *Spytime: The Undoing of James Jesus Angleton* (New York: Harcourt, 2000)
* *Elvis in the Morning* (New York: Harcourt, 2001)
* *Nuremberg: The Reckoning* (New York: Harcourt, 2002)
* *Getting It Right* (Washington, D.C.: Regnery Publishing, 2003)

The Fall of the Berlin Wall (Hoboken: John Wiley & Sons, 2004)

Miles Gone By: A Literary Autobiography (Washington, D.C.: Regnery Publishing, 2004)

* *Last Call for Blackford Oakes* (New York: Harcourt, 2005)

Notes

1. Life before *National Review*

The principal sources for the sections on Bill Buckley's childhood and family background are his own *Miles Gone By* and *Nearer, My God* (for bibliographical information on WFB, see the Appendix, p. 323), plus the memorial volumes for Will and Aloïse Buckley and their daughter Maureen, privately published by the family: *W.F.B.—An Appreciation by His Family and Friends*, edited by Priscilla L. Buckley and William F. Buckley Jr. (1959); *Maureen Buckley O'Reilly, 1933–1964*, edited by PLB and WFB (1968); and *Reminiscences of Aloïse Steiner Buckley, 1895–1985*, edited by Aloïse Harding Buckley, John Buckley's younger daughter (1987). John B. Judis's *William F. Buckley, Jr.: Patron Saint of the Conservatives* (New York: Simon & Schuster, 1988)—until now the only full-length biography of WFB—contains, in Dan Seligman's description, "much good reporting but suffers from . . . Judis's inability to suppress his horror of conservative ideas." Other sources: *Gleanings from an Unplanned Life*, by James L. Buckley (Wilmington, Del.: ISI Books, 2006); *Manqué*, by John W. Buckley (Hartford, Conn.: Sacré Bleu Press, 1986); *At the Still Point: A Memoir*, by Carol Buckley (New York: Simon & Schuster, 1996); and conversations, viva voce and by e-mail, with PLB.

For the sections on Yale, on WFB's marriage to Patricia Taylor, and on his time in the CIA: WFB's *God and Man at Yale* (especially the introduction to the 1977 edition), *Miles Gone By*, *Let Us Talk of Many Things*, *Saving the Queen*, and *In Search of Anti-Semitism*; Judis's *Patron Saint*. Also, a delightful little article by WFB for the *New York Times* (11/10/76), "Of Wives and Their Skills, of Men and Their Dreams"; this has not made its way into any of his collections, but thanks to an enormous undertaking by Hillsdale College, nearly his entire oeuvre is now available online at www.hillsdale .edu/Buckley.

WFB has more than once described *Facts on File* as "indispensable," and the present authors second that motion. Ever since World War II, *FoF* (New York: Facts on File) has provided weekly news summaries, bristling with names and figures; these are issued as weekly fascicles, then bound at the end of the year with beautifully detailed indexes. *FoF* gives a view of events undistorted by hindsight, and we have relied on it heavily for historical context, starting with the Soviet Union's salami-slicing of Central Europe and the 1952 presidential race.

The Conservative Intellectual Movement in America since 1945, by George H. Nash (New York: Basic Books, 1976), wonderfully summarizes the different strands of the conservative movement and depicts its principal figures. Other sources for the pre-*NR* period: *Will Mrs. Major Go to Hell?*, by Aloïse Buckley Heath (New Rochelle, N.Y.: Arlington House, 1969); *String of Pearls: On the News Beat in New York and Paris*, by PLB (New York: St. Martin's, 2001); *James Burnham and the Struggle for the World: A Life*, by Daniel Kelly (Wilmington, Del.: ISI Books, 2002); *The Secret History of the CIA*, by Joseph J. Trento (Roseville, Calif.: Prima Publishing, 2001); and WFB's *The Fall of the Berlin Wall*, *Miles Gone By*, and (with Brent Bozell) *McCarthy and His Enemies*.

2. Forging the Conservative Movement

Once *National Review* came on the scene, the bound volumes of the magazine itself were invaluable—especially the "marked copies" residing at *NR*'s offices, in which the authors of unsigned editorials are noted. From this point on, we used *NR* along with *Facts on File* for historical context. (The *NR* archives are now available on NROnline [www.nationalreview.com], though as of this writing the search engine is rather capricious.)

Other sources for the founding period of *NR*: Nash's *The Conservative Intellectual Movement*; the memorial volumes on Maureen Buckley O'Reilly (especially J. P. McFadden's contribution) and on WFB Sr. (especially WFB Jr.'s contribution); *Living It Up with National Review*, by Priscilla L. Buckley (Dallas: Spence Publishing, 2005) and an interview with PLB by Tamara Tragakiss in Litchfield County's *Passport* magazine (Winter 2005); *William F. Buckley Jr.: A Bibliography*, edited by William F. Meehan III (Wilmington, Del.: ISI Books, 2002); *The Making of the American Conservative Mind: National Review and Its Times*, by Jeffrey Hart (Wilmington, Del.: ISI Books, 2005); "Scrambled Eggheads on the Right," by Dwight Macdonald (*Commentary*, April 1956); Judis's *Patron Saint*; and WFB's *Miles Gone By*, *Did You Ever See a Dream Walking?*, and *Let Us Talk of Many Things*.

Priscilla Buckley, Bill Rusher, and Frances Bronson kindly supplied information in conversation and by e-mail. Elsie Meyer, during her time at 150 East 35th Street, told many stories of the early days (as, over the course of many editorial lunches and drinks sessions, did WFB, PLB, WAR, and Jim McFadden). When one of the present authors wrote about the Willmoore Kendall Memorial Couch some years ago (*NR*, 12/31/96), she received a letter from Gertrude Vogt, from her retirement in California, correcting one detail. W. H. Auden's letter to WFB is in the Buckley Papers at Yale. Information from WFB's calendar comes from a "Chronology" kept on computer by his staff. Entries are spotty for the early years of his public life, increasingly full starting in the early 1960s.

3. Goldwater for President

Principal sources for the early 1960s are: "The Right Stuff," by Michael M. Uhlmann (*Claremont Review of Books*, Summer 2005); *Wall: The Inside Story of Divided Berlin*, by Peter Wyden (New York: Simon & Schuster, 1989); *Fighting the Good Fight: A History of the New York Conservative Party*, by George J. Marlin (South Bend: St. Augustine's Press, 2002); Judis; Meehan; and WFB's *The Fall of the Berlin Wall*, *Rumbles Left and Right*, *Let Us Talk of Many Things*, and *Miles Gone By*.

Principal sources for sections on the Draft Goldwater movement and the subsequent campaign: *Rise of the Right*, by William A. Rusher (New York: Morrow, 1984); *The Conservative Revolution: The Movement That Remade America*, by Lee Edwards (New York: Free Press, 1999); and WFB's *Let Us Talk of Many Things*. Also, personal recollections of the Goldwater campaign in Southern California by one of the present authors.

For the birth of the pre–New Left/New Right on the campuses, *Revolt on the Campus*, by M. Stanton Evans (Chicago: Regnery, 1961). Also, personal recollections of events at UC Berkeley by the other of the present authors.

For the civil rights movement: "Liberty," by WFB (in a publication, *Centennial*, celebrating the hundredth birthday of the Statue of Liberty, 1986); and *Special Counsel*, by William A. Rusher (New Rochelle, N.Y.: Arlington House, 1968).

4. The Raging Sixties

For the mayoral campaign and its aftermath, WFB's *The Unmaking of a Mayor*; plus Judis; correspondence in the Buckley Papers at Yale; and conversations with Daniel Oliver, Agatha Schmidt Dowd, and David P. Stuhr.

One of the present authors prepared the annotated catalogue of all the *Firing Line* shows for WFB. This went with the *FL* archive to the Hoover Institution at Stanford; it is available at http://hoohila.stanford.edu/firingline/. Also, some *Firing Line* clips appear on the DVD *William F. Buckley Jr.'s 80th Birthday Celebration*, available from *National Review*.

For the Buckleys' homes, see WFB's *Overdrive*, *Miles Gone By*, "A Place in the City" (*Private Clubs*, September/October 1991), and "The Proust

Questionnaire" (*Vanity Fair*, September 1993). Also "Skiing at 70," by Alistair Horne (*Condé Nast Traveler*, January 1989).

Lee Edwards's essay in the Philadelphia Society's fortieth-anniversary souvenir program offered much useful information, and WFB put several of his addresses to the society into *Let Us Talk of Many Things*.

An American Life, by Ronald Reagan (New York: Simon & Schuster, 1990), is not as spontaneous as his collected letters, but it makes good use of his personal diary and gives a clear account of his remarkable life.

The Making of the President, 1968, by Theodore H. White (New York: Atheneum, 1969), offers a thoughtful and sweeping picture of the period. *Miami and the Siege of Chicago*, by Norman Mailer (New York: World, 1969), gives perceptive and surprisingly sensitive portraits of the candidates and the kids.

For two contrasting views of events on the campuses, see *The Kumquat Statement*, by John R. Coyne Jr. (New York: Cowles, 1970), and *The Strawberry Statement*, by James Simon Kunen (New York: Random House, 1969).

Additional sources: "On Experiencing Gore Vidal," by WFB (*Esquire*, August 1969) and *"Buckley v. Esquire": Libel and a Legendary Editor*, a dissertation by George Andrew Sullivan Jr. (Indiana University, 1999); *Radical Chic & Mau-Mauing the Flak-Catchers*, by Tom Wolfe (New York: Farrar, Straus, and Giroux, 1970); *The American Dissent: A Decade of Modern Conservatism*, by Jeffrey Hart (Garden City, N.Y.: Doubleday, 1966); *Radical Libertarianism: A Right Wing Alternative*, by Jerome Tuccille (Indianapolis: Bobbs-Merrill, 1970); and WFB's *On the Firing Line*, *The Fall of the Berlin Wall*, and *Let Us Talk of Many Things*.

Beginning in 1969, published information about WFB and *NR* is supplemented by the authors' personal recollections.

5. The Long Detour

Personal observations of the Nixon and Ford administrations by one of the authors have over the years been recorded in articles, reviews, and books, among them *The Impudent Snobs: Agnew vs. the Intellectual Establishment*, by John R. Coyne Jr. (New Rochelle, N.Y.: Arlington House, 1972), and *Fall In and Cheer*, by JRC (Garden City, N.Y.: Doubleday, 1979).

Comments by William F. Gavin on Richard Nixon came through conversations, e-mails, and an article, "His Heart's Abundance: Notes of a Nixon Speechwriter" (*Presidential Studies Quarterly*, June 2001).

Relations between Richard Nixon and the conservative movement are treated at length in WAR's *Rise of the Right* and "The Long Detour" (*Claremont Review*, Summer 2005).

Essential sources for students of Richard Nixon are the three volumes by Stephen E. Ambrose: *Nixon: The Education of a Politician, 1913–1962; Nixon: The Triumph of a Politician, 1962–1972;* and *Nixon: Ruin and Recovery, 1973–1990* (New York: Simon & Schuster, 1987–1991). Also, an interesting juxtaposition: *One Man Alone: Richard Nixon,* by Ralph de Toledano, an old friend and supporter of Nixon's (New York: Funk & Wagnalls, 1969); and *President Nixon: Alone in the White House,* by Richard Reeves (New York: Simon & Schuster, 2001)—a fine study of a quirky man by a quirky man.

The post-resignation literature on Vice President Agnew is surprisingly slim, consisting primarily of a quickie book by reporters Jules Witcover and Richard Cohen, *A Heartbeat Away: The Investigation and Resignation of Vice President Spiro T. Agnew* (New York: Viking, 1974), fed by prosecutors and rushed into print shortly after the resignation; and Agnew's own book, *Go Quietly . . . Or Else* (New York: Morrow, 1980). Agnew's book centers primarily on his refutation of charges brought against him and on what he believed were administration attempts, led by Al Haig, to force a quick resignation with no chance to make his case. The *"Or Else"* in the title refers to that and more. Agnew believed there might have been a plan to assassinate him if he failed to cooperate. Far-fetched? No doubt. But whatever his flaws, Agnew was very serious man, and the Nixon White House was a very unusual place.

Sources on the Buckleys in this period: WFB's *Cruising Speed, Airborne, Four Reforms, Let Us Talk of Many Things,* and *United Nations Journal;* an interview of Pat Buckley by George Gurley in *The New York Observer* (12/19/05); Priscilla Buckley's *Living It Up;* WFB's "Almost Nothing Hurts More than the Loss of Your Dog" (as reprinted in *Happy Days Were Here Again*); and a letter from Christopher Buckley in *Reminiscences of Aloïse Steiner Buckley.*

Additional sources: *The Emerging Republican Majority,* by Kevin Phillips (New Rochelle, N.Y.: Arlington House, 1969), and *Richard Nixon and the Quest for a New Majority,* by Robert Mason (Chapel Hill: University of North Carolina Press, 2004).

6. New Directions

Especially interesting on the first month of the Ford interregnum is *31 Days: The Crisis That Gave Us the Government We Have Today,* by Barry Werth (New York: Nan A. Talese/Doubleday, 2006). The subtitle is a tease, referring primarily to Cheney and Rumsfeld, both of whom made their bones under Nixon, then transferred their loyalties to Ford. But it does point to the split loyalties that started the Ford administration off on a dysfunctional note from which it never recovered.

On the Buckleys: "The Genesis of Blackford Oakes" appears in both *Let Us Talk of Many Things* and *Miles Gone By*; WFB's account of his first transatlantic sail forms the backbone of *Airborne*.

On the political climate: WAR's *The Making of the New Majority Party* (New York: Sheed & Ward, 1975).

7. Time to Regroup

Material on Starr Broadcasting comes from Judis and from one of the authors' personal recollections; on Catawba, from *Overdrive*.

The account of the Panama Canal debate is based on WFB's *On the Firing Line*. Daniel Kelly's biography is the principal source for Jim Burnham's failing health.

WFB's Notre Dame commencement address appears in *Let Us Talk of Many Things*.

Sources for Reagan's trips abroad: "Ronald Reagan: An Extraordinary Man in Extraordinary Times," by Richard V. Allen, in *The Fall of the Berlin Wall: Reassessing the Causes and Consequences of the End of the Cold War*, edited by Peter Schweizer (Stanford, Calif.: Hoover Institution Press, 2000); *Ronnie and Nancy: Their Path to the White House, 1911 to 1980*, by Bob Colacello (New York: Warner Books, 2004).

For Christopher Buckley, his own *Steaming to Bamboola: The World of a Tramp Freighter* (New York: Congdon & Lattès, 1982); plus interviews with the Literary Guild newsletter (1986) and *Newsweek* (2005); and his entry in *Current Biography* (1989).

There seems to be no one good place to go for discussions of the religious right. In the authoritative *American Conservatism: An Encyclopedia*, edited by Jeffrey O. Nelson (Wilmington, Del.: ISI Books, 2006), there are no entries for "Religious Right" or "Christian Right." For the purposes of this book, however, both Bill Rusher and Lee Edwards provide good summary treatments of the role played by the religious right in the success of the conservative movement.

The single best biography of Ronald Reagan, with detailed accounts of his governorship and his 1976 and 1980 campaigns for the presidency, is Lou Cannon's *Reagan* (New York: Putnam, 1982). The single best *inside* book on Reagan, his campaigns, and his presidency is *My Turn*, by Nancy Reagan (New York: Random House, 1989). Here's where you go if you want the *real* story on matters like John Sears's campaign strategy.

For WFB's 1980 sail: his own *Atlantic High*.

8. The Reagan Years

WFB's account of his "ambassadorship" to Kabul appears in *Let Us Talk*. Ronald Reagan's take on world events is drawn from *An American Life*. The account of how the Reagan administration sought to undermine the Soviet Union's power comes from "NSDD-75: A New Approach to the Soviet Union," by William P. Clark, in Schweizer's *The Fall of the Berlin Wall*.

In honor of the *Dartmouth Review*'s twenty-fifth anniversary, two alumni compiled an anthology: *The* Dartmouth Review *Pleads Innocent: Twenty-Five Years of Being Threatened, Impugned, Vandalized, Sued, Suspended, and Bitten at the Ivy League's Most Controversial Conservative Newspaper*, edited by James Panero and Stefan Beck (Wilmington, Del.: ISI Books, 2006).

Lou Cannon's second volume, *President Reagan: The Role of a Lifetime* (New York: Simon & Schuster, 1991), is as authoritative as his first. Cannon is especially good on the campaign of 1984, as is *NR*'s Richard Brookhiser, in *The Outside Story: How Democrats and Republicans Re-Elected Reagan* (Garden City, N.Y.: Doubleday, 1986). Absolutely indispensable are the letters: *Ronald Reagan: A Life in Letters*, by Ronald Reagan (New York: Free Press, 2003).

The paperback edition of *Overdrive* (Boston: Little, Brown, 1984) contains, as an "Introductory Epilogue," WFB's spirited reply to his critics; in it he quotes in its entirety David Brooks's parody.

Other sources: *Reminiscences of ASB*; *Man without a Face*, by Markus Wolf with Anne McElroy (New York: PublicAffairs, 1997); WFB's *High Jinx, Stained Glass, A Very Private Plot*, and *The Fall of the Berlin Wall*; WFB's "Marjorie's Slow Boat to Paradise" and PTB's "A Mate's Mutinous Thoughts," in *Condé Nast Traveler* (October 1988); CTB's *The White House Mess* (New York: Knopf, 1986); and PLB's *Living It Up*.

9. New World Order

WAR's *Rise of the Right* brings us up to the opening years of the Reagan Administration. In *The Conservative Revolution*, Lee Edwards takes us through the great Gingrich-led conservative congressional revolt and on into the last years of the Clinton administration. And in a booklet-length Heritage Foundation Lecture (#811), *The Origins of the Modern American Conservative Movement* (2003), Edwards takes us into the administration of George W. Bush and the invasion of Iraq.

Also valuable is *The Right Nation: Conservative Power in America*, by two reporters for *The Economist*, John Micklethwait and Adrian Wooldridge (New York: Penguin, 2004). George Will calls this "the best political book in years."

Other sources: *The Art of Victory: Fulfilling Mankind's Potential*, by Gregory R. Copley (Washington, D.C.: Defense & Foreign Affairs Publishing, 2004); *Roughnecking It: or, Life in the Overthrust*, by Chilton Williamson Jr. (New York: Simon & Schuster, 1982); *The NR College Guide*, by Brad Miner and Charles Sykes (New York: National Review Books, 1991); *The Art of Persuasion: A National Review Rhetoric for Writers*, by Linda Bridges and William F. Rickenbacker (New York: National Review Books, 1991); *Unkilled for So Long*, by Arnold Lunn (London: Allen & Unwin, 1968); and WFB's *WindFall, The Fall of the Berlin Wall, Let Us Talk of Many Things, In Search of Anti-Semitism*, and *Brothers No More*.

10. Passing the Torch

For the political scene: Micklethwait and Wooldridge's *Right Nation* and Lee Edwards's *The Origins of the Modern American Conservative Movement*.

For the overview of WFB's career: Meehan's *Bibliography*; Rusher's *Rise of the Right*; "The Right Man," by Dan Seligman (*Commentary*, October 2004); "The First Conservative: How Peter Viereck Inspired—and Lost—a Movement," by Tom Reiss (*The New Yorker*, 10/24/05); "Old School," by Joseph Rago (*Wall Street Journal*, 11/12/05); "The Conservative Lion in Winter," by Dan LeRoy (*New York Times*, 10/9/05, Connecticut weekly). Plus WFB's *Let Us Talk of Many Things, Last Call for Blackford Oakes*, and *Miles Gone By*.

Index

Senate and, 128–130, 135, 138,
158–159, 176, 195

Buckley, Jane (sister), 9, 10, 11, 12,
16–17, 31, 100, 148, 180, 269, 285

Buckley, John W. (brother), 8, 9, 10, 11,
12, 13, 14, 31, 196, 242, 243, 312

Buckley, John (grandfather), 5–6

Buckley, John (uncle), 6

Buckley, John Alois (nephew), 243

Buckley, Lee (niece), 312

Buckley, Lucy Gregg (daughter-in-law),
98, 241, 242

Buckley, Mary Ann (sister), 9, 88

Buckley, Mary Ann Langford
(grandmother), 5–6

Buckley, Maureen (sister), 9, 11, 39, 44,
49, 50, 59, 77, 87–88, 325

Buckley, Patricia Taylor (Pat) (wife), 1,
11, 22, 24, 31, 32, 61, 77, 97, 98,
135, 139, 140, 144, 149, 208, 227,
247, 251, 265, 269, 292, 303, 324;
charity events and, 131; fashion and,
131, 148; hip replacements of,
241–242; marriage and family of,
20–21, 30; personality of, 20, 100,
242; sailing and, 172, 173–174,
217, 259–260; social life of, 45,
98–99, 100–101, 225, 281

Buckley, Patricia (Trish) (sister), 9, 10, 11,
12, 16, 19, 30, 31, 42, 78, 122, 143

Buckley, Priscilla (aunt), 6

Buckley, Priscilla L. (sister), 8, 10, 11, 12,
31, 44, 72, 76, 77, 87, 88, 100,
130, 143, 148, 166, 168, 197, 202,
218–221, 231, 233, 235, 243, 260,
264, 269, 274, 285, 325; memoir
by, 137; at NR, 2, 49, 50, 52–54,
56, 57, 59, 62, 92, 108, 109,
132–134, 141–142, 156–158,
170–173, 177, 179, 202, 247–249,
256, 323; at UPI, 19, 33–34

Buckley, Tasa (sister-in-law), 243

Buckley, William F., Jr.: accomplishments
of, 327–329; on anti-Semitism,
16–17, 41, 250–251, 270–271;
awards to, 130, 183, 278, 302, 303;
bêtes noires of, 157–158; birth of, 9;
Catholic policies and, 78, 106;
celebrity status of, 95, 97, 130–131;
CIA post of, 19, 22–23; on Cold
War's end, 276–277; as conservative,
3, 5, 26, 65, 75, 85–86, 197, 322,

326–327; critics of, 23, 26, 237,
297; dogs and, 139–140; early
career of, 19, 22–23, 24, 29–30, 34;
editorial management style of, 249,
272, 273, 309; eightieth birthday of,
272, 273, 322–326, 328; e-mail
and, 265–266, 324; eye problem of,
149; family background of, 5–13; on
father's death, 56; few people
despised by, 14; on Ford's debate
gaffe, 192; friends' deaths and,
312–313; friendship and, 14, 15–16,
304; homes of, 24, 97–100, 132; on
Iraq war, 326–327; language and,
9–10, 101, 128, 157–158; lecture
circuit and, 60–62, 131, 172, 173,
277, 302, 327; lifestyle of, 237;
literary autobiography of, 2, 73, 98,
303–304, 313–316; mannerisms of,
130; marijuana views of, 146–147;
marriage of, 20–21, 30; McCarthy
and, 19, 29, 30, 31–32; Messiah
Party of, 45, 99; mother's death
and, 242–243; motorscooter of, 97,
131–132; musical interests of, 2, 10,
45, 98, 99, 269, 308, 315; New
York mayoral bid of, 91–95, 96,
104, 127, 135; Nixon obituary by,
283–284; as novelist, 168, 175–176,
181–185, 243–244, 292–293,
320–322; NYC police speech by,
90–91; on Panama Canal treaty,
199–202; personal traits of, 50, 130,
131, 211, 244, 284–285, 309,
315–316, 323–324; popular culture
and, 107, 130; retirement and, 2–3,
260, 271–272, 277–278, 301, 302,
308–309; routine of, 131–134;
sailing and, 44, 108–109, 131,
172–174, 208, 211–212, 215–217,
259–260, 266, 278, 284, 284–285,
308, 309, 316, 323; schooling of,
10, 11, 13; SEC battle with,
195–196; Sixties clarity of, 115–21,
124; skiing and, 44, 61, 99, 101,
280–81, 282, 285, 308; social circle
of, 44–45, 98–99, 100–101,
277–278; Swiss writing retreat of,
61, 79, 95, 99–101, 131, 147,
168–169, 173, 277, 280–281, 292;
syndicated column of, 2, 74, 79,
131–133, 172, 236, 277; television